To Arnie &

Institutions per

Buildings crumble

but ideas live on !

Fondly

Rudi Elstein

2
14
76

IN SEARCH OF LOVE AND COMPETENCE:

TWENTY-FIVE YEARS OF SERVICE, TRAINING, AND RESEARCH AT THE REISS-DAVIS CHILD STUDY CENTER

In Search of Love and Competence

Twenty-Five Years of Service,
Training, and Research at
the Reiss-Davis Child
Study Center

Edited by

RUDOLF EKSTEIN, Ph.D.

Published by

REISS-DAVIS CHILD STUDY CENTER ● Los Angeles, Cal.
Distributed by Brunner/Mazel, Inc., New York, N.Y.

Copyright © 1976 by
THE REISS-DAVIS CHILD STUDY CENTER

Published by
THE REISS-DAVIS CHILD STUDY CENTER
9760 West Pico Boulevard, Los Angeles, Calif. 90035
Distributed by Brunner/Mazel, Inc., New York, N.Y.

Library of Congress Cataloging in Publication Data
Main entry under title:

IN SEARCH OF LOVE AND COMPETENCE

"Papers Published in the Reiss-Davis Clinic Bulletin."
    Includes index.
    1. Child Psychotherapy.   2. Reiss-Davis Child Study Center.   I. Ekstein,
Rudolf.   II. Reiss-Davis Child Study Center.   III. Reiss-Davis Clinic
Bulletin.
RJ504.15   618.9'28'914   75-31732
ISBN 0-87630-112-X

MANUFACTURED IN THE UNITED STATES OF AMERICA

To

ANNA FREUD

for her 80th Birthday

Contents

PART III

THE DIAGNOSTIC PROCESS, ASSESSMENT,
AND TRAINING

PART IV

CLINICAL STUDIES AND TREATMENT

PART V

RESEARCH AND EXPLORATION

IN SEARCH OF LOVE AND COMPETENCE:

Twenty-Five Years of Service, Training, and Research at the Reiss-Davis Child Study Center

List of Contributors

BUSCH, FRED, Ph.D.

Past Function at Reiss-Davis: Postdoctoral Fellow in Child Psychology.

Presently: Associate Chief Psychologist, Children's Psychiatric Hospital, University of Michigan Medical Center; Senior Staff, Child Analytic Study Program, Children's Psychiatric Hospital, University of Michigan Medical Center.

CAMPBELL, MIRIAM, C.M.S.W.

Director, Psychiatric Social Work, Reiss-Davis Child Study Center.

CARUTH, ELAINE, Ph.D.

Past function at Reiss-Davis: Research Associate, Childhood Psychosis Project.

Presently: Assistant Clinical Professor, Department of Psychiatry, Child Division, UCLA Medical School; Consultant, Psychology Department, Cedars/Sinai Medical Center; Senior Faculty and Supervisor, Los Angeles Institute for Psychoanalytic Psychology.

EIDUSON, BERNICE, Ph.D.

Past Function at Reiss-Davis: Director of Psychological Services, 1959-1961; Director, Division of Research, 1961-1970.

Presently: Professor, Department of Psychiatry, UCLA School of Medicine; Principal Project Investigator, Child Development in Alternative Life Styles.

ERRATUM

COOPER, BEATRICE, M.A.

Senior Psychiatric Social Worker, Childhood Psychosis Project, Reiss-Davis Child Study Center.

EKSTEIN, RUDOLF, Ph.D.

> Director, Childhood Psychosis Project, Reiss-Davis Child Study Center; Clinical Professor in Medical Psychology at UCLA; Training Analyst, Los Angeles Psychoanalytic Society and Institute and the Southern California Society and Institute.

FRIEDMAN, SEYMOUR W., M.D.

> Director, Clinical Services, Reiss-Davis Study Center; Research Associate, Childhood Psychosis Project; Senior Faculty, Los Angeles Psychoanalytic Society and Institute.

HEINICKE, CHRISTOPH M., Ph.D.

> *Past function at Reiss-Davis*: Director, Division of Research.
>
> *Presently*: Associate Professor, Department of Psychiatry, UCLA Medical School.

HOROWITZ, MILTON, J., Ph.D.

> *Past function at Reiss-Davis*: Associate Director, Professional Services; Director, Training Program.
>
> *Presently*: Psychotherapy Supervisor and Instructor, Child Therapy Training Program at Reiss-Davis Child Study Center; Faculty, Los Angeles Institute for Psychoanalytic Psychology.

LANDRES, PETER D., M.D.

> Staff Child Psychiatrist, Reiss-Davis Child Study Center; Lecturer, Center for Early Education, Los Angeles.

LIEBOWITZ, JOEL, M., Ph.D.

> *Past function at Reiss-Davis*: Postdoctoral Fellow in Child Psychology.
>
> *Presently*: Supervisor, Child Therapy Training Program; Research Associate, Childhood Psychosis Project at Reiss-Davis Child Study Center.

MEYER, MORTIMER M., Ph.D.

Past function at Reiss-Davis: Director of Psychological Services; Director of Training.

Presently: Consultant at Reiss-Davis Child Study Center; at Vista Del Mar; at V. A. Hospitals; and at Patton State Hospital.

MOTTO, ROCCO L., M.D.

Director of Reiss-Davis Child Study Center.

NELSON, J. THOR, Ph.D.

Past function at Reiss-Davis: Postdoctoral Fellow in Clinical Psychology.

Presently: Research Associate, Childhood Psychosis Project, Reiss-Davis Child Study Center; Director, Child and Adolescent Program, Resthaven Community Mental Health Center.

PERNA, DORIS, M.D.

Past function at Reiss-Davis: Fellow in Child Psychiatry.

Presently: Assistant Clinical Professor, UCLA Medical School, Children's Division, Department of Psychiatry; Assistant Acting, Cedar/Sinai Medical Center, Los Angeles, California.

ROSOW, LEDA W., M.A.

Senior Clinical Psychologist; Supervisory Child Therapist; Supervision (Treatment and Testing); Team Coordinator at Reiss-Davis Child Study Center.

RUBIN, KENNETH, M.D.

Past function at Reiss-Davis: Supervisor of psychiatric residents; Research Associate, Childhood Psychosis Project.

Presently: Senior Faculty, Los Angeles Psychoanalytic Society and Institute.

JANET SWITZER, Ph.D.

Past function at Reiss-Davis: Senior Supervising Psychologist.

Presently: Executive Director, Switzer Center for Educational Therapy, Torrance, California; Education Extension Lecturer, UCLA.

TUMA, JUNE M., Ph.D.

Past function at Reiss-Davis: Postdoctoral Fellow in Child Psychology.

Presently: Associate Professor, Division of Child and Adolescent Psychiatry, Department of Psychiatry, University of Texas Medical Branch, Galveston, Texas; Associate Professor, Graduate School of Biomedical Sciences, UTMB., Galveston, Texas; Clinical Assistant Professor, Department of Psychology, University of Houston, Texas.

WAGNER, RALPH, M.S.W.

Training Supervisor, Reiss-Davis Child Study Center.

WEITZNER, LILLIAN, A.C.S.W.

Training Supervisor, Reiss-Davis Child Study Center; Clinical Associate, UCLA Department of Psychiatry; Guest Lecturer, Los Angeles Psychoanalytic Institute.

WHEELER, W. MARSHALL, Ph.D.

Past function at Reiss-Davis: Director, Division of Research.

Presently: Supervisor, Psychotherapy; Instructor, Psychoanalytic Theory at Reiss-Davis Child Study Center.

WILE, SIMON A., M.D.

President, Board of Trustees, Reiss-Davis Child Study Center.

Foreword

Books are permanent records of an author's concepts, his thoughts, his work, and to share with readers insights gained, knowledge and skills acquired. Books may also record shared interests, common objectives, and collective efforts in achieving those objectives.

This book, while commemorating the Silver Anniversary of the Reiss-Davis Child Study Center, is not merely to mark a moment of festivity, of joy and pride. It is primarily a documentation of a work direction, a collaborative enterprise, a philosophy, and a developing technique in helping children and adults. The book, which evidences the successful development of a well-conceived program, results from the combination of dedicated lay support and professional effort. It is a tribute to the unanimity of purpose and cooperation between the Trustees and the professional Staff of Reiss-Davis.

The Reiss-Davis Child Study Center, now 25 years old—a short span of time for an organization—has made a strong imprint on professional and scientific work on the American scene. All the articles in this volume are by present or former members of the Reiss-Davis Staff or its trainees. Characteristic of the wide range of endeavors carried out at the Center, they demonstrate a unity of purpose and commitment in a world beset by disunity and shifting goals.

Since I am a pediatrician, I know the magnitude of emotional and mental illness among children, the difficulties of parents, the disrupted family life, the school problems, the lack of trained professional personnel. I recognize the need for intensive, one to one, long-term treatment commitment to seriously disturbed children. As President of the Board of Trustees of Reiss-Davis, it is my intent to be a link between the authors of this volume and the supporting lay community. I see this volume, the collective product of the Staff and the Board, as a permanent record of their working alliance and a gift to the community which produced it. May it give additional strength to the Staff, further inspiration to the Trustees, improve our service to children, and encourage all of us in the professional and lay world to continue our support and our efforts in the interest of children everywhere.

SIMON A. WILE, M.D.
President, Board of Trustees

Introduction: Past, Present and Future

ROCCO L. MOTTO, M.D.

A book often is the result of the creative and productive work of one mind. This book represents the collective efforts of a group who have worked together in the period being commemorated by this anniversary volume. It is important to remember that the chapters represent but a small fraction of all the papers published in *The Reiss-Davis Clinic Bulletin,* and, more importantly, an even smaller part of all the scientific books and papers that have been published by members of our staff and by trainees in a wide range of professional journals and volumes in psychiatry, psychoanalysis, psychology, and social work. In order to provide a backdrop against which the work reflected in these articles can be better appreciated and understood, I shall describe the developments at the Reiss-Davis Child Study Center that have enabled us to mark this twenty-fifth year through this book.

Since entering private practice in 1948, I was keenly interested in knowing of any community agency to which I could refer families who could not afford private care. I had heard about a new child guidance clinic being established, but until 1952 there was very little community awareness of this small young institution. Then, early in 1953, I was asked to be the Director of the Reiss-Davis Child Guidance Clinic. In considering the post of Director, I spent much time in learning about the clinic.

I learned that Dr. Oscar Reiss, a pediatrician, very active in our community, had long been interested in establishing a child guidance clinic. He had spoken to many of his colleagues, to civic leaders, and to various philanthropic groups. His efforts had begun in the 1938-1940 period, had been interrupted by World War II and immediately resumed thereafter, only to be ended by his sudden death in 1948. Family, friends, and colleagues decided to establish a memorial fund aimed at "making Oscar's dream a reality": establishing The Oscar Reiss Child Guidance Clinic.

The efforts of this founding group were ably led by a younger pediatrician, Dr. David Davis. He had worked with Dr. Reiss, had known of his hopes and plans for another child guidance clinic for this community, and had shared his dream.

In 1964 the Reiss-Davis administration met with all the founders who were still alive and we compiled an oral history of the significant events that led to the founding of Reiss-Davis. Invariably one heard of the significant role played by Dr. Davis as he persuaded the founders to establish the following objectives for this new clinic.

1. To render diagnostic and therapeutic services in the field of mental hygiene to all children in need of such care, regardless of race, creed, or color.

2. To provide a teaching facility to medical students, psychiatric social workers, psychologists, and other students in allied fields.

3. To provide a facility for research and advanced study in the field of mental hygiene.

With the cooperation and enthusiastic help from many sectors of the community, the new organization was incorporated as a nonprofitable, charitable child guidance clinic to serve the diagnostic and therapeutic needs of the mentally ill child and his family. A warehouse building was offered on the most generous terms by the landlord. To remodel it, many community businessmen donated lumber, paint, floor and acoustical tile, doors, hardware, etc., along with pledges of money to enable this young organization to open its doors to those in the community who were in need. Dr. Davis was elected President of the newly created Board of Directors, a psychiatrist served as Director, and the full-time staff consisted of a clinical psychologist, a psychiatric social worker, a secretary, and a clerk-typist-receptionist.

Thus, in the period when the world began to rebuild after the global holocaust of the Second World War, the efforts of two pediatricians and a group of citizens were intent upon rebuilding and repairing the already disrupted lives of mentally ill children.

In September 1950, the clinic began to receive applications for service. It soon dispelled the anxious concern of some of the founders as to the real "need for another child guidance clinic in Los Angeles." I learned that most of the energies of the staff and the Board had been absorbed in developing a program capable of responding to the requests for diagnosis and treatment. The objectives of training and research were correctly recognized as areas to be developed after establishing a secure base of operating and supporting the diagnostic and treatment services.

When Dr. Davis died suddenly in 1951, the first crisis was faced by the young organization. A successor to Dr. Davis was elected from the ranks of lay Board members and the name of the clinic was changed to Reiss-Davis Child Guidance Clinic. The successful transition in leadership demonstrated how well guided the institution was: concern that without Dr. Davis to provide medical leadership there might be problems in carrying out the stated objectives of the founders proved unnecessary. The sense and the meaning of those objectives had been instilled in all the Board members and they were able to proceed with strength and assurance.

Early in 1953 the board learned that the first Director had decided not to continue after his three-year contract expired. I was then asked to take the position.

Since 1953, I have frequently been asked, and I occasionally wonder myself, why I gave up a busy and lucrative private practice in the field of child psychiatry and psychoanalysis and chose instead the stress and strain of guiding a community agency. This agency is a complex with a Board of Directors, supporting philanthropic groups, many and varied relations to the community, regional, state and federal sources, and with a staff composed of several professional disciplines. It is much removed from the relative simplicity of private practice. My answer to the question must draw upon the psychoanalytic understanding at the time of identity and character formation as developed by Erik Erikson and Anna Freud. My late teen and early adult years were greatly influenced by my activities and experiences in a Settlement House where after three to four years of enjoyable participation in the program and the facilities, I was asked to become a volunteer leader of a young boys' group. I later served as counselor in their summer camp and then as their representative to the city-wide inter-Settlement House Council. I was so deeply involved in these activities that all the Settlement House staff members were surprised when I enrolled in college as a pre-med student rather than for pre-social work. The Director of the Settlement House, however, revealed both her understanding and her ability to predict when she said, "In your future practice of medicine, I am sure you will always be able to find the community and social worker in you."

The opportunity presented me in 1953 allowed me to apply my psychoanalytic and psychiatric training and experience to the community in its broadest sense.

In the 1953-1956 period I asked for and was given complete freedom to restaff and to re-orient the clinic program along a psychoanalytic orientation. Concerned as we were with the development of our philosophy and purpose during those years, we found ourselves also engaged in meeting more primitive and basic needs like arranging for additional office space, and finding nearby parking space.

Response from psychoanalytic colleagues was most encouraging. They agreed to serve on our professional advisory committee, as consultants attending weekly sessions of the entire staff, and working as volunteer diagnosticians, therapists, and/or supervisors of psychotherapy. It was a time of intense stimulation and excitement. We practised the interdisciplinary approach to the total diagnostic and treatment service for the emotionally disturbed child and his equally disturbed, perplexed, and confused family environment. Our experiences with this approach continued to strengthen our conviction as to its value and deepened our commitment both to its practice and to increasing our understanding of its function in the therapeutic process.

Training programs were soon established. By 1956 we had

trainees in clinical psychology, psychiatry, and psychiatric social work. Between 1954 and 1958, these trainees were all enrolled full time in training programs elsewhere and were sent to us for a field placement in obtaining practical experience with emotionally ill children and their families. As the word spread through the professional community about the work of our staff, our consultants, and our supervisors, we were frequently petitioned to accept more trainees for varying periods of study. The Board of Directors responded by agreeing to create a position of Director of Training and shortly thereafter also created the position of Director of Research. The Board responded eagerly to all aspects of our developments. It was a common sight on evenings and weekends to see its members on hand to paint, to repair, to rebuild, or to lay plans to raise funds to hire more staff. This growth was mirrored in a budget expansion that reflected the increasing external financial support. The budget grew from $65,000 in 1958 to $209,000 by 1959, then to $658,000 in 1965, and over $1,000,000 in 1969.

In 1956 a "crisis" developed. The situation began with optimism and high excitement when the Dean of Medicine at UCLA offered us an opportunity to merge with them so we could build a greatly expanded facility on their property. There followed nine months of intensive discussion, negotiations, and finally, the painful recognition that by accepting the conditions of the offer we would lose identity, independence, and autonomy of our program. Early in these negotiations, I had recognized those dangers and was greatly relieved when the Board of Directors declined the offer in June 1957. We all recognized that in the umbrella of a university there would be many diverse programs, each operating within a specific area, but for us the critical issue was the opportunity to continue to develop in the direction we had taken. Subsequent discussions of possible mergers with other institutions confirmed our experiences of 1956-1957 that such action would mean a loss of our program.

Soon after the events of 1956 we began a vigorous search for a site on which to build a new facility. In February 1961 we moved to our present location with an expanded staff, a larger training program, beginning efforts in research and community education.

Most of all, there was a renewed commitment to our interdisciplinary approach and to our identification with our tripartite model of diagnosis and treatment, training, and research based on a psychoanalytic orientation.

Our commitment to the application of psychoanalysis grew and deepened as significant contributions were made in our clinical services of diagnosis and treatment. We were strengthened by additions to our staff of individuals trained in the Hampstead Child Therapy Program with Anna Freud, as well as those who had been trained by, or had taught in, the Menninger Clinic and other psychoanalytic training programs. Our training program was accredited by the AMA in 1962 for child psychiatric training; programs in postdoctoral clinical psychology and postmaster's psychiatric social work were also developed. As a reflection of the widening nature of our programs, our name was officially changed in 1965 to the *Reiss-Davis Child Study Center.*

Interest in a Day Treatment Program grew, and in 1966 funds were received from the Hill-Burton Hospital Construction Act enabling us to construct a new wing in which to conduct such a program for severely disturbed children. Here, too, application of ideas derived from psychoanalysis were combined in a clinical-educational program for autistic, psychotic, and borderline children and proved to be most rewarding. Unfortunately, the funding for this program was quite precarious and in 1970 we had to acknowledge that to continue with such a weak base of support was a threat to our entire program. One-third of our budget was cut, our Day Treatment Program was closed, our out-patient services were reduced by twenty percent, and significant areas of research dealing with the treatment of psychotic children in our community had to be terminated.

At that time there were suggestions of converting to other kinds of programs which were then in favor and for which funds seemed available. None of these, in my opinion, would have allowed us to continue with our commitment to psychoanalytic principles, and for this reason the staff and I recommended not to pursue them. Along with the negative and critical views expressed toward psychoanalysis, we were finding a fall off of interest and support of our endavors—increasingly we were asked to defend our practice of "long-term, intensive, individual psychotherapy for child and family." These questions were posed to us by our funding sources private, community and governmental agencies and in many instances it was suggested that we change in order to satisfy the source of the funds. Our consistent reply was to demonstrate that significant contributions were being made as a result of our diagnostic and treatment practices. We also knew how many children were in need of and could benefit from long-term therapeutic programs. Therefore, we felt that it was for our community to decide whether such patients were to have an opportunity for such services or not. We were unwilling to change the nature of our practices just to have it appear that we were "treating the masses," since we remained completely convinced of the need for a long-term, intensive individualized psychotherapeutic help for those who could avail themselves of our program and who had chosen to do so.

The contributions in this volume most certainly demonstrate that in the course of applying our principles to the diagnosis and treatment of these children, we have provided a meaningful contribution to a child and to his family. Moreover, in the psychoanalytic tradition established by Sigmund Freud, we have tried to utilize every therapeutic experience as a contribution to our total body of scientific knowledge. In addition, through our training endeavors, we have imparted this knowledge and this concept of treatment to a significant number of trainees who, in turn, are influencing other trainees and treating patients in many parts of this country and the world.

This volume is an example of what is possible in an experimental undertaking that rests upon the collaborative efforts of a serious and concerned group of citizens working side by side with experienced and competently trained professionals. Each lends the specialized skills and knowledge from his own discipline to the integrated and cooperative aspects of a psychoanalytically oriented child guidance program. It should be clearly evident that the results, as exemplified in the chapters of this book, could not have been accomplished except through an alliance of Board and staff and in an understanding which emphasizes the mutual and integrated efforts of treatment, training, and research.

It may well be that our society will turn its back on solid achievement such as this. In times of crisis with demands for many and varied services, one may find the child and the family who need long-term, intensive, individual psychotherapy ignored. We recognize this as a distinct possibility for the future, but we also know that ways can be found to continue this commitment to psychoanalytically oriented programs for mentally ill children, including, we hope, many who cannot afford private care. Within each of us is the hope that somewhere, somehow, the worth and the value of the application of psychoanalytic thinking to diagnosis and treatment practices in a community setting will be *recognized, accepted, and supported.* This would enable continuing the alliance of layman and professional who make these therapeutic services available to all socioeconomic levels and would also enable the application of psychoanalytic understanding and philosophy to be extended to the field of education. As Freud indicated his faith when he stated: "The voice of reason is soft, but it is persistent until it gains itself a hearing," we, too, can express our faith. We look forward to a fiftieth anniversary of Reiss-Davis which would witness the recognition and acceptance of the intrinsic and humanistic value of applying psychoanalytic principles to a community-wide endeavor that reflects the mutual respect and support of concerned citizens and mental health clinicians.

IN SEARCH OF LOVE AND COMPETENCE:

TWENTY-FIVE YEARS OF SERVICE, TRAINING AND RESEARCH AT THE REISS-DAVIS CHILD STUDY CENTER

Part I

THE REISS-DAVIS CHILD STUDY CENTER: ITS HISTORY, ITS PHILOSOPHY AND PURPOSE, ITS SCOPE

Chapter 1

❧

A Reaffirmation at a Time of Crisis: Concerning the Philosophy and the Scope of Work at the Reiss-Davis Child Study Center*

ROCCO L. MOTTO, M.D.,
MIRIAM CAMPBELL, M.S.W.,
RUDOLF EKSTEIN, PH.D.,
SEYMOUR FRIEDMAN, M.D.,
CHRISTOPH HEINICKE, PH.D.,
MORTIMER MEYER, PH.D.

In these times of stress, constant pressures are put on our educational institutions, welfare agencies, clinics, and training centers. Vital agencies cannot and must not withdraw to the ivory tower in order to protect their vested interests, nor may they simply yield to pressures of the short-lived fashion of the day. Too frequently, agencies under stress give in to demands without careful consideration of the long-range effect of such change, or they with-

* This statement is derived from a working paper which was submitted to a joint Board-Staff Committee on January 11, 1970, as a basis for the reorganization of the Clinic, made necessary because of the task of retrenchment. While community support has not wavered through the years, inflation and the fact that hopes for additional financial support had not been fulfilled, forced us to rediscuss our philosophy and our commitments. The working paper was accepted by the joint Board-Staff Committee as well as the total Board of the Reiss-Davis Child Study Center.

3

draw into isolation in the hope that the storms will pass and all will be as before. Each of these approaches is a betrayal to the community which has a right to expect and which ought to insist upon a more thoughtful, scientific response. Professionally mature agencies will respond to community need and not merely give in to pressure. Each need must be examined in terms of the actual means which have to be mobilized in order to meet it, and the agencies must find a place for themselves which permits an optimum use of their strengths in meeting needs. Thus, there must be a constant review of basic philosophy and program so that the work can remain vital, important, and stimulating, rather than a program of public relations with its attendant concessions to the shifting fashions and slogans of the market place. The constant review of our philosophy and program must always recognize the crucial importance of commitment to an integrated approach based on common action. We want our work to remain vital, important, and stimulating enough both to unite staff and board and to help our friends, our supporters, and our professional world so they may understand our program, and stay committed to it.

We refer to our commitment to and for a psychoanalytic clinic. For a vigorous program which will continue to make us outstanding in our community as a Center dedicated to the individual; for a quality and viable program to inspire staff, students, and the community, we must avoid the danger of developing into an eclectic and unfocused organization. We, therefore, want to make clear that instead of a non-clinical university model, we will embrace a model of operation which aims at the synthesis between ideals of programs such as envisioned by the Menninger Foundation in Topeka and the Hampstead Child Therapy Clinic in London.

Both programs predominantly stress individual treatment on a psychoanalytic basis. Child psychoanalysis, analytic child psychotherapy, and dynamic child psychiatry are combined on a psychoanalytic basis in these programs. The notion of a psychoanalytic clinic or a psychoanalytic child study center implies that the hub of our work must and will remain individual therapy. Such work has always created the main impetus for advance in our field, including the creation of opportunities for applications of psychoanalytic knowledge which should and must become part of a child-guidance operation.

A viable program can only be carried out if we see as indivisible the trinity of clinical and social service, training, and research. Neither treatment nor professional education nor scientific activity could survive independently; these three activities need each other. Each must feed upon and contribute to the others in order to keep alive progress and change and hope for finding ways of tackling the more serious forms of emotional and mental illness in childhood. Service organizations without training and research functions will not even render very good service. They will neither attract competent leaders nor very competent practioners and they will usually yield to pressures which dilute the work with the usual rationalization of social needs.

Such individual work must and will encompass both long-term and short-term psychotherapeutic services including concomitant work with the parents of our patients. We will also want to maintain a special, an almost unique feature of our Clinic; that is, the skill, the enthusiasm, the vast experience, and the research attitude around our work with severely disturbed children as we have developed it in the Childhood Psychosis Program. We have vital and competent therapists in this area who have contributed widely known and accepted work. We intend to maintain this special program which is equally important to those who need this kind of help, and attractive to students who turn to us for training. Moreover, this specialty should also be a powerful tool for our supporting groups in their efforts to appeal to the community at large.

But we can and must do more. Psychoanalysis must not merely be considered a therapeutic application, although this application is the center of our activity. Because of many years of experience in this area, we are also stressing work with teachers, with public and private school systems, and with parents. We are speaking about the application of psychoanalysis to pre-school and school education as it is designed for the average, the normal child. There is enormous need for this application in all areas, including the economically, culturally or otherwise deprived ones. Such work must be directed towards parents and all school systems on every grade level. We are interested in family education and school learning and we see in psychoanalytic application to education not merely a preventive force, but a progressive and positive power.

We are proposing that all these activities be interrelated. For example, we suggest that research carried out in this Center be oriented around the activities of the clinic. This research will be related to meaningful human experiences and will help to elucidate and to enrich these. It should be research centered on problems concerning diagnosis and treatment, education and training in school and home, and methods utilized in professional training. In this way, the research dollar would never merely be used for academic purposes but would actually represent an indirect application to the current task, and would therefore really be also a training and service dollar. We consider these three functions inseparable in any viable project in which we want to be engaged. Such a basic philosophy is applicable regardless of how small a staff is made necessary by retrenchment, even while it will be equally applicable the very moment when we can move forward again in terms of manageable size and the introduction of additional programs. If such a basic philosophy is to guide us, we are left with the question of how to distribute each budget dollar, and what work we may wish to do if and when the budget can be increased again.

At times one must be satisfied if one can only carry out a token program, a model, perhaps, which tests out a new idea and which prepares for larger action. But then one must also indicate directions for that time when the expansion of the budget will be possible.

Among many other proposals, we think, for example, that the current activities with teachers in schools might be increased considerably. We would want to go beyond extension courses and to develop a full training program for teachers as we now have for the clinical professions; a program which might offer diplomas after the end of three or four years of training. We are thinking of training programs for early education people, for pre-school people, for parents, for child-care workers, for people who work in depressed areas, and the like. We are thinking of new projects concerning short term psychotherapy, work with individuals and groups in emergency situations and in situational crisis. We are also thinking of the establishment of a therapeutic nursery and elementary school and the restoration of extensions necessary for the psychotherapeutic work with seriously disturbed children who need more than individual psychotherapy.

Each of these steps must be planned if and when more money becomes available, but the presently considered token programs, even if they have to be maintained for a considerable time, will be useful preparation. They will develop the needed thinking and skills until we once more have the means to put these programs into full effect. Such preparatory steps will give us the opportunity to evaluate where our greater efforts can be best and most effectively used. They will be cautious explorations to acquaint us with some of the many directions which could be traveled.

In a world which seems to be almost overwhelmed by social pressures, by demands and counter demands, we wonder at times whether one can mobilize sufficient enthusiasm for such programs. We wonder whether one can do that in spite of the serious crisis of each small institution today within the larger national crises. We feel that a psychoanalytic center cannot use the usual advertising methods of Madison Avenue to gain support. Our kinds of truth, our convictions can only be conveyed to people, to potential supporters, if we establish a public education program. Public education in our sense must be based on personal relationships rather than on public relations.

As we are trying to make optimum use of our budget, we realize that each budget dollar must be used for service, training, research —including scientific and professional publications—and the administration and maintenance of our beautiful plant. We must decide how we wish to split each budget dollar. Some of these decisions are actually made for us; e.g., we must accept certain basic expenses for the maintenance of buildings and certain administrative costs, even if, temporarily, we may have to keep some of our offices empty. We owe to the late Will Menninger the apt phrase that in our field money should be spent for brains rather than for bricks. It is noteworthy that many fund drives in these United States have stressed the buildings, the monuments of charity, rather than the people, the professional brains needed to put life into the bricks. We hope that our public education efforts will allow us to bring about again a situation in which the brains out-weigh the bricks. Our total budget, of which about thirty percent is derived from grant money primarily used for training and re-search, is approximately split up in the following way: of each budget dollar, forty-five cents is used for direct services; twenty-five cents for training (which incidentally, is a kind of service to the community since it trains students to do service activities), twenty cents for administration and maintenance, and ten cents for research. Any curtailment of budget will, obviously, limit our total program. But if the ratio is maintained, we will be able to keep up a competent, efficient base which can instantly absorb new personnel, additional training, added service, and new vital programs as the budget can be increased.

As a beginning experiment, we have already initiated a leader-ship group composed of Staff and Board. This group will do the preparatory work in order to help the Board to see the tasks ahead clearly and to support our philosophy with active programs and the necessary means.

A vital part of the present reorganization lies in the fact that a continuous and permanent Committee of Staff and Board has been established. It will get together and agree on new moves in order to bring about full identification for each introduced pro-gram and to guarantee a decision-making process which will safe-guard all these programs in terms of continuity and quality. This should help us to expand resources and to build a new unity so that we can move beyond crisis meetings and emergency appeals and again dedicate our strength to a creative application of our knowl-edge.

This statement of our philosophy and the scope of our work is well illustrated, we believe, through the professional contributions published in this particular issue. They deal with research, with professional training, with the application of psychoanalysis to education, with psychotherapy, with our work with parents, and also show what our students have learned from us. Thus, we want this statement to be not only a statement to inform the Board and our supporters about our work, but one which appeals for pro-fessional support. Each subscription for our scientific publication, *The Bulletin of the Reiss-Davis Clinic,* each referral, each student who applies to us, each grant given to us, each individual gift, small or large, will be used by us in order to maintain a small experimental model organization for psychoanalytic service, training, and research in the children's field, a hope for the future.

An old Greek myth tells us about Pandoras' box; opened, it let escape one evil creature after the other into the world. Most people just remember that when Pandora opened the box, out flew all manner of evils, troubles, and diseases—before unknown to man—which spread over all the earth. They forget that the last to become visible from the bottom of the box was Hope. In this world of unrest, small places like ours, community and crisis oriented, but at the same time holding on to professional and scientific knowledge, to skill, and to quality work, represent hope. We must maintain that hope. In this sense, the Reiss-Davis Child Study Center will remain at the bottom of the box which represents current mental-health discipline.

Chapter 2

❧

Brief Therapy Versus Intensive Therapy – Or: Patient-Oriented Treatment Programs

RUDOLF EKSTEIN, PH.D.

Are the emergencies which our patients bring to us acute social problems crying for an immediate answer? Or, are they emerging inner conflicts which need more than a hasty response? Must we find an instant answer to the problem, or must we avail ourselves of time, and turn the crisis, that one emergency point on the time-line, into continuity, into a process towards growth? This seeming conflict between emergency and process, impulse and emerging, is not a new, apparently unresolvable contradiction in our field, but an eternal, repetitive task for each clinician, for every new generation of students, and for all people seeking help.

In times of social emergency, anxiety, unrest, and political fragmentation and polarization, the struggle between established forces and those who want immediate change, all aspects of societal life are drawn into the conflict. This is also reflected in the competitive struggle on the psychiatric market place. With claims and counter-

This paper was stimulated by Dr. Alfred Flarsheim, Editor of the *Bulletin of the Chicago Society for Adolescent Psychiatry*, who invited me to write a "Letter to the Editor" concerning crisis-intervention and long-range treatment programs. The two observations cited here were published in the Fall, 1971 issue of that journal (p. 74).

claims, emerging therapeutic schools slogan new promises as they struggle for power and recognition, and try to enlist the support of the public as well as the fund-granting private and government agencies. The clamor for something new, the anti-establishment cry, is taken up by the public, by the patients, by the students. Much time and energy, instead of being invested in research, training, and service, have to be utilized just to stay afloat. One of the dichotomies of the current crazy-quilt scene which constitutes today's practice in the clinical professions, is said to be the contest between those who insist on crisis intervention or brief psycho-therapy, and those who are dedicated to long treatment processes.

The quest for the development of short-term services, instant interventions, is frequently defended in terms of having to meet immense social needs, in terms of its immediate accommodation to the help-seeking public, in terms of democratically sharing limited resources, even if the claims for effective total cure are not fully believed by most of the innovators.

Long-term psychotherapies are seen as luxuries for the few, not truly proven, and are considered to be in the way of today's quest for fast solutions. We speak about brief encounters, emergency ar-rangements, time-limited short hospitalizations, etc., and meet thus a social need, a responsibility which I cannot help but accept and wish to share in meeting. But is that all that we have to do?

I recall how surprised I was when somebody once asked me whether I knew which one of the medical discoveries had contri-buted most to the health of the peoples of the world. I was told that plumbing in the large cities, the introduction of sewer systems, had contributed more to the physical health and well-being of people than any other single medical contribution. I recalled then the masterful book of the physician Hans Zinsser, *Rats, Mice and History* (2), in which he documented how the health of nations, even the wars of nations, their future, may be controlled by pre-venting the spread of infectious disease. In times of total need, it is easy to rationalize the introduction of a single element in order to meet an emergency and to obviate the rest of acquired knowledge and skill. One throws out the baby with the bath water.

Recently, two teaching experiences brought me face to face with this problem.

The first one was a visit with the staff of the Orthogenic School in Chicago, a group of dedicated people who were willing to meet with me very late in the evening, far beyond the hour that most professionals usually schedule staff meetings. These people, originally under the leadership of Bruno Bettelheim but now under the directorship of Bertram Cohler, always met after the children had gone to bed. Late staff meetings were just one expression of total commitment to their task. They took up with me issues about the treatment of schizophrenic children and adolescents, particularly the issue of countertransference. I looked at the faces of these people, many of them quite young and some middle-aged. All expressed commitment and dedication, and each person considered it an indisputable fact that schizophrenic children usually need years and years of treatment, frequently years and years of life in a residential treatment center. Thousands and thousands of hours are invested in each of the children, many of whom make remarkable recoveries, through which we gain new knowledge which helps others as well. In addition to the usual therapeutic opportunities made available to them, these young patients live in a therapeutic milieu which is constructed in such a way as to allow them to begin meeting the tragic dilemma of their lives. Although they experience their life as a constant emergency, endless time is given in order to allow for a process which will facilitate the slow emergence of emotional strength.

The staff and I talked about the overwhelming nature of the illness, the deep commitment which almost devours them who dedicate their professional life to such work. This commitment could be considered the countertransference counterpart of the equally deep commitment of the schizophrenic patient to sustain his world, autistic or symbiotic. He defends it against the onslaught of those who want to lead him *back to reality*, since they are convinced that this style of life is destructive and does not lead towards a resolution of the self-sustained psychotic dilemma. In order to characterize for the staff the nature of the commitment of the caretakers, social workers, psychologists, psychiatrists, psychotherapists, and teachers, I borrowed an analogy from a short story.

Written by analyst Allen Wheelis (1), it is about a man who

wanted to be a writer. In searching for an opportunity, he found a position which required that he write the fortunes for a fortune-cookie factory. He was employed to feed the fortune-cookie machine, a kind of computer-type-writer-fortune-cookie system which was to deliver the cryptic messages he was to invent. He was intrigued by this task. The fortune-cookie machine produced such elegantly enigmatic messages that finally all the restaurants wanted to buy fortune cookies from this particular factory because of the appeal of these "fortunes." The machine—or, was it the employer?—made more and more demands on the young writer, and even as he fed the machine with more and more of his sayings he became more and more dedicated. Eventually desperate, as the demands turned out to be beyond endurance, he fed himself into the machine—a final sacrifice to create that ultimate saying, oracle, proverb, that interpretation that was to top everything that went before.

Many lessons can be read into that short story of never-ending, always-increasing commitment of the young man. The one that I drew from Allen Wheelis' fantasy of ambiguous oracular pronouncements allowing multiple meanings, concerned the inner fears of those who dedicate themselves to work with severely disturbed children. It concerned the worries about the nature of severe mental illness, and the endless professional training required in order to feed that fortune-cookie machine which feeds the children of the residential center.

As I discussed the implications of this story for an understanding of the nature of countertransference, I told the staff that I had become acquainted with the story in an entirely different situation: a staff meeting in a crisis-intervention hospital ward at the county hospital in my home community. The chief of that particular staff had told me about the story because it seemed to him to express the dedication, conviction, involvement, and moral pressure, which characterized his staff. They, too, dealt with severely mentally ill people, but rather than being prepared for years of treatment of these patients, they made it their task to meet the emergency and then to get these patients out of the hospital situation in as short a time as possible. They are then sent to comprehensive mental-health facilities, halfway houses, clinics, private therapists, etc. The staff's fear was that long-term hospitalization creates eternal dependency and hopelessness, and does not lead to cure. Instead of the starting point for a new kind of life, they felt that the hospital becomes a human warehouse as Albert Deutsch so aptly described it.

The staff of that center believed that the stay in the hospital should be as short as possible while treatment "elsewhere" should be as long as necessary. The staff seemed to me almost the same as the one at the Orthogenic School, except that they had to cope with acutely demanding, and constantly changing pressures. At the crisis-intervention ward, the staff had to size up patients' needs in a few hours or a few days, and then to try to contribute to a kind of recovery which would allow the patient to leave at the very earliest moment. They were often deeply troubled as to what would happen to the patients afterward, deeply unhappy if they misjudged the situation and did not help the utmost possible. They were not unaware that their hope and expectation about treatment elsewhere and as long as necessary were very frequently about as realistic as the hope of the man that he could ever satisfy the increasing demands of the fortune-cookie machine.

Sometimes I felt that the staff in the crisis center maintained itself by having a kind of deep private faith in their own construction of a sort of delusion that a couple of weeks of hospitalization could cure schizophrenia. This was a private, not a publicly expressed, position. It was actually a part of the omnipotent as well as omni-impotent countertransference position, for those who work under such conditions, and who know the limitations of the succeeding resources. No doubt this group saw its mission in dealing with acute breakdown, with the most dangerous phase of the psychotic or depressive experience, as the most important aspect of the total work. How could one develop such a degree of dedication and such highly professional morale unless willing to assume that one's own intervention in the disturbed life of a deeply sick individual could create the decisive turning point, if not the cure?

Both groups of practitioners, I suspect, would look at each other with great misgiving and would believe—I gather from the literature—that they are depending on entirely contradictory philosophies of treatment. Perhaps both need such faith in their respective philosophies in order to sustain the work, but faith is not enough. As Emily Dickinson suggests:

> *Faith is a fine invention*
> *For gentlemen who see;*
> *But microscopes are prudent*
> *In an emergency.*

These extreme polarities of an experience are magnified versions of the more usual problems. They suggest that we are not dealing with unbridgeable dichotomies, but rather with different levels of treatment or with different levels of social and therapeutic action. These ways of dealing with patients, seen as contradictions on the same level, may be synthesized if one is aware of the level on which one is dealing with the issue.

The immediate intervention of the medics at the battlefield may very well be decisive for the recoverability or treatability of a wounded soldier. This is true even though the long-term medical help and rehabilitation that he will need may seem to make the medics' emergency help on the battlefield but a tiny point in the long treatment process. The emergency help may be experienced by him who offers it as absolutely decisive; may create in him a kind of absolute faith concerning his definitive role in the cure of the patient. Thus he accepts his dangerous mission on the battlefield with a sense of a powerful calling.

In similar fashion can the social intervention of a medical doctor in public health be considered. In insuring a pure water supply or establishing a reliable sewage disposal system, his actions could be seen as more important and more decisive than the most complex medical or surgical advance. This is so because such action is applied on a completely different social level of effectiveness, and a different moment of appropriateness. And in like manner, a good many medical or psychiatric problems can indeed be resolved by short-term intervention.

Once this had become apparent to me, I found myself equally helpful to that group of practitioners who have but hours or days to effect therapeutic changes as well as to those dedicated to long-lasting treatment of severely disturbed children and adolescents.

Moreover, psychotherapy needs both levels of application. The danger of each school of thought does not lie in what it does, but in what it may think others should do, and that it alone has an exclusive monopoly on therapeutic effectiveness.

Much indeed depends on whether a society is willing to maintain investments on all levels. In a societal situation of dissolution, and disintegration, the emergency-help factor will be pushed by existing anxiety, while long-term attempts will be seen as a luxury. In emergency times one overlooks the strategies of treatment and gets over-involved in tactics of emergency. In quieter times, one may overlook, unhappily so, even the most demanding social aspects of psychiatry since one may feel safe on the island of one's specialization.

It is fascinating to observe how the knowledge that comes from specialization, from long-term treatment, is actually applicable in short, emergency interventions as well. One application cannot function without the other. I believe that crisis-intervention professionals and long-term professionals, if their skill and their knowledge are derived from basic clinical insight, will and must unite their endeavors instead of fighting each other in a meaningless ideological battle.

If my point carries, crisis intervention will turn out to be an important part in the whole process of treatment instead of being the delusion of the cure. It also will become a part of the genuine cure of the delusion. And long-term treatment, instead of an unobtainable luxury, will become the essential part of a total approach which, alert to the crisis of society, might help rid society of a mere crisis approach.

The Reiss-Davis Child Study Center tries to deny neither emergency nor long-term needs, but to experiment with therapeutic methods after careful consideration of the needs of each patient. Treatment techniques must be modified according to the specific needs of the patient. It is necessary to continue to reduce the ideological and political basis of our clinical activities and to strengthen the scientific by thorough diagnosis, careful training of staff, and appropriate application of the whole range of treatment possibilities. Notions of "maximum" and "minimum" must be supplanted by that of optimum service for each person in search of help. While society at large is not always ready to meet such utopian expectations, a small child guidance center can and must attempt to organize a model service. It must attempt to provide a pilot project to show the way towards the synthesis of service, training, and research, that indispensable trinity of therapeutic effectiveness. The range of activities at the Reiss-Davis Child Study Center concerns problems of diagnostic procedures, brief interventions, emergency interventions, long-term psychotherapy, as well as work with parents. The patient population covers a wide range of ages as well as of mildness or severity of illness. The emphasis of our treatment approach is on the specific need of the child rather than on a premature commitment to merely one modality of treatment. Our compassion for the child's suffering is supported by our faith in helping, but the methods of therapy are based on faith in the microscope.

BIBLIOGRAPHY

1. WHEELIS, ALLEN. *The Illusionless Man—Some Fantasies and Meditations on Disillusionment*. New York: W. W. Norton, 1966, pp. 111-144.
2. ZINSSER, HANS. *Rats, Mice and History*. Boston: Little, Brown, 1935.

Part II

THE TRAINING OF THE PROFESSIONAL

Chapter 3

✄

Training in Child Psychotherapy

MILTON J. HOROWITZ, PH.D.,
ROCCO L. MOTTO, M.D.,
MORTIMER M. MEYER, PH.D.

In the United States, there are relatively few training programs for psychiatrists, psychologists and psychiatric social workers in intensive, individual psychotherapy with children. Even in settings committed to training in child psychotherapy it is rather unusual to find that the training opportunities are similar for the several disciplines.

Moreover, it is at present considered timely to establish community centers (1, 2, 4, 7, 8) with action-oriented programs designed to serve large numbers of people as rapidly as possible. Clinical programs prepared to commit as much time as may be necessary to serve individual patients and their families may appear unfashionable. To provide training in intensive, individual psychotherapy may be considered that much more out of step with the times. Yet, we believe that training in intensive, individual diagnosis and psychotherapy is a necessary and vital focus in the preparation of all clinicians.

The training of psychotherapists, for both adults and children, has been a subject of long debate and concern (5, 9, 10). Proposals for the establishment of a new training program for psychotherapists are receiving renewed attention from representatives of the disciplines concerned (3). Though less attention appears to be paid to the training of persons in child psychotherapy than for those in adult psychotherapy, there seem to be similar problems concerning background, preparation and directions.

Reiss-Davis Child Study Center has long been committed to the training of persons in psychiatry, psychology and psychiatric social work in intensive, individual psychotherapy with children. The Center's Constitution states that one of its purposes is to offer training to all three disciplines and that training will be within the psychoanalytic framework. There is the additional statement that "an opportunity shall be afforded for continuous professional growth and development in the already acquired skills applicable to work in a child guidance clinic." Thus, training is offered to staff members who wish to develop additional skills as well as to those who come for the express purpose of receiving training. We take it as a basic premise that becoming identified with individual diagnosis and psychotherapy is a necessary part of the growth of professional identity* in persons who are preparing to work with children and their families.

We also take as a basic premise that intensive work with the individual child is necessary whether the eventual field of work will involve short-term or long-term procedures. Many new avenues of activity are currently being suggested for the clinician. The work involved, however, still depends on a thorough knowledge of the principles of human behavior and supervised experience in

---

* In a discussion of the training of psychiatric residents, and how this training fits in with preparing psychiatrists for community responsibility, Modlin (7) has observed: "We feel it vital that the resident be trained first in dynamic psychology, hospital practice, and intensive long-term psychotherapy to the point that he has a defined realization of the professional role of psychiatrist. We would counsel the same procedure for members of other mental health disciplines. Once professional identity is familiar and secure, then modifications and ramifications can be assayed with relative comfort. Community mental health practice requires flexibility, as does good psychiatric practice generally. It is important at times to separate diagnostic and therapeutic functions from professional role definitions. A well-integrated psychiatric team is able to see each patient or client as its responsibility, not just the psychiatrist's, and assign necessary professional ministrations for the patient and relatives to the team members most appropriate to the particular circumstances in the given case. This flexibility is best achieved through modification of settled professional role, ease and competence."

the applied use of this knowledge. Only when the clinician has the confidence associated with training in depth can he truly feel himself ready to tackle the demanding clinical problems in which quick judgments are necessary. As we know, the clinical process often requires making decisions on the basis of inadequate data. Only after extended training and experience, are we cognizant of the limitations and challenges of the clinical process, including our strengths and limitations as clinicians. Expressed another way, it may be said that the more rapidly a judgment must be made, the more a professional person must call upon his own resources. In-depth study of the patient helps provide these resources.

With mental-health professionals continually being asked to provide assistance in a variety of new ways within more limited periods of time, the need for careful intensive training becomes even more urgent. There is a temptation to provide a smattering of knowledge related to the many new fields in which mental health is applied. Thus, it is especially important for training programs to provide opportunities for the professional person to learn how to think, to make decisions and to assist in solving a variety of problems. In our diagnostic and therapeutic processes, much attention is given to the development of what might be called the "thinking process." It is generally what Klein has described: "The way clinicians work and how they think about cases" (6).

At Reiss-Davis, instead of many cases being seen for diagnosis and treatment, a smaller number of cases is studied in great detail. This provides the opportunity for the student to participate with a senior person in thinking through the processes of diagnosis and treatment. Long-term relationships between student and teacher around the supervisory process become critical. Training centers on understanding as well as the use of knowledge and skills, on what things mean as well as what may be done.

The basic assumptions underlying training in child psychotherapy are:

1. The focus of all clinical activity is the commitment to the individual patient and his family; correlatively, the focus of the educational enterprise is the individual student and his training needs.

2. All training centers around the student's clinical experiences.

3. Other methods of teaching are: individual supervision; courses, seminars and other didactic exercises; attempts at helping the student integrate the didactic, clinical and supervisory experiences; and collaboration with other disciplines involved in the therapeutic process.

4. The staff recognizes that the preparation of the well-trained child therapist requires more than two years of training. The programs, therefore, are seen as but a beginning in the further development of the individual clinician's knowledge and skills. Fellows in child psychiatry and clinical psychology completing the program usually seek to continue their training as therapists.

Though training in individual psychotherapy with children is a major emphasis, it is not identified as the exclusive objective in any of the training programs. In each discipline there are continuing activities in the work specific to the skills and identity of the discipline concerned. In addition, diagnostic work is regarded as having an important contribution to the trainee's efforts in psychotherapy, as described elsewhere in this issue by Friedman. For individuals in each of the disciplines, however, work in psychotherapy comprises more than fifty percent of his total training experience. This includes direct contact with patients, supervision, courses, seminars and other didactic experiences.

Described below are the highlights of the various parts of the training program in psychotherapy. It should always be kept in mind that they are interrelated with experiences with the patient which provide the focus for learning.

A. *Individual Experiences in Psychotherapy*

Though most trainees have had some experience in psychotherapy with adults, most have had little to no experience in treating children. Consideration is given, therefore, to selecting for assignment those children who, according to detailed diagnostic evaluation, seem suitable for these trainees. In the selection of training cases, attention is given to the following characteristics:

1. Despite other manifestations of emotional illness or disturbance, there are indications of strength and treatability in the child.

2. There is a likelihood the family and child are and will continue to be motivated for treatment.

3. The family is likely to support the treatment.

In 1965-1966, the total of eighteen Fellows (persons in training full-time), interns and residents in training was comprised of one career-teacher; three full-time Fellows in child psychiatry; five part-time residents in general psychiatry; four postdoctoral Fellows in child clinical psychology; two predoctoral interns in clinical psychology* and three Fellows in the newly developed program for social work clinicians. A total of fifty-four children were in treatment with these Fellows and residents.

Psychotherapy is conducted with children with a variety of emotional disorders. Slightly more than half of the children treated by students carry diagnoses in the Psychoneurotic Reaction categories. Most of the remaining cases have been diagnosed as Personality Trait Disturbance. Approximately half of the children seen in diagnostic study at Reiss-Davis are between the ages of six and eleven. About seventy percent of all cases in treatment with persons in training are between the ages of eight to twelve at the start of treatment. Boys outnumber girls in the ratio of two to one. Only one out of five children is a transfer case; the others are beginning treatment.

Patients are treated from one to three times weekly; most are seen twice each week. The average length of treatment is eighteen months. Parents are studied carefully and are given help with the individual and family problems which affect their ability to function as parents. In most cases, parents are seen by someone other than the child's therapist.

With the opening of the new Day Treatment Program, clinical services will be available to children ages three to twelve who, because of severe emotional disturbances, are unable to utilize normal daytime settings or the specialized settings already provided by nonresidential agencies. A smaller unit will be established for preschool children and a larger unit will provide service for older children.

---

* This was the last year in which training was offered to predoctoral candidates in clinical psychology. Training is now offered only to postdoctoral Fellows.

B. *Individual Supervision*

Experienced child therapists serve as therapy supervisors. Each Fellow in child psychiatry is assigned three therapy supervisors in the first year. In the second year, the number is reduced to two. Additional supervision is provided in continuous case conferences. The Fellows in child psychology and in social work are each assigned two therapy supervisors in the first year. Part-time residents in general psychiatry each carry two cases in therapy and have one therapy supervisor. In 1965-1966, a total of fifteen supervisors provided supervision. The articles by Wheeler and Dorn in this issue describe the experiences and philosophy of two supervisors.

A supervision seminar has been established to review the relationship of supervision to the structure and functions of the Center, to the educational program and to other administrative, clinical and training matters. Ongoing supervision is reviewed. All new supervisors, including supervisors of casework, psychological testing and therapy, are expected to participate in this weekly seminar.

Individual supervisors are permitted considerable latitude in the conduct of the supervisory process. They are responsible for periodic evaluations of their trainees. These evaluations are part of the trainee's record and are reviewed by administrative officers who have the final decision concerning action that may need to be taken.

C. *Courses, Seminars and Other Didactic Exercises*

There are several core courses for all persons receiving training in child psychotherapy; simultaneously, didactic exercises are offered on topics in the various disciplines. The latter need not interest us here. The core courses are:

1. Psychotherapy I: As described in this issue by Ekstein and student participants, this course covers generic problems encountered in psychotherapeutic work in a child guidance clinic. Problems considered include: the beginning of psychotherapy, the use of time, transference, the nature of play, of acting out, of fantasy, the nature of interpretation, collaboration, the use of the clinical team, termination and transfer.

2. Psychotherapy II: This course extends the course above but centers on specific questions such as how different development phases and symptoms influence the psychotherapy with the child. Efforts are made to consider cases typical of different diagnostic conditions and the therapeutic issues they entail.

3. Psychotherapy III: This course covers the available body of knowledge on the diagnosis and analytic treatment of psychotic children. Detailed consideration is given to ongoing work with children in intensive treatment as part of the research project on childhood psychosis. Tape recordings of therapeutic sessions are reviewed. The work reported is related to the literature. Throughout, attention is focused on current case material as presented by therapists within the Center.

4. Psychotherapy Conferences: Two conferences are designed with the objective of following specific cases in considerable detail. Fellows engaged in psychotherapy with children present their work regularly to consultants throughout the course of the training year. Cases are selected to demonstrate different kinds of problems. Emphasis is given to the discussion of psychotherapeutic technique. Pertinent literature is also reviewed.

5. The Child Study Course: This two-year course is provided for all persons in training and is especially designed for those in two-year Fellowships. The topics covered in the first year include child development, psychopathology and diagnosis, methods of assessment and child psychiatry and the community. In the second year, the work in psychopathology and diagnosis is extended. Attention then centers on reviewing ongoing therapeutic work by Fellows, methods of consultation with schools and other agencies in the community and research approaches to child development and child psychopathology.

D. *Integrating Didactic, Clinical and Supervisory Experiences*

It is, admittedly, difficult for a teacher to attempt to integrate the various orders of experience for the student. Rather, it is the student who must do so for himself. Throughout the training programs, therefore, efforts are made to help the Fellow integrate the various clinical supervisory and didactic experiences. Increasingly, with his cumulative clinical experience and participation in the supervisory process and in the various didactic exercises, the Fellow becomes able to integrate what is occurring in his training.

In the seminar on psychoanalytic theory (see Wheeler's article Ch 5), an attempt is made to relate psychoanalytic literature to current clinical work supervised by the leader of the seminar. In a seminar in the second year of the child study course, trainees present ongoing therapeutic work; here, the objective is to help the student integrate for himself and for his colleagues aspects of the clinical experience and selected foci of the supervisory process. In the seminar on psychotherapy of the psychotic child, increasing attention is given to the literature and to the findings from the Project on Childhood Psychosis conducted at Reiss-Davis. In all seminars, of course, readings are suggested and in selecting them, attention is given to the clinical and theoretical contributions. The use of supervisors as instructors in the didactic program is especially helpful in the integration process.

E. *Collaboration in the Therapeutic Process*

Interdisciplinary collaboration is a major emphasis in training as well as in service. This extends into the therapeutic process as well as diagnosis. In a continuing manner, the therapist-in-training is acquainted with the efforts of all who are working in both the diagnosis and treatment of the child and the family. There are no standardized collaboration procedures, however. In selected instances, for example, collaboration between therapist and caseworker may be minimized in order to allow the therapist-in-training to develop for himself as fully as possible how the child's internal conflicts mirror the external situation and his role within it. In other instances, the therapist-in-training works very closely with caseworkers in the therapeutic process to see where casework may make special contributions. Fellows in psychiatry and clinical psychology are encouraged in selected instances to do the casework themselves to learn about the work with the family as well as the child. Also, the traditional roles of the Fellows in the several disciplines are varied so that in addition to having all persons gain experience in treatment of children, members of each dis-

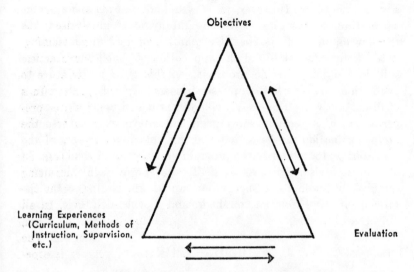

Fig. 1 — A Model of the Educational Process: Interrelationships of
Objectives, Learning Experiences and Evaluation.

cipline may work therapeutically and diagnostically with all members of the family.

Educational programs have long been schematized as a triangle consisting of three principal components: objectives, learning experiences (including curriculum, methods of instruction, use of supervision, teaching material, facilities, etc.) and evaluation. Each component affects and is, in turn, affected by the others. As shown in Fig. 1, educational objectives help determine the selection of learning experiences and what is done to evaluate the extent to which objectives are realized. Responses to learning experiences and results of evaluation provide insight into the relevance of the educational objectives. Each component, then, may be demonstrated to be dynamically interrelated with the others.

In a clinical setting in which professional training is offered and in which the principal instructional methods center on the integrated and dynamic use of clinical experience, individual supervision and seminars, the interrelation of the several components in

Fig. 1 is evident. However, as is well known, evaluating professional training programs is difficult. Many problems are found in the development of systems of evaluation of an individual candidate's knowledge, skill and the application of that knowledge and skill in handling specific problems. At this time at Reiss-Davis, evaluations by psychotherapy supervisors, derived in the course of discussion with trainees, provide the principal mode of assessing performance. Attention is being given to developing increasingly useful evaluation methods that will not only help assess performance, but will also clarify the program objectives and the adequacy of the supervisory process itself. Two by-products of the newly established seminar on supervision would appear to be the improvement of evaluation methods and clarification of program objectives.

BIBLIOGRAPHY

1. BRICKMAN, H. R., SCHWARTZ, D. A., and DORAN, S. M. The Psychoanalyst as Community Psychiatrist. *Amer. J. Psychiatry,* April, 1966, 122:1081.
2. Community Psychology: A Report of the Boston Conference on the Education of Psychologists for Community Mental Health, Boston University, 1966.
3. HOLT, R. R. New Directions in the Training of Psychotherapists. *J. of Nervous and Ment. Disease,* Nov., 1963, 137:5.
4. Joint Information Service of the American Psychiatric Association and the National Association for Mental Health: The Community Mental Health Center — An Analysis of Existing Models, Washington, D.C., September, 1964.
5. KIRKPATRICK, M. E., et al. Training for Psychotherapy with Special Reference to Non-medical Fields. *Amer. J. Ortho.,* January, 1949, 19:1.
6. KLEIN, G. S. Credo for a Clinical Psychologist. *Bull. Menninger Clinic,* 1963, 27:61.
7. MODLIN, H. C. Community Mental Health Planning. Discussion of Papers Presented at Symposium, American Orthopsychiatric Association, April, 1966, 61.
8. SMITH, M., and HOBBS, N. The Community and the Community Mental Health Center. *Amer. Psychol.,* June 1966, 21:499.
9. WELSCH, E. E., et al. Qualifications for Psychotherapists. *Amer. J. Ortho.,* January, 1956, 24:35.
10. WYATT, F., et al. Training of Clinical Psychologists. *Amer. J. Ortho.,* 1952, 22:138.

Chapter 4

❧

Notes on the Teaching and Learning of Child Psychotherapy Within a Child Guidance Setting

RUDOLF EKSTEIN, PH.D., FRED BUSCH, PH.D.,
JOEL LIEBOWITZ, PH.D., DORIS PERNA, M.D.,
AND JUNE TUMA, PH.D.*

In 1923 Freud acknowledged receiving a book which Fritz Wittels (5) had sent to him. Although not altogether happy with this biography that his student had written, Freud wrote Wittels:

> On the other hand I willingly concede that your penetrating observation has divined quite correctly in me features well known to myself; for instance, that I am compelled to go my own way, often a roundabout way, and that I cannot make any use of ideas that are suggested to me when I am not ready for them (4).

---

* Contributing members to the minutes of the course whose work was either directly quoted or summarized were: Morton Bramson, M.D., Fred Busch, Ph.D., Patricia Flynn, A.B., Gale Goldschmidt, M.S.W., Esther Hecht, M.S.S.S., Peter Hood, M.D., Margot Kohls, M.S.W., Joel Liebowitz, Ph.D., Kaj Lohmann, M.S. (auditor), David Meltzer, M.D., Clinton Montgomery, M.D., Evelyn Motzkin, M.D., Doris Perna, M.D., Michael Silverman, M.A., June Tuma, Ph.D., Elinor Weissman, M.S.S., Frank Williams, M.D., and Abraham Wodinsky, M.D. (auditor).

This observation contributes a germinal insight into the nature of teaching and learning. The professional teacher of psychoanalysis is certainly aware that students cannot make use of new ideas that are suggested to them unless they are good and ready for them. The challenge of our training work in child psychotherapy consists of creating situations which help prepare students for new ideas that they can use.

How is one to go about creating a training structure which permits such readiness that the teacher truly teaches rather than lectures, and students truly learn rather than parrot the teacher's words? How will the teacher accept the fact that in some small way every student, and certainly every gifted student, must go his own, often roundabout, way? One of the great teachers of psychoanalysis, the late Ernst Kris, is said to have suggested that the good teacher, rather than merely imparting knowledge, offers inspiration to his students. How is one to live up to so great an expectation within the boundaries of administrative requirements? And how is one to develop teaching techniques which will stimulate independent thinking within the boundaries of Freud's concepts?

In order to highlight the complexities of the teaching situation, I should like to quote from the self-evaluation of a psychiatrist in our training setting. Writing about his learning experience with his first supervisor in child psychotherapy, he states:

> As well as I can recall I came to Reiss-Davis for several reasons. First, I had had some experience with children at another hospital which I had found unsatisfactory. Secondly, I felt that it was important to understand pathology in children in order to be able to work more effectively with adults. Work with adults was at that time my primary interest and I felt that my experience at Reiss-Davis might be informative but probably not extremely enjoyable.

This man took an assignment here without knowing whether he would be truly interested in doing therapeutic work with children. He thought of such work as a "roundabout way" of learning more about adults. The seasoned administrator of psychoanalytic training programs certainly might hope that all people who work with adults would also have had experience with children. Yet he must see this student as one deeply engrossed in issues of professional choice; must consider him confused about his professional identification; and must be aware that such a student is trying to cope with powerful obstacles in his use of either supervision or lecture and seminar experience. These obstacles cannot be understood if we over-simplify and call them learning resistances. The young doctor soon found out that he would have to involve himself deeply. Much of his learning with us, rather than being only an issue of information, must have turned into an issue of pain, decision making, immense self-doubt and an unexpected kind of involvement.

Much of our supervisory work is aided by a seminar for supervisors. In this seminar an attempt is made to apply to work with children insights on the training for adult psychotherapy (3). The "Clinical Rhombus" (3) concerning the clinical training setting, has to be modified to meet the special countertransference problems when children and parents are involved. The whole problem of authority takes on magnifications of a completely different order from that in work described earlier (2).

All of our students come to us with different backgrounds, different expectations and different levels of training. They come with different ambitions, different hopes and, above all, with different methods of making use of professional teachers. In other words, they come to the training situation with different patterns of learning, in addition to all their individual idiosyncrasies.

These highly unlike individuals are the students that I meet at the beginning of each year and must try to involve in the basic principles of psychotherapy. At the end of this section is the current outline of the course. There is a "curriculum." But I try to bring a body of knowledge to the students in such a way that there will develop between us an interchange, a process, a lively coming-to-grips with the central issues that they will encounter. They will bring questions from their previous studies or their current clinical settings. We will revive the "ideological warfare" between the different psychological or psychoanalytical schools once more. And though I will be quite outspoken about my views, I try to bring the students more than doctrine. I want to bring them a way of thinking, a way of working and a commitment.

Through the psychotherapy seminar I learn what concrete and overconcrete use is made of my teachings, and how I am understood or misunderstood. Frequently I get a little frightened about the effect that I seem to have on the students and the distortions that occur during the transcribing of knowledge. Sometimes I am amazed at how much use could be made of the material. And I have come to appreciate an insight that I came by rather late in my life as a teacher: the success of a good teacher depends on having good students. Yet as I listen to my students I cannot help but have some misgivings. Though I listen at times with delight to the student summaries of lectures and discussions, other times I listen with pain because I feel misunderstood or suspect that I have been unclear and dull. But each time I have learned a little more and have felt less need (if only in fantasy) to censure them in order to correct their impressions of material I presented.

Every teacher, of course, hopes that his students will identify with his teachings and will have reason to be proud of him. But it is equally important that he be proud of the students. It is for this reason that I am glad to be listed as co-author of the following notes which illustrate what has transpired between us and in which way they have acquired new ideas about child psychotherapy. They are working notes about teaching and learning and, perhaps, will inspire us to work more thoroughly on methods of teaching and learning in our field. Learning cannot take place without the willingness to show one's weaknesses and difficulties, and the willingness to ask questions for which one has no answers as yet. This collaboration shows agreement with Freud that one can make use of new ideas only when one is ready for them, and that one is frequently compelled to go one's own, often roundabout, way. But there are no shortcuts for either the students or the teacher.

R. E.

SYLLABUS

I. *Conceptual Framework*

Aim of course
Definition of Psychoanalytic Child Psychotherapy
Training for Child Psychotherapy (place of personal analysis for students)
Team Approach, Team Functions
Crisis Intervention (emergency and emerging conflicts)
Application Procedures and the Diagnostic Process

II. *The Beginning Phase of Psychotherapy*

Purpose, Goal, Function
Method—Theoretical Framework
Commitment—Patient's and Therapist's Commitment
Structure, Limit Setting, Positive Use of Structure, Equipment of Consulting Room
Initial Interview—the Opening Gambit

III. *Transference in Child Psychotherapy*

Definition
History of Concept
  The early positions of Melanie Klein and Anna Freud
  An attempt at synthesis and current views
Positive
Negative
Institutional
Countertransference (obstacle or road to empathy)

IV. *Communication—Modes of Technical Intervention*

Definition
Purpose
Development of Language Function (communion to communication, signal to symbol)
Psychoanalytic Theory of Development of Thin king (frustration, delay leading to thinking)
Revised Model of Thinking (foreplay, act and after-play)
Bühler's Model of Language
Pleasure Principle, Reality Principle and Adaptation
Play as Communication
Play as Psychic Work
Microcosm and Macrocosm in Play
Play Acting, Play Action and Acting Out
Setting the Stage—the Therapeutic Situation
Continuity, Play Disruption
Play and Games
Interpretation, Nature of; Direct and Indirect; Metaphoric
Identification and Identity
Work and Play as Communication
Receptor-Perceptor Paradigm
Age-appropriate Play
Adaptive Function of Play

The authors, trainees at the Reiss-Davis Child Study Center, consider this a rare opportunity to present the student's view on how he is being trained. The presentation focuses on the thoughts and feelings as communicated by Dr. Ekstein to students in his psychotherapy seminar.

The primary purpose of this seminar is to teach the generic nature of intensive child psychotherapy within the structure of a child-guidance setting. The course deals with the philosophy of psychotherapy and is not intended as a prescription for psychotherapy. That is, we learn process and not technique. This becomes an exceedingly difficult task because the seminar participants bring a great variety of background and knowledge to the course. In order to make contact with the seminar as a whole, Dr. Ekstein works with a formal structure within which there is great flexibility of content.

Each seminar begins with the reading of minutes from the previous session, after which there are questions and discussion around the minutes. The case material dealing with the particular area to be covered is then introduced and discussed, and questions are raised. This is the structure of the seminar. The aridity of this description is matched only by the richness with which the material in the seminar is covered. No topic is discussed in isolation. During discussion in any one area, Dr. Ekstein will cover the historical factors and difficulties in the area; references to pertinent literature, past and present; the merits and difficulties of other modes of treatment; the implications for treatment within a child-guidance setting. In this way Dr. Ekstein tries to present material not as fragmented bits of information, but rather as an integrated whole within an organized, continuous process. He incorporates literature, myth, politics, philosophy, former treatment cases, personal experiences and his own unconscious into the material. These astute connections among seemingly diverse areas serve to make the seminar more meaningful and enjoyable.

This paper also deals with some of the major topics covered in the seminar. For organizational purposes these have been divided into various subheadings, but it cannot be emphasized strongly enough that these are artificial separations. An area discussed is never left to lie dormant, but is continually returned to and re-synthesized within the larger framework of the seminar objectives.

In order to give the reader a feeling for the spirit within the seminar, selections from the minutes of the seminars are presented below. The minutes reflect the give-and-take between teacher and student, the confusion, the reflection, the questioning that leads only to more questions from the student struggling with the elusive entity known as psychotherapy.

DIAGNOSIS

Although separation of diagnostic and therapeutic phases is taught, this separation is an artificial one, since diagnosis is continuing process and not merely a static prelude to therapy. Diagnosis is a difficult task, viz., to maintain the child without being intrusive or violating the privacy of his thoughts. The best method of handling many patients in a diagnostic phase is to invite them to give what material they wish without deliberately attempting to extract information. The style of psychoanalytic help is one of complete respect for the personality and its defenses and consideration of the ego-organization. In contrast, diagnostic procedures (psychological testing, for example) can circumvent ego defenses. Herein lies an important and crucial distinction. Since the administration of psychological testing as well as giving a physical or neurological examination, or taking a social history, affects unfavorably the sensitivity required for psychoanalytic therapy, none of these should be done by the therapist.

This could be one of the serious disadvantages of private practice. Dr. Ekstein urged that Freud's example of sending his patient for physical treatment to another doctor and thus not polluting his own role as the patient's analyst be followed by those in private practice.

Dr. Ekstein was asked a question which he rephrased: "Should we accept, bypass or engage material which might be inappropriate because of its being premature?" He responded by saying that what one did with it would, to a large extent, depend upon the "school to which one belonged." The Kleinians, who deal with content alone, would probably seize upon it; such a move often creates hostility, paranoid and persecutory feelings and depressive states. Other schools would use a more tactful approach; while not denying the material, they would not make use of it at the time. Dr. Ekstein indicated that he would lean toward the latter technique, adding that he would seek to discover the relationship between the personality structure vis-à-vis the meaning of the material and its emergence at this particular time. He did caution, though, that while he respects the total personality, his tactical maneuver would be governed by the situation at the time. By this he meant that should material be presented which would threaten the immediate safety of therapist or patient, he would interpret it and/or deal with it, regardless of ego structure.

While a prolonged diagnostic workup is useful, it must be kept in mind that material received in a diagnostic phase must not be imposed by the therapist. Otherwise indoctrination, rather than therapy, occurs. The non-intrusion principle must be maintained insofar as it is possible so that the psychotherapeutic relationship will not be violated.

GOALS AND PURPOSE OF PSYCHOTHERAPY

This particular area can be roughly divided into three subheadings: goals and purpose *within* the psychotherapy process (macrocosmic view); goals and purpose as process in psychotherapy (microcosmic view); goals and purpose as dependent upon environmental pressures.

Goals within the psychotherapy process may be formulated as the attempt to gain an understanding of the patient for the purpose of restoring continuity of functions which have become, for one reason or another, unavailable to him. This restored inner continuity must make available for the individual the word as well as the act, the limerick and the fantasy, the emotions, sensitivities and violence.

It is important to note that understanding, for those involved in intensive child psychotherapy, is not the same as reassurance or giving. Understanding is the untangling of an extremely complex web of structures and systems which leads the therapist to find causes for the patient's behavior. This is a great shift from the early analytic position that bribery must be used to get children involved in therapy. The child will realize, through the therapist's attempts to understand him, that the therapist is on his side.

After the reading of the previous minutes the session began with the following question: "Is revealing the feelings of the therapist to a patient worthwhile?" Dr. Ekstein answered that analytic treatment is based on inner continuity. Many aspects of the patient are disorganized or repressed. The goal is not to give an experience of intimacy but to restore the patient's capacity for normal intimacy. This can be compared to a male therapist dealing with a female patient with intimacies. Offering intimacies burdens but does not help the patient.

Dr. Ekstein recalled an occasion which had occurred many years ago when he put his arms around a boy patient. The boy immediately asked, "Why are you doing this?" The boy was obviously not ready for intimacy but saw it as a homosexual seduction. Yet, every psychotherapeutic experience is exactly that to some extent: conveying a sense of intimacy by accepting the patient, and by being mild and human. One cannot say that intimacies are never indicated, but only in specific cases. They are certainly not a basic core of psychoanalytic thinking. A corrective emotional experience may be helpful once, but this is not basic analytic therapy.

Someone else asked, "What good does a remark like 'You're trying to make me feel angry,' do?" Dr. Ekstein answered that the isolated remark is of no value but must be made into an interpretation leading to insight in the patient's behavior. Sometimes, in cases of repetitive behavior, the repetition itself could be pointed out. We do not want to be educating, moralistic, accommodating or apologetic. We want simply to hold a mirror in front of the patient, and even this may be an affront.

There are numerous inherent dangers in attempts to practice intensive child psychotherapy. The commitment to finding the unconscious conflict must not be diverted to outside reality (parents, school, etc.) despite the provocation from the material to do so. This process can be likened to a river flowing in a riverbed. The riverbed must be maintained even as the river is undermining it.

A question was raised concerning the "lack of commitment of scientists." Dr. Ekstein stressed that he used the example to evoke in the participants a sense of commitment which is absolutely essential in child therapists. This sense of commitment can be dispensed with in some other fields but not in intensive psychotherapy. In psychoanalytic thinking, every outer reality has to be interpreted in terms of the inner reality.

Another participant wondered what happens if the therapist's mind is preoccupied with the outer reality. Dr. Ekstein commented that the better analytic writers have written on this subject. In every culture there are crisis situations. One of Freud's patients wanted to marry Freud's daughter, who was then seriously ill. Some of Dr. Ekstein's Viennese colleagues who remained in London had opportunity to analyze the "Blitz." If one wants to be a child therapist, one has to give up many other reality focused activities. The notion that social consciousness requires one to drop what one is doing any time to put out fires may be tempting, but in child therapy, the dedication to the patient is essential. If one finds difficulty in keeping one's mind on the patient and his inner reality, he should carefully examine why he is unable to do so. If he is unable to maintain this dedication, he should give up child therapy and commit himself to being a social reformer.

One of the participants regarded this view as too black and white; there are many hours in the day outside of child therapy practice. Dr. Ekstein cleared up this misunderstanding. The point is that while one is doing child therapy, a complete commitment is essential. He warned that we would find that we would not be able to have two identities. A former patient of his, on reading one of his articles and recognizing herself in it, wrote to him. She was, at that time, fluctuating between her commitment to her husband and having a child or getting her Ph.D. Finally she decided to do both and wrote, "I will be, I guess, a part-time mother, but not a part-mother." One can be a part-time therapist, but never a part-therapist.

Another question connected the concept of commitment with the influence of culture, which might override the disposition of individuals. Dr. Ekstein felt that Lenin, a fundamentally inner-directed person, would have gone out to organize Watts. One can have commitments to outer reality just as to inner reality. He gave the example of a patient of his who broke his appointment in order to go to Berkeley with a friend. When asked why he had not cancelled his appointment, he said he knew that if he had heard his analyst's voice, he would have kept his appointment and disappointed his friend, and he wanted to go with his friend. This is, of course, an impulse-ridden person who responds to every stimulus.

Also, those doing intensive psychotherapy must resist the efforts of social psychiatry to make us feel guilty for choosing to treat one person adequately, rather than one hundred inadequately. The trends in "crisis intervention" are not new and crises have traditionally been handled in the mental health clinics. Patients always come into therapy with a crisis and the therapist doing intensive therapy handles this not by pushing the crisis down, or trying to wipe it out, but by making the crisis into a process. The need is for clinicians who can respond to a crisis and offer a process, and not those who try to separate the crisis from the process.

A participant said that earlier in the course Dr. Ekstein had made the point that brief forms were not the preferred methods of treatment and that he felt it wasteful for people trained in psychotherapeutic techniques to become involved in them. In a later session, however. Dr. Ekstein seemed to be making the apparently contradictory point that certain brief forms had validity and applicability.

To Dr. Ekstein, the preferred emphasis would be on intensive training out of respect for the individual and without reference to social and political considerations. For those who have invested in an M.D. or a Ph.D. and subsequent training, to devote themselves to doing "patch-up" work in a crisis-intervention program, he would view as wasteful, though he would have no objection to occasional involvement in such a program. He expressed himself as specifically opposed to the replacement of intensive, serious training by the more superficial preparation indicated in the current efforts of social psychiatry. It is perhaps unfortunate that, in our culture, belief in the magic powers of the psychiatrist has become so overestimated that the psychiatrist is being used for advice-giving that could just as well be sought from other sources.

Psychiatry seems to have taken upon itself the role of being competent to contribute to the solution of all social problems, which is not a valid role. Its involvement in the Watts riots, for example, was inappropriate since psychiatrists are not trained in crisis-intervention techniques. Psychiatrists do know treatment, however, and should remain focused there.

Crises such as suicide attempts, which are truly psychiatric problems, do occur and have traditionally been handled in clinics. For those in the crisis-intervention field to claim that this is not so is pure fabrication. In a clinic such as ours, the social-work staff is prepared to intervene in a crisis, to offer emergency appointments. Every good family agency since the days of Mary Richmond, in fact, has believed in crisis-intervention. There is nothing new about the concept. What is new is the financing by government of large-scale projects, and the entry of the sociologist into the psychiatric field with the idea that psychiatric methods, which are oriented toward the individual and toward psychotherapy, can be replaced by the kinds of mass media used in totalitarian states.

A seminar participant felt Dr. Ekstein was speaking of an ideal rather than a real situation in that the large number of patients seen in crisis clinics could not be handled in existing psychiatric settings. Dr. Ekstein felt all such short-cut methods are ineffective and are, in fact, dangerous to young people. They may see in the crisis-intervention concept a means of solving social problems and may thus be diverted from the primary purpose of developing into competent psychiatrists, psychologists or social workers. The field seems to attract those who are intensely dedicated to the one purpose and stay with it, and those who will dilute their efforts. The late John Benjamin commented on this field. Using the analogy of little boys with phallic ambitions, he said, "There are those who cut a wide arc with a urinary stream to show how powerful they are, and those who hit the target." Dr. Ekstein's choice is the target. The satisfactions in staying with a schizophrenic child for ten years and thereby contributing to the body of knowledge on schizophrenia would be greater to him than seeing four hundred patients in a crisis-intervention setting.

Goals and purpose in therapy can also be looked at as part of the process in therapy. Since each phase of therapy brings with it a phase-dominant purpose, the purpose will always be changing. Compared to the phases of life, therapy also has its beginning stage (birth), its phases in which dependence and independence are highlighted, and its problems of separation (death). As in Freud's and Erikson's conceptualizations of the developmental process, where all phases must be lived through effectively in order to achieve a well-balanced life, so all phases of therapy must be worked through in order to render effective help. Though certain therapeutic purposes seem to be phase-dominant, no purpose is ever completely resolved or finished, only relatively so.

A question arose as to whether separation from therapy can be equated with "death." It was contended that end of therapy should be experienced, instead, as a "rebirth." Yet we know that every separation, regardless of the nature of the experience involved, brings forth feelings of loss, guilt and mourning. In order to grow up, one must separate from one's parents. Despite the positive nature of this separation, feelings of killing the parents are also present. In pathological cases the separation is compared to the birth process, that is, the emergence from safety and dependency into dangerous and

destructive reality. In the myth, Oedipus at birth was sen-
tenced to die in the wilderness. Since one must become an
Oedipus, one must die. Birth and death go hand in hand in
the unconscious. When we speak of birth, we really speak of
having given up the early paradise and having come to the
world which is only second best. And, when we speak of death,
we see it as a return to "mother earth" and going to heaven
which is a form of rebirth. Thus, on the one hand, we regard
individuation-separation from therapy as death; on the other
hand, the non-individuation could also be experienced as a
form of death and paralysis.

Goals and purposes in psychotherapy do not exist in isolation,
but are dependent upon environmental pressures. One has only to
look at clinic waiting-lists to see how far we have moved from the
early analytic position, that children be taken into analysis only
when their parents were analysts or thoroughly identified with
the analytic movement. Yet there still remain certain factors
which cannot be overlooked in accepting a child for intensive psychotherapy. In treating the very disturbed child within a clinic
setting, the therapist must consider not only his own personal
comfort with such a case, but also such factors as the skill and
temper of those formulating the clinic's policy and the sophistication of those supporting the clinic. Methods of treatment are
as much dependent on society's readiness to accept them as on
the technical skill of the therapist or the advancement of science.

> The need for stability in a family as a criterion for accept-
> ance of the child to therapy was discussed. One person stated
> that our data are insufficient, and research in this area is
> indicated.
> In 1926 Anna Freud's methods of selection were influenced
> by the sentiments of the time. Psychoanalysis was then an
> embattled science in its early stages of acceptance. To protect
> it, she did not want to treat children who might act out and
> thereby provoke the public criticism that analysis perverts
> children. Kraepelin and Bleuler, who knew psychotherapy,
> did not have the social environment for practicing it and
> therefore are associated with the reactionary state hospital
> system where condemned people were placed in back wards.
> In our society today there is no readiness for treating au-
> tistic and schizophrenic children although we have the skills.

Dr. Ekstein is happy with the Reiss-Davis environment where the level of sophistication is high enough to permit this type of work. He is hopeful that his students will continue to carry on this work elsewhere. He recognizes that our values will be derived from that which permits our own sense of creative development rather than from indoctrination of a particular training program. However, only free prosperous societies can afford analysis.

BEGINNING PSYCHOTHERAPY

Beginning of formal psychotherapy is the period of making contact and establishing the psychotherapeutic situation. In beginning therapy there is a conscious purpose present as well as a counterpurpose. For example, the initial conscious purpose of the patient may be to make himself eligible for treatment. Existing concurrently is the counterpurpose, "Do I really want to start therapy? Can I face the material?" Initially, neither party is ready. The participants cannot agree on the method of help necessary to create internal change. The initial meeting, a process of primarily unconscious negotiation, has these goals:

1. The establishment of purpose: the child is ill, he has symptoms of which he is to be rid.

2. The establishment of method or structure: a design not to create limits but to make possible a process; there are rules of the game but the rules change as the game progresses.

3. The establishment of commitment: this can be broken by either patient or therapist.

The therapist's initial problem is to set up a situation that fits the purpose. Usually the purpose of the interview has been defined differently by the therapist and the child, and a common purpose must be reached. The beginning phase of therapy, for example, is one in which commitment, structure and purpose are the phase-dominant purpose, but commitments arrived at in this phase are only relative ones.

An example of this may be seen by reference to case material of an eight-year-old boy with symptoms of passivity and enuresis.

The child referred to the therapist as his teacher, and the therapist reaffirmed that she was a doctor who was there to discuss feelings and problems. A card game was then started at the patient's suggestion. The therapist then asked the patient to put the cards away and to draw some pictures. The patient complied, although he stated that he would prefer to play cards. Dr. Ekstein pointed out that here each tries to cope with the situation. He suggested that the child says, in effect, "Teacher, teach me," and the therapist says, "I am a doctor and I help with feelings." The child then says, "Let's play," and brings in the very structured game of cards. This game gives the therapist no opening; unlike play, rules are set for games. This kind of structured game gives away the least amount of information about the patient. Dr. Ekstein used the analogy of a patient in the early 1900's giving the therapist all of the phone numbers that came into his mind. Here, when the therapist asks the patient to draw, she wants him to play something that will let the patient reveal something about himself. He says, "Let's have an id purpose," and she says, "I appeal to your superego; let's use the time for a purpose." He resists and she tries to get around the resistance by asking that another game be played. She shows him that he plays a game instead of playing. She observes that the patient gives her compliance, and that compliance does not give her what she wants.

The patient then drew a squirrel and said that it looked like a cat. The therapist commented on what a bushy tail it had, and the patient complied and made it bushier. Here, Dr. Ekstein pointed out, he tries to comply to get the therapist to love him. This is a problem because we have compliance, not production. He then states, "I know what I left out—a sun." She asks if it is a happy sun, and he says, "Yesa" and draws a smile on it. This is more compliance. Dr. Ekstein noted that the patient and therapist have not yet reached the purpose of the session.

There are at least three problems that immediately confront the child therapist. These are the questions of how to communicate with the child (which will be considered later); the problem of setting the stage so communication can best occur; and, the need to convey to the child that the therapist is identified with him and his problem.

In working with children Dr. Ekstein noted:

There is usually a prelude in the child's play, setting the stage for what is to follow. An analogy was made to the setting of the stage in a drama which helps to put the play across more effectively. In addition to the child's effort to put the therapist in the proper mood for the play to proceed, the therapist, likewise, sets the stage for his child "actor." In adult psychoanalysis this task is simplified by a set ritual, and the analyst does not have to struggle with the problem of how to prepare his room for each individual patient. Child analysts, however, must necessarily be intuitive and inventive and cannot take the "stage setting" for granted. The object in therapy with children is to make available the material by means of which the child can express himself without influencing the themes of his play. At the same time, the therapist must vary the material he provides according to the age, sex and therapeutic needs of the child. Perhaps the best therapeutic setting would be comparable to the modern stage à la Brecht. Here the setting and stage set may appear irrelevant but are purposely flexible to allow for maximum self-expression by the actors.

The notion of identification with the child is an extremely important one. The best remarks in the beginning of therapy are those that aid the flow of material and assure the child that the therapist is identified with him and his problem. Although it is a necessary prerequisite to be identified with the child, one may be too much on this side. That is, child therapists may ally themselves with the child against him (the child's) parents, in a sublimation of their rebellion against their own parents. In working with children many phases of our own childhood are revived. Unless the therapist can identify with the child and maintain in himself a certain degree of childishness and rebelliousness, he is unable to deal successfully with children in a therapeutic situation. However, the therapist may identify so closely with the child that he is not able to work well with the parents. The problem is to identify with the child without losing one's identity with society as a whole. This is a very difficult process.

The therapist and child need to experience a togetherness. Dr. Ekstein alluded to a play titled, "O What a Lovely War!" and noted that psychotherapy, too, has the aspects of confrontation which create immense anxiety for the child-patient, the adult-patient and the therapist, as well. "It is not a confrontation with bullets but . . . with one's self." In the interview between patient and therapist, even though each one is attempting to impose his or her structure upon the other, there emerges a psychological movement toward one another, i.e., togetherness.

TRANSFERENCE IN CHILDREN

Transference is a conscious or unconscious reaction the patient has to the therapist, and it must be understood as a replica of early relationships with the parents. Transference used to be experienced as resistance, but Freud showed that it is the very existence of this resistance that allows for treatment. The patient revives and ascribes to the analyst hopes, wishes and fantasies which in his early life were of great significance to him. Thus, what we get in adult analysis is a development of transference neurosis which is a repetition of infantile neurosis. A person cannot be analyzed without the revival of his infantile relationship to the parents. No infantile life is free of neurosis. This neurosis is not pathological since it springs from the natural dependency of children on parents.

Anna Freud initially believed that since transference neuroses are repetitions of infantile neuroses, they are possible only for adults and not for children. The Kleinians, on the other hand, claim that children have transference neuroses exactly like adults.

Dr. Ekstein accepts the conviction advocated by Melanie Klein that the concept of transference is indispensable for understanding child analysis. However, he considered of equal importance Anna Freud's observation that the clinical manifestations of the transference in children differ from those observed in adult analysis.

The philosophy of handling transference material was dealt with in response to a question concerning case material.

A question was raised as to why the therapist did not deal with the immediate interpersonal message between himself and the patient but rather it kept it on the level of the patient-grandmother relationship. He might have said, "You want me to control you." Dr. Ekstein commented that both approaches were not completely right. Always to talk of the interpersonal relationship would detract from the therapeutic situation. Always to guide it to the grandmother would be distancing one's self from the patient as if she had no conflict in the office. The therapist, rather, needs to show her what she does with him is a reflection of something outside. This is especially difficult to do with children who bring not only generic repetitions of what has been done in the past but also displacements of what they are still doing on the outside. The therapist must then show that what the patient does with him is a displacement and a repetition. It is difficult to find the proper compromise between showing the interpersonal aspect and guiding it back to Grandma. Ingenious wording to which the child can catch on helps, but one obstacle is that for the child the here-and-now is so important while the capacity for reflection is weak.

Material illustrating a case of transference was brought in by a Negro therapist who was seeing a boy whose problems include fire-setting. The session reviewed was the one immediately following the Watts riot in Los Angeles.

The boy sadly asked his therapist whether he had heard about the riots. When the therapist answered that he had, the boy screamed at him, "You are one of them, you are one of them," and was on the verge of tears. The therapist responded by sympathizing with the boy's feelings that it must be pretty upsetting to him to feel this way. He brought out that he had implored his mother not to make him come twice a week for a year for therapy and then desperately asked, "Are you one of them?"

Dr. Ekstein commented that this was hard on the therapist. What does it mean that H. accuses his therapist of being a firesetter and implores him for reassurance? What happened to H. was a powerful paranoid transference, and he needed the therapist to restore his sense of reality. Children's fantasy material often spills over so much into reality that they cannot keep the outer and inner reality apart. This powerful transference reaction has to be interpreted. The problem is to react in such a way that the patient, even in a rage, gets his self-observation restored. If some of this can be created in H., he and the therapist can then understand it together. If this is not done, there is no therapeutic gain; there is no real flood control but only an emergency measure.

H. pleaded for reassurance that the therapist "was not one of them" and the therapist struggled to get more of the child's feelings. The boy then expressed, "All should be locked up except you, Dr. W., and other nice colored people." At the same time he squirted water over his therapist. The therapist remarked, "Then you don't feel I am one of them?" and the boy replied, "No, you are my friend." At this the therapist suggested "Then perhaps you can stop squirting water on your friend," and H. laughed and stopped. Dr. Ekstein pointed out that if the therapist had been too full of Watts, he would have been reassuring or educational. Instead he showed the boy, by sympathizing with his anxiety, that he was not contaminated by it, and the boy brought in the waterplay, which had interesting sexual implications.

H. is actually telling his therapist about his conflict; he is desperately afraid of his father, but he also wants to identify with him. He brings up that he had told his mother that she is bad and mean because she sends him to this angry dangerous man who will hurt him and will stop his nice squirting fantasy game with his mother, which is expressed in his bedwetting. This is a strong negative transference. All his material comes into the open because of the external reality material which is comparable to the day residue in a dream, and it was handled so that it furthered therapy.

In H.'s case, the boy used the material to underline his tremendous anger at his father. The relevancy of outside material is that it reflects inner material. When you analyze you follow the transference; the transference uses Watts and *not* the other way around. There are patients who completely ignore outer crisis; others constantly use outside events.

Patients transfer to us their good and bad feelings; these are powerful positive and negative transferences. Freud said, "Patients cure themselves by means of transferences." All we have to do is to interpret the transference.

COUNTERTRANSFERENCE TO CHILDREN

The concept of countertransference is one area of difficulty for all therapists and the therapist's method of blaming himself when something goes wrong. Of course, things go wrong for other reasons, too.

Countertransference is the revival in the therapist of unconscious material in relation to parents, siblings, peers or others which does not belong in the present. This reaction may be in relation to the material the patient presents or to the patient himself. These are two entirely different situations.

Countertransference to material is exemplified when the patient's material revives conflicts in the therapist. The revival of the therapist's own past difficulties sometimes traps him among his own past, the patient, the patient's parents and the therapist's parents. Thus may occur the technical mistake of offering injunctions not related to the total person but only to the material presented.

In total person countertransference, the patient is reacted to as a person as a whole as the therapist reacted to a person from the past. Total person countertransference reactions may be either positive or negative. It has been said that one cannot work with a child unless one feels some positive feelings toward that child. While it may be possible to be a successful analyst with an adult in the face of overwhelming attraction or repulsion, this may not be the case when dealing with children.

For years the term countertransference has been used in a derogatory fashion. Allegedly it is "not a good" reaction to have, yet it does have both positive and negative aspects. If one follows one's countertransference reactions to their conclusion, they often lead to countertransference insights which, in turn, can further the psychotherapeutic process. In fact, a psychotherapist should be analyzed, not to fill in his blind spots, as is usually stated. There may be people in whom there are no blind spots of significance. Even such a person desperately needs the sensitivity and contact with his own self to invent the techniques needed to deal with his own and the patient's material. The patient's material takes the analyst down paths of his own, leading to countertransference insights which further therapy.

When a child makes the therapist anxious, it is wise to assume that the anxiety is caused by the material. One's own countertransference feelings must be utilized in an attempt to get the patient to be better aware of what it is that he, the patient, is doing. The thoughts that are aroused in the therapist by the patient should not be used confessionally, but to help the patient gain in understanding.

Case material dealing with a fourteen-year-old girl, C., who was referred for severe depression and suicidal ideation illustrates manifestations of countertransference.

> C. sent Dr. W. a poem called "The Ooze," which deals with Mommy, Daddy and the Ooze. Daddy and daughter love the Ooze; Mommy does not and attempts to come between the daughter and her father. At the same time C. writes a letter which tells of her panic, wild emotions, love, hate and confusion directed toward herself and toward her mother.
>
> In C.'s letter, Dr. Ekstein comments, is the heart of both the transference and countertransference implications of this case. It is a moving appeal which of necessity evokes in the therapist a reaction of wanting to help this girl; she must not go down into the Ooze and must recapture something which never existed. The Ooze is, of course, the phantom father. The only way which C. feels she can recapture him is to go back into some primordial Ooze where he exists, since her real information about him is negligible. She knows that the information that comes from her mother is distorted. We use the patient's own imagery because we have no better imagery at this time.
>
> C., as with children who have no parents, attempts to reconstitute parents from fantasies and stories. Therefore, the transference reaction will be part phantom father and part real mother, and she will attempt to make what never existed; that is, her phantom father the real one in the person of the therapist.
>
> The countertransference potential of this case is enormous, C. makes the plea that, if taken seriously, can be overwhelming: rather than be a therapist, she needs him to be a father. The therapist must avoid the trap of giving more than he should and becoming a real person rather than a therapist. This is giving too much help. On the negative side, her needs can be viewed as overwhelming demands which act like a seduction to which the therapist may react with fear and reject the patient. As in the Baron Rothschild analogy, a Jew comes to him with a multiplicity of terrible complaints. After his pitiful story is over, Baron Rothschild tells his servants to "throw him out. He breaks my heart."

The transference and countertransference situations are analogous to two sides of a coin, in that transference is that indispensable road to recovery, whether the transferences are workable, unworkable, positive or negative. The other side of this situation is that the therapist cures the patient via his countertransference reactions, whether these reactions, also, are workable, unworkable, positive or negative.

COMMUNICATION

It is important for every child therapist to recognize the various types of communication applicable to child therapy; not only the way they are presented by the child, but also the way they may be used therapeutically. The modes of communication discussed in this paper include language, play and acting out.

Initially, the therapist tries to make contact with the child. The first problem is finding an optimum way of communicating, i.e. the choice of language must be negotiated. The therapist often tries to talk in adult language, due to his own inhibitions about relating as a child does. Such feelings make him ineffective. Instead, he must show the child that he understands the child's language by trying to match his style to the child's and commenting in the child's language.

An example of this difficulty is seen in the case of the patient who said he would draw a little boy but drew a monkey. The therapist asked if little boys are like monkeys. By saying this, the therapist was trying to get the patient to communicate on an adult level, instead of himself speaking the child's language.

The ability to communicate on the child's level requires the therapist's awareness of the level of language development at which the child is communicating. There are three reference points in language development. The therapist may be presented with language as an expression of an internal state (symptom language), as is demonstrated in play when the child tells something through the play that he does not necessarily want to reveal. The child may also use language as a signal (signal language) to which he expects the therapist to respond. However, as the child matures, he finds symptom language and signal language less effective and communicates directly with symbol language, i.e. words.

On the other hand, the therapist may not immediately be able to grasp the child's language, and as a result, may make the wrong overtures. Even so, if the child senses they are overtures, they will work. The child will then attempt to make contact.

The next dilemma for the therapist is what mode of communication will be so convincing to the child that it will enable him to gain insight into his psychic organization. We know that the ability of the child to listen and be convinced depends on early interrelationships. In therapy, the child should be permitted to use all modalities for insight which are available to him.

Play is the child's best means for communication of unconscious conflicts. Although play may be equated with free association in the adult, it is usually thought of only in terms of impulse gratification. However, even more important in therapy is play's function as psychic work used to solve conflicts, by bringing about a synthesis between the different aspects of internal life. As such, play is utilized for higher integrative capacity.

Play may also be seen as controlled motor activity which develops into language. Originally the infant expresses impulse through motor activity, in an attempt to master reality immediately. As the infant's means of problem-solution grow richer, the motor discharge of impulse is modified by delay and is known as play action. Play action combines the gratification of the play with an attempt at resolution of the conflict. Although the child can now give up immediate gratification, play action is still near primary-process thought. As mental development continues, the child slowly replaces elements of play action by expressed fantasy, in which the need for action is given up. The child then attempts to master the future experimentally by role-taking. This aspect is seen in play-acting, where fantasy is woven around an external object. The transition from this stage to that of adaptive behavior is achieved when reality testing and secondary-process thought are firmly established.

Sometimes, the child may be unable to communicate through either language or play, but may be able to express the conflict only through the more primitive mode of acting out. Here, we see an unconscious repetition of a conflict of the past, while actually behaving as if the object around which fantasy is woven is real.

The therapist should try to understand acting out as a means of communication when it is presented to him.

An example of acting out was seen when a five-year-old boy was playing hide-and-seek with his therapist. He took some candy from the desk and later asked for more. When the therapist refused, the patient began to scream. The playing out had turned into acting out, with the therapist forced to counteract out. Instead of being able to show the patient that he had become more and more demanding and unable to accept limits in his relationship with his mother, the therapist was forced by the boy's behavior to say, "Well, that's the end." Here the therapist ended the act, but also the play. The reason for this is that the patient now has an argument with the therapist as well as with the mother, an argument which prevents the acting out from returning to playing out.

A problem of play therapy is letting the child play while allowing time for fantasies to develop. A five-and-a-half-year-old girl returned for the next session with two animals from the previous session and made contact with the therapist via telephone play. It was as if she were saying, "Since the last time I've had the impulse to phone you. I am telling you now that I was thinking of you and wished to be in touch with you." An interpretation by the therapist at this point would have been premature, leading to discontinuance of the free association.

Direct questions or initiation of play activities by the therapist will also hamper the free association process. This is illustrated by the child who drew a squirrel. When the therapist commented on its bushy tail, the child complied and made it bushier, thereby ending the fantasy and including the therapist's theories in his play.

The therapist must be alert to scene shifts in the play. As the child expresses himself, he may come to a point where he is overwhelmed by feeling. The play suddenly becomes the real life and is too painful to maintain in open fantasy. The child therefore interrupts it. This point of disruption is where the conflict lies. A five-and-a-half-year-old girl showed the therapist how well she could print her name, but actually made frequent mistakes. She became anxious when she realized that her exhibition was deficient and asked to do something else. The child will eventually repeat the same play over and over, many ways, being unable to escape from his central concern.

Eventually, the question arises about when to make interpretations. In therapy, one usually gets more material than one can use. For this reason, interpretations are unnecessary in early sessions, except about resistance to communication. The therapist should react only to the part of the interview that will make it flow. These remarks assure the child that the therapist is identified with him and his problems. Later on, when the therapist has more information, and the pattern of the case becomes clear, he can make more far-reaching interpretations. At these times it is important to emphasize the continuity of material from hour to hour, but not at the expense of losing the significance of the immediate material. The experienced therapist can listen to the material as presented and relate it to past material. Although the child may appear to make rapid insights, the therapist should remember that they may only be passive imitations of the therapist, and not true insights.

The therapist should maintain the child without being intrusive and without violating the privacy of his thoughts. The child should be invited to give whatever material he wishes. No attempt should be made to extract information from him. Every confrontation in therapy is experienced as violation since the need of all patients is to make a good impression by presenting themselves in the best light. The therapist's asking a direct question may be seen by the child as a challenge, not an interpretation. The child may then withdraw.

The therapist must be sure the child understands that interpretation is not direction. The therapist should try not to direct the child, but to show him direction in his life. The child can then employ the insight gained through play and metaphor, and finally come to believe interpretations made on a secondary-process level. Once the child has reached this level of verbal understanding, he has reached the final point in a successful therapeutic situation.

WORKING WITH THE PARENT IN A CHILD GUIDANCE SETTING

Child guidance clinics are usually most dogmatic about stressing the importance of working with the parents. Many clinics do casework with the parent and focus on the parent relationship with the child, rather than treating the parent's intrapsychic conflict. Depending upon the needs of the case, however, a variety of techniques of working with parents can be utilized within a clinic setting. For example, there are situations in which psychotherapy with the parents may be necessary. That is, sometimes before parental support of treatment can be obtained, work with the parent's problem may be necessary. In other cases, the parent may need no help but is seen anyway. In still other cases, a minimal amount of contact with the parents is necessary, as is often the case in working with adolescents.

A seminar participant wondered why we did casework with the parent and focused on his relationship with the child rather than treating the parent's intrapsychic conflict. He questioned whether treatment could really be effective if we avoided focusing on the parent's conflicts, and whether any real change could occur without this intrapsychic focus. Dr. Ekstein agreed that unless the work with the parent was related to his internal conflicts, there was little chance of helping him. For this reason "guidance," in the strictest sense of the term, seldom worked. However, there were situations where advice-giving had its place. Dr. Ekstein cited the case of a four-year-old girl with separation anxiety who was supposedly phobic about attending nursery school. The mother's transference to Dr. Ekstein as the parental figure had allowed her to let the child go and to trust the nursery school teacher as advised. In this case the mother's anxiety about letting the child go was transferred to Dr. Ekstein, the authority figure. This had given her sufficient reassurance to accept his advice, but the doctor had given advice only after he was certain that it was the mother and not the child who was phobic.

Thus, if the child's symptom is not an expression of an internalized intrapsychic disturbance, guidance with the parent could be highly preventive in this regard, assisting the parent to allow the child to grow and develop more adequately.

The philosopher William Ockham described the need to reduce the solution of problems to their simplest principles. The rule of Ockham's Razor refers to the economy of energy principle in that more energy is used only when necessary. Applied to therapy this means that change can take place short of analysis. Neurotic conditions are not "all pervasive" and do allow for change to take place within the context of the neurosis. A small change in the child's environment can make a significant difference in the patient's personality. This can be accomplished in many cases without even touching the parent's neurosis. We do not resort to analysis of the parent when it is indicated that change is possible without analysis through working with the intact aspects of the parent's ego. These conflict-free areas are enormous and can be worked with to the benefit of the child in treatment.

However, knowing when to do casework and when to do psychotherapy with a parent is a problem in diagnosis.

A question was raised concerning the pathological family in which the emotionally ill child is the family scapegoat. Generally the real problem is a marital one, and the child is being used to divert attention from this to allow the parents to function with less anxiety. A good caseworker has the capacity to discriminate the problems and focus the parent's treatment accurately. Establishing the dominant obstacle is often a difficult diagnostic problem in the treatment of child. Another difficulty is knowing where to intervene.

It was suggested that we intervene according to what is dominant and what is workable. The advice was to throw our strength where we could most effectively move the process toward change. During the course of treatment it might be necessary to intervene in different directions. The important thing to remember in psychotherapy is to remain flexible in terms of what is needed in treatment of both parent and child.

In working with parents, an ambivalence is revealed. We depend upon them to bring the patient, to pay for treatment, etc., but every parent who brings a child to a treatment center comes with positive and negative feelings.

To explain this more fully, Dr. Ekstein discussed some aspects of fathering and mothering and alluded to the book, *How to Be a Jewish Mother*. The author is an apparently middle-aged, accomplished male, but the book contains portraits of himself as a baby, being fed by the mother, and as an adult, also being fed by the mother (as if some of us are not allowed to out-grow our mothers). His mother read the book, of course), enjoyed it, and seemed to be proud to be depicted as that kind of mother. It was as if she said, "I want my son to be an accomplished man (doctor, lawyer, analyst, author), but he is to never leave my breasts. I must feed him."

This provoked Dr. Ekstein to fantasy another book entitled *How to Be a Greek Mother in Antiquity.* He spoke of Thetis, the mother of Achilles, who envisioned that her son's fate was to become a hero. She aided him to the extent of dipping him as an infant in the river Styx to protect him. However, she, too, was ambivalent for she forgot to change hands, and this left him with his famous vulnerable spot. Her ambivalence is further reflected by her attempting to protect him by disguising him and thereby hoping to spare him from combat, peril, destruction and damnation, as if one could possibly become a hero if confined to safety and security. She seemed to be saying, "I want my son to be a hero, a man of valor, but don't dare take my baby from me."

This is the same thing as the cry of the distressed neurotic person. He comes to the therapist asking and pleading for relief from the distressing symptoms, at the same time he builds up all the resistances and says, "Hands off. Don't you dare disturb my neurosis." This ambivalence seems to be a must for it is clearly seen in the parent-child relationships of all cultures. It does not implicate the parent as the faulty party for no parent can avoid the ambivalent-dependency situation. Therapists who adhere strictly to one philosophy of treatment (as seeing the child solely and having no contact with the parent) are strongly identified with one side of the ambivalence. Those who adhere to collaboration only are identified with the other side of the ambivalence. Even the excellent analyst himself brings with him to the treatment situation the vulnerable heel of Achilles. It seems to be the eternal link of parent and child. The parent who adheres to the heel does everything to maintain the relationship with the child. The child struggles to gain autonomy but the parent must struggle against it. The father, as well as the mother, has his heroic-vulnerable ambivalences, and these too are reflected in the therapy process. The therapist must ask himself, "What is the state of the parental relationship to the Achilles' heel and its role in the psychotherapeutic process? How can it enhance further this process?"

In order more clearly to understand the current notion of working with parents in a child-guidance setting, the history of such work is traced in this course. Included are the views of Hug-Helmuth, Melanie Klein, Anna Freud and the present approach in which the parent, too, is viewed as a human being who needs help as a parent.

> Still recognizing and highly regarding the intrapsychic conflict, one is aware that the realities of the treatment center and of the child and his parents cannot be denied. How then can the various modalities be coordinated with the psychotherapy of the child who presents an intrapsychic conflict? Dr. Ekstein pointed out that if the child is viewed solely as an extension of parent-ambivalence, this may greatly interfere with intrapsychic work.

It need not necessarily. One can, with skill, handle the realities and yet maintain the structure, purpose, and commitment of the therapeutic process. Ideally, the child therapist is focused on the unconscious conflict of the child during the course of the psychotherapy. He does not allow himself to be veered from the course by external realities, but, especially for a child, they cannot be denied. In fact, knowledge of the external realities furthered by collaborative work with the caseworker can enhance and support the child therapist in his task of focusing on the child's intrapsychic conflict. For even if the therapist could control the environment, the strength of therapy is ultimately in the therapy room.

Further reference to previously cited case material will clarify this.

> Dr. W. annotated H.'s case by saying, "This was the hour following the week end of the Watts crisis." H. said, "I'm wild and my behavior is wild." Dr. Ekstein then quoted Goethe: "What thou hast inherited from your fathers, acquire it and make it thine." Our little fellow was saying, "I'm a wild boy, that's why I am seeing you." H. had symptom awareness. He expressed his anxiety during the hour by having to run to the toilet. He said, "I couldn't urinate in your office, could I?" Dr. Ekstein interpreted H.'s authoritative manner and daring attitude as, "You tell me I'm a fire setter? You tell me that, Daddy, who, yourself, are a fire setter."
> That devastating week set off in all of us feelings of "thank God, I'm not down in that area," and then a universal guilt. H. brought these feelings to the session when the Negro therapist was vulnerable. At that point, Dr. W. could not say that he was against fire setting in order to become an educator for,

at this moment, he was experienced as that self-same black man who set fires and was wild. Dr. W. might have feelings of both, "Who am I to try to help this boy who sets fires?" and "I really don't have anything to do with those who are down there." Yet he did not fall into the trap laid by counter-transference feelings. He maintained his therapeutic role. H. played checkers by Dr. W.'s rules but began to cheat, and then called Dr. W. a cheat. H. was very angry with Dr. W. and then, when he was confronted with this behavior, said, "Dr. W., did you hear about those riots?" As we can see, children have a very clever way, as do adults, of bringing to therapy a material piece of reality that cannot be ignored. The reality of Watts is so much to the point that it is difficult to show the child the real point. One of the great problems of the therapist is to have the eyes upon the unconscious and not upon Watts. Though it may be agony not to keep one's eyes upon Watts, it is ecstasy and real therapy to keep one's eyes upon the unconscious.

BIBLIOGRAPHY

1. EKSTEIN, RUDOLF. Psychoanalytic Notes on the Function of the Curriculum. *Reiss-Davis Clin. Bull.*, 1966, 1:36.
2. EKSTEIN, RUDOLF. Special Training Problems in Psychotherapeutic Work with Psychotic and Borderline Children. *Children of Time and Space, of Action and Impulse: Clinical Studies on the Psychoanalytic Treatment of Severely Disturbed Children and Adolescents.* New York: Appleton-Century-Crofts, 1966.
3. EKSTEIN, RUDOLF, and WALLERSTEIN, ROBERT S. *The Teaching and Learning of Psychotherapy.* New York: Basic Books, Inc., 1958.
4. FREUD, SIGMUND. *Letters of Sigmund Freud.* Ernst L. Freud, ed. New York: Basic Books, Inc., 1960; p. 346.
5. WITTELS, FRITZ. *Sigmund Freud: His Personality, His Teaching, and His School.* New York: Dodd, Mead, 1924.

Chapter 5

❦

On a Method of Supervising Psychotherapists

W. MARSHALL WHEELER, PH.D.

This essay on the supervision of psychotherapy is also about psychoanalytic psychotherapy. Since this is so, my view of psychoanalysis will inevitably come into it. First of all, therefore, I want to point out that I do not teach psychoanalysis. Proof of this lies in the fact that if any student of mine is in personal analysis, it is without official bearing on the training program of which I am a part.* But I want also to point out that everything I teach is based on standard psychoanalytic sources (see appended reading list for the seminars) and that my own definitive training in the psychoanalytic treatment of children was at the Hampstead Course and Clinic in London. A predicament faces me when I try to describe anything about my teaching that varies from psychoanalytic educational practice. The clinic framework, i.e., the training situation, is different from that of an institute. There appears to be nothing

---

* The observations contained in this essay are based on my experience during the past five years in supervising and instructing staff members and USPH Fellows in child psychiatry and clinical psychology in a child guidance clinic where emphasis is on intensive, long-term treatment of disturbed children. Classical psychoanalytic theory is the framework within which instruction of the students and treatment of the patients proceed. All supervision of the psycho-therapeutic work of the psychiatric and psychology Fellows and staff members has been by psychoanalytically trained personnel.

else that varies outside the rather wide range of psychoanalytic educational practice. For example, in reading the description of training in the United States given by Lewin and Ross (4), I was struck by the ease with which the Reiss-Davis program could be fitted into the general pattern of institute instruction, except for the absence of systematic personal analysis, as already noted.

Authors writing about psychoanalytic education—Ekstein and Wallerstein listed twenty-nine on training in psychoanalysis and sixty more on training for psychotherapy (1) and there are still others—have expressed views compatible with many I state here, e.g., Searles (5). Perhaps the main reason for this article, then, is to show that the principles of psychoanalytic education apply in a clinical setting where unanalyzed students train.

To avoid any misunderstanding about the level of the students (Fellows and staff in separate seminars) with whom I am concerned, let me emphasize that they are not beginners. All have had at least one or two years' experience treating patients and many have had several years. The problems of the beginner are different from those discussed here. (See "Training in Child Psychotherapy" in this issue.)

The first observations in the supervisory process are those made at the time the student is presented with a case folder. His reactions frequently indicate the gentleness, caution, thoughtfulness (or their opposites) with which he will approach the actual patient. It has been remarkable, though not surprising, that the medically trained students are more judgmental in their approach and also less prone to accept the passivity essential to the psychotherapeutic relationship than non-medically trained students. The latter tolerate their confusion better, but are hampered by the confusion itself, and have no easy doctor role to facilitate their early engagement with the patient. Often these students resent the supervisor's reluctance to give them rules for patient management.

Supervision which is directive is as ruinous and contradictory as "directive" psychoanalytic psychotherapy would be. The spontaneity of the therapist is often a very tender attribute which wilts and dies under the fire he feels from his instructors and patients. To comment without criticizing, to correct without squashing and to indicate misunderstanding without implying stupidity, all comprise the supervisor's most difficult task. Obvious tact, overtly politic manner and indirection are useless since the supervisor himself must value spontaneity.

One phenomenon frequent in supervision is helpful in fostering spontaneous development in students. It is customary for them to interrupt their descriptive recounting of therapy sessions to comment as an aside on their thoughts at the time patients gave associations. If the supervisor says, "You thought you understood something. Did you put it into words?" the way is open for the student to discover that he withheld expression of his thoughts. Then the student can examine whether such an inhibition was wise. This approach has the advantage of freeing the therapist and of leading to greater spontaneity. It remains remarkable to me that as treatment progresses, it is the positive and empathic responses that follow this course. Just as patients run from positive transference* so students flee from positive countertransference.

> A male student was very upset by the direct physical approach that an eleven-year-old patient was making toward him in the sessions. In trying to prevent the approach, the student became involved in a sadomasochistic struggle very similar to the one between the boy and his mother. Only when it was pointed out that the approach he had experienced from his patient as an attack was much more sexual and much less aggressive than he had thought was he able to interpret in sexual terms and desist from the struggle that had previously ensued.
>
> Another student who had gone on a long and sudden trip returned to find his patient refusing to come to treatment. Interpretation in negative terms got nowhere, but the student was finally able to tell his patient that it had been difficult for him to tolerate the therapist's sudden and prolonged absence, not because he felt angry, but because he had felt deserted and unloved. Then the patient could more directly reveal his deep attachment to the therapist.

As the students begin treating their cases under supervision, they begin their seminars, the function of which is to give the theory

---

* I am using a technical word incorrectly, but I can find no substitute. Perhaps it will suffice to say that "transference" and "countertransference," as I use those terms in this essay, mean not only the current re-experiencing of reactions derived from previous object-relationships but include elements contributed by projection and externalization as well.

which will serve as a base for their clinical experience. The supervisor who is lucky enough to have his students in both kinds of situations can serve as a bridge from case material to theory. This is true for me. Often a student will not recognize a mechanism typically used by his patient when it is discussed theoretically. The same student can gain quick understanding of either theory or practice by the use of his case material to exemplify a theoretical point. The opposite does not appear to be true: putting case material into the frame of theory during supervision is inhibiting rather than thought-provoking.

During a seminar in which the use of denial as a mechanism of defense was under discussion, a student commented that he understood only very young children or children whose contact with reality was impaired could use this mechanism. The seminar leader (supervisor) was able to remind him how a neurotic adolescent whom he had in treatment typically said, "I don't care" to any deprivation or frustration to which he would have been expected to feel appropriate affect. The student had not seen this as denial of affect and had been in the habit of saying to his patient, "I'll bet that made you angry when your mother wouldn't even listen," to which the patient would say, "No, why should it make me angry?" After the link made in the seminars, the student's interpretations began to be directed toward the defense rather than the presumed affect, and he could say, "Whenever you feel something you don't like, you announce you don't care and turn away from it."

A student had great difficulty in comprehending the concept of externalization of parts of the personality. I reminded her of her new patient who had insisted, over her objections, on doing his homework in the psychotherapy sessions. In later meetings of the seminar, she was able to report how he made her do the problems because it was so much easier for her than him. If he did do any himself, he would demand that she tell him whether his answer was right or wrong because he couldn't tell. At first she thought this might be externalization of the superego, but why not transference as well? With the help of the seminar members, she was free to consider that he had assigned some of his own skills, duties, perceptions to her. Most important, in subsequent sessions with this patient, she no longer tried to prevent him from bringing homework, but saw that this was a source of material with which she could work.

Two kinds of case material are used in the seminars. The more effective is the use of illustrative material from the students' own cases, as illustrated above. I think of these as internal cases. External ones are those in the literature or those presented by non-members in some formal Center meeting. One such case has been extremely useful, but it appears to be an exception (3).

My approach to theory in the seminars is so loose that only a few comments about it are possible. I have tried many things—frequently at the suggestion of students. While each seminar always has a current task, paper or topic, any member feels free to digress. Events in the Center or in the larger world of psychotherapy, psychology and psychiatry often cause long and fascinating diversions. The description of the "external case," noted above, created a diversion that lasted a month!

> One approach suggested by the students was to center the seminar around technical papers—i.e., papers on the technique of psychotherapy. This failed because it was the students who had no grasp of underlying principles who wished to substitute a rote learning of rules of behavior. The good students, on the other hand, objected to rules and in questioning the basis for technique requirements we found ourselves right back in the province of theory.

Another approach I anticipated would be effective was to start with a theoretical area where the students felt comfortable; the area of ego psychology suggested itself. Yet there was more difficulty with this than with instinct theory, a previously used starting point. I have since reverted to the practice of leading off with close attention to Freud's "Instincts and Their Vicissitudes." Psychology students especially have an idea of the ego which diverges significantly from the classic psychoanalytic view. Since their ideas of "instinct" are vaguer, those ideas are less difficult to re-form.

At one point I was inclined to think that the relationship to the supervisor was intensified for non-analyzed trainees by the absence of an analyst-figure. Subsequent observations do not support this opinion. There is one major modification in supervisory technique which the absence of personal analysis seems to have made necessary: I have found it impossible, or at best unwise, to try to use or even to indicate countertransference elements in the reactions to patients of students who are not in analysis. The student is dependent on his feelings about the patient for his deepest understanding of the patient; i.e., on his spontaneous reaction to the patient's behavior. He must, it appears, trust these reactions, even if they are neurotic ones, for if he wonders whether his reactions are inappropriate he invokes maneuvers and defenses which obliterate understanding of the patient. I handle this rather delicate point by agreeing with the student who suggests his spontaneous reaction may be determined by his own psychodynamics. I then go on to remind him that, neurotic or no, it is his most dependable tool, and if he forbids himself its use he has hamstrung himself. This solution does not make up for the absence of an analysis which could free him as a therapeutic instrument. It is a compromise which retains the student's tentativeness without forbidding the use of feeling in understanding the patient's material. This compromise helps the student preserve a degree of spontaneity despite the constant glare of attention and criticism from his patient, his supervisor and himself.

The supervisor's aim, the psychotherapist's aim, and the patient's aim all become identical: understanding. Sometimes we speak of understanding as empathy; sometimes as comprehension. It has a rational, logical element and an irrational, feeling element. The goal of psychoanalytic treatment has been described (2) usually in terms reminiscent of Freud's dictum, "Where id was, there ego shall be." I believe that psychoanalytic treatment reaches its goal through understanding, and that the novice or the expert who thinks he can reach this goal by other routes makes major mistakes. If we in psychoanalytic psychotherapy emphasize our therapeutic goals too much and our analytic method too little, our aim becomes cure or symptom removal or adjustment and we make mistakes. If we attempt to understand the patient and his material, forgetting any other purpose, we and our patients stand a better chance. If we can develop this view for ourselves, our students and patients, we listen and look far more and we interfere far less. We can be sure of understanding only if we can put our understanding into words. And even there, if we are doing it for ourselves rather than to convince someone else, the process is far more successful. Often a student tries to distort this view to include the notion that understanding is all very well, but we must communicate understanding to our patient. This is another mistake in understanding. If that view is taken, the psychotherapist starts telling and explaining instead of perceiving and attempting to comprehend. One must put his impressions into words for himself. He must put his ideas into a clear state, but not in order to make them clear to someone else.

It helps the student to achieve this attitude as a therapist if he is able to consider himself stupid. I often commiserate with him on how difficult a job that is. How easy to be smart and knowledgeable; how immeasurably more demanding to be helplessly uninformed and dumb! Only if one recognizes one's stupidity is it possible to learn, to see, to find out, to discover.

READING LIST

SIGMUND FREUD:
 1900: "Interpretation of Dreams." Chapter 7.
 1911: "Formulations on the Two Principles of Mental Functioning."
 1914: "On Narcissism: an Introduction."
 1915: "Instincts and their Vicissitudes."
 1915: "The Unconscious."
 1917: "Mourning and Melancholia."
 1923: "The Ego and the Id."
 1926: "Inhibitions, Symptoms and Anxiety."
 1937: "Analysis Terminable and Interminable."

ALICE BALINT:
 1943: "Identification."

EDWARD BIBRING:
 1941: "The Development and Problems of the Theory of Instincts."

ANNA FREUD:
 1937: *The Ego and the Mechanisms of Defense.*
 1965: *Normality and Pathology in Childhood; Assessment of Development.*

BIBLIOGRAPHY

1. EKSTEIN, RUDOLF, and WALLERSTEIN, ROBERT S. *The Teaching and Learning of Psychotherapy.* New York: Basic Books, 1958.
2. FREUD, ANNA. *Normality and Pathology in Childhood; Assessment of Development.* New York: International Universities Press, 1965; p. 216.
3. GREENSON, RALPH R. A Transvestite Boy and a Hypothesis. Presented at the 24th International Psychoanalytical Congress.
4. LEWIN, BERTRAM, and ROSS, HELEN. *Psychoanalytic Education in the United States.* New York: Norton, 1960.
5. SEARLES, HAROLD F. Problems of Psychoanalytic Supervision. In *Psychoanalytic Education.* Jules H. Masserman, ed. New York: Grune & Stratton, 1962; p. 197.

Part III

THE DIAGNOSTIC PROCESS, ASSESSMENT, AND TRAINING

Chapter 6

The Diagnostic Process as Part of the Treatment Process

SEYMOUR W. FRIEDMAN, M.D.

Psychiatrists, psychologists and social workers training in the child guidance clinic always consider the diagnostic and therapeutic relationships with the live child-patient and his parents the highlight of this experience. Didactic teaching is essential for the understanding and intellectual elaboration of clinical experience. Supervision enriches the emotional involvement in the training process and enhances professional skills. But each trainee regards direct work with the live patient as the *sine qua non* that animates his training experience, and initiates the formation of his clinical identity.

The rewards of this work, however, are not unalloyed. The diagnostic evaluation, particularly, has often been regarded by the student as an abortive procedure which abruptly terminates a germinating relationship with the patient. In so doing it seems to betray an implied promise of continued service, and to violate a basic attitude of professional service. It seems to the trainee that the patient is provoked to feel rejection and disappointment rather than the trust and commitment with which the young clinical trainee would like to be identified. All too often, the diagnostic evaluation is regarded as merely a routine procedure for the collection of data about the patient. It leads to diagnostic classification in order to satisfy the need of the administration of the clinic for statistical data. Perceived as a routine preparation for the treatment process, the diagnostic procedure is often seen as having no merit in itself. Nor is it seen as having value for the patient except to inform him of his need for treatment. If treatment is unavailable to the patient, the entire diagnostic process may then be considered as having been a waste of time.

In short, although conventionally and intellectually recognized in the modern psychiatric setting, the meaningful nature of the dignostic evaluation is often not genuinely understood by the trainee. Also, it may not be truly accepted by the training administration. Yet, this is an area of training that can be exploited with great benefit in the development of the student, and may make an important contribution to the patient and to the training center.

Psychiatric diagnosis evolved out of medical diagnosis. In its own development the latter passed through various stages of conceptualization and practice paralleling the predominant modes of understanding. In their evolution and historical development, medical diagnosis and notions of illness were influenced by supernaturalism, mysticism, magic and then by naturalistic, mechanistic and rationalistic considerations. In accordance with accepted scientific rationalistic demands, the aim of diagnosis was to gather and organize the most complete and available compendium of information bearing on the problem under clinical observation. The purpose was to arrive at a valid designation of the disturbance for the purposes of correct and precise labeling and classification. Presumably, such classification would automatically lead to appropriate treatment.

In the psychiatric setting in which the basic medical orientation and philosophy predominate, the approach to the diagnostic procedure may advocate a formal structure. This might specify, for example, the number and spacing of interviews as well as the variety of attitudes and techniques to be used at different stages in the evaluation. The procedure could consist of daily or less frequent interviews proceeding, in general, from an initially passive, accepting unstructured free-play situation to one in which increasing demands are put upon the child. The focus could shift from total interest in whatever the child brings to an insistence on dealing with certain specific material. Thus, the initial contact may be an attempt to relate to the child's anxieties over the total situation in an accepting, welcoming, non-directive fashion. Subsequent interviews proceed on the assumption that such an opening has some kind of trust relationship and mobilized some strength in the child. They begin to present demands to the child which are for the purpose of learning something about him. Various techniques may be utilized, such as questioning, focusing, projective play devices (e.g., the exciting scene technique of Erikson), task-setting, or others. All these techniques require the child to do something for the examiner. Generally of a projective nature, these techniques are expected to serve as the vehicle by which the child will externalize his inner psychological structure, content and conflicts. In addition, the physical examination of the child is included in the diagnostic procedure in some medical psychiatric facilities. Conducted by the psychiatrist as part of the psychiatric evaluation, it is expected to furnish additional concrete information— albeit occasionally of an explosive or trigger nature—about body image and castration anxiety. Such an evaluation helps gather information. In essence, it represents a medical approach to diagnosis in which the accumulation of data helps identify and classify the patient's illness so that the recommended course of treatment may be prescribed to the parents.

In contrast to this orientation to the diagnostic process, there evolved the psychological orientation. This is supported by dynamic, process-oriented, psychological, explanatory concepts directed towards understanding and explaining disordered human behavior. A basic difference between the two approaches springs from the underlying attitudes toward and assumptions about the nature and goals of the helping process as they emerge in a diagnostic evaluation. It is this difference, rather than techniques used, that provides the unique nature of the diagnostic evalution as an instrument for helping the patient. For we discern that the evaluation with its variety of techniques is essentially a variation of the basic clinical tool in all therapeutic work with patients. The evaluation is an interview situation between two people who have met for a mutual, conscious purpose, around which there is meaningful communication in the language of words, action or play. However, the very tool of the clinician is also part of his goal. Be he therapist or diagnostician, the clinician uses the tool of the potential relationship within the structure of the diagnostic interview and the total evaluation. With this tool he seeks to set in motion a process between himself and the patient which will lead to changes within the patient and between the patient and himself. An unfolding communication process must change; as it does, it will produce and reflect the changing nature of the intrapsychic processes of the patient. The diagnostician, therefore, becomes a part of the very process which is the object of his evaluation. One is reminded here of an all-purpose microscope: The doctor simultaneously is the one who looks through the eye-piece; is the reflecting and refracting mechanism into which he looks; is also the stain impregnated in the specimen which brings out the specific characteristics being studied.

The goal of the total evaluation within this philosophy is to assess what the patient is like, how he thinks, behaves or misbehaves, and deviates from the normal or the healthy. But the even more important goal is to evaluate the strengths and forces which push towards health and which can be assessed, in part, by the very attempt to mobilize them within the diagnostic evaluation. In essence, the clinician is assessing the capacity to change through this sample within the assessment procedure itself. The basic goal is to evaluate those potential forces that can foster appropriate action away from the adaptation to the illness, as expressed through the symptomatology which indicates the patient's means of coping with the pathology.

Thus the immediate goal of a dynamic diagnostic interview is different from that of one conducted within the traditional orientation where one wants certain information from the patient. In the latter, one may describe the interview as a way of inquiring as to what the patient can do for the doctor so that he can obtain the desired information. But the former can be described as an inquiry as what the doctor can do to help the patient (1) experience that he is applying for help and (2) to begin to become aware of the forces of resistance that will interfere with the presumed need to change himself.

Typically, the request for help may be application for relief of pain to be administered by the physician, or at least prescribed by him. The assumption here is that an emotional disturbance is a complete illness in itself, and that it is not the intact, mature aspects of the ego that bring the patient to the doctor seeking help. Rather, the patient comes seeking surcease from the pain of the symptomatology, that is, those disturbing experiences which are the consequences of the illness, and not the illness itself. The illness itself can be thought of as the identification of the patient with those forces that have made him ill. Since identification with the forces of illness has become his major mode of adaptation, the patient must inevitably bring to bear resistance to the notion of getting well. He must also give up this form of adaptation, based on a psychic homeostasis, and be helped to achieve a means of coping with his inner and outer environments.

The diagnostic interview as an instrument of the total diagnostic evaluation, therefore, must assess the interplay of forces among (1) what troubles the patient sufficiently to bring him to the clinician for help to maintain this adjustment (make it more ego-syntonic, as it were); (2) what can be done to mobilize within him the desire to change himself, and (3) the desire to move towards the action to bring this about. Consequently, there are three main functions of a diagnostic interview. One is to provide the kind of emotional climate that permits the patient to begin to experience the difference between health and illness. The second is to begin to develop an emotional understanding of his disturbance and of the existence of forces within him that presently give him no other choice but illness (even though other choices are potentially available). The third is to indicate the support for action towards achieving health and freedom to choose means other than illness to master problems.

Objectors might ask if it is not the parent who really must experience the need for treatment, who really makes such choices and takes appropriate action. One can only point out that the basic assumption in the treatment of children is that they do possess the potential for inner change, including their capacity to influence their environment. In point of fact, the sick child is often one who has exchanged roles with the parent in that he dominates and tyrannizes the family through his illness.

Such an approach to the diagnostic interview may well engender anxiety in the student. The technique is one of becoming involved in a relationship for the purpose of the resulting process rather than one of using physical co-existence to avoid a relationship through fact-gathering. Thus, objections to this approach are often voiced in the rationalization that it is unfair to encourage a relationship which will lead only to rejection. Therefore, the rationalization goes, it is preferable to avoid a meaningful relationship if it must end in "separation and rejection." More sophisticated versions of this concern are expressed around the issue of whether this approach is not actually treatment and therefore a by-passing of the process of diagnosis.

The essential issue set forth is that the diagnostic evaluation is the initial phase, and an integral part, of the total treatment process differing in function and purpose but not in essential process. The diagnostic and treatment functions can be separated and differentiated, although both are part of the total treatment process. The diagnostic function serves to evaluate the psychological and emotional difficulties of the child as they appear currently, how they have developed and how they may be assessed with respect to the capacity to change. Assessment depends upon the use that the child can make of the diagnostic process and whether it can enable him to experience his illness as ego-dystonic and to recognize within himself forces which interfere with his capacity to change. This initial aspect of the therapeutic process should serve as a tool by which the patient can develop an awareness that there exists a problem that is not yet understandable. But he should become aware that there is a way of getting help and that he, himself, can help initiate action in this direction, even though he cannot yet change.

The diagnostic evaluation offers a cross-sectional microscopic view, as it were, to the patient of what he can do with the treatment process. In his unconscious, the patient, no matter how much explicit structuring there has been regarding the limited nature of the diagnostic service, expects to receive the desperately needed help at once. In a sense, the patient is correct to the extent that the first step in the treatment process is to accept the idea of help and to identify with the helping doctor rather than with the illness. The diagnostic function contains the initial function of the treatment process. It is thereby differentiated from the total treatment process with respect to its limited structure, difference and variety of techniques, and its more limited and specific purposes and goals. It is concerned with the initial therapeutic problem of mobilizing the patient to permit himself to move to some appropriate action in the process of understanding his illness and to continue the beginning identification with those forces allied with and directed toward change. The time limit itself helps to mobilize the patient to commit himself to continue the process of understanding his illness, and to continue the beginning identification with forces towards changing rather than with those maintaining the status quo. The purposes of the diagnostic process are helping the patient develop both emotional understanding of his situation and a feeling of hopefulness that he can do something to change it. In addition, it helps him to learn a little about the process of change, and that it will develop out of the process between him and the therapist. All, in fact, constitute the essence of the total treatment process.

Chapter 7

꧁❈꧂

Some Observations Concerning the Choice of Time in Applying to a Child Study Center

MIRIAM C. CAMPBELL, M.S.W.

As a medium of communication, the telephone offers the possibility of a connection and the safety of distance. Using it, many individuals seem able to express themselves and their secrets with a degree of freedom not possible in a face-to-face encounter. Others find it a frustrating instrument imposing a distance-barrier on meaningful communication. In the Child Study Center, the telephone line is most frequently the medium for the first tentative connection and exchange between the parent and the intake worker who symbolizes, as it were, the portal of entry to the institution where help may be possible.

Here, in this brief and tenuous beginning of the diagnostic process, are ambivalently expressed hope and expectation, doubt and confusion, desperation and pressure. The parent attempts to describe the child's immediate need for help, but the feeling she conveys is of her personal crisis. As one explores many of these calls and follows the course of the diagnostic evaluation, it is striking to note the sharp contrast between the urgent nature of this request and the long history of the many objective signs of the child's disturbance.

Frequently the incident or behavioral symptom the parent describes with such anxiety seems to us minor by contrast with the more serious symptoms, inadvertently described, which appeared to have caused little or no anxiety. Some parents express a feeling of the shock of sudden recognition that all is not well with the child. It is as if they have suddenly perceived the child as alien and unfamiliar to themselves. Some express fleeting awareness that the child has been disturbed for some time and regret or rationalize their not having sought help earlier. Others need to give, even at this first contact, both the diagnosis and prescription for the cure. Frequently, the initial description concerns a precipitating behavioral incident which appears to create intolerable anxiety for the parent. These presentations usually give us very few clues concerning the nature of the child's disturbance. They are most revealing, however, of the nature of the mother's involvement with her child and of that which creates intolerable stress for herself. As one follows the mother through the full diagnostic process, one learns that the child's emotional turmoil with which he has been living was not experienced as such as long as she felt capable of coping with her child.

In our preliminary exploration of these initial calls and in reviewing the total diagnostic process, we are seeking to understand not why the parent—usually the mother—has called at a particular moment but what has made it possible for her to wait this long. Many individual familial and social factors influence both the stress of the moment and the delay. In this presentation, however, observations will be confined to three aspects of the problem.

Foremost among these are human ambivalence and resistance to change (2) which create a barrier to applying for help until the situation seems critical and can no longer be handled alone. The very need to place that call for help is in essence the true crisis for the individual. It contains all the fear of change, of facing even momentarily a breakdown in one's capacity to function. Simultaneously, the applicant is expressing a hope for the help which another human being may be able to offer.

There are differences, however, in making that move toward help for oneself and that of a mother requesting help for her child and only indirectly for herself. Regardless of the nature of the parent-child relationship, be it benign or malignant, a sense of the child's being a part of the self, belonging in a basically private way, is always present. Inevitably, the child is perceived as a representation of the parent, be it total or partial, positive or negative, depending upon the nature of the involvement and upon the stage of development of both parent and child. Personal feelings of disbelief, shame, guilt and fear that one's own child may be disturbed, make it very difficult to acknowledge this even to oneself.

Some parents may have long been aware of the fact that all has not been well with the child. Others may have been so involved in their own life problems or with the child that they truly do not perceive the child's problem in any separate or objective terms. For all, however, making that step to ask for professional help brings to the foreground the hope and fear, the movement toward and resistance to, the possibility of change for either self or child.

A second contributory factor to the delay in recognizing the need for help for one's child and in acting on it is the meaning of time itself. Perhaps no other aspect of our existence carries with it such universal and highly individualized meaning as the variations in the human being's attitude toward time.

The psychological meaning of time for the parent can become an important influence affecting her readiness and capacity to act upon a problem (4). Some hope that time itself will take care of the child's problem, others fear that there will never be enough time. Frequently, there is real confusion for the parent. How often is the advice given and the words heard: "He's still young; he'll grow out of it. Give him time." How often, too, does it seem that time is the miracle, for the symptom of one year may disappear and thus, for the parent, the problem no longer exists. One parent wants the clock to stop because the child is so rewarding at one stage of development. Another looks forward to becoming a pal to an adolescent and finds the earlier tasks of mothering tedious. She cannot wait. One parent needs more time for herself before she can give full attention to the child's needs. Another, in denying her own needs, sets her time clock solely by the child's.

Perhaps most important, the third factor which emerged from this preliminary study relates to the nature of the adaptive capacities of the parent and the state of equilibrium between parent and child. Ideally we could expect that parents have achieved such a level of ego integration that they are able to see the child through the many normal crises of his growth process. In many cases, however, such maturity and ego integration have not been achieved. At times, the tasks of parenthood create intolerable pressures on the adaptive capacities of the ego under the best of circumstances. When this occurs, two processes are in motion simultaneously. The child, in his age-appropriate phase of development, is reaching for freedom and support in attaining his own identity through a gradual differentiation process. The parent is constantly faced with the need for adaptation to the differing phases of the child's development.

The process of individuation and separation from the parent is a slow and sometimes painful one for the child (1, 3). Equally slow and, at times, more painful is this same process for mothers who in previous relationships have not worked out their own individuation problems and thus displaced them onto the child. Role reversal; seeking self-esteem by way of the child's achievements; gaining narcissistic gratification from the child's positive emotional response to her; controlling the child's aggressive expression which may stir her own conflicts; merging into a more total symbiotic state; these are but a few of the relationship patterns we observe.

For those mothers, in particular, whose sense of identity and ego-integration are tenuous, their inner state of equilibrium and functioning capacity is frequently dependent upon the child serving as a benign alter-ego. For this, the child must corral the proper behavior, the kind of response which does not too greatly threaten the mother's inner stress. So long as this borrowed strength is given, boundaries between mother and child are not clearly perceived by the parent. However, the inevitable steps that a child must make toward differentiation and growth, feeble or frantic as they may be, can, at times, threaten the mother's own state of equilibrium. Her denied or repressed conflicts may be stirred up by the child's moves to loosen the tie. She feels threatened, alone. Indeed, the child seems to threaten to remove himself, the prop which has supported her own defensive ego organization.

Many parents, in that first call for help, express their shock at suddenly perceiving that their child is not well or that he has changed. The mother puts out to us an expectation that we restore the child to her as he used to be. It would appear that the true panic, overtly or subtly expressed, is the sudden recognition that the previous capacity, real or illusory, to function as a good parent is being undermined and is no longer available to herself. Her plea to restore the child as he was is but the inverted plea to restore her capacity to function as a parent.*

Frequently the child can find no way to make his own plea to be allowed the room and support to grow except by drastic action. He will explosively express anger directly to the mother, present to her a bad report card or bring himself to the attention of a neighbor, the police or the school authorities.

Consider the many applications where the parents have been almost forcibly pushed by the school, the pediatrician, the courts or a complaining neighbor, to make that first ambivalent call for help. It appears that the nature of the tie and emotional involvement in this child has been such that the mother perceived and experienced a very different child from that which was perceived by outsiders. Thus, it was a shock to her to view her child as others did. Along with this she felt panic at the threatened exposure of her own illness, so long denied though, in essence, carried for her by the child.

In summary, an attempt has been made to explore the time lag between the objective signs of a child's disturbance and the moment the parents make that first call for help. We have highlighted three factors. Ambivalence toward change, which that request for help symbolizes, may be intensified because of the very nature of the tie between mother and child. Time as a psychological factor may affect the parent's attitude toward self and child. Finally, it has been suggested that the initial call for help is most frequently the mother's emergency, her overwhelming fear that she can no longer cope with her inner stress or the child's pressure. In many instances, her fear concerns the individuation and differentiation of the child and of herself.

Just as the child's illness serves both a positive and negative adaptive function for himself, so does illness serve an internal

---

* Informal communication with Rudolf Ekstein, Ph.D.

need and purpose for the parent. While the parent is experiencing gratification from the child or feeling able to cope with his problems, she experiences little need for help which implies change. It is the nature of the mother's strength and illness that allows her to "look through a glass darkly," and thus be unable to see the child as he is.

The first overture towards help with its tenuous connection will be heard and responded to as a positive plea for help to restore the capacity to function as a parent and a desire, no matter how tentative, to allow room for the child's positive growth and change.

BIBLIOGRAPHY

1. COLEMAN, R. W. E., KRIS, E., and PROVENCE, S. The Study of Variation in Early Parental Attitudes: A Preliminary Report. *Psychoanalyt. Study of the Child*, 1953, 8:20.
2. FRIEDMAN, SEYMOUR W. The Diagnostic Process during the Evaluation of an Adolescent Girl. In *Children of Time and Space, of Action and Impulse*, by Rudolf Ekstein. New York: Appleton-Century-Crofts, 1966, p. 15.
3. MAHLER, M. S., and ELKISCH, P. Strengths about Development and Individuation. *Psychoanalyt. Study of the Child*, 1963, 18:307.
4. TAFT, JESSIE. *The Dynamics of Therapy in a Controlled Relationship*. New York: Dover Publications, 1962.

Chapter 8

The Therapeutic Potential in the Application Process

RALPH WAGNER, M.S.W.

The request for help that carries through to the point of application offers opportunities and challenges to the caseworker who responds to it. The atmosphere in the initial interview is charged with emotion, crisis, hope and resolve. Resistances ase not yet as well mobilized as they will be later on. There is a freshness and a freedom for both patient and worker. A sense of urgency is born out of the decision finally to move toward help and away from further postponement. There is a conscious readiness to make commitments, to risk familiar modes and patterns in the hope of changing an unhappy situation. The atmosphere seems fertile with possibilities. As has so often been said, "All of the dynamics of the case are presented in the first interview."

On the other hand, the patient is not without his defenses and distortions as well as his resistance to change even in the face of suffering. Nor does he come empty-handed. More aften than not, he brings his own definition of the problem and prescription for its cure.

"The problem is my daughter steals." "Yes, there are problems in my family but if my son would only stop making in his pants." "The foul language I can't stand in anyone much less in my own daughter." "He's aggressive and I'm afraid of what will happen

84

later." "He's not aggressive and I'm afraid of what will happen later." "Help me to get the school off my son's back, they sent me here." "My son is very fearful of everything including growing up, please help him with these fears and return him to me." "The whole problem is his father, how could any boy grow up normal with a father like that?" "My own problems are such that I have nothing to give to my children, maybe you can help them." "After her weekend visits with her father she is uncontrollable for days."

The central task in the application phase is the clarification and resolution of the discrepancy between the "wished-for" treatment services and the available ones. Coupled with this are an assessment and an attempt to release forces in the patient and/or in his environment which might provide perspective on the request for help and offer a more promising and healthy direction. Outcomes of this process may involve: (1) redefinition of the problem, redesignation of patient and movement toward another treatment service; (2) crystallization of the problem and the need, and movement toward the service available; (3) decision not to proceed as in the completion of a service at intake when coping capacities seem to have been restored.

Friedman (1), in his discussion of diagnostic process as treatment process, sees the diagnostic evaluation as an instrument for helping the patient. This occurs through the use of the technique "of becoming involved in a relationship for the purpose of the resulting process rather than one of using physical co-existence to avoid a relationship through fact-gathering."

He speaks of providing "the kind of emotional climate that permits the patient to begin to experience the difference between health and illness . . . to begin to develop an emotional understanding of his disturbance and of the existence of forces within him that presently give him that no other choice but illness (even though other choices are potentially available) . . . to indicate the support for action towards achieving health and freedom to choose means other than illness to master problems."

Friedman's formulations are very provocative when considering possibilities for helping in the application process.

The question arises: Can or should such a process be initiated in an application period where one or two interviews are often followed by a long delay before the next step can be taken? Notwithstanding the fact that in all cases the patient comes for help, are there opportunities for truly helping at this stage? How is this help defined, implemented? How does the caseworker effect the process? How does he move to help? By what method? To what end? This paper will attempt to address these questions.

In the application interview, the clinic process and the hopes and expectations of the parent (or those urging the parent) come together. In this clinic, the parents make the application and appear on behalf of the child. The child is usually not seen at this point. The assessment process is twofold in that a clinical picture of the patient must come from the parents' presentation. Often this occurs simply enough. A mature stable parent can offer a sufficiently clear picture of the child's symptoms and behavior to make the next step in the process a natural one. In other situations, however, the process is complicated by the intensity of emotional disturbance of the parent or in the family, which obscures reliable information about the patient. How the parent experiences the caseworker's attempts to gain a picture of the child's situation is the heart of the matter at application.

Out of this encounter the caseworker develops the data base for important decision-making with regard to the patient-family. The interview follows the model of treatment process in that the caseworker provides an atmosphere and continually moves from patient material but with the full recognition of the press of time. The hour or two that is given to the application should produce a plan for the patient-family which it can endorse and begin to follow.

Accepting the time-limited nature of the experience, and capitalizing on the patient-family's motivation to do something now, involve the case worker in a very active role in the situation. He needs to evaluate the parent, the problem and the strengths and weaknesses in the patient-family. Techniques of clarification, confrontation, interpretation are used to bring together the patient-family's hope for cure and the clinic's assessment process. Ultimately the areas of meshing of these two processes provide indications of the patient-family's motivation and capacity to handle their problems without professional help, or their recognition of and commitment to the kind of help that is needed.

Having to appeal for professional help for one's child is an act inevitably involving intense emotions. Such an appeal comes after a failure of best efforts, no matter how puny or distorted these may seem to an observer. It culminates a history of powerful efforts to deny, avoid or accommodate to an emotional illness. It involves an exposure most difficult for a mother to make. It hurts deeply. One mother, then, may hide her child in her defense of him. Another may shower herself with blame for her child's problems. Another may feel bereft of any emotion save anger toward the child. Yet another may be finally responding to continued demands from school to get help but still holds the hope the school misunderstands. The theme, "take him, he's mine!" is played out in many variations. We do not know enough about the timing of these appeals for help or the shifts in family equilibrium which bring them about. Campbell, in Ch. 7, addresses herself to a particular group of mothers who experience a "shock of recognition" regarding their children as they finally move toward help. More study in this area is necessary.

Time, at the point of application, is "now." Mother's feeling of urgency; the decision to act; the opportunity for action; the caseworker's interest and readiness to begin; all focus on the current situation and the immediate precipitating circumstances. Time, as experienced by the mother, is a major source of stress or crisis. Time, as offered by the caseworker, implies hope.

It is in the nature of emergency or crisis situations that they threaten totally the state of equilibrium and draw on all of the available resources without significantly reducing the threat. The tremendous need to "solve" the emergency becomes the reservoir of hope for the future and the walls of the dam crack. This is the presenting situation at intake.

The assessment tasks in the application phase are manifold. They involve the development of information for understanding the presenting complaint, the child as a whole, the parent as a participant in and witness to the events, the pattern and quality of family relationships and their characteristic problem-solving resources. The focus of the caseworker shifts as elaborations of certain relationships, experiences and/or activities, past and present, promise understanding of the current situation, offer possibilities

for diagnostic assessment and opportunities for therapeutic leverage.

The caseworker must attempt to draw on those energies being
used ineffectively in the service of emergency and to apply them
towards a fuller appreciation of the total situation. The presenting
complaint is generally overdetermined and its ramifications overestimated. The mother's special definition of the problem and prescription for its cure represent a narrowing of her perspective, an
identification with the child's problems and a reduction in her
capacity to choose alternative actions. In a word, it is a fore-
closure on the mother's own inner resources, or resources possible
in the environment, which leaves her feeling helpless and inadequate to deal with the problem.

To test the mother's freedom to look beyond her preconceptions
and to begin to utilize latent strengths, the caseworker engages her
in an active, mutual exploration of the child's problem in all its
aspects. The fact that the caseworker does not immediately accept
the mother's clarion call both offers support and sets the process
in motion. The detailed examination of the meaning for the mother
of the child's problem encourages expression of the feelings, hopes
and expectations that have become identified with the problem.
The discussion of the vicissitudes of the child's behavior invites
the mother's observations beyond the confines of the problem and
begins the differentiation between adaptive and disturbed reactions. The recapitulation of the chronic and the acute reveals the
previous accommodation and offers clearer perspective on the current stress. A more dimensional picture of the child emerges as does
an enhanced conception of the family as a whole.

The mother's capacity to engage in the relationship offered by
the caseworker and her ability to begin to identify with the helping
process provide the gauge for the therapeutic potentials at the
point of application. The caseworker drives the process to demonstrate the resistances to help, to clarify the meaning of the child's
problem for the family and to develop alternative courses of action
available to the family. It is this process which produces the shifts
in designation of patient and/or problem and reorientation regarding the help needed. It is here that family strengths and resources
are freed sufficiently to support the decision that no further treat-

ment is indicated now. It is here, also, that the child's problem is stripped of its encumbrances so that the mobilization of commitments to the treatment confirmed as necessary is begun.

The following case illustrations may help to describe the process:

A 38-year-old divorced mother, employed as a secretary, made urgent application on behalf of her only child, a 16-year-old son. The presenting complaint listed poor school achievement, irresponsibility in the use of money and in keeping proper hours, along with fear of his involvement in juvenile delinquency. The mother was frightened by her loss of control over her son and certain he would be led into trouble by bad associates.

The mother's description of her son was interesting. He was a tall, handsome, blue-eyed, blond who was athletic, popular and had a great sense of humor. His life was full, active, exciting and dangerous. In contrast, her life seemed drab and uninteresting. She was not happy in her work and had few social outlets. She dated infrequently because most men seemed to make immediate sexual advances. She suffered periods of depression. A religious person, she visited her pastoral counselor from time to time to discuss her problems.

Discussing this contrast, the mother recognized that her most pleasureful and most painful moments were involved with her son. She was given to excesses in permissiveness and restriction in regard to curfew and in giving and withholding money. For his part, her son seemed to demur and rebel in accordance with his own problems in growing up and becoming separate from his mother.

It developed that the mother was not concerned about her son's school grades, not about juvenile delinquency, nor even about his future success. Identifying him with his absent father, she felt frustrated and angry about her need to hold on to him while feeling subjected to his exploitation. She had bought him an expensive guitar on condition he practice regularly and go to work to help pay for it. Her son worked for one week, quit his job, and was "looking" for another without success. This broken promise and show of irresponsibility was the crowning blow that led her to seek help for him.

In the application process, the mother recognized that the gift of the guitar was a way of tying down her son's free time both inside and outside of the home and, moreover, that it was one of many such efforts she made with this in mind. She decided to withdraw the application at the clinic, feeling she understood the situation better and could manage. She wanted to try a more consistent approach with her son and make an attempt to develop her own interests and social activities. She was also considering the possibility of treatment for herself.

The above case illustrates the problems encountered by a mother who is not fully prepared to deal with her son's emerging independence, especially when her own sources of gratification and self-esteem are minimal. Her anxiety in the situation left her with only dire predictions about the future and led to the request for help. As she was able to examine her own involvement with her son, she could consider his behavior in a different perspective and mobilize resources in herself to deal with the inevitable separation.

In another case, a couple in her mid-40's applied for help for their eight-year-old son. The marital history was chaotic and there was one lengthy separation. At the time of the application the parents were legally separated but were living in the same home. The father, an angry, resentful person and reportedly a very heavy drinker, was unemployed. The mother, an aggressive, embittered woman, was the head of the household and held a responsible job.

In the call to the clinic the mother was not specific about the request for help, implying perverse sexual behavior and stating that the school psychologist had recommended treatment for the boy. In the interview it was difficult to get any consideration of the child's situation because the parents contradicted each other continually and pursued their marital conflicts.

Confronted with their inefficient use of the interview time and encouraged to focus on a discussion of their son, the parents acknowledged they were not very aware of the nature of his difficulties. They were certain, however, that their marital difficulties had no effect on him. As the boy's situation was examined, the mother revealed the school recommendation for treatment had been made the previous year when she had not acted on it. Instead, she called the clinic soon after she found her son in suspected sex play with another boy. She was shocked because he had always been extremely modest. From this she moved to her son's "beauty," his artistic ability, his fussiness about being clean, his dislike of his resemblance to his father, his hatred of his three-year-old sister and, finally, to her fear he would become homosexual.

Prior to the second interview, the mother arranged a school conference. She learned that her son was aggressive and attacking with others, that he had little tolerance for frustration, lacked self-control and that he often appeared worried and unhappy in school. She supplemented these observations with more of her own. She related becoming aware of her son's attempts to win friends by offering his possessions. She revealed the long hours he spent alone and his terror when his parents fought.

She wished to admit her neglect. She began to realize that her intense involvement in her occupation had necessary elements of self-justification which served to ward off feelings of helplessness to deal with a hopeless marital situation. She became aware of how she postponed decisions regarding the marriage and her son in the hope she would not have to make them. This bargaining for time in the future came to an abrupt end in the incident of the sex play which brought the application. The mother was initially motivated by guilt for having destroyed her son's masculine identification. In the process she was able to examine the situation beyond this central concern and to consider experiences which contributed to the boy's problems as well as those which had the potential for more adequately meeting his needs.

In the end, she remained uncertain about what would happen in the marriage. She had an enhanced appreciation of her son's need for help, however, and wanted to pursue the application for an evaluation. In the interim, she felt she now had means to reduce the stress for her son and herself.

The situation in this case involved parents so tightly locked in their own marital struggle they failed to notice the extent of their son's problems. The task was to draw their attention, and give weight, to those observations which promised greater recognition of the boy's needs and conflicts, and to explore their readiness to move to protect him from the excesses of parental conflict. As the mother became aware of her defensive operations, and as she could permit the full impact of her son's situation to become real to her, she could consider actions to alter the unhappy course of events in the family.

To sum up, the point of application can be of critical importance to the patient-family and have far-reaching consequences in the way they deal with their problems and in their attitudes about the nature of help. The initial request indicates a shift of forces in the family and a decision to act. It is this motivation, no matter what burden of other family problems it carries, which provides the opportunity for helping. The family situation has become somewhat fluid, and the previous pattern of avoidance, denial and/or distortion no longer serves the purposes of postponement. The patient is designated, the problem defined, the resolution invested with hopefulness, and this program is presented to the helping person in the first interview. The emergency surrounding the presenting situation serves to bind the resources of the family to the terms of its hoped-for resolution.

The caseworker in the application interview offers the parent a relationship designed to permit a mutual exploration of the problem and its many implications for the family. A process is developed which attempts to divest the presenting situation of its overdetermined aspects and of the unrealistic hopes, anxieties and identifications which have become associated with it. The beginning acceptance of the problem, in its derived state, releases forces previously bound to the family definition of the problem. These forces can now be utilized to initiate movement toward change in the family without further help or movement toward and commitment to an appropriate course of treatment. The parent is left to carry his responsibilities either with his own resources or with an enhanced understanding of the help that is needed and an increased awareness of how the help will come about, both for himself and for the child.

BIBLOGRAPHY

1. FRIEDMAN, SEYMOUR W. The Diagnostic Process as a Part of the Treatment Process, *Reiss-Davis Clin. Bull.*, 1966, 2:62.

Chapter 9

❧

Inner and Outer Reality Testing
on the Rorschach

MORTIMER M. MEYER, PH.D., AND
ELAINE CARUTH, PH.D.

CARD V

(Reprinted with permission of Hans Huber, Berne, Switzerland.)
1.—A bat, eating people. Vultures.
2.—A cat.

The Rorschach has long been used as a means of evaluating the reality testing function of the ego. However, a comparison of the above two responses poses an interesting but heretofore unex-

plored aspect of the individual's relationship to reality as is reflected in his test performance.

In the first response, the subject uses appropriately the shape
and boundary of the blot and integrates it correctly into the percept—"A bat." However, the inappropriate attribute of "eating
people" ascribed to the percept represents a severe distortion of
ideation. In the second response, the subject uses the shape and
boundary of the blot inappropriately, although the content of the
response is without evident distortion of inner ideation. Both of
these responses are inappropriate but they differ in the manner in
which they misuse the material. In each instance the relationship
to reality is impaired in a different way. In the first response, "A
bat, eating people," an unrealistic interpretation is assigned to a
correctly perceived bit of reality. In the second instance—"A cat"
—a realistic concept is arbitrarily assigned to a misperceived
reality.

Examination of the nature of the difference between these two
responses has led to the consideration that the concept of reality
testing must be refined and elaborated. These two responses suggest that the ability to evaluate experiences which come from the
outside must be differentiated from the ability to exaluate those
experiences which come from the inside. Clinically, such a distinction is implied by the recognition that there is both an inner and
outer reality. Historically, however, philosophical and scientific
psychology were primarily concerned with the acquisition of
knowledge about external reality. Consequently, research was
primarily focused upon such epistemological problems as the relationship between stimulus and reaction, and the means by which
the psychic apparatus evaluated the stimuli from the environment.

Studies using techniques of introspection about the content of
mental life were relatively rare before Freud. With the development of psychoanalysis, however, and particularly after Freud's
discovery that the heretofore postulated sexual trauma were, in
actuality, most often of fantasy origin, the emphasis upon the inner
reality became paramount clinically. Currently, it would be truly
a psychological anachronism to limit the definition of reality to
those experiences which can be defined only in terms of their ob-

servable sources of stimulation. Nevertheless, residuals of this historically rooted reluctance to give full and equal weight to "the world within" as well as "the world without" are present to this day in the clinical use of the concept of reality testing. The theory and use of Rorschach technique for the purpose of evaluating reality testing has also continued to be tied to the original emphasis upon outer reality.

Reality testing was first described as the capacity to judge the source of perception with reference to whether it came from within or without. Freud's original formulation stated that perceptions which can be made to disappear by motor activity are recognized as "external, as reality, where such an action makes no difference, the perception originates within the subject's own body—it is not real" (1). Gross distortions of reality would, thus, be exemplified by hallucinations.

Reality testing, however, includes more than the ability merely to differentiate the subjective or objective nature of the source of the perception. It is generally only in the most gross disturbances that such a perceptual impairment does exist. Nevertheless, the relationship to reality can be defective even though the capacity to differentiate between inner and outer reality is relatively intact. A delusional system may not impair the perception but it will impair the interpretation of the perception and, thus, reflects a distorted relationship to reality. Hartmann has suggested such a distinction when he stated, "Actually, as mental phenomena are no less real in the outer world (although we often refer to the latter only in speaking of 'reality'), it might prove useful to include testing of the within as well as of the without . . . we could say that with the neurotic testing of inner, with the psychotic testing of outer reality is interfered with. However, a higher complexity is introduced by the fact that among others, that the two aspects of reality testing often interact" (3).

Subsequently, he elaborated this differentiation both between inner and outer reality as well as inner and reality testing: "Problems of acceptance, of distortion, of denial occur in relation to inner as well as outer reality—About the distorted picture of inner reality, . . . it seems reasonable to speak of a testing of the within, in addition to testing of the without—that is, to distinguish inner reality testing from outer reality testing" (4).

It has been less clearly recognized, though Hartmann seems to imply it, that these two aspects of the relationship to reality may vary independently of each other. The emergence of primary process in the content of the response has not generally been considered a discrete parameter of the reality testing function. Rather, the content of the responses has been considered merely as reflecting the individual's fantasy as it is projected onto the blot and therein giving evidence of the kind of ongoing internal life. Schafer, for example, describes the relatively low incidence of good form responses in schizophrenia as "indicative of the extent of the breakdown of reality testing and the suffusion of a perception with pathologically autistic thought content" (6), without considering the possibility that these two aspects should be dealt with separately.

Hartmann, however, was concerned primarily with the neurotic-psychotic dichotomy to which he had referred. In the understanding of patients whose pathology is characterized by fluctuating ego states, such as the borderline and schizophrenic patient, a knowledge of the vicissitudes and permutations of inner and outer reality testing might improve our understanding of how these patients experience their inner and outer worlds. Such understanding could give us greater insight into the nature of their particular ego disturbances.

We would like to suggest now a working definition of these two concepts. By outer reality testing, we refer to the process of perceiving external reality. By inner reality testing, we refer to the process of evaluating the accompanying fantasy in terms of its appropriateness to the circumstances involved and the realistic possibility of its fulfillment. Thus, an individual may indulge in many unrealistic fantasies, fed by either the primary or secondary process, but still retain the critical ego functions which make for recognition of their inappropriateness or unrealistic nature. On the other hand, an individual may indulge in the same fantasies but be unable to recognize their inappropriateness. In the latter circumstance, the inner reality testing is impaired, regardless of the effectiveness of the testing of outer reality. Where the fantasy has been guided by the primary process, we have evidence of the intrusion of a more chronic and pervasive thought disorder.

In differentiating between "the world within" and "the world without," it must be recognized that this is not a topological distinction. "The world within," is defined as the individual's world of thought and fantasies. The content of this world consists of the psychic representation of the individual's experience with outer reality, from which it is differentiated, although it follows certain parallel laws. The "world without" includes stimuli arising from the body of the individual so that distortions in bodily sensations, such as functional physical complaints, would be attributed to an impairment of outer reality testing. We are including the entire gamut of enteroceptive, properoceptive and exteroceptive input. This is opposed to the more usual distinction between enteroceptive and exteroceptive stimulation which is of significance in the development of the differentiation between "I" and "non-I," a differentiation which we usually refer to as *external* reality testing. Thus, disturbances of body *image* would be attributed to a distortion of inner reality. Obviously we deal here with a relative rather than an absolute distinction. Outer reality is perceived on the basis of the internal image, and the internal image is derived in part from outer reality. We might postulate that the experience of a fantasy limb is a product of a temporary impairment of both inner and outer reality testing. In this instance, sensations are misperceived as emanating from a non-existent piece of reality. At the same time, the psychic representation of the body image has not been readjusted to the new external reality of the change in the body. Loss of contact with reality can be similarly differentiated. Loss of contact with inner reality, such as feelings of depersonalization, may occur without concomitant external reality distortions. Loss of contact with outer reality, as exemplified by the "classic" bizarre-hallucinating schizophrenic, can occur in a patient firmly in contact with his inner reality, crazy though it may be.

Such a differentiated use of the concept of reality testing becomes of immense value when applied to the evaluation of the Rorchach. Here, too, reality testing has been traditionally regarded as a single entity which is reflected in the ability of the subject to perceive appropriately the boundary and shape of an object; that is, in Rorschach terminology, to use good form. The appropriateness with which the form of the blot is used is interpreted as the degree to which the individual pays appropriate attention to the boundaries of a reality situation in the environment. Thus, the handling of form reflects the readiness with which the individual perceives appropriately the external observable reality. Returning to the illustrative responses above, it becomes apparent that the subject making the first response was able to evaluate appropriately the external reality but permitted evidence of primary process functioning to emerge. By contrast, the subject making the second response misinterpreted the external reality but did not permit emergence of primary process functioning or distortion of inner ideation.

Within this frame of reference of two kinds of reality testing, it is suggested that a disturbance of outer reality testing would be evidenced by a misperception of the environment and would be reflected in the Rorschach by a disturbance in form. On the other hand, a disturbance of inner reality testing would be evidenced as an inability to judge the appropriateness of the fantasy and would be reflected in the Rorschach by the attribution of inappropriate or bizarre qualities to the percept.

Observing this differentiation in interpreting the Rorschach can contribute to a clearer understanding of the subject's potential for coping and adaptation. The subject, who can maintain adequate form in spite of inappropriateness of content, demonstrates an ability to relate to external tasks so that, objectively, his reality testing appears adequate. He can deal with that part of the task that can be separated from the inner image as if the reality testing were unimpaired even though the one aspect of reality testing is actually impaired, as evidenced by the inappropriate content. Such an intra-psychic constellation is observed in the ambulatory schizophrenic patient who is capable of maintaining a job in spite of peculiar and bizarre fantasies. This is the kind of patient who gets into difficulty primarily on the rare occasions when the external task makes demands upon internal imagery in order to complete the task.

The particular responses where the form, as well as the content, shows reality violation are then suggestive of those areas in which the patient is likely to experience the external environment as impinging upon the unrealistic imagery. This results in the impairment of outer as well as inner reality testing and concomitant failure in coping. This differentiation is thus particularly useful in understanding the seemingly erratic and shifting behavior of the borderline patient. It explains why at times he is able to behave as if there were no impairment in reality testing and at other times appears to be suffering from a complete breakdown of reality testing.

The records of children in the Project on Childhood Psychosis at Reiss-Davis Clinic furnish many examples of this kind of differentiation. Reproduced below are two different responses to Card IX from the protocols of two adolescent girls evaluated and treated in the Project.

The first subject responded with two birdmen, formed of a carrot's body and a man's head, bowing to each other. This re-

CARD IX

(Reprinted with permission of Hans Huber, Berne, Switzerland.)

Subject A.: "Two birdmen, formed of a carrot's body and a man's head bowing to each other."

Subject B: "Oh, I see another monster. This monster is scary . . . fat and big. Pink, two eyes, holes also. A long nose and hanging down . . ."

sponse reflects complete indifference to the ideational distortion inherent in this kind of contamination, yet there is careful documentation in the response with respect to form. This particular subject demonstrates clinically a similar discrepancy in her functioning. She was quite capable in her handling of reality, and the underlying thought disorder did not intrude into her handling of external reality. Eventually, however, the inroads of the pathology into her total personality organization led to a more acute overt break with reality.

The second patient, however, who was clinically unable to handle external as well as internal reality, responded to this card as, "Oh, I see another monster. This monster is scary . . . fat and big. Pink, two eyes, holes also. A long nose and hanging down. . . ." This response reflects complete indifference to the form of the stimulus. The content also is suggestive of some ideational distortion, although it is difficult to evaluate what would be a realistic description of a monster. For this particular patient, the monster within was occasionally projected and seen as a monster without. This patient also had difficulty differentiating inner from outer reality in a variety of other situations.

Certain aspects of the recent work in the area of sensory deprivation, or to use Kubie's more precise term, "afferent isolation" (5), may be interpreted within this proposed frame of reference of both an inner and an outer reality testing function. We would like to suggest some of the possible implications. In a study on sensory deprivation and interference with reality contact, it was stated: "Man is to a large extent dependent on continual commerce with his usual environment to maintain his highest level of thought functioning. Many of the effects of isolation may be understood as the emergence into awareness of a kind of thinking usually found in dreams, psychosis, and artistic creation" (2). We would like to suggest that this "continual commerce" might be thought of, to paraphrase Menninger, as a "vital balance" between inner and outer reality testing which is needed for the individual to maintain an optimal level of functioning. These studies suggest that when the opportunity for outer reality testing is minimal (except for those stimuli arriving through enteroceptive sensations), the individual will experience a breakdown in the inner reality testing and will evidence the intrusion of primary process functioning. In some instances he will undergo a breakdown in the outer reality testing and develop hallucinatory experiences. This need of the normal person for continued interaction between the external world and his inner world is reflected, perhaps, in the often reported phenomenon of psychological disintegration following retirement in many effective working people. It is also one of the problems that has to be faced in space-age aviation.

In closing, we would like to suggest that not only does what is real exist both internally as well externally, but what is unreal may be attributed to both the internal as well as the external.

BIBLIOGRAPHY

1. FREUD, S. Instincts and Their Vicissitudes (1915). *Collected Papers*, Vol. IV, pp. 60-83. London: Hogarth Press, 1946.
2. GOLDBERGER, LEO, and HOLT, ROBERT R. Experimental Interference with Reality Contact: Individual Differences. *Sensory Deprivation*: Symposium held at Harvard Medical School. Cambridge, Mass.: Harvard University Press, 1961.
3. HARTMANN, HEINZ. Contribution to the Metapsychology of Schizophrenia. *Psychoanalytic Study of the Child*, 1953, 8:195.
4. HARTMANN, HEINZ. Notes on the Reality Principle. *Psychoanalytic Study of the Child*, 1956, 11:50-51.
5. KUBIE, LAURENCE S. Theoretical Aspects of Sensory Deprivation. *Sensory Deprivation*: Symposium held at Harvard Medical School. Cambridge, Mass.: Harvard University Press, 1961.
6. SCHAFER, ROY. *The Clinical Application of Psychological Tests.* New York: International Press, 1948, p. 69.

Part IV

CLINICAL STUDIES AND TREATMENT

Chapter 10

The Young People's Problem Center: An Adolescent Drop-In Clinic

LILLIAN WEITZNER, M.S.W.

There were two reasons for the organization of a brief treatment service for adolescents within a psychoanalytically oriented child study clinic. One was to increase experimentally our understanding of the nature of the manifestations of psychopathology of current youth. The second was to attempt to adapt our psychological understanding and methods to meet the increasing demand for mental-health service during a time of general curtailment of support for intensive individual psychotherapy.

The Young People's Problem Center, as the drop-in adolescent service was known, was staffed by psychotherapists of the Reiss-Davis Child Study Center, who volunteered their services.* Their clinical experience and empathic maturity were vital qualities for the therapeutic tasks involved. The interest, sensitivity, and knowledge brought to each patient and problem were reflected in the results and enthusiasm which marked this endeavor.

The structure of treatment was based on the hypothesis that the quixotic upheaval in mental equilibrium, so characteristic of

---

* Therapists included Ruth Bro, Beatrice Cooper, Sylvia Dilman, Albert Ellenbogen, Gale Goldschmidt, Esther Hecht, Herbert Rosenfeld, Ralph Wagner, and Lillian Weitzner. Ida Shulman volunteered important secretarial service.

adolescence, often responds quickly to intervention. The powerful maturational thrusts to impulses also influence the ego and super-ego, creating a fluidity of defenses and heightened self-awareness. The adolescent, consequently, is receptive to understanding the exaggerated conflictual forces within the personality and is able to change to more adaptive defenses.

The adolescent who comes for help has been feeling the distress for some time, and the driving force is the feeling that nobody understands him, least of all himself. He feels himself in an emergency because of the qualitative and quantitative changes in almost every respect of his personality: physical size, strength, genital sexual demands, and aggressive expression. These changes arouse a sense of danger, but he cannot turn to his parent for help because the accompanying break in the attachment to the parental object requires a reorientation to new objects. Confiding in, or closeness to, a parent places him in a position in which the newly aroused genital impulses will connect with his old love object. Thus he externalizes, displaces, and projects his impulses and disappointments.

These changes require him to make a change, demand a choice, turn passivity into activity. He may physically run away; without leaving home, he may actively leave the family circle for peer activity; he may isolate himself. If he does not turn to activity, he feels uprooted. He cannot be patient because patience is a condition of inactivity. This intolerance of the status quo, in combination with the urgent demand for action, creates the emergency state which brings the young adult, or his parents, for help. It is, therefore, important that he be seen immediately, since waiting increases the need to act out and delay adds to the discouragement and negativism towards treatment. Further, when a request for help is appropriately responded to, the initiator perceives himself as having actively accomplished a task and is thus not in the painful position of passively waiting. If he is further included in making decisions about himself, some of this satisfying activity continues in the mastery of the task.

The structure and location of the Center attracted those adolescents who could follow the suggestion of school authorities, physicians, etc., to seek help. Others came via their friends. Occasionally, parents initiated the contact. The young people who came were mainly white, middle-class adolescents, still living at home. Their ages ranged from 13 through 20, but the 15, 16, and 17 year olds were highly represented. More than half of the families in our population had been disrupted by divorce or death of a parent, and many parents had remarried.

All patients were seen individually, although conjoint interviews occurred, according to the discretion of the therapist. The vast majority of those who sought help were not reacting primarily to the impact of adolescence, but to the acuteness of stress in this developmental stage on previous, even long-term psychological disorder. Severe disturbances—borderline, psychotic, severe character disorders—were referred to other agencies or private therapists, with much care involved in the selection of the resource, as well as the referral process. The frequency and number of interviews were not predetermined, but varied according to the nature of the situation. Half of our adolescents were seen once or twice, and half between three and fourteen times.

Six months after having been seen, a follow-up telephone call was made to the patient and to the parent, if he had been seen. Our questions had been designed to ascertain the patient's subjective evaluation of his contact, the effectiveness of the service, and information about specific problems.

Two areas of difficulty, presented by the young and middle adolescents (the majority of our patients), center around the task of dissolving the tie to their parents and the struggle to find new permanent objects, especially in a mobile community. Broadly, early adolescent youth are driven away from parental involvement by their increased aggressive impulses and the impact of their revived pre-oedipal impulses. They are drawn to their peers as transitory objects in the step away from the object, but frequently seek help to cope with the anxiety, depression, and fear of acting out their displaced inner conflicts with their peers.

At 15 or 16, then, young people may turn to their peers, especially those of the opposite sex, as displaced oedipal objects. In addition, however, the turn to their own social groups is part of their widening social awareness and increased ego functioning. The degree to which an adolescent frees himself from the parental tie allows him to turn to this larger social world and search for his own destiny. The help needed at this time is to cope with those difficulties which impede the movement to peers or with the impulse to break away from the family prematurely by leaving home.

Throughout this age group there is a trend towards making an overall effort to bypass internal conflicts and discomfort, especially those to which adult opposition contributes. There is a push to imitate the patterns of older adolescents who engage in drug-taking, sexual involvement, and school avoidance. The recent trend in films and T.V. towards greater abandonment of sexual and aggressive control sometimes serves as sanction for such behavior. At times the struggle appears to be in the direction of avoiding struggle, with the aim of acquiring a sense of ease—physical, moral, and social. A few of the patients assumed the continued casual acceptance of parental material support, with angry rejection of the parents' opposition to such expectations and little or no comprehension of the meaning of the parents' position.

Most of our patient population could not find a group within which they could work out their individual emancipation. Their own psychological difficulties kept them bound to the family pathology. They were unable to organize their activities in a firm cohesive body in opposition to parental ideals. They were equally unable to identify with parental ideals or even with those ideals which they felt their parents had abandoned. In families disrupted by death and divorce, the adolescents' ties too often were involved with idealized and unavailable parental figures, or they actively sought the absent parent. The significant number of patients in our population with single parents, or remarried parents, presented us with information about circumstances compounding the difficulties with which today's adolescent often must cope.

The thrust of our brief intervention was to find the progressive forces in the individual, to locate and delineate the most important and accessible conflict, and to mobilize the progressive force to deal with the conflict.

Each therapist had complete autonomy in treating his cases. The therapeutic staff met weekly as a deliberating group, during which each case was reported and discussed. These weekly discussions continued through the completion of the follow-up telephone calls, at which time the patient's reported statements and evaluations were analyzed vis-à-vis the therapists' opinions as to whether there had been a therapeutic gain. For the most part, the therapists were less sanguine about beneficial results than the patients, since the latter reflected the not uncommon "glow" of having benefited from the caring nature of the relationship. The 41 or 79% of the 52 adolescents seen, reached by telephone, commented favorably on their experience, even when they reported they had not been helped. It had been important to them that the therapists "cared" and that there had been a place where they could be seen immediately. The follow-up telephone call was cited as additional evidence of attentiveness and concern.

A brief intervention is not sufficient to meet the needs of severe disturbances, such as depression, panic, and schizophrenic thought disorder. Referral to a more appropriate agency did take place, except when parents were unable to accept their child's plight, or where a good treatment resource was not worked out. In such situations it does seem necessary to have a period of intermittent interviews, in which one can develop the parent's trust and work through the recurring erupting upsets, before the referral will be acted upon. Some such situations came to our attention during the beginning period of our project and were successfully referred. Had the project been in existence longer, it might have been possible to have completed more referrals.

No benefits were experienced in those instances involving adolescents with long-term personality disturbances in families which were inadequate, unable to establish controls, or disrupted by continuing crises, alcoholism, etc. These adolescents were frequently involved with drugs, truancy, and behavior which brought them to the attention of the Probation Department. Parents then sought additional help for which our service was inappropriate. In general, where there were gross defects in ego integration and where the family environment was ineffective and diffuse, brief therapeutic effort had little or no effect on course of behavior.

There were, fortunately, many adolescents with more intact ego functioning whose difficulties were more circumscribed and available for examination and clarification. In these situations, the therapists were able to free and mobilize the healthy portions of the personality so that the adolescents could move on into more gratifying activities.

Initially, most of the patients presented their discomfort with themselves, although they were unclear as to what it was. However, they usually externalized the problem as due to their parents' or teachers' difficulties, in which they were caught and unable to extricate themselves. Their parents or teachers were too restrictive, unreasonable, angry, punitive, or just "weird," and certainly not understanding. There was a feeling of isolation and a fear of becoming more involved in the drug scene or of suffering the effects of past drug involvement on their brain (although the latter fear was not expressed overtly). A good number were able to maintain some involvement in school work, despite their concern about decreased interest and wish to drop out.

The therapist's rapid assessment of the situation led to a focused point of exploration. Uppermost was the acknowledgment of the patient's affect, the mood and its possible effect, the mood and its possible effect on the person's self-perception and activity. One then explored the reasons for the mood by eliciting the events and background which the adolescent thought contributed to the situation. When the affect and self-perceptions could be linked with a specific event or constellation of family events past or present, the therapist was effective.

Although most adolescents externalize their difficulties, the early pubertal adolescent is unable to modify this defense and maintains his stance of being misunderstood and being attacked. Therapeutic help is limited, except as one can meet a need, modify the reality situation and, if indicated, deal with guilt. One can help the parents to tolerate the situation better. The 16 and 17 year olds, however, are usually more introspective and able to tolerate self-scrutiny and gentle probing.

Thus, a 13-year-old depressed girl and her parents were all puzzled by her recent temper outbursts and antagonism, especially towards the stepfather. She was irritable with friends and provocative to teachers. The girl acknowledged to the therapist her self-dislike and shame because she was ugly and wished she could hide her face. Her unexpected mood swings were confusing to her. The therapist took up the girl's positive feelings towards her deceased father. He had been separated from the mother when the patient was four and had subsequently died in a drunken brawl, a fact known to the girl, although believed by the parents to have been kept secret. The mother had never spoken to the girl about her father, which contributed to the barrier between them and to the confused and distorted self-image.

Her therapist discussed with the parents the girl's need for the idealized lost parent as well as her confusion and need to defend against her stepfather's affection. The girl then questioned her mother for details of the former marriage and divorce, to which the mother openly responded. This allowed the girl to display a formerly hidden photo of her father. The noticeable change in mood and activity continued to improve, especially after the onset of menses several months later. There was also evidence of more age-appropriate peer relationships. It is problematic whether the full mourning process for the deceased father can take place later, but just the removal of the taboo against affectionate feelings for the lost father and re-establishing him as a love object were helpful as this girl was entering into adolescence.

Serious parental illness, psychological or physical, exerts an overwhelming impact on the adolescent whose own instability acts on and reacts with the parents' lack of control. The adolescent's defensive reactions of avoidance or denial against his fears, especially of contracting the illness, and his helplessness in not being able to alter the parental illness, lead to despair, withdrawal, and hysterical suicidal gestures. In two girls, 14 and 15 years old, the situation was further compounded by the absence of the father, which was experienced as abandonment. The lack of another substitute adult contributed to the confusion about their own reactions. They could not test or clarify their observations. Both girls had managed to live relatively calmly, devoting themselves to their school work, which was a source of gratification, until a short time before they came to the Clinic.

The 14-year-old girl's stepfather was in the home but removed himself from the constant embroilment. The girl was psychologically fragile and had withdrawn into an extensive fantasy life, based on romantic literature. She had made several suicidal gestures. The frightened, somewhat paranoid, mother would not allow psychological exploration nor further treatment. In this instance, the therapist engaged the girl in a search for less unreliable allies. One such ally was her natural father, whom she visited and who, after an interview, re-established his interest, which he had relinquished because of past frustrating hopelessness. When the mother refused to bring her daughter for her interview, the therapist's phone calls resulted in the stepfather bringing her in, thus engaging him in the process. The patient reported that, despite her mother's disapproval, she went out with some newly found peers, after which she found it more difficult to regress into her fantasies. The mother could even allow an Easter holiday away from home, after which the situation calmed considerably.

On follow-up, the mother reported that despite her continued disapproval of her daughter, there was decreased tension between them. The girl verbalized her disappointment about no further treatment. She continued to see her father, but he, too, was disappointing since he was fearful of confronting and stopping the mother's irrational behavior. The revived affectionate feelings had been tied to an idealized fantasy oedipal father. The reality of his existence permitted more effective perception and resolution of the idealization. She has also turned to an adult female cousin who is less disturbed and is interested in her. She has friends with whom she talks and finds understanding. Although serious personality problems still exist, the daughter is not interlocked in the pathological relationship with her mother. Her relationships outside her home and her school activities provide sufficient gratification and outlet so that complete withdrawal no longer threatens.

In the other instance, the therapist confirmed the girl's awareness of her mother's indeed very serious paranoid psychotic condition. She was helped to deal with her guilt and encouraged to call on her father for support and protection for herself and her younger brother. The ambivalent father needed the therapist's corroboration of the accuracy of his daughter's perception of the family circumstances and was supported in removing the children to his own home.

If the disturbed parent is seen, one tries to find access to reduce the identification with the child, so that he is no longer seen as a victim, but as a separate individual able to move on. If this is accomplished, decreased guilt tends to reduce the anger, and the home need not remain the battlefield between fear and guilt. However, it usually is necessary to see the older adolescent without the parent, since he seeks help for himself in the attempt to establish a degree of his own separateness and to distance himself from the object of his current anger.

A bright 16½-year-old boy intermittently appeared for appointments. Chronically agitated, he had made desperate sporadic attempts to flee from his intense ambivalent attachment to his parents and from his suicidal gestures. Determined to become a doctor, he was obsessed with the fear of failure, as well as the possibility of losing his mind before he reached his goal. Conflicted about outdoing his unsuccessful father, his main concern was with his very disturbed mother who was suffering from an advanced neurological illness. The patient's obsessive-compulsive defenses were unable to withstand the increased pressures of adolescence, and he attempted to reinstate them by ritual. He tested and punished himself by appearing ridiculous before his peers and took flight into grandiose fantasy. The therapist linked some of his anxiety to his fear of becoming ill, as had his mother, at the age of 17. Further, his intense need for exceptional intellectual prowess was clarified as his need to hold up his family as equal to his wealthy successful relatives. But it was even more important to the patient to become capable of reversing his mother's illness. He achieved some insight into his ritualistic behavior prior to exams, which allowed him to relinquish it slightly. His inability to keep appointments led to the surmise that the connections between his mother's illness and his symptoms were too difficult to tolerate, especially as they aroused his death wishes and fears. On follow-up, the mother felt there had been no change, but he expressed himself as doing better, was looking forward to high school graduation, and going away to college. He appeared to be coping with this difficult situation.

Among the 14- and 15-year-old boys living with their single mothers, the increase in aggressive and sexual drives played havoc on their relationships to their mother. Alternately denigrating and needing her, the tie to the absent father was on an idealized pre-oedipal level, with a wish to be cared for by him. Passive wishes were aroused with the fear of being weak and inadequate. Drugs relieved the pain, decreased the need to act on impulses, but increased feelings of passivity. The overwhelming anxiety led to feelings of fear of thought disorder, seen as drug-induced brain damage.

This, in part, describes the situation of a 15½-year-old boy who arrived strung out on a variety of drugs. Deeply involved with drugs, he was referred because he had taken part in minor delinquencies. The boy had had no contact with his father since the age of two, and the mother worked and was studying a profession. In addition, the boy was subjected to his younger brother's physical violence.

After two visits, arrangements were made for a diagnostic evaluation and long-term treatment. The referral process and wait were lengthy, but could be carried through by maintaining intermittent contact with his male therapist. It is doubtful whether, without this holding line, he could have sustained the long wait, during which he was at times less involved with drugs and occasionally even drug-free.

A handsome, sensitive 16 year old lived with his divorced mother and youngest sister while a middle sister lived with the father. The boy was bogged down in truancy, lying about it, avoiding or having arguments with his mother. His one area of functioning was his music, which he pursued with initiative and achievement. He came to the Clinic on his own, was very depressed, and in talking steadily, indirectly revealed his fear of having harmed himself.

He quite correctly pointed out that his "brilliant," but volatile, father had been attempting to use him to effect a remarriage with his mother. The father harshly berated the mother's indulgence and lenience, while she, in turn, displaced her helplessness in controlling the father onto the son. The son was unable to remove himself from this position since it fit into his omnipotent fantasies as he assumed the responsibility for resolving his parents' problems. The situation also provided punishment for his victorious oedipal position. His anxiety, when unable to stop his parents' frequent fights, led to two suicidal gestures. His first sense of relief was when the therapist discussed and accepted his natural adolescent wish to turn away from the problems and to pursue his music interest. The therapist further mentioned that at this age one also again tries to be the heroic big daddy, as one did as a youngster, only to feel again the rejection and failure, since one cannot replace one's own father. The boy then told of his chagrin at learning that his parents had been divorced previously and then remarried when he was little. His fear and guilt emerged while telling of the fatal accident to the son of his mother's fiancé, a boy his age whom he had liked. The accident occurred during a rebellious act in opposition to the parents' demand. The patient then traced his past work history, which had been vigorous until the accident, and he could see how he shared his mother's and her fiancé's depression and feared punishment for his rebelliousness. The mother's love relationship was now teetering and he felt that he was to blame. The oedipal conflict was not interpreted but the sense of omnipotence was.

This patient was one of those seen as often as nine times, so that we could trace his movement away from and back to his parents. At times he succumbed to his father's caring for him, only to rebel at the latter's manipulations, especially as it aroused a wish for closeness. However, it was not until the therapist pointed out how he avoided his fear of his inability to concentrate, or to think clearly, that he agreed to undergo psychological testing. When brain damage was ruled out, he withdrew from his involvement with his battling manipulative parents.

The mother was helped to support this move and to realize the effects of her own guilt-provoking complaints. She became quite aware that she could not depend on her son to ease her own situation but had to resolve her own relationship to her ex-husband. She felt her son had been greatly helped, although the other problems around the divorce remained. The gains, which the adolescent described as receiving "relief," resulted in better school adjustment, employment, and markedly decreased family fights.

Several 16- and 17-year-old girls, of divorced parents, presented similar patterns of difficulty. They were unable to resolve their oedipal attachment to their parents and defensively maintained an ambivalent splitting of the objects, which they perceived as "loyalty" conflicts. The heightened adolescent competition with the mothers was increased by the mothers' dating and social activity. They suffered from feelings of inadequacy and depression.

When they could not tolerate their anger, they fled by moving to their father's home, adopting a motherly role towards him. The fathers' dating or remarriage, usually to a younger woman, again confirmed their infantile feelings of inadequacy and exclusion and they found themselves unable to remain. In strife and in limbo, they were unable to maintain their competence in school, which added to the low self-esteem. They either avoided sexuality, or wished to act out on it, in the attempt to achieve a feeling of closeness. The lure of school truancy and drugs then aroused further conflict in the attempt to avoid pain.

It proved possible to decrease the diffuse anxiety by pointing out the conflict with the mother. One could interpret the derivatives of the revived oedipal longings, affects, and the guilt, where they are operating. One could discuss a girl's fear of not being lovable and her feelings of increased paternal rejection by linking what happened when one was young and had affectionate feelings towards the father, felt rejected, but got over it. It was then possible to point to the specific reasons why it was hard to effect a resolution and why the patient reacted to the present situation with such intensity.

When the therapist makes interpretations under such circumstances, it is not always clear to what aspect of the interpretation the patient is responding. Experience indicates that these interpretations, helpful and acceptable in brief therapy, are usually not as acceptable to adolescents in more intensive therapy. The resistance in intensive therapy may be aroused by the specific transference conflicts which evoke anxiety and the regressive pull so feared by adolescents.

Mrs. Sheila Mason* described a similar observation in her work with adolescents in London. She felt that one finds a quality of openness at the point where no relationship has been established which allows adolescents to hear and see explanations, uncolored by the effects of the transference.

When interpretations are made during a very limited contact, it cannot be clear whether its ultimate effect is one of progressive use. The therapist may perceive a reduction of anxiety and a par-

---

* Presently in the Department of Psychiatry, Adolescent Service, University of Michigan, in personal communication.

tial freeing of ego functions, but this result may operate against working through of conflicts when further therapy is indicated and available. Thus, an 18-year-old girl, was quite depressed and suffered from phobic attacks in which she was fearful of being alone and of not seeing her mother. There were only two sessions available, and the therapist linked her symptoms with the anniversary reaction of her brother's accidental death. This led to her expressed anger that her parents do not appreciate her, no matter what she does. She felt much relief and returned two weeks later, looking very well indeed and pleased that she was able to remain at home alone, as long as there was someone available by telephone. She now wanted to discuss her fear of something happening to her mother, and during the course of the discussion a generalized oedipal interpretation was given and again received with much relief. She wanted further treatment and the referral was made.

Six months later, both she and her mother reported that she had received little help. Although she was functioning better, had graduated from school, and gotten a job, her phobic anxiety returned intermittently. She had not followed through on the referral, in fact had forgotten it had been made. On her request, another resource was named but she did not act on that. The limited symptom relief, and possibly the reaction to the interpretive remarks, set up defenses against further exploration and working through.

Before concluding this summary of the work and findings of brief treatment with adolescents, it is necessary to report that the staff felt that closing the Center after only a six-month operating period made it quite difficult to deal with those people who required some time before they could use our services; those who needed to return after an interval; and those who came at the point of closure and who needed more than a few interviews. A longer interval than six months, or a year before follow-up, might provide different information.

This limited study demonstrated the possibility of helping some adolescents in a brief time, but also raised many questions about technique and long-term results. Reiss-Davis is continuing to explore brief therapy with children and parents in another project which, it is hoped, may provide a few answers to some of the urgent questions to young people's problems and their solutions.

Chapter 11

✳

Identity Formation in the Treatment of an Autistic Child

Leda W. Rosow, M.A.

No one who has worked with autistic children will
ever forget . . . how desperately they struggle to
grasp the meaning of saying, "I" and "You." How
impossible it is for them, for language presupposes
the experience of a coherent I. Work with deeply disturbed young people confronts the worker with the
awful awareness of the patient's incapacity to feel the
"I" and "You" which are cognitively present and the
fear that life may run out before such feelings may
be experienced—in love.

—Erik H. Erikson

In the recent past, the phenomenon of infantile psychosis has
increasingly become the subject of clinical and research studies.
Whether the organic or psychogenic point of view is emphasized,
the complexities are still too great to be certain about the etiology
of this personality deficit. Nevertheless, there is a growing body of
clinical evidence regarding the psychogenic nature of autism with
special reference to certain typical psycho-dynamic conditions in
the life experience of infants who develop such severe ego disturbances. One such condition is the absence of a positive emotional nurturant relationship with a mothering person in the early
months of life.

The effects of such deprivation are especially important during the normal autistic and symbiotic phases of infancy. Mahler places emphasis on this period: "I believe it is from the symbiotic phase of the mother-infant dual unity that those expected precursors of individual beginnings are derived which together with inborn constitutional factors determine every human individual's unique somatic and psychological makeup" (9). The normal separation-individuation experience, she states further, is the first crucial prerequisite for the development and maintenance of a sense of identity.

This clinical presentation is concerned with the treatment of Kenny, whose development took place in an environment characterized by deprivation and trauma, resulting in the inhibition of speech and avoidance of human contact which comprise the autistic syndrome. The essential purpose of this paper is to focus on and delineate the achievement of a sense of identity and integration of the ego in this autistic child during the three and a half years of long-term psychoanalytic psychotherapy. "Identity" is used in the sense that Erikson found useful: to consider the sense of self or various selves as part of but different from the functions of the ego (5).

At four and a half, Kenny was a slight child who stood passively and silently, head to one side and one shoulder slightly raised. His head was bent so low that it was not possible at first to see his delicate, sad features. Kenny's symptoms included limited, primitive "scribble" speech alternating with mispronounced words; seeming inability to understand what was said to him; inability to make contact with other children or adults; and withdrawal from all activities except as a passive "victim" in sadomasochistic interaction with his brother, who was also extremely disturbed. On psychological testing in which he expressed no spontaneity at all nor interaction with the tester, who later became his therapist, his speech score was approximately below the age of two. However, on the form-board test he achieved scores approaching age level, characteristic of psychotic children whose behavior combines primitive arrested reactions with fleeting, more age-appropriate performances. His score fell in the retarded range of intelligence, but the scatter of his performance gave the impression that he had a potential for at least low normal functioning. The symptom pattern inevitably raised questions regarding the possibility of an anlage of brain damage or traumatic psychosis as important factors in Kenny's ego development. The diagnosis was that of infantile autism.

Kenny was born into a gravely troubled family that was incapacitated by severe emotional difficulties. The family consisted of the mother, father and the brother, Stuart, two years older, who had been in treatment for about two years when Kenny was brought to the Clinic. Stuart's treatment had begun when he was three years, four months, because of symptoms including autistic-like withdrawal alternating with fits of maniacal rage, and long periods of uninterrupted screaming. His speech consisted of grunting, growling noises, and his parents were not certain whether he understood what was said to him. His diagnosis was "atypical childhood psychosis." His father had punished him by beatings and forcible ejection from the house. The parents, in their own childhood, had experienced beatings, seductiveness, forcible enemas and cleaning of the genitals in the service of "good hygiene." The mother suffered beatings from her husband and criticisms from her own mother as being unworthy to have attractive children. She thus lived in the center of a whirlwind of emotional and physical violence, and became literally paralyzed in her attempt to be an adequate mother. On the day of Kenny's birth, she was warned that another screaming baby would not be tolerated. Throughout the years of treatment it was not possible to recover precise details of Kenny's early days. All the parents remembered was that at birth he was a quiet baby and had a gentle cry. He did not sit up until ten months old, provoking the father's concern about his slow development which, however, was judged to be normal by the pediatrician.

Throughout his first year, Kenny was left very much to himself, the family being preoccupied with Stuart's problems. Kenny's crib became a sounding board for the screaming and primitive rages of his brother. When the parents realized that Stuart would poke his fingers into Kenny's eyes, ears and mouth as well as attack his body, they locked him out of the nursery, leaving him standing outside screaming endlessly. Kenny was left alone "to cry it out."

The children's screams upset the father to such a degree that at seven months of age Kenny was beaten about the face.

In a psychic environment of constant screaming terror, physical assault and non-availability of a nurturant person, trauma was added to isolation. This phase in Kenny's life corresponds generally to the normal child's emergence from the symbiotic phase as described by Mahler. Although the mother could describe Kenny with empathy, in actual fact she was not able to show such feeling overtly. She was a rigid, deep-feeling, seemingly emotionless woman who worked incredibly hard, seemed to give endlessly of herself but in essence could not express warmth.

During his second and third years, Kenny was left with a succession of baby-sitters who were reported to have either neglected or mistreated him. Kenny developed autistic defenses to cope with these unbearable tensions. He remained on the periphery of the family milieu except when he permitted himself to be a passive victim for the hostility of others. When he came into treatment he was toilet trained, could partly dress and feed himself, and managed to remain in a small nursery school mainly by not participating in any of the activities.

STRUGGLE TO SURVIVE

Several months after the diagnostic evaluation, Kenny and the therapist started out on an odyssey into his inner life which, in effect, turned out to be a search for his identity. It was soon apparent that he was not a child whose extreme mechanical withdrawal is associated with failure to perceive emotionally, i.e., cathect the mother from birth. The initial treatment hours revealed autistic as well as symbiotic characteristics. These are highlighted in the following excerpts from the first therapy hours.

First hour: Kenny came quickly into the room, ran around touching everything quickly. He jumped from the desk, the chairs, the play table over and over paying no attention to me. He tried to pull things from the wall, broke crayons and threw everything out of the boxes, etc., until it was time to go. At times he perched himself in a very precarious position so that I had to follow him around to protect him. I stayed with him, told him I did not want to see him hurt. If I offered him anything to play with, he promptly threw it up at the electric fixture. At no time did he behave as if he had ever seen me before.

Fourth hour: Kenny appeared on a warm day wearing a very heavy jacket. He would not allow me to unzip it and he would not take it off himself, although he appeared hot. (This jacket, which he wore to every session, unfailingly, was not removed for another year and a half.) After frantically playing out a scene with dolls in which the boy doll was injured, Kenny quickly left the table, turned away completely and walked to a corner where he found a toy milk bottle which he filled full of marbles and began sucking on it. It was as if symbolically he had indicated that he got rocks instead of milk. He found a toy toilet and immediately left the room saying, "Bapoo," his word for bathroom.

Twelfth hour: Kenny was more relaxed today. He stayed very close to me almost as if he would melt into my body if he could. He grabbed my hand and then my fingers, pushing them in a hurtful way toward my arm. He jumped down from the table over and over. Once he got tired of that he found a piece of a plane which he had broken previously when he had thrown clay on it. He glanced at it and began to pound himself over the head. He found a toy train which he had broken and once more said, "Bapoo." It appeared that this word had a dual meaning: bathroom and broken.

These first hours revealed the range of ego states available to Kenny. They revealed the silent, hyperactive, non-speaking child who does not seem to perceive or relate to the therapist as if "inherently autistic." The fact that "bathroom" and "broken" were associated in his own language, revealed a very crucial fact about him: he felt broken or damaged and wanted to be fed like an infant. Although it seemed that he could function on higher levels of psychic organization, as suggested by the "instant play" with the dolls, it soon became clear that such levels were only fleetingly available to him. Although he wanted contact he could not bear to have it, and although he wished to be completely defended in his autistic state, he could not maintain it. He was thus in a chronic state of tension, and panic states erupted almost constantly. Ritualistic play with water, the toilet and mechanical toys and objects, as well as complete withdrawal, seemed to serve as defenses against his impulses, ineffectually controlled by fluctuating ego states.

An important factor in the early weeks of treatment concerned his reactions to his brother who was in treatment at the same time. One day as he permitted himself to come near the therapist, he heard his brother yell in the hall and immediately scratched the therapist's arm. It was as if he had momentarily fused with the aggressive, screaming brother. He threw my phone on the floor. When I gave him a toy phone, he made a sound into it and threw it away. He made garbled sounds of all kinds, to which I responded by repeating some of them. I hoped to let him know in this way that he was not alone in his terror and that we could build an empathic bridge. His voice became louder and he tried out various sounds and even what seemed like snatches of song. He was using sound to contact the therapist rather than words. As I repeated everything he did, he became more excited. He lay down on the floor, seemed to withdraw into rapt isolation and began to make infantile sounds. I said "Now Kenny is a little baby," and handed him a toy milk bottle. He began to suck on it and I noticed his lips moved soundlessly as if he were saying "La, la, la" (his word for milk, I learned later). From then on each successive sound became more and more infantile until he was gurgling. It is possible that the soundless lalling may have indicated that precursors of speech had progressed this far in his first weeks of life. He seemed to be far away, not hearing anything I said, when suddenly, with a fierce expression on his face, he got up, grabbed hold of my arm in a vehement gesture and ran out. This significant treatment event revealed that he seemed to respond to whatever cue was given him and to take off from there as if he himself had no inner direction, and was not a separate being. The danger of becoming separate was constantly expressed in impulsive erratic behavior, as well as in reaction to the danger of relating to the therapist. He seemed to borrow the identity of anything or anybody within his vicinity which led to changes in the direction of what preoccupied him.

Kenny was constantly filling himself full of water and going into the bathroom. His apparently senseless activity in the bathroom gradually revealed the meaning of his struggle. I am reminded here of a wonderful title given to a paper by Alice Balint, "On Being Empty of One's Self." Indeed, as Kenny drank and immediately seemed to empty himself, one wondered what remained with him. The struggle of the "self vs. the non-self" as Bettelheim (2) puts it, was constantly expressed in this kind of activity. It was on the lowest level of body function, that of taking in liquid and emptying oneself in the bathroom, where his awareness of himself was most dominant at that time. The minute the water would gush down, Kenny would be in terror as if he felt he would go down also. It was only at moments of such total fear of annihilation that he could tolerate the therapist's nearness.

The first year of treatment was characterized by Kenny's constant struggle to dare to exist. Every hour was filled with restitutive maneuvers to ward off a chronic anticipation of fragmentation. He moved around in the treatment hours constantly watching for the possible unleashing of destructive forces around him. He always seemed to be looking for external reassurances that if objects were in good working order, so would he be. One day, on his way back from the bathroom, he noticed that a cooler fan was not connected. He immediately muttered "Bapoo." I connected the fan and showed him it was not broken. He turned away from me and looked up at the picture on the wall. When we had first walked down the hall, I had shown him these pictures. He was now using this remembered experience to contact the therapist as if to indicate his relief. But having come so close to the therapist, he became anxious and so another form of defensive repetitive play was introduced. This was a game of "knock-knock" (so named by me). It entailed pushing the therapist out into the hall and then permitting her to come in. Later, he would go out and return. His object relationships seemed to be characteristic of the first level of separation of the infant from the mother, at an emerging minimal level of self-awareness.

Later, as he further identified himself with a cooler operated by a fan and water-filled system, he revealed that inanimate as well as animate objects were fused in his own inner experience. One day when he was unusually tense he ran through the Clinic searching for his mother. When he could not find her he drank enormous quantities of cold water and blew at the therapist like the fan. Having lost his mother, he substituted transitional objects, fountain and fan; with these he reconstituted himself to avoid the agony of feeling fragmented. This play, continuing for hours on end, emphasized the need of his primitive ego to be concerned only with defense. He was both frightened and fascinated by the fan, and became very excited when he learned that he could make it go and stop. I played a game with him saying, "Go," and then connected the fan. I would say "Stop," when we disconnected it. This became a ritual. However, one day when *his* saying, "Go," coincided with the actual rotation of the fan, he ran up and down the hall in terror as if he fantasied that his word, i.e., his impulse, had unleashed destructive forces. I had another clue regarding his inhibitions against talking. Kenny maintained his autistic defense by fusing with mechanical objects in his world, since this permitted him to remain silent and to keep his impulses unexpressed but, nevertheless, alive. By introjecting the power of mechanical objects, Kenny was able to cope with his sense of helplessness by using a kind of mechanical auxiliary ego.

In relationship with his brother, however, these defenses did not hold. Then he was forced to express affect through cue-taking from his brother. This was revealed one day when Stuart, in a bad mood, yelled at me, "Shut up," as soon as he saw me with Kenny. This strongly agitated Kenny. With great rapidity he hit me, broke crayons, wrote on the wall and rattled the water cooler. It was as if he had actually become his brother, fused with him and hated me through him. When he ran to the fan and tried to push his fingers between the rotating blades, I stopped him, and he hit me again. I could not understand the intensity of his rage, but I soon found out that previous to this hour, Stuart had told Kenny that I was going to leave him. It seemed that although other people could not get through to Kenny, Stuart always could.

Self-destructive behavior persisted throughout the treatment in the beginning years whenever he felt enraged or "bad." When I managed to convey to Kenny that I knew how he felt, that it was not true I was leaving him, once more he sent me away to play the game "knock-knock." He suddenly ran off to the bathroom and then came back. For the first time he had used the toilet and invited me in to show me his "anal gift" which he called "doo." It was as if he indicated that he wished to keep the therapist from going away by getting rid of his bad self (12). However, having dared to give up part of himself, he became frightened once more. He ran from one fan to another to make sure they weren't disconnected. Through this expression of his need for the therapist, it became apparent that Kenny had made an important step in the process of his own self-awareness.

In approximately the third month of treatment I realized Kenny warded off contact by becoming completely mute and ignoring me whenever I used the first or second personal pronouns regarding myself or him. I habitually began to refer to both of us in the third person. This defense made it possible for him to feel safe in an intensive pursuit of a symbiotic relationship with his mother, which was also brought into the treatment relationship. For his fifth birthday, I gave Kenny a toy car and a birthday card. He immediately left for the lobby to show this to his mother. When she did not look up, he stood there and showed her the card again. She glanced at it briefly and went back to her reading. His passive appeal was ignored and he came shuffling back slowly. He regressed and became silent, very restless and destructive, and he was not to be reached at all for the rest of the hour. He did not touch the gift I gave him, as if now both it and he were worthless. During this incident his behavior was reminiscent of Mahler's (10) description of the shadowing of the mother in the separation-individuation phase, i.e., a desperate appeal to and wooing of the mother which he carried on persistently at home in his wild and provocative behavior. He flushed the toilet endlessly in such fury that it seemed he would break it. He did break the radio in the car, the symbol of his hopeless attempt to reach his mother. He was severely punished and felt overwhelmed by the enormity of what he had done. His increased use of "broken" revealed that he felt not only that he was destructive, but also that his mother's anger annihilated him.

Shortly after, a favorite family cat was accidentally killed. This threw Kenny into unrestrained panic. He turned on all the electric lights and once more drank water so frantically he could barely swallow. During this time his mother reported that while in a store, Kenny noted that a band-aid display usually in motion was not working. He screamed uncontrollably until this display was turned on once more. Thus, following the death of the family cat who had become his central, libidinal object, Kenny created the role of a "band-aid" mother who would not let him get killed. He felt magically restored and a new phrase appeared in his vocabulary. He brought a little box from home and asked me to "fikit" (fix it). He would repeat the word followed by my name, saying "fikit-fafow," over and over. He felt clearly that the therapist now had become his auxiliary ego and he fantasied her as having a purpose in his life as a needgratifying object and as the "fixer" who would repair the broken boy.

However, the fragile state of his tenuous identity was clearly highlighted in the following incident around the time of the cat's death.

> At Halloween time, Kenny "to be like other kids," was dressed up to go "trick and treating." He came to this interview hour after a school party dressed in a clown costume, with makeup on his face. His normally pale countenance was now chalk white. He was completely disoriented, with a vague lost expression, as if he literally no longer knew who he was but was "moving in a trance of agonized anonymity . . . as if he became almost impersonal, as if the escape from selfhood was complete" (14). Kenny's *in*voluntary "escape from selfhood" was his reaction to the fact that the cat had died and he felt his fragmentation to be imminent. An effort was made to include him in the production of a little clay cat, hoping this would induce him to express how he felt, but there was no response. He really was completely lost within himself. I then started to talk to him about Halloween. I told him that the clown suit did not belong to him and that when he would go home he would take it off and would be Kenny again. There was a burst of incomprehensible sounds. Although I made some empathic response to him, Kenny withdrew completely. This time he revealed that understanding of his affects by the therapist was not enough. When the hour was over, he went as he had come, shuffling his feet, walking slowly down the hall, one shoulder higher than the other, his tall hat askew on his head, a very sad, grotesque little figure in a clown suit.

Fused identification with the dead cat as the victim and the destroyer made him extremely vulnerable at this time to triggering-off stimuli. One day when Kenny heard Stuart screaming outside the treatment office, he immediately resonated with his brother's terror as well as his own. He ran up and down the hall destroying everything in sight and then retreated to the usual water and bathroom play. His identification with his brother's wildness and rage soon revealed that the most acute sense of self concerned being bad and guilty. The word "bapoo" was now replaced by "boy, do da," a repetitive declaration of omnipotent and omnipresent destructiveness. One day Kenny saw an accident on the freeway where two trucks had collided. He came into the Clinic and with a burst of speech exclaimed, "Moto twuck go boom, boy do da?" The mother also was quite frightened by the accident and Kenny shared this emotion with her. As she stood by listening to him, she wondered why he was always saying that. I explained that Kenny felt that in some way he had caused the accident. She expressed her regrets that she had not understood, since she had felt this way when she was little. She said sympathetically, "I wanted so much to help him." Kenny heard his mother and now entered another progressive step in his development. It was no wonder that for Kenny merely to exist had been so dangerous. It had been impossible for him to identify clearly whose rage he feared, having been unable to distinguish between his own destructiveness and that of the external environment.

Now, people in his life could be presented in their different roles and he gradually began to show me the frightening as well as the supportive aspects of his home life. He used the clay dog and cat that I made for him and had them fight. He fed the cat giving it more and more water and tested the temperature of the water with his finger, identifying with the function of a mother who was taking care of her sick child. He thus signified that he had deepened the symbiotic relationship with the therapist. She evoked his panic when he felt punished as the aggressor, but also she restored his identity in the role he assigned to her as the fixer and maker of things who could restore the dog's tail, or make a cardboard gun on Kenny's demand. He yelled excitedly, "Ya fafoo," (therapist's name) as if she had at this instant become magic. As the magical protecting object via the things she made him, she clearly was being incorporated. Signs that he could accept delay and anticipate the future appeared when he was able to wait for a promised ride. In the past, it was reported by his mother that Kenny would have "screamed and been in a crazy panic all day."

APPEARANCE OF A TRANSITIONAL IDENTITY

Having restored the need-satisfying symbiotic object, the therapist, Kenny now seemed literally to integrate into a new identity "under the eyes of the therapist" (1). I had given Kenny a toy wagon for Christmas, his father helped him assemble it, and Kenny felt accepted. He brought the toy to the Clinic and wanted to play with it, tried very hard to do it himself, and finally succeeded. I exclaimed, "Why, Kenny, you fixed it," to which he replied, "No Cluddy!" It gradually became apparent that Kenny had taken on a seemingly transitional identity (8), who could do and feel things that Kenny was afraid of or could not do. As Cluddy, he started a new kind of building play with blocks. High walls were built with nothing between them, the symbolic representation of his perception that his ego boundaries or the shell of his self was being restored and constructed. This step in psychic integration has been described by Mahler: "As the child begins to retrieve the symbiotic object and cathect its representation with libido, we observe more ego filled moods and emotions. These manifestations mark the first state of giving up and replacing autistic defenses. They also mark the ego emergence as a functional structure of the personality" (9).

The fluid shifting of ego states and ego functions continued for many more months of treatment. During the tenth month, the effect of heightened annihilation anxiety on perceptual distortions was graphically revealed after Kenny had been harshly punished for his increasingly provocative behavior at home. In this hour he was unusually pale, with deep circles under his eyes. Once more he seemingly found that all the things were broken. He sat listlessly, looking at pictures of railroads and engines. He pointed to a blue fence (which he had seen before) calling it water. It was as if he had regressed once more to an undifferentiated state. Gradually he began, as if reintegrating, to recognize the inanimate figures and objects in the book. However, when he came to the picture of a movable, open guard rail on the railroad track, he became very tense and cried out, "Bapoo" (broken). He kept turning to the next page where the closed guard rail was shown. He did this over and over to reassure himself that it was not really broken. He kept putting my finger on the broken part as if this would restore it (himself). He insisted that my finger remain there. This seemed to reduce his anxiety. I tried to help him talk about the beating that he had received. There was no response. To the question, "Did you cry?" Kenny answered, "Cluddy cwy." Neither tears nor affect were permitted to Kenny, but for Cluddy, his blossoming identiy and "stand-in," hopefully they could be risked without absolute threat of annihilation. Once more he returned to the open guard rail and since he realized that putting my finger there did not actually restore it, nor had it prevented him from being beaten, he tried another tack. He had me put a band-aid on his heel, which was not sore at all. In his magical, delusional thinking this restored both him and me—as a "fikit" object—and he went out, limping, with satisfaction.

Kenny had now begun to learn to swim. When I talked about it to him, he said, "Cluddy afwaid." It was as if he now began to be aware of his own feelings, but was able to let me know only by projecting them onto his alter-self, instead of the machines that formerly had been his vehicle for such communications. Now we had another sign that his psychic organization had integrated to a somewhat higher level. One dramatic day it became obvious he was approaching an acceptance of Cluddy as himself. He noticed that there was some scribbling on a checker board that we had played with in the past and he called out, "Keeky do da, Cluddy do da?" Cluddy served as that part of himself that tentatively tried to reach out to the world and dare to face reality. Ego mastery was also attributed to Cluddy in "art" products made at school. Panic states no longer appeared as frequently, since, through Cluddy, he was able to express his feelings.

Therese Gouin-Decarie (7), writing on the relevancy of Piaget's theories for clinical child psychology, emphasized that the "maternally deprived child is also inevitably a sensory-motor deprived individual . . . although physically intact, the play of assimilation and accommodation will remain defective." Kenny's behavior certainly bore this out. His defenses served mainly to protect the ego from being overwhelmed, at the cost of depriving the ego of its cathexis for various functions. In the service of his autistic defense system, Kenny had successfully blocked or retarded the functions of affect and perception. With the unfolding of his self-awareness, energies were released for exploration of his world.

In one of the interview hours he became aware of and responded to different metallic sounds. This became an act of discovery that was infused with pleasure and was followed by actively sought sensory and perceptual experiences. "It was as if the frozen deanimated wall" (1) was removed. Explorations of inner and outer aspects of the Clinic building and of my car occupied him almost exclusively. One day when he was given a candy life saver, he looked at the hole and said very slowly, "Do-nut." In the past he had put a candy in his mouth without looking at it and would more often than not refuse to take it. He was now making associations and links between his perceptual experiences and motoric executive implementations. There was a noticeable decrease in his hyperactive, aimless behavior and his activities became more focused.

Although he was now almost six, his responses in some areas were reminiscent of an infant's. The concrete nature of his thinking appeared when he began to distinguish colors, as when he was busily turning the gears of a plastic toy. I helped him associate the names of the colors with the different gears, but he could only name the colors by calling, "White, paper; green, bathroom." He seemed unable to maintain an abstract concept of color without associating it to some firm facet of his experience. Kenny continued to present himself as helpless and needing care, as being unable to function except in the presence of an auxiliary ego, thus slowing down the process of separation from the symbiotic object. One day he asked me to sing. When he was invited to sing also, he said, "No, Cluddy sing," and began to clean the dollhouse and arrange things neatly, involving me in this activity. In this behavior Kenny revealed that speech was still dangerous; it was associated with being a messy child who deserved punishment. What he seemed to say symbolically was, "If I am put in order, perhaps I can sing-talk." Kenny informed me through symbolic action rather than speech that he felt disarranged.

The central meaning of this little vignette, however, was that he seemed to be inviting the "good mother," as in a happy primary relationship, to be part of the experiencing duo. He suddenly got up from the play table and began to go through a learned set of gestures he had been taught in school. As I sang to him I watched his rigid movements, so like the dance of a marionette pulled by strings. Nevertheless, for the first time, his face was alive, his eyes shining with an intense expression of concentration while he performed his awkward little dance.

STRUGGLE TO SPEAK

Although Kenny began to use speech more freely, he still maintained his rigid defensiveness. He was now able to express rage through screaming, especially towards his brother. This release of aggression was usually followed by a further integration of ego functions. One day at the start of an hour, in the second year of therapy, he sat quietly, racing cars very vigorously.

I greeted him saying, "How are you, Kenny?" He replied, *"Am fine!"* I expressed my delight to which he quickly responded, "No, Cluddy talk." (I had been too intrusive and had not respected his defenses.) I asked, "Can't Kenny talk?" He said, "Fafoo afwaid." Suddenly a siren sounded outside and he sped to the window as if he were propelled, perhaps fearing punishment. On the way back he picked up a doll, turned it around, looked at its face, put his hand on its mouth and screamed, "Shut ut." I interpreted his fear of getting hurt when he screamed, as if someone is going to come to hurt him, whereupon Kenny let out a sharp scream with a piercing panicky sound to it. He kept screaming for the longest time, yelling, "Shut ut, shut ut." His face became infused with blood, the veins in his neck stood out, the sound of his voice became increasingly guttural. He stopped suddenly, completely worn out. I remarked, "Now I see why you are so afraid to talk. You're afraid that whenever you make a sound, someone will hurt you and now you're screaming and screaming to let me know." Kenny immediately ran to fill himself full of water. Before he left, he took the baby bottle with him but indicated that I was not to come.

The intrusive therapist had become dangerous by interpreting instead of offering herself as a symbiotic partner. However, through a conciliatory gesture, Kenny offered me the Fixit book to read. As I told him the story via the pictures, Kenny acted it out as if once more he could use his thought processes to tell me his inner meaning. He acted out the crying of the child in the story in such a realistic way that I could hear how Kenny must have sounded after crying for a long time. He made sounds of sobbing which became fainter and fainter with an increasing tone of abandonment appearing in his voice. He acted out his loneliness by projecting it onto the picture child. When he came to the picture of a boy who was watching a slashed tire being fixed he said, "Boy goof?" (Am I guilty?) At the end of the story he held the book for a moment. He sighed, stopped abruptly as if his breath were suddenly cut short, and then let out the remainder of a long deep sigh. His act had made his inner feelings visible. He seemed to be communicating a memory that had suddenly arisen to the surface (3).

This dramatic event revealed the disorganizing effect of trauma on his developing function of speech. The cry, the infant's first means of influencing the environment, had become negatively cathected so that to be vocal was to invite disaster and become helpless. During this hour the eruption of painful experiences associated with his crying in infancy was graphically play-acted. Concurrently he was also being punished at home for being so noisy, and probably it was Kenny's way of communicating something about his present experiences as well. Up to this time, Kenny could organize his experiences only with act, gesture and pantomime but now vocalization was added.

With each discovery in the outside world, further separation of self indicated that he was beginning to feel unified. He would pull me out to the parking lot to show me the place of absent cars by saying, "One, one, one." When he was helped to grasp the concept that more than one, that many absent cars and people would come back, he eagerly began to count his fingers and toes and mine as well. It was quite moving to watch him make "his discoveries." For the first time since therapy began one and a half years before, Kenny took off his heavy jacket.

He now actively expressed the wish to be made whole. Whereas formerly the fountain and fan served as vehicles to express his need for survival, now he used the talking machine, the ediphone, to express his feelings about wishing to talk. At the beginning of a new kindergarten semester, he brought a photo of himself with his mouth open as if to speak. He denied this and said, "Boton"—a new version of "broken." He turned to me and asked, "Me, you fix?" But with the heaviness of basic distrust still weighing him down, he turned from me to the machine and said, "Do da,"—turn it on. He was encouraged to talk into it and tell about the picture which he called "teeto." The therapist verbalized his feelings and he listened as the conversation was played back. He responded to the machine as if it had become the therapist in reality and reacted with great excitement as he recognized our voices. He picked up his picture, put it in front of the machine and said, "You see teeto, you see teeto."

The animate and the inanimate, the therapist and machine, were still fused by him and he endowed human as well as mechanical attributes to both. It was clear that Kenny was very much excited about deliberately wanting to talk. It also became clear to him that he could not voluntarily make the sounds that he wanted to. When he did try to talk, each word had to be forced out and the muscles on one side of his face would draw back in a tic-like facial movement. His voice tended to be a little flat, each word was separated by an effortful pause before the next one appeared.

One day he came in very angry and said, "You no fen me"—you are not my friend—"no fix words." It was characteristic of him that he would suddenly say or do something that seemed to reflect the existence of a more complex psychic structure than his behavior indicated. At school he had become aggressive and troublesome, and the teacher was beginning to ask questions about the level of his intelligence. He knew about this and started the hour by picking up a gun and shooting at me. He ran out of the room and started shooting into the hall. At that moment a woman walked down the hall and he said in fear, "Na shoo lady." I interpreted his anger toward me for not fixing his words. I told him that I knew he was angry and shooting his gun because he couldn't say his words. Kenny became angrier. Suddenly he stopped shooting, put the gun down and began slowly to prowl around the room, gradually becoming more and more active and excited. He picked up all the books and papers from my desk, looked underneath and went to the cupboard, picked up everything in his search for some unknown thing. When I asked him what he was looking for he said, "Look for word!" I told him that he had not shot his words out with a gun, they were still inside of him and that he would find a way to say them. His wish to speak led to added awareness of his own experiences and his responsiveness to them (13).

A very important aspect of his burgeoning ego was revealed in his growing body awareness. He had been subjected to abusive sexual play, but this had not been brought into treatment. However, he had had an accident at school one day and in his inimitable style, with a great deal of encouragement, was able to say: "Faw dow, hut head, fleet bed. Cold ladel." (Fall down, hurt head, sleep in bed. Cold water.) He pointed to his head where he had been hurt. The next hour revealed that another source of body concern had to do with sexual differences. In all the time he had been coming to the Clinic he had seemed to ignore totally or avoid the girls' bathroom. Now he pulled me into it and indicated that he was afraid to go in. He pulled back into the treatment-room and play-acted a "seduction" scene by inviting me to stroke his genitals. He had experienced this with someone else and it was with a strong sense of excitement that he tried to communicate it. Kenny was busily sorting out all the dangers in his life but this time the emphasis was on body functioning. One day just as he was about to say something he passed flatus which he called "poo sou." He did not seem to be frightened by this so I remarked that he could make noises with his behind and that his mouth could make sounds too. His response to this was, "No nay noit." (My mouth doesn't make noise.) He told me that he made poo sounds but that was all. It was obviously still too dangerous for him to make any sounds vocally. In fact, he had behaved in the past as if all his body emissions were bad. However, the fact that he could make anal noises pleased him very much. I laughed. He immediately took the cue, looked delighted and, for the first time, Kenny and therapist laughed together.

He could now come to the Clinic with greater ease. One day he tore off his shirt in a great hurry. When he tried to put it back on he kept forcing his elbow into the sleeve. I offered to help him, but at first he wouldn't let me. Suddenly he looked directly at my face and asked, "Anri?" I said, "No, I'm just trying to help you put on your shirt." At this Kenny looked at me directly and said, "Oh."

He had become aware that non-verbal cues from the human face could now be visually engaged without fear.

At this time the school counselor called to report that although Kenny had completed his second year in kindergarten, he did not seem to know what was going on and that he had become more aggressive, less inhibited and less fearful of the children. The counselor raised the question of mental retardation. He suggested that Kenny would do much better in a school for mentally retarded children. However, the counselor accepted the explanation that Kenny's behavior was a kind of defensive pseudo-stupidity and he was permitted to enter a special class in the same school. Because of the co-operation of the school counselor, Kenny was able to continue in an encouraging educational environment (4). Learning inhibition at school reflected that he did not feel as yet that he could function as a separate self. Although autism as a defense was not so rigidly maintained, inactivity was another expression of it. To function alone was to destroy the possibility of return to symbiosis. This was vividly apparent when he was encouraged to fashion a clay animal. He insisted that he couldn't do it. To help him start the process I put my hand on top of his. As this happened, his hand seemed literally to fuse with mine as if he could function only in this way. Gradually his own muscles took over and he uttered a cry of satisfaction at his success. He felt as if he were now infused with power.

In spite of the primitive nature of his functioning he recognized that he was a failure at school and in desperation searched for another identity. One day he announced, "No call me Cluddy, no call me Kenny, call me Hal." This particular borrowed identity belonged to a real boy, his brother's friend. This was soon given up, since the magic was not sustained, but is was obvious that Kenny was separating his essential self from his part identifications. He would still savor his brother's triumph as if it were his own and still use him as an auxiliary ego to express his own anger. As the process of identification continued he internalized the brother's strength and power through the experience of the brother's absence. The brother was no longer coming to the Clinic when Kenny was. One day the confusion about who he was appeared when he played the "knock-knock" game and after opening the door said,

"Tuie?" (Am I Stuart?) I reassured him that he was Kenny, not Stuart who was away at school. Concomitantly his building structures began to have better planning and coherence and very slowly the synthetic functions of the ego began to integrate.

Towards the end of the second year of treatment the interview hours became full of material about a new baby accompanied by self-punitive activity. When Kenny voiced his apprehension, the mother denied that she was pregnant. She said that she was concerned about the fact that he sat about at home undressed all day. In the past he was the one "who always was independent." It was Kenny's way of telling his mother that he wished to be the baby, to be cared for. In spite of the mother's denials, Kenny's fantasies about the baby proved to be true. Anticipation of the new infant was very upsetting to everyone in the family. Outbursts of mutual hatred heightened the two boys' aggressive behavior. They reacted as if the baby were already there and chose each other as the objects of their jealousy. In imitation of his brother, Kenny acted out what seemed to be negative transference reactions in the treatment. When he became aware that he was being led to express hate directly to me, he became very frightened. However, he also seemed to be aware that I was not the true object of his rage and he yelled, "Throw a baby dead, throw a mommy dead."

The mother reported that he was having "morning sickness" like herself and would go to the bathroom many times to try to throw up. Worries about her own condition were projected on to her disappointment in Kenny's improvement. For the first time she expressed dismay about the slow appearance of understandable speech. There now began a round of visits to doctors and dentists. At this point, contrary to the therapist's advice, Kenny was enrolled in a speech class. Once more, autistic defenses were fully evident so that at times it seemed that he literally could not hear, although hearing tests revealed no deafness. The speech tests were inconclusive and recommended that psychotherapy continue so that Kenny's "confidence would improve."

The birth of a baby sister triggered off intensive anxiety. Regressive play in the bathroom returned and once more ego boundaries seemed threatened. Kenny sat in the bathroom with the door opened which was unusual, as if oblivious to everything except the imminence of his own destruction. He held on to his penis looking forlorn and fragmented. He said pathetically, "My penie?" I named each body part and reassured him of his continuing ownership of all of these, including his penis. I tried to talk to him about the differences between himself and the new baby sister. He sat without a sign of response until I said, "When Mommy comes home she will want you to have your penis." At this his expression changed and once more he reintegrated. Again he was concerned with his badness and he asked me whether his loud or soft noises would be acceptable.

It was difficult to contact him at this time and he gradually subsided into silence, at times appearing robot-like. However, because of the strength of the therapeutic bond, he could reconstitute more quickly following the emergence of archaic rage. He felt that his own badness and loudness had triggered off the heightened anxieties at home. When I was able to help him to understand, he said, "Call me Kenny." He regressed briefly once more to infantile dependency but this did not satisfy his needs. After holding a baby bottle he decided, "I no baby, I Kenny."

Family circumstances again interfered with his life and the progressive course of his treatment. The family moved to a new neighborhood which would, in effect, be a new start in life. The boys' jealousy and aggression grew to such a pitch of intensity that the parents talked of placement. After saying, "I be baby, no talk," Kenny for the next three months became a wild, silent physical expression of rage. He had been given a longed-for toy for his eighth birthday which his brother immediately destroyed. After this, Kenny's very silence vibrated with rage, but at first he could not offer a sound about this latest cruel injustice. I reminded him that babies could not talk, and that he had told me he was not a baby. His response to this was, "I wan' be hater." I wondered who he hated since he knew that his brother had destroyed his toy but he would not tell. I urged him to tell me, to say his brother's name. I pronounced the name very slowly and when I accented the sibilant first syllable, Kenny became frightened. He blew with his lips instead. He protested, "I no do da. I be dead."

Nevertheless he felt that I understood he had a right to express his angry feelings; still fearful of talking, he once more put them into action. He would bound into the Clinic, dash straight to the therapy room and once inside, would throw large building blocks at the window, door, light fixture and me. Interpretation of his feelings toward the therapist, who threatened the release of such dangerous thoughts and feelings, of his anxiety about losing his mother because of the new sibling, did not reach him. It wasn't until a few weeks later, when the move to his new home became imminent, that I fully understood. Kenny felt that he was going to be thrown away because all old broken things were abandoned like old homes and babies (himself). His actual fear was of being left behind in the old house and being replaced in the new by the new infant. It wasn't until this precise interpretation was given to him piecemeal and repeatedly that he was able to calm down.

Negative transference manifestations appeared more consistently and were expressed in body language. Instead of throwing things at me when he was angry, he would bend over and seemingly deliberately pass flatus, or spit. At times he filled the room with foul odors to indicate he felt bad, dirty, rejected and wanted me to feel it, too. Suddenly one day, he said to me after we had survived his unremitting aggressive hostility, "Why you like me for?" I gave him all the reasons and then reminded him of how he used to feel and that he used to say, "Boy do da." He then demonstrated, "I go like this," and assumed the old head down, withdrawn autistic posture. He had become more reality oriented, and past and present were now clearly separated in his experience. Memory was being restored.

He had begun to learn spelling and arithmetic at school, subjects he seemed able to grasp relatively well, after the initial resistance to and fear of new learning experiences were overcome. Numbers, like his developing speech, became organizing, cognitive principles, and he was preoccupied with them. He wanted to know why the clock had only twelve hours (does one die then) and asked, "Why so little numbers on the clock, why is it no got 13?" He kept testing me to see if I wanted him alive or safe. He was now using abstract concepts in an obsessive defensive way. He wanted to know if he could live to be 99 and would flip the calendar and would ask me on which day did I think that he or I would die. His preoccupation with living and dying finally led to his ability to tell the therapist that, "If I get real, real angry, I die."

In the fall of that year, in imitation of his brother, he wanted to join a boys' club. This imitation was not like the former fusion with the brother during which boundaries were confused. It was a true imitation of the activity of a separate person. At his initiation, he was able to go to the head of the room where his father and many other people listened as he responded to the initiation rites over a microphone. Even though his speech at this time was unintelligible, he played his part. He came to the Clinic afterwards flushed with pride over his performance and the acceptance by his family. He was transformed. He walked into the room with an erect posture, head up, eyes bright with his newest dream. He asked me, "What I do be club leader?" He revealed his fear of failure by asking the therapist, "What you do if I no make it?" I replied that perhaps we should think of the things that he needed to do. I reminded him that he was learning to read and write and do arithmetic at school; that he was going to speech class; that he came to the Clinic so that I could help him with his worries. Kenny thought this over very seriously and looking up at the therapist said, *"I not afraid to live!"* Kenny had declared his commitment to life. For the next few weeks he was busy trying to figure out the exact meaning of words. He would ask, "What means friendly; what means sad; what means hate; if a clock is fast does it mean it can go no farther?" Kenny now seemed to be preoccupied with the basic elements of life itself.

Obstacles to Kenny's development appeared very early in his life and the events of the separation-individuation phase resulted in psychotic fixation. Traumatic events and conditions continued to accompany him as he grew older. Treatment in the postautistic phase, therefore, continued for several years but in spite of his unhappy life experiences he continued to improve. When at the age of 14, Kenny graduated from the eighth grade, there were 3 A's and B's on his report card. Understandably he was very elated. Even though peer relationships were still fraught with unhappiness, he was encouraged by his mother to go to the school dance accompanied by his father. He was triumphant. When I complimented him on going even though he was afraid, I remarked that everyone in the family deserved credit for the mutual help they were giving each other. To which Kenny replied slowly and with effort, "Another person deserves credit, you helped me get my grades up." I reminded him that *he* had done the work and I wondered how he thought this change had come about. He replied, "It's like a light, a bulb. It went out, it went on and off. You helped me and the light went on." It was fascinating to observe the emergence of the meaning of this former ritualistic acting out now being revealed in Kenny's symbolically apt verbal statement. He exclaimed, "When I go to high school, I'll go to the school dances, this one woke me up!" This was a declaration of hope for the future and beyond his competence at that time. Nevertheless, the establishment of the self now helped him further to cathect the world of people.

To sum up, when Kenny began treatment, he seemed to be completely preoccupied with the struggle to make certain of his place in his chaotic world. He did this by alternating between psychotic incorporation of "the good mother" and ejection of the bad self as if this were the only way he could be defended against further fragmentation of his empty and disorganized self. The primitive form of his defenses and identities was revealed by the defective differentiation of self from animate or inanimate objects in his environment. Very early in infancy, Kenny's sensory and perceptive functions had become involved in avoidance mechanisms, so that he appeared not to look or listen. Preverbal elements of language as well as words became negatively associated with feelings of his own badness, in part, because of his harsh parental introject. The result was that language did not develop beyond its rudimentary elements, and all human contact was avoided.

When Kenny began to develop an attitude of trust and to form a secondary symbiotic relationship with the therapist, he was able to move out of the undifferentiated phase, and sensory-motor perceptual and cognitive functions were expanded. As each regressive phase was worked through, energies were released for further separation of the self and for gratifying experiences. Each step led to the expansion of the perceptual system, which could thus become more responsive to an increasing variety of stimuli.

The tenacity of his bad self-image prolonged the time in which this became the battleground for further individuation. It was not until he began to sort out inner and outer experiences that aggressive impulses and affects became available for the task of ego mastery.

His primitive defenses were highlighted in the choice of animate and inanimate objects around which he wove his conflict of survival. When self and non-self were undifferentiated, Kenny acted as if he literally became the object with which he identified. When the therapist entered Kenny's psychic orbit as a kind of magical auxiliary ego, Cluddy, a transitional identity, appeared. Now that he began to modulate feelings within himself, Kenny seemed to be changing the "shape" (13) of his self-awareness by becoming this non-existent imaginary child. This permitted him to have affects, to feel and to be vocal about fear, to experience ego mastery and to sort out reality while gradually giving up autistic defenses.

Part identification with Cluddy was given up since it was limited in its usefulness and Kenny's ego was not integrated sufficiently to maintain synthesis and structure through a relationship with a fantasied object (6). The next short-lived choice in his quest for identity was that of Hal, his brother's friend. This identification, which might be characterized as a borrowed "ideal self," served as a defense against disapproval and loss of love since it appeared at a time when Kenny was faced with school failure. In the boys' club episode, when Kenny identified with his brother, he no longer fused with him but imitated and attempted to be like him. This process characterizes Kenny's attempts to incorporate every positive identity as a spur to progressive personality organization.

When Kenny had attained a unified self-representation he was able to exclaim, "Call me Kenny." His beginning tender feelings for the therapist made him wish to please her by taking on the identity of Kenny. This case, treated by psychoanalytic psychotherapy, illustrates the genesis and dynamics of the generation of a sense of human identity in a child who presented both autistic and symbiotic elements of infantile psychosis.

BIBLIOGRAPHY

1. ALPERT, AUGUSTA. Reversibility of Pathological Fixations Associated with Maternal Deprivation in Infancy. *Psychoanalyt. Study of the Child,* 1959, 14:173.

2. BETTLEHEIM, BRUNO. *The Empty Fortress.* New York: Free Press, 1967, p. 36.
3. EKSTEIN, RUDOLF, and FRIEDMAN, SEYMOUR. On the Meaning of Play in Childhood Psychosis. In *Children of Time and Space, of Action and Impulse,* chap. 10. New York: Appleton-Century-Crofts, 1966.
4. EKSTEIN, RUDOLF, and MOTTO, ROCCO L. The Borderline Child in the School Situation. In *Professional School Psychology.* M. G. and G. B. Gottesegen, eds. New York: Grune & Stratton, 1960, p. 249.
5. ERIKSON, ERIK H. *Identity, Youth and Crisis.* New York: Norton, 1968, p. 217.
6. GIOVACCHINI, PETER L. Integrative Aspects of Object Relationships. *Psychoanalyt. Quart.,* 1963, 3:403.
7. GOUIN-DEARIE, THERESE. *Intelligence and Affectivity.* New York: Int'l. Univ. Press, 1966, p. 63.
8. JACOBSON, EDITH. *The Self and the Object World.* New York: Int'l. Univ. Press, 1964, p. 48.
9. MAHLER, MARGARET S. Thoughts about Development and Individuation. *Psychoanalyt. Study of the Child,* 1963, 18:307, 309.
10. MAHLER, MARGARET S. and LA PERRIERE, K. Mother-Child Interaction during Separation-Individuation. *Psychoanalyt. Quart.,* 1965, 34:4.
11. PELLER, LILI E. Freud's Contribution to Language Development. *Psychoanalyt. Study of the Child,* 1966, 21:459.
12. RINSLEY, DONALD B. Economic Aspects of Object Relations. *Int. J. Psychoanalysis,* 1968, 49:44.
13. SANDLER, JOSEPH, ET AL. The Ego Ideal and the Ideal Self. *Psychoanalyt. Study of the Child,* 1963, 18:152.
14. TYNAN, KENNETH. *Kenneth Tynan, Right and Left.* New York: Atheneum, 1967, p. 112.

Chapter 12

❈

The Relation of Ego Autonomy to Activity and Passivity in the Psychotherapy of Childhood Schizophrenia*

RUDOLF EKSTEIN, PH.D., AND ELAINE CARUTH, PH.D.

Act from thought should quickly follow. What is thinking for?

—W. H. AUDEN

A useful approach to the understanding of the issues of activity and passivity in psychoanalytic theory and technique is to distinguish between ego activity and passivity, and motoric activity and passivity. The active ego, specifically the autonomous ego, can mediate between demands of id, superego and reality, and retain freedom of choice in the resultant behavior. However, the ego can be overwhelmed and considered liable to passivity to all three.**

Motoric activity can reflect ego autonomy, as in goal-directed

*This work partially supported by funds from the Annenberg Foundation. Longer version of paper presented at Midwinter meeting of American Psychoanalytic Assoc., New York, N.Y., Dec., 1966.
**This viewpoint represents a synthesis of the views of Rapaport (23, 24) and Hart (18, 19).

behavior, or it may reflect ego passivity, as in automatic behavior like echopraxia and echolalia. Similarly, motoric passivity (or inactivity) may reflect ego autonomy, as in the very potent yet motorically passive "acts" of civil disobedience, like those of Martin Luther King or Gandhi, or it may reflect the presence of ego passivity. A good example is the paralyzed obsessive who vacillates and cannot act—Buridan's ass who starved between the equidistant bale of hay and pail of water.

The healthy autonomous ego is capable of a greater or lesser degree of motoric activity in relationship to objects, to reality orientation and to instinctual expression. It is capable of establishing an optimal balance between active and passive modes of behavior and the inner degree of ego autonomy. The normal child's behavior tends to show relative consistency between the inner and outer state. When psychologically helpless and inundated by either inner or outer stimuli, he tends to be motorically inactive; when psychologically active, he tends to be more physically active or else engaged in behavior oriented towards future activities, such as school work or study.

When we deal with the schizophrenic child, however, we are faced with the lack of an autonomous ego and we come closer to Orwell's world of 1984. Black is white, up is down, active is passive. This world is characterized by the rules and logic of primary-process thinking which follows a different "grammar." Inside and outside are not clearly differentiated; self and object may fuse but seldom integrate (22), non-Euclidian geometry and non-Newtonian physics can reign (2) in defiance of our secondary-process laws of space and time.

Unsuccessful in mastering the individuation-separation task, the schizophrenic child is still struggling with early problems: restoring the positive symbiosis in the absence of the object and maintaining separation in the presence of the object. These patients frequently fear the act as destroying the object and self representations which are still so closely fused that they can maintain their separation only through artificial "distance devices" (2, 8, 13). Paradoxically, as we will see in the following case, they often maintain their closeness through what appears to be separation.

Carol is a deeply troubled borderline adolescent girl embroiled in a masochistic, suicidal, depressive reaction. Carol barricades herself in her room, writing suicide notes to her family and isolating herself from all contact, except the minimum necessary to continue high-school studies. She comes voluntarily to the therapist fully aware of her need for help and of some of the irrational elements in her pervasive feelings of inadequacy, worthlessness and rejection. Yet she gives the initial impression of coming involuntarily, against her will, even under force, although, in fact, her parents are so frightened of this child that they literally cannot exert any control except by cajoling and pleading. Also, she overtly gives the impression of sullenness, bitterness and resentment, and quickly demands to know how she can be helped if she does not talk. She has had several earlier "encounters" with therapy, the last terminating disastrously. The therapist had responded in anger to her expression of anger, after having previously berated her for not trying because she did not talk enough. Thus, she now presents herself with all of her inner helplessness exposed. Without choice and passively, she submits to the counter-cathectic forces which forbid any impulse expression; her worst fears have previously been confirmed that giving vent to her aggressive impulses leads to the loss or destruction of the object. She experiences the defense against the destructive impulses as ego dystonic, and she becomes, in a sense, a slave to her own projected superego. As the transference develops, however, there is an additional weakening of the defenses, and she begins to experience the counter-impulse of giving in to the destructive forces, equated with talking. At this point, she flees treatment.

Some time later, the mother, strengthened through her own treatment, has been able to reassert control to the extent that Carol no longer locks herself up. The mother can also insist that Carol return to therapy. The girl is now literally forced to come to treatment. One is immediately impressed by the fact that externally there is little difference between her present behavior and her earlier behavior when she had come under her own power. Now her silence is no longer ego alien, but rather can be experienced as a syntonic act. She no longer feels she cannot talk; rather, she can experience it as if she will not talk, that she has freedom of choice. She has relinquished the external activity of seemingly coming voluntarily, which had led to her experiencing the helpless passivity of being unable to talk, or else unable to control the destructive outburst. She has now reached the seemingly passive state of being forced to come, wherein she can feel that she will not talk and consequently not endanger the object. She now experiences as a voluntary act what she had previously experienced as a passive, choiceless symptom.

We are reminded of another borderline schizophrenic child, somewhat younger, who tells us endlessly through his play that without ego autonomy, there can only be the subjective experience of helpless oscillation between being passively driven to destroy the world, or else being passively destroyed by it. His play reflects the shifting dominant phase of the conflict between the wish to inflict and the wish to suffer aggression. He veers between being a "teeny mouth" swallowed by the whale puppet in the office or being, like Hansel, readied for cooking and eating by the therapist, and being the monster with big muscles and big teeth with which to eat the therapist. This seven-year-old boy's constantly fluctuating levels of ego states confuse parents and doctors who seek to see in him only the healthy aspects. For them, the healthy aspects mean "active." This is a desperate attempt to deny his more withdrawn periods during which, in fact, he is able to exert some modicum of control over the impulse-driven behavior, even though forced into a kind of autistic fantasy world.

Let us turn now to another adolescent schizophrenic about whom we have written previously (5, 6, 7, 9, 11). Her first attempts to move from a kind of autistic psychotic position into a world of secondary-process functioning, of reality and actuality, were communicated through a series of psychotic acting-out episodes, following which she developed some capacity to move from a primary-process level of functioning to a beginning capacity actually to fulfill tasks and promises on a minimal level. She has achieved now a kind of pseudo-normal facade of seeming adjustment. She is able to handle everyday details of budget, transportation, minimal encounters with peripheral kinds of social experiences, etc. She seeks to maintain this relatively stable balance by persistent and endless variations of counter-cathectic maneuvers. While rendering her seemingly paralyzed and immobilized in outer reality, these actually serve to master and bind the impulse-ridden, primary-process core. She misses appointments, comes late, spends her days in endless preparations that lead nowhere. In the treatment hours, she slowly begins to recover and reconstruct memories that were previously reconstructed through the psychotic acting out (9, 12). But she must restore these memories and at the same time defend against the regression to the helpless impulsing of earlier days. Thus, she begins to experience a pervasive feeling of paralysis, of inactivity and inability to accomplish in external reality, which culminates finally in a conviction of being a ghost, both dead and alive (6).

As she is safely immured in this kind of frozen position, she begins to communicate to us what it is that is defended against. She approaches this through her characteristic distance device, the use of borrowed TV and movie fantasies. In the 578th hour (12), she relates the story of a street cleaner, rummaging in the sand for trash, who comes upon a part of a statue of a Roman soldier that was destroyed in the earthquake that wiped out Pompeii. As the statue is removed to a museum, it becomes alive and menacing. Thus, she tells us of her attempts to immobilize her own destructive power, which, like the earthquake, are so violent they can destroy the world. And she tell us also of her fears that she cannot maintain this control. She begins slowly then to recall an actual earthquake, which is followed by her memory of a subsequent nightmare about this earthquake in which her little dog is killed. In a succeeding hour, she arrives announcing that she has a burden that is both a mystery and a miracle. She is like the old woman who never was, she is a ghost, one that is both dead and alive at the same time, a sleepless ghost that is made out of flesh and blood. She comes now to remember that this little dog, which she both loved and hated, suffered because of her guardian's neglect, clearly revealing that she is striving to ward off the actual memory of having herself threatened and mistreated the dog, which we know from the history.

We can now understand the meaning of her current preoccupation with a variety of trivia and minutiae that literally paralyzes any positive action by her. We see developing a kind of psychotic obsessionalism that, although seemingly in the service of her primary-process relationship to time as infinite and unchanging, serves also to develop inner structure that helps control the drive organization. This very process of reconstitution and restitution makes possible the kind of symbolic reconstruction of which she is slowly becoming capable, and demonstrates the complex vicissitudes of the activity-passivity conflict that can occur with such a patient. Initially, she appears passively overwhelmed as she reports the borrowed TV fantasy of the menacing statue that has suddenly become alive, a kind of borrowed external representation that serves as a *screen delusional fantasy*. Subsequently, she is able to recall her own *screen nightmare,* no longer borrowed, of the volcanic eruption (of which she knows not whether it be inner or outer) which defended against the actual memory of her violent, aggressive acts against the dog, prior to his subsequent death from unrelated causes.

To the extent that the reporting of the delusional material is in the service of restoring the function of remembering, we can see that the passivity referred only to certain aspects of the ego. Simultaneously it was also in the service of those aspects of the ego which had not been overwhelmed, and aimed at the restoration of active, secondary-process memory function. As this is restored, the girl comes, two hours later, to a more conventional screen memory, the aunt's mistreatment and rejection of the dog. This becomes an acceptable substitute screen idea for the unacceptable memory of her own violent rage which had led to her abuse of the dog.

Thus, now that she has achieved the capacity to still the helpless, driven activity of earlier days, even though in such massive measures as to achieve a living paralysis, she can begin to remember. We can hope now that the soft but persistent voice of an autonomous ego (to paraphrase Freud) will have begun to be heard; for if she can still the act, she need not fear so desperately the primary thought which can still turn so quickly into an uncontrolled act.

In subsequent visits to her therapist, she begins to play with the thought that she can moderate the acts without having completely to suppress them. She begins to exert mastery over the loss of the object when it is no longer present by instituting a kind of peek-aboo game with the therapist. She knocks on his exit door, as if to show that she can still make an entrance only by way of a departure. This in itself is a reconstruction of her own life history with its constant exchange of mother figures, about whom it might be said that she had a more stable relationship in their absence than in their presence.

We would like to end by referring to a rather unique aspect of the activity-passivity issues in the treatment of borderline and psychotic children. All analytic treatment requires of the therapist a constant kind of balancing between a seemingly "active" and a seemingly "passive" position. He must listen and he must intervene; he must understand and he must interpret; he must experience and he must observe and reflect (17); he must identify with and he must confront; he must "regress" empathically with the patient and progress with the analysis; he must accept the endless dalliance of the patients for whom time is interminable and he must press for the working alliance that implies finite goals. But with these children, the nature of the regression—to a symbiotic fusion, to primary-process archaic levels of functioning, to fragmented and discontinuous contact and communication—creates special countertransference problems which at times seem to echo and make him an echo of his patients (3, 10, 21). His task becomes then to sleep but not to dream (10), to mirror but not to echo, to accept the symbiosis but not to become attached to it, to enter the autistic wonderland but to reserve passage for a return.

It is for such reasons that the treatment of these children within a research program can not only enrich but facilitate it. Such patients provide the therapist with the opportunity for the continued search for understanding that requires his own integrative and synthesizing functions to make the necessary empathic regression (10) truly in the service of a therapeutic and autonomous ego, which is to say, of an active psychic organization.

BIBLIOGRAPHY

1. ANDERSEN, HANS CHRISTIAN. The Red Shoes. In *The Fairy Tales,* 1835.
2. CARUTH, ELAINE. The Onion and the Moebius Strip: Rational and Irrational Models for the Secondary and Primary Process. *Psychoanalyt. Rev.,* 1968, 3:416.

3. CARUTH, ELAINE, and EKSTEIN, R. Certain Phenomenological Aspects of the Countertransference in the Treatment of Schizophrenic Children. *Reiss-Davis Clin. Bull.,* 1964, 2:80.
4. EKSTEIN, RUDOLF. Discussion of "Transference and Countertransference by A. Aberastury et al. Presented at 2nd Pan Amer. Psychoanalyt. Cong., Buenos Aires, Argentina, August, 1966.
5. EKSTEIN, RUDOLF. The Opening Gambit in Psychotherapeutic Work with Severely Disturbed Adolescents. *Amer. J. of Orthopsychiat.,* 1963, 33: 862.
6. EKSTEIN, RUDOLF. The Orpheus and Eurydice Theme in Psychotherapy. *Bull. of Menninger Clin.,* 1966, 30:207.
7. EKSTEIN, RUDOLF. Puppet Play of a Psychotic Adolescent Girl in the Psychotherapeutic Process. *Psychoanalyt. Study of the Child,* 1965, 20:441.
8. EKSTEIN, RUDOLF, and CARUTH, E. Distancing and Distance Devices in Childhood Schizophrenia and Borderline States. *Psycholog. Reports,* 1967, 20:109.
9. EKSTEIN, RUDOLF, and CARUTH, E. Psychotic Acting Out: Royal Road or Primrose Path. In *Children of Time and Space, of Action and Impulse* by R. Ekstein. New York: Appleton-Century-Crofts, 1966.
10. EKSTEIN, RUDOLF, and CARUTH, E. To Sleep but Not to Dream. *Reiss-Davis Clin. Bull.,* 1965, 2:87.
11. EKSTEIN, RUDOLF, and CARUTH, E. The Working Alliance with the Monster. *Bull. of Menninger Clin.,* 1965, 4:189.
12. EKSTEIN, RUDOLF, and FRIEDMAN, SEYMOUR. Object Constancy and Psychotic Reconstruction. *Psychoanalyt. Study of the Child,* 1967, 22:357.
13. EKSTEIN, RUDOLF, and WALLERSTEIN, J. Choice of Interpretation in the Treatment of Borderline and Psychotic Children. *Bull. of Menninger Clin.,* 1957, 21:199.
14. ERIKSON, ERIK H. *Childhood and Society.* New York: Norton, 1950.
15. ERIKSON, ERIK H. Reality and Actuality. *J. of Am. Psa. Assoc.,* 1962, 10:451.
16. FENICHEL, OTTO. *The Psychoanalytic Theory of Neurosis.* New York: Norton, 1945.
17. GREENSON, RALPH. Empathy and Its Vicissitudes. *Int. J. Psychoanal.,* 1960, 61:418.
18. HART, HENRY H. The Meaning of Passivity. *Psychiat. Quart.,* Oct., 1955, p. 595.
19. HART, HENRY H. A Review of the Psychoanalytic Literature on Passivity. *Psychiat. Quart.,* Apr., 1961, p. 331.
20. KNIGHT, R. P. Borderline States. *Bull. of Menninger Clin.,* 1953, 17:1.
21. LINDNER, R. M. The Jet Propelled Couch. In *The Fifty-Minute Hour.* New York: Rinehart, 1955.
22. MATTE-BLANCO, IGNACIO. Expression in Symbolic Logic of the Characteristics of the System UCS. *Int. J. Psychoanal.,* 1959, 40:1.
23. RAPAPORT, DAVID. Some Metapsychological Considerations Concerning Activity and Passivity. *Archivos de Criminologia Neuro-Psiquiatria y Disciplinas Conexas,* 1961, 9.
24. RAPAPORT, DAVID. The Theory of Ego Autonomy: A Generalization. *Bull. of Menninger Clin.,* 1958, 1:13.

Chapter 13

The Phaeton Complex: Play Disruption in the Service of the Acquisition of an Integrating Capacity

JOEL M. LIEBOWITZ, PH.D.

Phaeton sought proof as to the fact of his being the son of a god. He sought out his father, Apollo, . . . who rode the sun across the sky creating day and night, who wishing to confirm that Phaeton was indeed his son said, . . . "To put an end to your doubts ask what you will, the gift shall be yours as proof of what you ask." Phaeton immediately asked to be permitted for one day to drive the chariot of the sun. His father begged Phaeton to withdraw his request, explaining that it was not safe nor one suited to Phaeton's youth and strength. The first part of the way, he explained, is steep, and such as the horses when fresh in the morning can hardly climb. The middle is high up in the heavens, from where I myself can scarcely, without alarm, look down and behold the earth and sea stretched beneath me. The last part of the road descends rapidly and requires the most careful driving. The road is through the midst of terrible monsters. You will not find it easy to guide these horses . . . I can scarcely govern them myself . . . It is not honor but destruction you seek.

He ended but the youth rejected all admonition and held to his demand. So, . . . Phaeton mounted the

chariot and was off. The steeds soon perceived that
the load they drew was lighter than usual. . . . The
horses rushed headlong and left the travelled road.
Phaeton is alarmed and knows not how to guide
them, nor if he knew, had he the power.

When hapless Phaeton looked down . . . he grew
pale and his knees shook with terror. . . . He loses his
self-command and knows not what to do—whether to
draw tight the reins or throw them loose; he forgets
the names of the horses. He sees with terror the mon-
strous forms scattered over the surface of the heavens. Here the scorpion extended his two great arms,
with his tail and crooked claws stretching over two
signs of the Zodiac. When the boy beheld him reeking
with poison and menacing with his fangs, his courage
failed, and the reins fell from his hands. The horses
then dashed headlong and unrestrained off into the
unknown regions of the sky now up in high heaven,
now down almost to earth. The clouds . . . smoke . . .
the mountain tops take fire; the fields are parched . . .
the plants wither, the trees burn, the harvest is
ablaze. Great cities perished . . . whole nations . . .
were consumed to ashes. Earth . . . called on Jupiter, . . . "we fall into ancient chaos. Save what yet remains. . . ." Then Jupiter . . . brandishing a lightning
bolt . . . launched it against the charioteer and struck
him . . . from existence. Phaeton with his hair on fire
fell headlong like a shooting star (1).

Although there are many aspects of this story of Phaeton that
lend themselves to analytic interpretation, one, in particular, is
singled out for the purpose of this paper. It is the question of appropriate occasions for the expression of impulse, especially in therapy with severely disturbed children. That is, how does one understand the occasions for the expression of impulse in the borderline
child's play and the adaptive means of dealing with the premature
expression of such impulses by play disruption? As child therapists,
we are ordinarily accustomed to reacting to the child's play in
terms of the content. This is understandable and, as Erikson (4)
points out, "Play is to the child what thinking, planning and
blueprinting are to the adult, a trial universe in which . . . past
failures can be thought through, expectations tested." But what

if the "blueprint" reveals the presence of inner forces too great to be managed? What if Phaeton had in some way perceived what lay ahead? Would he have proceeded? If he could have fathomed the terrors that awaited him, we would have considered him wise to heed the warnings and hold fast; that is, to disrupt the activity. Had he done so he would have had good reality testing, good control, and good judgment, and there would be no need to refer him to a therapist. He was, however, filled with unrestrained inner forces seeking only to be expressed but, in expressing them, he was led to his doom for he was unprepared to cope with them.

Ordinarily, play is disrupted at such a point, broken off, and the usual interpretation is of the defensive nature of this disruption: the ego is too threatened by the emerging material and avoids it by disengaging. For example, Eric, aged nine, comes to one therapy session obviously upset and distressed. He is an active child who is having problems in school. His concentration and attention are poor, he daydreams and is below grade level in achievement. And yet, his life outside of school is generally more appropriate and reasonable. The middle child of three boys, Eric has reasonable interaction within his family and good relationships with his friends. His sessions are typically filled with play of aggressive fantasies— airplanes battling in the skies overhead, bombs exploding the buildings below, secret forts and hideouts built with the help of trusted allies. When he comes to today's session quite tense and restless, the therapist remarks on this. Eric denies that anything is wrong in a manner typical of latency-aged children by saying, "And besides, I don't want to talk about it." He wants to play a game instead.

This is unusual for Eric, for usually we play with our imaginations and he does not rely on the external support of a game. But feeling shaky at the moment, he picks the game of "Concentration," one he hopes will absorb all his conscious thoughts with the necessity of concentrating and remembering the location of the "hidden" pairs of cards to be matched. The therapist remarks on this search for the hidden, how in this game we must look for that which is missing, pressing further by adding that perhaps Eric is troubled about something that he, too, wishes to hide, something which if revealed will make him feel worse than he does already.

Tears begin to well up on his eyes and after a while, Eric "confesses" to the therapist about an incident at school earlier in the day. With great emotion he tells how some children picked on him because he did not know the right answer to the teacher's question; i.e., he did not know what was hidden. In the subsequent associations he reveals how he becomes so upset when he is called upon in class, so fearful that the other children will make fun of him (i.e., attack him) and tease him. He tells the therapist how he becomes so upset that he forgets what he knows and then feels silly and embarrassed.

Here, the interpretation of the defense that "nothing is wrong" is the focus as it is pointed out to Eric that "nothing" can be wrong, it is only "something" that can be "wrong." The attempt on Eric's part is to deny the upsetting feelings. The interpretation that the therapist realizes something is hidden allows Eric enough assurance to reveal what he ambivalently held secret. The positive transference, the feeling of safety, the pressure and wish to confess, all combine to help him let go of what is troubling him. The tension relaxes and the disruption is over. He is able to continue. What was disrupted in Eric's case was his "usual" play with fantasies while the "game" itself became the form of defense intended to prevent the upsetting fantasies and feelings from emerging. The game of Concentration quickly finished, Eric is once again able to return to his own style of play. Thus, the ego helped to avoid the release of upsetting material by disengaging from its usual play until the interpretation encourages expression of feeling so Eric can proceed.

Laurie, aged ten, a somewhat more disturbed child than was Eric, also has a relatively age-appropriate level of ego functioning. She has fantasies in which she is convinced that she possesses special powers—psychic capacities. She reveals these fantasies only to her parents, her absolutely closest friend, and the therapist, thereby reflecting the ambivalence of her "belief." Initially, treatment goes well; Laurie comes to her sessions eager to talk about the fantasies which make her a very special person, indeed. Gradually though, after three or four months of therapeutic honeymoon, Laurie becomes somewhat reticent, less communicative, and more withholding. She begins to censor her comments and becomes increasingly tense, apprehensive, and uncomfortable. Eventually she wants to stop the treatment altogether and puts great pressure on her parents to allow this. Previously we had talked often and openly about her secret powers but now this talk no longer takes place. She denies that she has these powers any longer, claiming that she was just kidding all along. Where have all the powers gone? Long time a-hiding.

Interpretations focus on her fearfulness about revealing any more to the therapist—how she'd rather switch than speak—focus on her avoidance of "something private" which she fears may either be taken from or used against her. By her manner she evidences that her very identity is threatened if she says anything more. Yet even as she holds on tight to her private world, literally to herself, she demonstrates this struggle to the therapist. By doing this she also demonstrates her wish to let go and allow the therapist to understand what it is she cannot tell. The interpretations then focus on the wish to let go and the fear to do so. Finally, after weeks on the seesaw of ambivalence, Laurie, overcome, breaks down and pours forth her heart, explaining that she fears if she speaks about her special powers, "you will steal me away." Further work helps to clarify for her her transference fears that the therapist's powers will be increased by the amount that hers are diminished. Her fear is that in the process of giving up her secrets she will lose her very self, her identity as a special person with special powers. She listens, and little by little over the ensuing weeks the gates are re-opened. The secret paradise of special powers is once again visited and explored and found, indeed, to contain some remote corners that are more hellish than idyllic.

The interpretations in Laurie's case helped to allow the secret fantasies and impulses to find expression. The disruption of play, a lengthy and torturous one, helped Laurie to prevent the emergence of material experienced as too threatening. With interpretations focused on the defensive aspect of this disruption, the material could, once again, emerge. Erikson (4), too, has pointed this out when he notes that "play disruption is an example of the way in which an ego, flooded with fear, can regain its synthesizing power via disengagement of play." One ordinarily thinks of a disruption of play, perhaps particularly in latency-age children, as indicative of defensive operations, as a means of preventing the emergence of material which the child does not wish to reveal. As with all human functioning, however, the situation is not completely clearcut, but in the treatment of borderline or psychotic children the therapeutic stance of interpreting play disruption as a defensive avoidance of emerging material can, and often does, lead to even greater disruption in functioning. The disruption of play in the severely disturbed child can also serve an extremely important adaptive function. To overlook this and interpret only the defensive aspect is frequently to miss the point and provoke an even more chaotic situation.

It would have been an adaptive move on Phaeton's part not to take the reins of horses he was unprepared to control. Had he declined, it would have been folly to interpret to Phaeton his defensive avoidance in the hope of provoking him to accept the impulses that he found threatening. Blind to the fact of his inabilities, Phaeton was in no position at that point to question his impulses and could only feel the surge of excitement. The refusal to accept the expression of impulses or fantasies in his situation would have represented a matter of good, sound judgment in recognizing that one may not be prepared to cope with what emerges. Phaeton's refusal to accept these feelings, these impulses, would have represented an adaptive acceptance of his ability and limitation and not a defensive avoidance. The disruption of psychotic-like acting out actually protects the therapeutic situation and leaves options for the future.

In the inner functioning of any human being there is a continuous ongoing struggle between impulse expression and reality testing. We assume that in the "normal" child the age-appropriate ego "chooses" those conditions in which impulse can find its most satisfying expression while reality receives its just consideration. In the neurotic, the ego, seeking more or less of a compromise, may end up perversely tricking itself. Nevertheless, the ego still attempts to function in a mediating and compromising fashion. There are some individuals, however, in whom the ego is either not sufficiently developed or else so labile or erratic that it cannot perform its functions in an age-appropriate fashion. In children, this incomplete ego development is partially a developmental issue, but it is possible to judge the ego's adequacy relative to age. The mis-implication is to assume that the ordinary logic of treatment applicable to the neurotic child can be applied to the borderline or psychotic child, as well. This is a gross misunderstanding of the nature of these children's personality organization so, for example, the assumption that play disruption is a defensive operation which must be interpreted as such may interfere in work with such children. As Erikson (4) points out, "Play is dependent on protection from unmanageable conflict." The key word is "protection"—meaning the capacity of the ego to bind the impulse, the structure to keep it within operational bounds. When this capacity is not present and the impulse is expressed, there occur the states ordinarily referred to in the cliché as "nervous breakdown"; that is, the overwhelming flooding of impulse and the subsequent regression into psychotic functioning. Thus, for the borderline or psychotic child, arresting the development of play must not be viewed as simply an operation of defense nor an operation to ward off awareness and recognition of what is experienced as too overwhelming or too frightening to experience. Such an arrest may also be seen as an entirely appropriate adaptive maneuver—a putting off of the expression of impulse for which there does not yet exist the structure necessary to keep it within bounds.

This view of defense and adaptation with regard to the ego's functioning has concerned psychology for many years. Analogous to the question of adaptation/defense is the parallel question of figure/ground. Which is which depends upon the aspect in focus but the viewer must always be cognizant of the total picture. It is not that one interpretative stance is always correct and the other incorrect for there are many situations in which an interpretation may focus on both the defensive and adaptive functions inherent in play disruption. Rather than stating as dogma that a borderline or psychotic child's play disruption should always be considered adaptive, the present point is that there are many occasions in the work with such children that this viewpoint may prove helpful and therapeutically indicated. In the cases of Eric and Laurie, situations familiar to all therapists who work with children, disruption is interpreted in the light of the defensive effort to avoid that which is feared to be emerging. But Eric and even Laurie are children with relatively intact, reasonably functioning egos.

The child with a borderline ego state or psychotic personality organization, however, does not have the luxury of control, synthesis, and integration. He must often struggle for every inch of appropriateness, sitting as he does on the lid of an ever-boiling caldron of intense, unbridled emotions, impulses, and fantasies. Though burned from the heat within, he is unable to let go of the lid for fear of the terrifying explosion that may result. Such children are truly caught between the devil and the deep blue sea. Rather than defense, play disruption for them may have much more significance as an integrating effort on the part of the battered, fragmented, often primitively integrated ego. The best therapeutic intervention for them may be help in turning off the fire or, at least, in turning down the flame. By responding to the adaptivity inherent in the play disruption, the therapist allows the child to break off the process of the emerging material thereby preventing further regression into chaos. To encourage these children to release the hidden, to interpret that "getting things off your chest," so to speak, is always helpful may drive them into the very psychotic regression that their disruption of the activity is intended to prevent. This is likely not the time to open the lid and peek inside the cauldron, nor to turn up the heat so that everything can bubble out to the surface. For these children it can be psychologically healthier not to let go before they are able to contain that which emerges. Otherwise, they may end up like Pandora, after having opened the inner "box," thereby letting forth all the demons of the world without any way in which to deal with them.

The truth does not always set man free: individuals whose psychic organization is too disturbed to deal with the "truth" may be rendered helpless prisoners of the demons of their own mind. The therapist ought not to encourage a crossing into the darkness of confusion and chaos unless he is able to provide transportation back into the light of reality. Thus, with children of borderline or psychotic ego states, the therapeutic implications may be quite different from those pertaining to children of relatively age-appropriate egos. The maintenance of self may crucially depend upon not letting go until the ego is able to keep mastery over what emerges. To continue the play may superheat the bubbling water of impulse beyond all controllable proportions throwing the individual, like Phaeton, to destruction by those forces.

Since a therapist does not sit by and wait for the ego to develop on its own the needed maturity and strength, it is suggested that with borderline children play disruption may be interpreted from the viewpoint of control and adaptation. For example, Ekstein (2) writes about a borderline child in therapy. Timid and inhibited, lonely and distant, he plays with blocks and builds fortresses in which he places little rubber horses. The horses appear trapped, seeming always to seek an exit from their apparent prison. As they continually smash down the walls, the process of building and rebuilding is never ending. Early in the treatment interpretations are offered that the horses wish to be released from the prison of the walls, to be free to come and go as they please. Nothing changes. The behavior continues unabated, it seems as if the repetitive, obsessive activity will go on for ever. Then the interpretive position is shifted from impulse expression to control. The focus is now centered on the walls. How necessary are the walls; how sad that the horses keep kicking in the walls because without them they have no place where they can feel safe; how strong walls are needed to keep wild horses under control. It is not freedom of expression the horses seek but freedom of safety, a haven in which to be contained, restricted, and controlled. Gradually the "unending" activity diminishes and movement into some other activity becomes possible.

Nor is it exclusively with borderline or psychotic children that play disruption may be seen as a positive indication. To confront many children with its defensive aspects may foster the defensiveness so that one ends up instigating the defensiveness rather than interpreting the defenses. As Erikson points out, "Never underestimate the power of the ego," and I would add, even the ego of a severely disturbed person. Thus, interpretation of the defensive quality only of play disruption can drive the person into a state of panic and true therapeutic disengagement. With Ekstein's case, the horses have no problem with their impulse expression: they are all too ready to break out. Rather, the child's anxiety is focused on whether or not the available structure is sufficient to keep the power of the horses contained. One cannot see content as something apart from structure. Indeed, it is the nature of the structure which is critical and of particular concern in children with severely disturbed and fluctuating ego states. There is no rational way to "force" the material, to provoke its expression—a sharp temptation particularly with young children when the therapist often understands, long before the children have awareness of, the nature of the inner turmoil. To rush in interpretively is perhaps error enough. To rush in when play is disrupted and confront the child with the nature of the impulse whose expression the child may have no structure to contain is to awaken a level of anxiety and panic which, like Phaeton's can lead to destruction. While doubtlessly true for work with all children, this possibility applies particularly to those children with borderline or psychotic states. The material seems so "transparent," so accessible, that the interpretive temptations to the therapist are quite strong. "Interpretation," however, may turn out to be the expression of countertransference difficulties.

The following clinical material is being introduced to help clarify the premise that play disruption in the borderline child may be viewed as an adaptive maneuver by the ego necessary to aid in the acquisition of an integrative ability. It is suggested that the therapeutic demand to reveal, implicit in interpreting play disruption as a defense, may be inappropriate in the treatment of children with severely disturbed ego states where the crucial need is a full assessment of the state of ego functioning in order to reach a therapeutic interpretive position. Interpretation of the defense would not, for example, have been applicable in the case of Phaeton where the ego organization was primitive, and reason was not the driver. The point is that it is inescapably incumbent upon the therapist to consider the personality organization and not to assume that all ego states are the same. The awareness of the specific personality organization should then determine the therapeutic stance.

Billy, whose adjustment is of a borderline nature, is 8½-years-old and the elder of two children in a family in which both parents are academically oriented. They value intellectual creativity and precocity and set a high standard on academic achievement. Billy attends a progressive school, one that would presumably provide him with the opportunity to become intellectually upwardly mo-

bile. All who meet Billy are impressed with his artistic ability;
with a simple stroke of a pencil, he can produce the endless characters of his imagination. These drawings are artistically impres-
sive and provide the visual accompaniment to his prolific fantasies
which are often told as narrative stories of carton sequences.
Through Billy's eyes the therapist has visited far-off Oosh-kan, a
planet deep within space, just left of the sun after one passes
Venus. The therapist has met with "Kwabos," animals housed in
the zoo in Billy's inner mind. The therapist has flown on a "fly-
mat," a non-polluting airship that takes us 3,000 miles in a moment's passage of time. He has met a "Fiodo," has conversed with
"Paul D. Piboto," and chatted with a "Libma." All this and more
have passed before our eyes as Billy weaves in and out of fantasy,
one moment here on earth and the next moment drifting free in
the limitless reaches of inner space. In addition, puppet play is one
of the hallmarks of Billy's therapy and the puppets help to allow
him to produce the imaginings of his mind. Each puppet has a
name, assigned from the outset of therapy and remembered with
unvarying accuracy. All the puppets have a relationship with each
other, which is maintained throughout. As indicated in a previous
publication (5), it is the nature of Billy's functioning to interrupt
a theme as the impulse comes to awareness and to move to other
material. This type of functioning, i.e., this disruption of play, has
been consistent throughout his treatment. The session presented
below clarifies the nature of his functioning and the thesis of this
paper.

> Billy began the session by drawing a picture of a monster
> named Big Oscar . . . a bulldog-like creature with great big
> teeth and a nasty scowl. Billy indicated that Big Oscar was
> rough and big and tough. I indicated that I wasn't afraid of
> Big Oscar and Billy asked to see my muscles. I made a muscle
> for him and Billy was duly impressed, indicating that perhaps
> I might be able to beat Big Oscar but not just because I was
> strong. He explained that Big Oscar and I had the same
> strength but that I was smart and could use my head to out-
> think Big Oscar who was kind of dumb. . . . Billy then drew
> some of Big Oscar's friends and proceeded to draw a collection
> of monsters. There were Big Dirt Pile and his son, Little Dirt
> Pile. Little Dirt Pile has three kinds of things to smoke in his

mouth—a pipe, a cigarette and a cigar—and is a rather nasty looking little creature. There were Fred and Tootsie, two close friends of Big Oscar. There was also the Krooked Troll, a hag-like creature with a long curved nose and an unfriendly grim-ace. There was Little Wolfie, a hairy creature who Billy in-dicated looked something like the Lorax, a character of Dr. Seuss fame . . . recently seen in a television show. Billy wanted to know if I had seen this show and we discussed it while he indicated that his favorite character in the show was the Lorax. Finally, at the bottom of the page appears the character who will be called forth to fight the monsters. . . . Super Trash. Super Trash is something of a mess himself for he has a beer can for a head, bear feet for legs, one hand is in the shape of a menacing mace and the other contains a long whip. Thrown over his shoulder is a cape and Billy laughed as he drew the cape and asked if I knew what the cape was made of. He said it was a dirty towel on which someone had gone poop. I then imitated Super Trash, throwing the towel over his shoulders with the poop landing on his clothing and as I brushed the poop away Billy indicated that it was quite a mess. I wondered how Super Trash could fight all these monsters and Billy in-dicated that Super Trash was smart and clever and had great strength in his hands. At this point Billy abruptly broke off the play, looked around the room and wondered why it was we had only pencils and paper and blocks to play with. Why . . . only . . . puzzles and dolls? He explained that he would like to have something else in the room that we might do together. He would like to have a Parcheesi game.

The contents tempt one to interpret many themes, such as Billy's change of topic just when Super Trash gets set to do battle. One could, with much apparent justification, point out how he avoids some inner conflict, or how Super Trash and the monsters all represent the conflicted inner parts of himself. However, the point being made here is that the play is disrupted just when the material becomes too threatening, but that this ought not be viewed simply as a defensive avoidance of the emerging material. Another possible explanation for this disruption of play is that Billy, unable to contain what pushes to emerge, disrupts the play to prevent a further breakdown in functioning that might occur should the play be allowed to continue. This play disruption can be considered to be in the service of acquiring an integrating capa-

city. Unlike Phaeton, Billy has come to "learn" through the therapy that to break off the play, to disengage, is adaptive. This
knowledge and awareness were not always apparent to him. Earlier, in the therapy, the play reached the panic point but was not
disrupted and continued to the disastrous conclusions that he is
now trying to prevent. A portion of a session from the previous
year shows what happened when the play was allowed to continue
beyond the point where the ego could cope.

At this point Billy suggested that we play the game of Hangman. Billy began in the usual way by drawing the gallows for
me and then the steps and having me guess the secret letters
for which there were blank spaces provided. I guessed the first
of these secret messages rather quickly and it read, "He sleeps
in a hamburger." When I puzzled as to how someone slept in
a hamburger, Billy, too, agreed that it was indeed very puzzling, and he, too, could not understand how this was possible.
Next, it was his turn to guess my secret message, which in
time, he did and it read, "Billy and Liebowitz work together."
The next was Billy's turn and he started to arrange the blank
spaces that I would be guessing but in the middle lost track
of what he was thinking about and so had to abandon this
secret which he could no longer recall to himself. It was clear
that he was becoming confused and he seemed unable to make
clear the thoughts of his own mind. Eventually he did place a
series of blank lines upon the page ready for me to guess what
turned out to be a random series of the letters of the alphabet.
When I understood that this was the alphabet arranged out
of order it was easy enough to supply each missing letter.
However, by mistake, I guessed the letter "u" twice so that
when it came time to guess the letter "z" there was no available space for this letter. When I remarked to Billy that he
had written down the letter "u" twice he acknowledged this
adding that this was his original intention. Thus, having committed himself to my error he then arranged the whole situation to appear as if it was under his control. I interpreted this
defensive maneuver to him and Billy sat impassively, making
no verbal comment but obviously becoming upset and dis-
traught. In the interpretation I had made reference to his
being confused and now that he was confronted he became increasingly troubled and upset. He asked if he could guess next
and I put down one blank space and as Billy began to guess
all the letters of the alphabet it was to no avail because the

caricature of the man, the man to be hung, was drawn and then hung upon the gallows. As it became apparent to Billy that the man had been hung, he began to cry. He clutched at his throat as if trying to rip open something that was tightening about his neck and he made the gasping sounds of someone struggling for air. Billy, himself, was now choking to death as the man hung from the gallows. In between the gasping for air, he wanted to know the correct letter that he had not guessed. When I told him it was a letter from the planet of Oosh-kan, a language he had taught me after our trip to this planet some months before, Billy stared at me in disbelief, filled with frustration, overcome with panic, and choking to death. Billy understood and then became more confused. In a series of frantic hangman "games" that followed he had me guess words from the planet of Confusion, "gorch," "prangle," "dizominowitz." These were not the words he intended when he laid out the blank spaces, if indeed he intended any particular words, for no matter what letters I guessed and no matter what order I guessed them in he put down every letter as being correct. There could be no mistake now—all was confusion and, out of disorder, chaos reigned supreme. For the moment Billy had gone over the edge and had no way to get back. He had no way in which he could structure what was emerging and all he could hear and see from the inner space of his mind was confusion, panic, and chaos.

The consequence of letting the play continue beyond the point where Billy could cope with what emerged is evident. Further evidence of the consequence of material emerging before there is structure with which to cope with it comes from a session which took place one month following the session presented above.

Billy proceeded to draw a picture of a monster which had very prominent sharp teeth and ears in peculiar geometric shapes, as he explained to me that this was a monster and that it was a very frightening one. He then shaped the creature into a hand puppet and put it on his hand while he started to make the noises of an angry, roaring monster. I drew back in mock horror and fright. Billy then explained to me as he put the monster aside that he had been taken by his parents over the previous weekend to see two horror movies, "The Frogs," and "Blacula," a black Dracula-like creature. He described first the story of "The Frogs," which he explained takes place in a small town where there is a swamp and people go into the swamp and never come back. The first to enter the swamp is a lady who goes in to collect butterflies, next a man, and so on, with none of the people ever returning. In the one scene that he recalled most vividly, a man goes into the swamp to shoot a big, yellow snake, but as he shoots the snake a bunch of frogs and lizards and "wet, slimy things that people are afraid to touch" come out and cover the man with their bodies. Then the moss comes down from the trees and the slime engulfs the man who suffocates and gets buried "like buried treasure." Billy went on to describe other scenes from the movie and then went on to talk about the film "Blacula." What particularly impressed Billy about this film was that this Dracula-like creature goes about biting people on the neck and thereby turning them into vampires. He spoke about this as very frightening to watch. He spoke about the fear of a kiss that turns into a kiss of death and how people are changed in the process of this contact. Billy then assigned me the puppet roles of Mr. and Mrs. Smith while he took the part of Olevo, a little boy, and the alligator. As the play began the alligator made menacing noises and threatening gestures towards Mr. Smith. Then the alligator devoured Mr. Smith, sucking him through his angry teeth and then evacuating him out the back and then the alligator became Dracula. Dracula went about kissing and biting everyone on the neck and turning each in turn into other Draculas, so that the original Dracula incorporated other Draculas into his legion of armies. Then the furniture became Draculas and then the walls became Draculas and the entire office became a living, enveloping Dracula that moved out into the hallway on its way to creating and then incorporating other Draculas. There was no escape. All within his path was devoured, consumed, and transformed. There was no safe place to hide. The forces of destruction had been unleashed and they were running rampant, out of control, and their own size by the very act of their expression grew into an enormity that was everywhere. And then as the interpretations focused not on the impulse but on the need for some control, for some force to limit this Draculinian beast, Billy broke off the play and turned to a blank sheet of paper on which he then drew some random lines. He then cut out some random shapes and asked me to fit together the pieces of this homemade "jigsaw puzzle."

These examples convey the spirit of what happens when Billy's play is not disrupted and reality is lost as the chaos is allowed to emerge. The examples clarify how play disruption serves an adaptive ego function in Billy's case. Some three months after the session quoted above Billy, himself, seemed to be developing an awareness of the necessity to disrupt the play in order to maintain the self. This beginning awareness is revealed in the following excerpt:

> He turned his attention to the puppets, this time taking Olevo and John and Mr. and Mr. Pandels. Billy played the parts of the Pandels, assigning me the roles of John and Olevo. Again, the play seemed aimless and without apparent direction, the puppets were greeting each other without any more to say as if to say anything would have been inappropriate. Rather, the puppets were assembled on the stage without any script to follow. As if to confirm this Billy then asked if I had brought the script that he had written at our last session and I remarked that I had not, that I had forgotten it thinking he was finished with it. He added, "Well, without the script we can't have a play." He then suggested that we sing some songs which "we know very well."

What would have emerged had the script been there? Whatever it was, it was clear that Billy was beginning to understand that there is something inappropriate about letting out the inner fantasies and impulses without benefit of structure and control.

These clinical examples seem to confirm that the continuation of play under certain conditions is not possible for borderline children because they have no structure available with which to bind the impulse expression should this play continue. Unlike Phaeton, Billy has come to perceive through therapy what he is getting into and rather than go on a trip for which he is ill prepared, he has learned to suspend the journey through a disruption of the play. Without structure and the knowledge of this structure as an integral working part of the self, Billy is left to the mercy of inner forces run rampant. Under these conditions discretion is the better part of valor; Billy has learned not to let loose that which he is not yet able to control. To have confronted him, in whatever way and no matter how gently, with the fact that his play was disrupted to prevent expressing the impulse is, in actuality, to request that he let loose this expression. To interpret to him from the viewpoint of control, that is, that disruption is an adaptive maneuver necessary to maintain a vitally needed control over the impulses, is to acknowledge that this control is needed before impulse expression can be tolerated. Billy's request for the "script" is, in its own way, a request for rules and structure. To push for the expression of the impulse or fantasy and to not allow the movement towards a script (i.e., structure) can only lead to panic, misunderstanding, and the terrifying sense of not being safe.

It is not the freedom of expression that concerns us with Billy and other children with borderline ego states. Rather it is respect for their need for structure, their requirement that a viable psychic organization is necessary and prerequisite before terrifying impulse and fantasy can safely emerge. The interpretive acknowledgement of this situation is often tension-reducing in and of itself. The child with a borderline ego state is all too easily subject to the capricious whims of a labile and fluctuating ego. Panic and confusion are frequently the everyday companions of these children. Impulse reigns supreme and fantasy is often the waking state while reality may exist only as a vaguely perceived shadow at the end of a dimly lit tunnel. The borderline child is already too "loose"; he is unable reliably and consistently to express the fantasies and impulses in a reality-bound fashion. As a way of thinking about the therapeutic position with such children it is suggested that one not push for the child to let go or to express. Rather, the therapist should act as a facilitator, focusing on the importance of control and structure so that when the time is right the inner forces can be safely expressed within this structure.

In considering the question of play disruption, this paper suggests that it may be considered not simply as a defensive maneuver but as an adaptive function of an ego attempting to acquire an integrative capacity. In particular, with the borderline child, respect and consideration must be given to the adaptiveness of the ego's maneuver as it expresses itself in play disruption. One ought never to underestimate the power (and wisdom?) of the ego, particularly in the severely disturbed child where the internal homeostasis is a fleeting labile, and sometimes thing, and where it is often not easy to recognize that the ego may be operating in an adaptive fashion. With the borderline child the disruption of play can serve to maintain the tenuous internal psychic balance so that eventually the ego can express the fantasies and impulses within a structured, controlled setting. To rush in with the therapeutic shibboleth that play disruption represents only a defensive aspect of functioning is to ignore the words of Apollo and listen only to the impulsive impatience of Phaeton. As Billy's case demonstrates, play disruption can be a positive maneuver, necessary to control the violent loss of impulse expression. When the play becomes too "poopy," when the outbreak of anxiety and the fear of destruction become too dangerous, when the inner monsters threaten to take over and devour all, play may be disrupted in order to bind the anxiety and thus the disruption is in the service of ego reconstruction, a necessary archaic defense when no more appropriate one is yet available.

To sum up, we ordinarily view play disruption as a defense to be broken down and given up. In the case of children with borderline ego states, however, we see disruption as a positive aspect necessary in order to give time for structure to develop and to mature. When this structure develops and is experienced the play can, of its own accord, proceed more safely. In fact, the expression of play and the extent to which it is allowed to proceed may be viewed in the case of severely disturbed children as an indication of the adequacy and maturity of the ego's functioning especially in regard to its integrative and synthetic capacity.

BIBLIOGRAPHY

1. BULLFINCH, THOMAS. *The Age of Fable.* London: Springbooks, 1966 (2nd edition).
2. EKSTEIN, RUDOLF. *Children of Time and Space, Action and Impulse.* New York: Appleton-Century-Crofts, 1966.
3. EKSTEIN, RUDOLF. *The Challenge: Despair and Hope in the Conquest of Inner Space.* New York: Brunner/Mazel, 1971.
4. ERIKSON, ERIK H. *Childhood and Society.* New York: W. W. Norton, 1963 (2nd edition).
5. LIEBOWITZ, JOEL M. Story Telling in Search of a Plot. *Reiss-Davis Clin. Bull.,* 1972, 2:112.

Chapter 14

On Self-Prescription of Instant Psychotherapy: Stop, Touch, Take, and Run

BEATRICE COOPER, M.S.

In the treatment of adolescents in different stages of illness, we have begun to make some observations that are consistently borne out: among them is that the condition for treatment, the child's way of maintaining the treatment program, is studded with many cancellations, interruptions, disruptions, and disappearances. We have come to the awareness that the treating professionals, who have a part in re-ordering the lives of these children, have merely ephemeral contact with them.

In some situations a social worker and a therapist individually see adolescents. The psychotherapist focuses on the internal struggle while the social worker focuses on social planning. It is as if the transference condition for such treatment as "presented" by the child is one of "touch and go." Some of our psychotic adolescents create impossible conditions for treatment by telephoning and hour of the night or at the exact time of the appointment, rather than coming to the therapist for the hour. We know that for them "out of sight" does not mean "out of mind"; on the contrary, it frequently means exactly the opposite. They think of us a great deal and expect us to be available immediately or simultaneously as the thought occurs, so that they telephone us, sometimes collect, long distance, any time, any hour, any day, and uncritically assume and presume that we are there for them.

In a previous communication (1), our research team has written about the lack of differentiation within the psychic organization as a phenomenon that is paralleled by the lack of differentiation of psychic structure from the environment. "Consequently, instead of internal conflict, the predominant conflict is seemingly between the patient and the environment which has become the external-ized projection of his opposing impulses. This is why the inner life of these children frequently seems to mirror and to echo, to reflect but not to reflect upon what they have experienced both in the past as well as in their present environment. Their external world seems also to reflect and mirror, to resonate with their inner reality. We may say of these children that they look into reality not to find what there is outside themselves, but rather to find outside themselves what lies within . . . and as the child succeeds in finding or provoking the objects in his outer world to echo the images of his inner world that are the archaic unstable introjects from his past, he thereby confirms the validity of and strengthens his al-legiance to his inner world" (p. 111).

Ekstein has described the specific nature of the anaclitic relation-ships of such children as one like that of squirrels who cannot develop a trusting relationship with human beings other than to accept and to depend upon a certain person as a human being who is there to provide the nut. The squirrel stops, touches the feeding hand, takes the nut, and runs. With our psychotic adoles-cent patients, we know that we must consistently be there to pro-vide the relationship, but they cannot allow themselves to trust, to depend upon, to commit themselves to the concept that we are there in our particular way. Instead, they know we are there as objects for them, but nebulous and distant objects, from whom they require that we are there for them whenever they are willing and ready, no matter what time or how far away they've gone. Terror structures their need to fashion us into make-believe char-acters, whose helping process is disguised by their fear of and need for the helping relationship. They verbally abuse us, demean us, accuse us of pursuing them, and at the same time are terrified when they are away from us. They telephone merely to hear the sound of our voice, to know we are there.

In one such clinical example, no matter who treated thirteen-year-old Dorie, she could not be attached to the therapist. At the same time she longed for the relationship, overcame tremendous physical obstacles in order to get herself to the hour, or to stay away from it. Initially her problems expressed themselves as inability to attend school but soon unfolded a more severe pathology of schizophrenic condition dominated by a negative symbiotic attachment to her mother. Dorie would appear at the clinic bizarrely attired in her mother's outdated, outmoded, discarded clothes, or exhibitionistically flaunting herself in as little as possible, and derisively commenting on the men who had responded to her provocative appearance. Sometimes she would lament that her now obese mother had once been able to wear these attractive articles of clothing which Dorie had rediscovered and unearthed—excavated —as she rummaged through the parents' drawers and closets in a desperate attempt to reconstruct the mother's happier past. From moment to moment her identity changed from fusion with the mother of the past to the present sexually promiscuous young woman. Constantly in flight, she'd run from home and school to hippie hangouts. She'd try to flee the evil forces that pursued her within herself by trying to make that internal-evil fear an external environment where she could project such impulses. She'd distance herself from ongoing therapy and attach herself for brief periods to Jesus freaks, heroin addicts, artists, writers, superficially experiencing the terror and glamour associated with such people. Living vicariously, and sometimes not so vicariously, in their degeneracy, she'd telephone the social worker and/or the therapist* to share the exploit of the moment.

Dominated by the fear of police persecution when she had, with her parents' permission, gone to a hippie community in Northern California, she had briefly attached herself to one commune after another. Once she telephoned the social worker, collect, to share the experience in which she had miraculously been rescued from

---

* Elaine Caruth, Ph.D., to whom we are grateful for the use of some of her material.

danger by the police whom she successfully convinced she was eighteen to avoid being treated by them as a runaway. By means of the telephone, she re-attached herself to the social worker to whom she appealed for help in getting from the parents a written statement giving her their permission to travel on her own though she was only fifteen and a-half. She also wanted the social worker to know that she had telephoned the parents and that they would be especially pleased if the social worker called them. In whatever way she could, she was constantly trying to maintain her distance, her separation, her separateness, from the helping person. At the same time she used the police rescue, the social worker's intercession, the parents' permission to travel, simultaneously seeking and denying the protection of the authority figures.

In the process of working with this adolescent, the therapeutic team frequently questioned how to proceed in such treatment conditions. Dorie required equidistance on the epigenetic scheme of anaclitic relationships, a kind of touch-and-go treatment process. In time we could perhaps develop it into a more appropriate helping relationship, but there was also the possibility of the development of a kind of chronic transference condition that could never lead to a genuine helping relationship. Dorie's particular style for survival had adaptive functioning in maintaining her psychotic psychic life. She had to keep a distance from us no matter who we were, Jesus freak, therapist, parent, teacher, police. Her touch-and-go style could be understood in terms of a stage in her growth and development. Coming together with us, the touching, as it were, was represented as possibly providing fuller gratification. But we were left with the unanswered problem of whether this would be useful enough for her so that, in time, the inner terror that drove her away would enable her to come back and trust. We did come to understand that she used the social worker somehow to get confirmation both that she could return to her family and receive the medical care she needed from to time to ensure her mental and physical well-being. But our need was to be able to reach her: we wanted to communicate with her that long-term intensive treatment was necessary and could be reliable. Her use of our professional selves perplexed and challenged us. It was as if she could only deal with a fragmented mothering-helping process. She could make us into an appeal-mother who provided instant gratification, but not a fulfilling, orally gratifying mother. She made us demanding mothers who relied on external structures, expected her to come for appointment times, imposed a kind of discipline that she had to resist and struggle against. Whenever she became almost trusting and seemed about to participate in an ongoing treatment situation, she would make us into incest-taboo mothers who stirred up her instinctual fears, her impulses, her fear of developing lesbian transference relationships from which she had to escape.

Painfully slowly we came to recognize that in running away from the object she could experience a sense of differentiation between self and object. She organized herself around running away from the object who, she felt, wanted to engulf or fuse with her, which would result in her loss of separation of self and object. In forcing herself to run away, she could separate in order to return to us.

Dorie insisted that she could not maintain ongoing therapeutic appointments with people who were paid to listen. She tried other alternatives: speaking with strangers whom she met on the street, faceless voices whom she would contact on "Help Line." At the same time, she recognized that when she thought she was getting too close to any one person she chose another option. From time to time she was able to use the social worker as someone from whom to run away; without that, she feared she might slip away entirely and return to the earlier deep depression which terrified her. Her rationale was that she had to move away the intensive therapeutic relation in order to maintain an independent position. We could accept her verbalized efforts to do things on her own even while recognizing that she was powerless to do so.

The social worker had to drift with her, meeting her on her terms outside the clinic and refuting her pathetic, provocative attempts to get us to give up on her. She would snarl her disgust with our allowing her to put us in this "humiliating" position. We consistently maintained the role of having the stamina, the inner strength, to meet her under any conditions. In a subtle way she began to identify with some of our values. She clarified certain concerns she had about her physiological condition, and referring critically to the way she "used" us, wondered if she was denigrating and wiping us out. Throughout these interactions, psychotic material emerged. Her fear of bugs devouring her if they bit her; her fear of fusing with us; her hallucinations both auditory and visual; and an outpouring of voluminous poetry which revealed the psychotic thought disorder but always concluded with the element of hope and faith that "maybe you will find that it can be what you make it and happy sometimes and be reborn again." These interactions communicated her acceptance of her illness as long as she could maintain some hope through her peripatetic hold onto the clinic program. But the hope was based on pessimism; it was an alibi, a form of ego passivity rather than ego activity.

She terminated her ongoing relationship with us at the point in which she was able to take private driving lessons and pass the driver's test. She did that not to drive an automobile since there was none at her disposal, but so that she could have a driver's license, an identity. She made much of the driver's license as filling the need to have concrete evidence of her identity. In the same hour, she was able to thank the social worker for talking to her at all hours of the night and to indicate her beginning awareness that perhaps it had not been appropriate to phone whenever she felt like it. "Her entire attitude today was one in which she was forcing herself to cope with herself, her limitations, her craziness. At the end of the hour commenting on how the social worker had changed, Dorie felt improved so that now she could split from Southern California, return to Northern California where she felt the new self, the more successful adaptation, was possible." In previous hours the contact with this young adolescent had been mainly a monologue in which she had held forth in diatribic, avaracious attack on the lack of helpfulness in the relationship. Towards the end of the treatment period she allowed for a beginning dialogue. There had been some sharing of her deep anguish in causing suffering both within herself and her family situation and of her incipient awareness of her sexual feelings towards the female social worker, which were related to her fleeing the original therapist, a woman psychologist.

We have the feeling that there is something not understood about the treatment process with such adolescent patients who experience us as not very useful when they are with us but quite useful when they are away from and yearning for us. In spite of all our best efforts to work with them, they cannot hold on to us. On a lower level of psychotic functioning, a more psychotic boy, Robby, aged nineteen, could not hold on even to the thought that we would remain with him. He would ask repeatedly, "Do you have faith that I will make it?" (2).

With this more overtly psychotic patient the assumption is that the first random communication system between the mother and child is never successfully organized and learned. He is never gratified, so that he hardly ever achieves a reliable responsible object. Regardless of what one offers him, it is not experienced as a satisfying, lasting enduring object. He chews up therapists like external objects, excretes us, and/or on a higher level, like Dorie, makes us persecutory objects from whom he must escape. At the same time, we serve as peripheral external organizing objects for him. Friedman (2) has described how Robby reached his adolescent stage without having already achieved stable self- and object-differentiation, individuation, and constancy. "His personality and psychic organization, primitive, fused, fragmented, are only weakly and tenuously integrated. For him the adolescent process becomes a ceaseless struggle between the omnipotent and omni-impotent, between the all-powerful and the abysmally helpless perception and experience of his archaic self on the most primitive, symbiotic level. In his desperate striving to avert fusion with the omnipotent object, he undergoes this terrifying struggle between devouring and being devoured, between destroying or undergoing dissolution by the object. He longs unendingly for the impossible attainment of self and identity as the culmination of his adolescent crisis, but its outcome continuously remains suspended and undetermined" (p. 96).

Robby creates a deanimated state of endlessness, while Dorie creates God in her image, in order to develop a sense of self and object. She creates a symbiosis, then struggles to get away from it in order to feel alive, really separate. Robby attempts to create the symbiosis but his God exists only to make demands upon him. He comes to treatment to be saved, to be protected, and to be fused. What can we create so that the therapist,* the supplier, can

---

* Seymour Friedman, M.D.

be experienced as a separate, independent existence? We have developed a program, a way of working to maintain such a child in treatment. In order to get the supplier, the therapist, to give, he must meet the conditions of the structure, the therapeutic environment. He escapes into psychosis; regresses to become more helpless in an attempt to get away from the symbiosis with the therapist. Robby reaches out repeatedly for what he cannot use except to struggle against. As long as he demands, he feels he exists. He has only the appeal function to reach the object, the therapist. Obviously, in gratifying him, in granting him his appeal, the object can never satisfy him. Robby can never hold on to him. He manages to create situations that require his return to a state hospital where he experiences being cared for, with little or no demand. But paradoxically, he responds positively to the demands of the state hospital in order to be discharged, in order to return to the object, the therapist, on an outpatient basis.

Prior to the hospitalization, his behavior was wildly bizarre, fragmented, and intolerable; he was protesting how impossible it was for him to meet the demands of the outside, the free world. His recurrent theme was, "What do you think will happen to me?" The meaningful people in his life were saying, "You need a state hospital because it is best for you." His pathetic appeal to his mother, "Can't you do anything about it?" was seen as his attempt to separate from her. Driven by the impulse to become an active self, he could not control the impulses. He thus created the feeling of omnipotence that he had made this happen. He became active in order to fight the fear of becoming passive. If he met the conditions of the treatment outside, he fought the sense of helplessness that overpowered him, thus triumphing over the subject, the therapist, whom he saw as pushing him to grow, to change. He regressed in this reverse way to master the sense of helplessness and forced upon the self and us the hospitalization, thus removing himself from the symbiosis with the therapist.

Whenever Robby was threatened by the loss of one board-and-care situation, he would explore other community resources in such a way as to make himself totally unacceptable; consequently, exploration became destruction. He was driven to repeat his history of the loss of good helping people whom he had experienced

178 In Search of Love and Competence

as meaningful but who would eventually have to "give up on him."
He felt that he made them disappear so that the bad Robby could
survive, a classic illustration of *the divided self*. It required the
collective efforts and strengths of the parents, the clinical team,
vocational workshop, board-and-care home, just to maintain him
each day. While all strove to achieve this, he was determined to
regress to the former sicker self.

The interplay was a strange kind of love-making. He would, for
example, say to the social worker after a tiring hour in which he
would force the issue of conditions necessary for him to be maintained outside of a hospital, "Good, that's good. You will make me
go to work so that I will grow stronger." At times he would squeal
with delight when the social worker would become firm: "You're
meaner and crueler than Dr. Friedman." At such times it became
apparent that he needed the social worker as a persecutory object.
When we would make it clear that we would have no part in his
pushing for hospitalization where he felt he would have everything
he wanted, no pressures, the right to die and be the bad Robby,
he would complain about how demanding the current situation
was. We would recognize that he needed to experience the outside
world as bad, as dangerous, in order for the bad Robby to co-exist
with the ever-growing, healthier Robby. Then he would review the
history of his losses of good people whom he now longed for. He
would cry at his fate in having been stuck with the persistent social
worker and analyst. Now they were the ones whom he had to experience as mean and cruel and bad just as in the past the people
whom he now experienced as the lost, good, helpful ones had been
experienced as his villains. But at the same time he knew that we
understood this was the nature of his illness. As well as he could,
he understood that we would not desert him; that he could not get
us to give up on him; that we could accept he was desperately ill
and therefore needed to experience us as mean and cruel. As long
as we knew who we were, he could not be powerful enough to hurt
us with his accusations. He would ask repeatedly if he could cause
anything bad to happen to us. When he realized that whatever
happened to us was determined by circumstances outside of his
control, he would be relieved. At the point of ending a session, he
would cling desperately to us, repeatedly asking one more question.

When he finally managed to bring about his hospitalization, he wondered whether we could cry. The social worker tried to make him understand that we would feel sad that the sick Robby had no faith that we could make it with him.

For three months we did not hear the anguished sounds of Robby's wailing as he would search the halls of the clinic crying, "Where are you, Mrs. Cooper?" or "Where are you, Dr. Friedman?" During the brief hospitalization, he held on by letter and telephone call in order to return to us.

The complex nature of the conditions necessary for maintaining the treatment process for some adolescent psychotics is partially illustrated by the behavior of Dorie and Robby. The development of a sense of self in such young people is often characterized by a thin and unstable line of contact. The "touch-and-run prescriptions" of these patients must be utilized to the fullest by the therapist to develop further treatment capacity.

BIBLIOGRAPHY

1. EKSTEIN, RUDOLF, SEYMOUR FRIEDMAN, ELAINE CARUTH and BEATRICE COOPER. Reflections on the Need for a Working Alliance with Environmental Support System. *Reiss-Davis Clin. Bull.*, 1969, 2:111.
2. EKSTEIN, RUDOLF, and FRIEDMAN, SEYMOUR. Do You Have Faith That I'll Make It? *Reiss-Davis Clin. Bull.*, 1971, 2:94.

Chapter 15

The Flawed Hammer

KENNETH RUBIN, M.D.

Some considerations from the treatment of a borderline psychotic little boy, Nick, born with an enlarged right hand and arm, apparently due to faulty lymphatic drainage, shall be presented. Special focus shall be made of the unconscious meanings of the big hand which caused the boy to react to it as being at one and the same time uncontrollable/omnipotent/destructive, and vulnerable/weak/helpless/destroyed.

Alfred Adler suggested (1) that possession of a defective organ could be reacted to by an individual by spurring him on to compensate or overcompensate for the resulting feelings of inferiority. He means to imply by this that the defective organ could act as a psychic organizer for that individual, around which the psychic apparatus could react and respond. In the child under consideration here, the defective organ indeed acted as a kind of psychotic organizer, since he had a psychic organization contaminated by psychotic processes, in the special ways that shall be described. But in this case there was the marked duality of reaction in which the deformed organ was viewed not just as inferior and weak but simultaneously as all-powerful.

Lussier has reported on the case of a boy, Peter, born with congenitally short arms (6). This boy, born with an apparent better ego endowment than my patient, reacted to his infirmity in more normal intrapsychic ways. For him the deformity acted as a psychic organizer that spurred him to activity, not just defensively applied, instead of passive masochism and self-pity. Castration anxiety, greatly heightened by the real deformity, was predominant. The use of fantasy as a prelude to actual accomplishments, just as denial, was an interesting feature.

Nick was five years and a few months old when he was brought to the Center. Nick was living with his mother; the parents had been divorced when he was 15 months old. The mother reported Nick's problems as difficulty in going to sleep, temper tantrums, rebellious behavior, and unresponsiveness to her attempts at discipline. However, the mother sought help mainly as preparation for hand surgery planned in a few months. She took the deformity itself, as did the child, as the cause of all his problems. The mother first became aware of Nick's problems when he was two. She had returned to work as a secretary when the child was 21 months old. Nick, enrolled in a nursery school, began resisting going to bed, verbalized anger toward the mother as well as kicking, biting, and hitting her. He showed considerable problems in adjustment in nursery school. He behaved in a rebellious manner by disregarding rules and, at the same time, in an infantile, dependent way. He was very sensitive about his big hand and complained that the other children called him "fat hand."

Evaluation revealed a borderline-psychotic child, still psychologically placed in a pre-separation-individuation, symbiotic relationship with his mother. There was a thought disorder of moderate degree. Intensive analytic-type treatment was recommended.

Treatment began, three times a week, when Nick was five years, nine months old. The mother was started in casework at the same time Nick presented his main problem in the first meeting with the therapist. Casually he held up his big hand in order to show and complain about a hangnail on the little finger. Thus began the theme which emerged over the years of treatment, in which his problem was presented in terms of a conflict between feelings of utter helplessness and utter omnipotence, as though the two extremes could not in any way be integrated or maintained together.

The therapist's description of Nick's large hand, two-and-a-half times normal size, is of interest in this regard. He originally described it as "a large, puffy hand, with fingers tapered down to normal size at the nails, like a boxing glove with separate tapered fingers." The therapist unconsciously recognized the omnipotent half of the meanings the big hand had for the little boy. The whole arm was somewhat fatter and longer than normal but overshadowed by the prominence of the hand.

In the first hour Nick elaborated his feelings about the simultaneous strength and weakness of his big hand. He drew a picture of a huge Brontosaurus. He described it as big but vulnerable inasmuch as it served as meat for Tyrannosaurus. In the background he drew a volcano, which was quiet at first and then erupted violently. He drew a cross, which he said was a German cross. This was the first hint of what was to develop as a strong identification with the aggressor.

Nick first presented these themes via a book about dinosaurs that he brought with him. In the twelfth hour Nick asked the therapist to draw a dinosaur, especially the skeleton, as shown in the book. The request quickly became a command that the therapist draw. This was the first acknowledgment on Nick's part of a feeling of helplessness in regard to the powerful forces that he struggled with, that he had an illness and he needed help with it. But the way the plea was couched he sounded as though he were an imperious potentate in complete command of the situation. Thus, the demand that the therapist draw contained the plea that the therapist master Nick's chaotic inner conflicts but in a context of Nick being in complete control. It was like Genghis Khan ordering his court physician to cure him. But Genghis controlled, prescribed, and supervised every move of the physician; held a sword over the physician's head, and indicated that death would reward any error. The physician clearly was seen as a mere extension of Genghis Khan. In this way another aspect of Nick's simultaneous omnipotent/helpless feeling was revealed, referred to the psychic representation of his self, which within the symbiosis was a self-object fusion. The Genghis Khan attitude was like a psychotic version of turning passivity into activity in the attempt to master anxiety.

In the next few months of treatment, Nick continued unfolding the picture, mainly of unbridled power. The vehicle for this was preoccupation with such things as huge dinosaurs. Tyrannosaurus was a favorite, stressing the primitive oral aggressive features in which the omnipotence was displayed at this time. The other side of the coin was shown from time to time as a dinosaur such as Brontosaurus which was depicted as large but clumsy and slow and so likely to fall victim to Tyrannosaurus. Along with the dinosarus, volcanoes became a favorite symbol of uncontrollable force.

The oral aggressive aspect of the omnipotent half of Nick's feelings was shown also in his fascination with the Flying Tiger P-40 planes of early World War II. These were decorated by large sharklike open jaws over the whole nose of the plane. Nick ordered them drawn or drew them himself, endlessly. Later on the same decoration was added to German planes as these attained the mantle of power.

Focus on the large hand itself was forced into the open because surgery had been planned on the hand before Nick had begun treatment. An attempt was to be made to reduce the size of the hand by removing some of the presumed inner spongy tissue. At the time there was insufficient leverage with the mother to modify the plans. Surgery had been set for a time four months after treatment began.

At the last minute surgery was postponed two weeks because Nick had a cold. In the hour after the postponement Nick drew a picture of a volcano. The volcano began to erupt. The fiery fingers of lava flowing down the mountain side were drawn in the exact image of the thumb and four fingers of a monster hand. It was as though Nick had hoped the surgery would remove his big hand, cure his uncontrollable, powerful, destructive self. With the postponement of surgery came the fear of uncontrolled, internal eruptions.

Two weeks later, at the age of six years, one month, the first surgery was performed, on the fourth finger, to test the results. Nick was in the hospital over a week end. A plaster cast on the finger and part of the forearm was in place for several weeks. On the surface Nick took the procedure quite calmly. But underneath he seethed. He became very touchy in school where frustration tolerance and impulse control always had been poor. He was in the first grade of a public school, with the usual large class. Nick became harder to handle. Finally, one day two months after surgery, apparently provoked by some confrontation with his teacher that made him feel helpless, Nick went wild, kicked his desk until it broke, attacked and kicked both the teacher and the principal. The two of them reacted with real fear, as though Nick were an uncontrollable monster. The next day in his therapy hour Nick drew a picture of Moby Dick, pin-cushioned with harpoons, enraged, vengeful, and at bay.

This rage reaction was like a psychotic version of identification with the aggressor, mother/teacher, as a necessary escape from the terrible feeling of helplessness at being overwhelmed by the symbiotic object. In this rage reaction and in other material from this period, Nick showed his reaction to the operated-on-hand-in-the-cast as the epitome of both damaged helplessness and a powerful, uncontrollable weapon.

One month later the second hand surgery, on the next three fingers, was performed, the first surgery having shown initial promising results. This time the cast was left on only three weeks. Nevertheless, Nick was even more terrified of the cast as the embodiment of a terrible weapon. He vacillated in his therapy hours and in school between maintaining a position of omnipotent control and one of utter helplessness.

In his therapy hours during this period Nick generally ordered the therapist to make drawings. Often these were of large World War II bombing planes. Their power was measured by the number of guns they bristled with. But their weakness showed through in Nick's uneasiness about the plexiglass nose cones. Though guns shot out through these bulges on the end of the plane, Nick pointed out that nonetheless enemy shells could penetrate through the exposed protuberance. This became the current expression of the imnipotent/vulnerable duality of feelings about his hand. Another expression of this theme was indicated by Nick's fascination with the Titanic, the mighty impregnable ship that nevertheless sank. Once he even drew the shark-mouth decoration on the prow of the Titanic, to enhance its impregnable strength.

For a long time Nick was very touchy about the drawings the therapist made at command. They had to be perfect in his eyes. He was especially intolerant of any line or portion of the drawing that seemed too thick or fat, as he called it, in obvious unconscious equation with his hand. Such drawings had to be thrown out instantly. Sometimes it was impossible to complete a drawing. Once Nick remarked about an allegedly thick line, "Can't you see it's going to blow up?" as he fearfully threw the drawing away.

As time went on it became apparent that the surgery was a failure. The fingers gradually resumed their former swollen appearance. Nick began to berate the therapist more and more for not being able to make the drawings come out right or to fix them. He was often irritable, critical, and unable to be consoled by anything.

In school, Nick's tendency to be triggered to rage attacks continued. Finally, five months after the second hand surgery, he had yet another explosion at school and was expelled for good. For the first time, Nick's father was called to the school during the episode. As the father tried to reassure him after talking to the teachers, Nick attacked him viciously and tried to choke him. The father reportedly was able to maintain a supportive attitude. However, Nick refused to come to the next two therapy appointments after this. He verbalized to the mother the fear that the father and doctor would be very angry with him and he clearly feared retaliation. The therapist spoke to Nick by telephone at this time.

On the third scheduled hour, the day he was to go for an interview to a new, private school, Nick came to the office, bringing a big book of the fighting ships of the world. He opened up to a double-page that showed a battle between British men-of-war and the Spanish Armada. The scene was very colorful and confusing. All the cannons were shooting. The right half of the picture was obscured by a big explosion, as though one of the ships had blown up. Nick's eyes were round with fascination as the drawing, better than any words, described his confusion over the fusion of self and object representation in the idea of the ship that simultaneously destroys and is destroyed. Later this same hour Nick announced he was going to draw the Titanic, "but not the one that was sunk by the iceberg; the way it was before," thus skipping over the vulnerable time and going back to the previous invincible one, as he hoped would happen in going to a new school. Nick looked through the book and pointed out ships that had one more smokestack than the Titanic or that were bigger than the Titanic. Nick was accepted into the private school and attended there profitably over the next year-and-a-half.

This school, with its smaller classes and more individual attention, was very helpful for Nick. He was better able to pay attention, and learning forged ahead. Further surgical intervention to produce a more normal-looking hand was abandoned, as it was apparent it was ineffective.

Over the next many months. Nick struggled with the awareness that his hand could not be fixed. Sometimes he reacted with despair at the conviction that his situation was hopeless, that he was doomed to be the way he was, internally as well as externally. But, in the course of therapy, as the symbiotic position was slowly given up, and especially, as ego structure and function grew, Nick could begin to deal more realistically internally with the reactions to his big hand. The need to be in absolute control of everything abated. He could express feelings of not knowing everything. He could allow and even insist that the therapist could do some things better than he. He could admit not being able to do some things at all. At first the expression of inadequacies represented the helpless side of the symbiotic omnipotent/helpless struggle. But gradually the awareness of "not being able to" stemmed from a more realistic appraisal of his capacities. He was, after all, a child.

Best of all, Nick became able at times to accept help from others and alter his way of doing things. This was shown graphically in drawings as he became a more sophisticated and talented artist, acknowledging what his teacher had taught him. Similarly in therapy he could take in more of what the therapist said. At present writing, Nick has completed four years of treatment and displays much more normal ego functioning.

Thus, from the first meeting with the therapist, Nick presented the important unconscious meanings of his big hand, which he felt as simultaneously uncontrollable/powerful/omnipotent/destructive and vulnerable/weak/castrated/helpless. Mainly, the hand stood for the psychic representation of the self. But since the child was in a state of psychic fusion with his mother when he entered treatment, it was the representation of the self object. Separation-individuation was very incomplete. Nick's object, the mother, herself displaying simultaneous feeling of strength and helplessness, added to Nick's feelings in this regard in his primitive and pre-identificatory processes. The hand also represented a manifestation of the functioning of the ego. For instance, insufficient impulse control allowed outbursts of violent and omnipotent behavior, which were a kind of strength but at the same time frightening to Nick. In a similar way, all the ego mechanisms of defense were unable sufficiently to contain impulses in the beginning, resulting in a feeling of inner weakness. The poor synthesizing and integrating capacities of the ego contributed to feelings of inner chaos and helplessness. And above all, the symbiotic position itself, in which he was stuck, felt at one and the same time all-powerful, as he fused with the object, and all-weak, as he was threatened by engulfment and loss of the self in the fusion.

In addition, the flawed hand was reacted to intrapsychically as a quasifetish, or better, a quasi-transitional object/fetish. Ekstein and Friedman have written (2) about a case of a psychotic little boy, Robby, who dismantled and hoarded doorknobs. These doorknobs represented for the child a quasi-fetish. They stood for parts of the mother that he tried to maintain. The doorknobs functioned not only to replace the absent love object but to secure narcissistic cathexis to help maintain his body image and sustain his precarious sense of identity.

Furer has written about (3) the case of a little psychotic boy, Malcolm, whose investment in an inanimate object, which he calls a "psychotic fetish" heralded a better prognosis for psychic growth in treatment. This child moved from an autistic world into a transitional world. The first link was an attachment to the corners of inanimate objects. Later in this child's mind his own feces, which he retained, took on the characteristics of transitional objects. The feces became the focus of the libidinal and aggressive cathexis of poorly differentiated images of self and object; at the same time, they indicated the beginning formation of this differentiation. The feces acquired importance, according to Furer, because of the increasing libidinal cathexis. The boy retained his feces as an attempt to prevent their loss by destruction; the overwhelming by aggressive cathexis leading to the loss of this beginning representation of both self and object.

I believe that the propensity to psychotic fetish formation is enhanced by the capacity to deanimate the psychic representation of human objects and animate the psychic representation of deanimate objects. This is a capacity that Furer's case and my own possessed to a marked degree, as do all borderline and psychotic children.

In two recent papers Greenacre has written about the relationship of the fetish to the transitional object (4, 5). She reviews Winnicott's original paper (7). The transitional object a normal device, born of a relationship to a good-enough mother, containing elements of both the object and the self, allows the infant, starting from the position of symbiotic attachment to the mother, to move to the position of secured individuation. The transitional object serves as a bridge between that which is comfortably familiar and that which is disturbingly unfamiliar while it facilitates the acceptance of the unfamiliar. Greenacre contrasts this with the fetish, arising from a reaction to a not-good-enough mother, a patch that covers up something that is disturbed in the relationship. An abnormal device, it, nevertheless, allows the individual to continue his psychic development. She further points out that the child's own body parts, hands, fingers, toes, lips, and tongue may be used in a playful way in the beginning, as a forerunner of toys, just as a transitional object may be used.

My patient, Nick, could figuratively hold up his big hand and think to himself, "Behold my fist, my powerful self, my intact self; or, is it my weak, incomplete, damaged self? Or is it Mother? Is it the Hammer of Thor? No, it is an albatross around my neck." All this as he moved along the treacherous road toward individuation. Thus, for Nick, the flawed hand represented simultaneously a helpful/hindering fetish and a protective/unprotective transitional object that aids/detracts from the illusion of intactness that is to be maintained.

BIBLIOGRAPHY

1. ADLER, ALFRED. *The Individual Psychology of Alfred Adler.* Heinz L. and Rowena R. Ansbacher, eds. London: George Allen & Unwin Ltd., 1958.
2. EKSTEIN, RUDOLF, and SEYMOUR W. FRIEDMAN. The Meaning of Play in Childhood Psychosis. *Children of Time and Space, of Action and Impulse.* New York: Appleton-Century-Crofts, 1966.

3. FURER, MANUEL. The Development of a Preschool Symbiotic Psychotic Boy. *Psychoanalyt. Study of the Child,* 1964, XIX:448.
4. GREENACRE, PHYLLIS. The Fetish and the Transitional Object. *Psychoanalyt. Study of the Child,* 1969, XXIV:144.
5. GREENACRE, PHYLLIS. The Transitional Object and the Fetish with Special Reference to the Role of Illusion. *Int. J. Psycho-Anal.,* 1970, 51:447.
6. LUSSIER, ANDRE. The Analysis of a Boy with a Congenital Deformity. *Psychoanalyt. Study of the Child,* 1960, XV:430.
7. WINNICOTT, D. W. Transitional Object and Transitional Phenomena. *Collected Papers.* New York: Basic Books, 1958.

Chapter 16

The Flawed Triangle

BEATRICE COOPER, M.S.

Nick's divorced mother came into treatment because of her son. Skillful at initiating relationships with people, she nevertheless always found herself home alone on New Year's Eve. As a condition for mothering, she required a transient lover. Using her body as barter for services, she could not identify with her own mother or her sister whom she envied and regarded as competent females. Instead, she felt she was more like her father, in both her actions and her selfishness. She had once had a handsome lover with a withered arm who had deserted her. Ever since she had feared dependence on this kind of unreliable "love" since "once you knew what it was like to have it, you were vulnerable because you needed it and you might lose it." She acknowledged that Nick's father had helped her transform herself through plastic surgery, contact lenses, and dyed hair, from an ugly woman into a glamour girl who could attract anyone. Nevertheless, she vowed never to become involved with handsome men because they could easily be stolen away by women who would find themselves attracted. She reluctantly described how she never reached an orgasm, just needed a man around during the lonesome evenings. These relationships required that the child, Nick, overlook the man's very presence. After about a year of weekly sessions, she continued to discuss her difficulty in maintaining the relationship with each current lover. She still expected Nick to overlook each man's presence and to remain unaware of the nature of the relationship. It is as if she had given the child an injunction, a demand to repress what he had obviously seen many times.

Nick had trouble getting to bed in the evening, so he usually could be counted on to sleep late in the morning, just enabling the lover to slip away before the child awoke. One particular day, Nick had wet his bed, an unusual occurrence. He had awakened early in the morning and had come to his mother. He observed her exposed naked shoulders in bed alongside a boy friend, who was sound asleep, as he plaintively complained about the wet bed. Flustered, she gently put her arms around him, and return him to his bed. At that moment he didn't seem to perceive the sleeping lover or to ask any questions, but throughout the day, she noticed that the boy was sensitive, easily moved to tears, irritable. In the evening, he said belligerently, "You tell Joe to leave"; somewhat later, he asked, "How come some people sleep naked?"

That night Nick wanted to sleep in bed with his mother, which she allowed him to do. When he fell asleep she gently moved him back to his own bed. The following day he again wanted to return to her bed. When she refused, he cried and hugged and clung to her, but they seem to have handled the situation satisfactorily. At her next appointment, however, she defensively and angrily demanded that we help her maintain both the lover and the child without hurting either. She couldn't see her lover staying away because of some six-year-old kid. She thought Joe was fabulous—he was cuddly, he was perfect. He was the first man with whom she had experienced orgasm. This led her to being able to allow herself to reffect on the gamut of feelings that she has in relation to her child's temper tantrums and mood swings. The rest of the week had been horrendous. Nick had a temper tantrum because there was no ice cream and the mother had reminded him that they had consumed the ice cream the day before, all three of them—she, the lover, and he. Nick became furious. He wanted the part the lover had eaten. He started to rage at her. She explained that it was impossible for her to give him the ice cream that Joe had consumed, that she would be glad to buy additional ice cream. Nick didn't want this; he wanted what Joe had consumed.

I tried to help her understand what the child was communicating to her, his difficulty in sharing her with another lover, one who was not available to him, and even consumed the little that was available to him. I tried to help her understand that if the man could exist for the child this might, perhaps, relieve some of the tensions. I explained this was possibly why she had such difficulty in getting Nick to bed, why he insisted on going to bed with her. She demonstrated how Nick screams, "I'm going to have nightmares! The only way I can go to sleep without them is to have you!" It is as if he knew he would need the loving mother instead of being visited in his dream life by the angry mother of the night. She realized that if she permitted this she'd be prevented from sleeping with her lover, who would have to leave and might not come back at all, or might be put out by having to return in the middle of the night.

One astounding thing to her was that all of her relatives and friends knew about her relationship with the lover and approved of him. They advised that she punish the child, place him if necessary. But she, because of our working together, knew that this would be ineffective and even harmful for Nick. He did not need to be disciplined, he needed to be understood. She questioned whether it was possible for a six-year-old to be cognizant of her relationship with her lover. She also wondered if Nick saw Joe as not providing anything directly for him, an experience typical of his relationship with his actual father—who provided legalized and then illegalized neglect. She told me she felt as if Nick never wants her to have a choice in anything—from a choice between two television programs, between Joe and himself, between work and motherhood. She sees Nick as constantly intruding, preventing her from getting her work done or maintaining a relationship with anyone but him. At one time he was so disruptive, slamming doors, that she hurt her finger, though this was not directly caused by him. He shouted, "I didn't do it; it was all your fault."

At times she told me that she would like to record what goes on at home so that the child's therapist* and I could better understand what goes on and see how things reach the point when Nick and she both become hysterical. Whenever I ask her to reflect on

---

* Kenneth Rubin, M.D. See "The Flawed Hammer," Ch. 15.

what causes the hysteria, what we always come to is Nick's fear that she will leave him, that she will choose work, lover, anything instead of him. All he has is she. She is his only constant love object. In sharing with her so many intruders and intrusions—loves, work—he has constantly to compete with some third person for her affection. As much as she loves Nick, she has repeatedly admitted how difficult it is for her to be alone with him. She always has to get involved with a third person. She married because she had become pregnant with Nick, and it was soon apparent that she would never be able to maintain the marriage. By the time Nick was two, she had had one lover who had really loved and cared for her intensely, but because of Nick, the relationship had ended. The lover with the withered arm could not tolerate to look at her child who had an enlarged hand—the triangle was unacceptably full of flaws. She projected onto Nick the power to destroy any opportunity for mature happiness and she also saw him as blackmailing her with the possibility that he might tell his father about her lover, causing her loss of custody. The husband still wanted to have a post-marital affair with her.

She began to see that the bedtime problems came because. Nick sensed she was trying to get rid of him in favor of some lover. He created difficulties to prevent sharing her with another person. I tried to indicate that if the lover were really available to him as a person, Nick would not feel so competitive. This became a focal point for our ongoing work, in the course of which she acquired a permanent lover, a man with whom she could perhaps sustain a marital relationship. This man became available to Nick as a friend; a father-figure who helped him with his school work, helped him develop co-ordination enough to participate in Little League as a star pitcher—the flawed organ had become now an expert hand—and supplied information to answer Nick's curiosity about sex.

The basic insight I wished to open up was that, out of desperate need, she constantly created a destructive hopeless triangle. I stressed the non-solution aspect rather than getting lost in the moral judgments that she wished to impose on me during the developing transference. Could she slowly see that a triangle situation could become functional and helpful? The therapeutic team developed a strategy by means of which she might have some kind of hope that there could be a stabilization of object love and self-esteem. For this, that third person was immensely important. Could there be a mature object love instead of mere primitive mothering? How could a therapeutic situation be created so that Nick, even though he would regress, could be sustained by his mother? The boy saw her as someone who must separate and keep apart father-figure and son so that they wouldn't kill each other. Her attitude tended to re-inforce and re-create this kind of repetitive triangular battle situation. She experienced the child as an omnipotent raging monster who destroys even the school situation. She was helped to accept temporarily his anxiety outbursts. The support system was structured so as to prevent and/or handle the rages. The teacher and the special school, confronted with a raging child, did not know, of course, that the child saw the mother sleeping with the lover. However, we wanted to permit a differentiation of objects to exist for the child. If the teacher were to know everything that the therapist knew, we would be maintaining an artificial intimacy, not allowing for differentiation of function and autonomy of individual helpers. In a support system the material does not have to be totally shared because differentiation of helpers' functions is basic. If everyone knew all that took place, we would create a dream world surrounded by a quasi-symbiotic sac, catering to the omnipotence of the illness where undifferentiated objects would fuse. In this collaborative effort, we meet the transference conditions by maintaining a consistent attitude.

Thus, in working with Nick's mother, the dilemma seemed to be that she experienced an irreconcilable dichotomy between being a mother and being a woman. She felt herself to be either a woman with a child, unable to have a mature companion, or as a woman with a lover, unable to have a child. Normally, the total woman has a variety of roles simultaneously, and interprets them. For this mother it was as if the different character fragments had no relation to each other; she lacked a core identity, the synthetic function. She gave the impression of being fragmented and probably, in part unconsciously, presented herself this way in therapy. Although she presented helplessness as a transference position, she appeared quite capable of handling situations outside the home.

The therapeutic task was to help her have the capacity to maintain a stability where formerly there seemed to be little or no structure. She felt that in order to love her child, she herself must be loved by a fatherly man, be someone else's child. Her difficulty with her kind of loving, a form of anaclitic love, is not being able to experience love as mature sharing, as mutuality. Since there exists no situation of unrationed and total love, her inner conditions for love were never totally met except in idealized memory or in fantasied anticipation. Every adult relationship is burdened by the fact that one has to give up early childish conditions for love in order to be able to reach heterosexual genital love. Nick and his mother were locked in a symbiosis in which the child could function beautifully within the symbiotic sac; once out of contact with the mother, however, in a school setting, he would fall apart and behave violently. In contrast, within the home, the mother would explode, dissolve in tears, become helpless; yet she would function beautifully and competently outside the home. This is one aspect of the treatment in which the focus was on this mother's need for promiscuity and for frequent changes of lovers, in order to maintain her role as mother to a sick child. Her gradually growing ability to enter into a deeper commitment with one man, enabled her to maintain a kind of constancy with her son, a commitment to ongoing, intensive treatment over a four-year period, during which time she developed a stronger sense of identity as a woman.

Nick's mother, a doll-like perfectionist, was actually a rigid person fearful of being emotionally involved. Initially, she heard our offer for intensive treatment not as an offer of help, but as an additional and intolerable demand upon her time. Filled with self-pity, she wept bitter tear over her plight; abandoned by an irresponsible husband-father; having to raise a malformed child; forced to work full-time with no one caring or offering to help her; without hopes for remarriage, for who would consider marriageable a woman with a damaged, uncontrollable son? In spite of this, she buried the anger and functioned as a competent, machine-like individual at work, never missing time, always in such tight control that no matter what happened to Nick during the day at school she showed up for work the next morning. Initially, seeing our offer of help as a demand to give even more, she originally experienced therapy as punitive, demanding, and non-giving. When she "submitted" to the "all-powerful" clinic, she saw us as the miracle workers who could tame the monster child. We, of course, explored other options for treatment, her thoughts about residential settings, placement, etc. But it was apparent she needed to hold on to her bad and helpless self and, indeed, to the underlying hope that we could make Nick happy and lovable. After all, she had sacrified for him. How come he wasn't ever happy or pleased or satisfied, but would stare at her with reproachful eyes, rendering her ineffective, helpless, and enraged, filled with guilt? Her only respite was a twice-annual visit from her parents when she would be "remothered" herself. Her child and she could then be provided for, even though the price for this help was to submit herself to the interrogation by her irascible, irritable father who made her feel guilty and see herself as bad and promiscuous, and who re-inforced her hopelessness about remarriage. She had lost, already, the one man she loved and had come close to marrying because he could not accept his own or her child's deformity. She was still behaving like a promiscuous adolescent, bringing men home and sneaking them out in the early morning before her son awakened, and she was still wondering why it was that the child had severe temper tantrums. When left with a sitter, he smashed his door, defaced the walls in his room, and used vile profanity.

Added psychological testing* confirmed the initial diagnostic impressions of this woman. The test revealed that the coolly aloof outward facade masks her insecurities related to her impaired self-image. She fluctuates between a narcissistic view of herself as special, attractive, desirable, and a depressed view of herself as being fat, unattractive, some sort of physical freak—not unlike the way she saw her son with his flawed hand. Uncertain about herself, she uses people around her as check-points, relying on their reactions to reassure herself of both her attractiveness and her ugliness. She relates to men by way of her body, the tool for her medium for expression; she needs them to reassure her that she is not some horrible, deformed thing. At the same time, she feels entitled to

---

* Joel Liebowitz, Ph.D., administered psychological tests.

be cuddled, to be loved, but is unwilling to face and accept these needs. She remains despairing and anguished, confused in her role as mother, wife, woman, person.

She comes to us for help while believing nothing would really change. With this in mind, our focus was to work through the feeling of despair about herself by way of her acceptance of her deformed son, the projection of her deformed self. The social worker, over a four-year period in once-a-week interviews, and occasionally twice-a-week, focused on her role as mother of and to this child, moving into a supportive relationship with a woman who had to mask and defend against her needs for acceptance. The worker did not challenge, in any way, the woman's need to have a lover. Instead, she subtly questioned how little the woman asked of herself, how little gratification she allowed herself even in these short-lived relationships which in no way carried over to her role as mother or as a functioning and highly competent person during the day. The woman was able to move away from seeing her child as a saboteur or an obstacle in a permanent relationship with a man, to seeing him as an asset. Gradually, she allowed her lovers and friends to know the boy, to include him in outings. It was on these occasions that his behavior improved markedly. He was a model child, conducted himself with poise and sophistication in the adult environment of restaurants, theater, trips, etc. On one occasion when he had exploded with the word "mother-fucker" she became depressed and enraged, feeling that unless the child were placed immediately she might kill him. Having learned that what she wanted to do was smother his accusations expressed in the word, the social worker's response was, "But you think of yourself that way," she wept then and softened. She told how much she loved the child. It wasn't that the child was accusing her but was acknowledging her needs and self-accusations. When she reached this stage, she was able to maintain an ongoing, strong attachment to one man for over a period of one year which led to plans for marriage. They lived together openly, the child then had a father in the home. He had no severe temper tantrums at home and was included in their total living situation, taken on long excursions, vacations, and was on friendly terms with his new siblings, the man's children from a previous marriage.

The relationship to the man whom she was going to marry puzzled her. She wondered how much fun he could have with his children from a previous marriage and with hers. While she dreaded any exposure to Nick's nasty behavior, this man was a parent who could talk with Nick about his behavior. Nick's classical rationalization would be, "Everything is fine, but there is just one thing wrong." Unlike the mother in the past, with her fiancé, she would now understand the one thing that was wrong; the damage to the hand was irreversible. She could bear the complaint not as a criticism of or a disappointment about her. The complaint was about the hand which would never fully respond to corrective surgery. In a tender moment when she had volunteered to stay at home with Nick when he was mildly ill, he responded that she could continue with her work because he would be all right; if he needed her he could telephone. Then he added wistfully and forgivingly that she couldn't after all, change his hand.

The mother had answered Nick's questions concerning her interest in marrying the man who would then belong to both of them. Nick would then chant a song about how the man would be marrying both of them. The mother would allow herself to recall dreams about beautiful modern kitchens with aromas of fine cooking (in the past she would demand the lovers take her to expensive restaurants). In these dreams, she and her husband were cooking delicious foods, developing gourmet skills; but lurking behind all this was the underlying fear that something might happen to destroy their plans.

The mother tried to avoid the fate of Jocasta who slept with her son of the flawed foot. But her lovers were merely anxiety-reducing parental substitutes. The help she received moved her to a man who accepted her on a mature level, as the mother of our patient. The flawed triangle dominated by the powerful past has now changed to a triangle which is future-directed and adaptive.

BIBLIOGRAPHY

Ekstein, Rudolf, Seymour, W. Friedman, Elaine Caruth, and Beatrice Cooper. Reflections on the Need for a Working Alliance with Environmental Support Systems. *Reiss-Davis Clin. Bull.*, 1969, 2:111.

Chapter 17

Transformation of the Flaw– Reevaluation via Psychological Testing

JOEL M. LIEBOWITZ, PH.D.

He looked like a little waif, somewhat on the thin side, and he was sitting in the room by himself. When the examiner introduced himself, he said nothing but immediately got up and started toward the stairs. During the testing he seemed to experience questions that he didn't know the answers to as an attack. He either responded with an annoyed manner or sat with a disdainful smirk.

It was in this way that Nick reacted to the first testing session some four and one-half years ago. The evaluation at that time revealed a little boy with a misshapen hand, filled with the roar of unbridled aggressive fantasies, consciously denying his fright everywhere expressing the inner fears and anxieties, while his over-all functioning was on a borderline level of adjustment. Even within the most structured and benign situation, Nick experienced threat and functioned erratically. As one listens to the words of the first test report, a picture of this little boy begins to develop. "Quite threatened," "ego must use extreme measures," "fragmented reaction to the environment," "reality distortions," "ego is crippled in dealing with anxiety-arousing situations." While these descriptive summary statements taken from the first test report create a useful picture, it might be helpful to look at the raw data themselves and review with them the changes that have taken place over the course of the treatment in the last four years.

Psychological testing was first carried out in January 1967 (1). Nick was five years and three months old at that time. In May 1969, he was seen for a re-evaluation (2), and in May of 1971, he was seen again for a re-evaluation (3). In attempting to understand the nature of the changes that took place, this paper focuses on three types of test data. First, the focus will be on the clinical impression as revealed through the test behavior and the test responses. Secondly, it will be on the test data themselves with particular reference to the Draw-A-Person test and with reference to one particular Rorschach item. Finally, it will be on the changes in intellectual functioning as revealed through the IQ assessment.

The clinical description of the first testing has already been noted. If one looks further at Nick's Draw-A-Person test that was completed at this time, there is, in obvious distorted display, a clawed right hand drawn on the male figure. It is drawn noticeably different from the left hand of this figure and different again from the hands which appear on the female drawing. It is clearly disfigured as the object which possesses the hand holds it high in the air. The appendage upon which the hand is located does not end in fingers but in primitive misshapen edges, ragged and formless —more like the edge of a cultivator, a tool that one uses to claw in the earth. The object itself that possesses the arm and hand is drawn transparent so that one can see inside where one glimpses the form of a locomotive, smoke pouring from its stack, fire belching from the furnace—literally the inner fury of this little child, a fury also represented by the symbolic claw. It is a claw which represents both power and uselessness.

Concurrent with this visual impression of the Draw-A-Person test, Nick responded to the very first Rorschach card by saying, "That looks like a monster." He goes on to explain, "Giganter's nose. This is the part that looks like his nose." In the inquiry he explains further, "Because it has a point on it." Anything else? "No. You know, a monster's head is funny. It's all crooked and has holes in it." At this point, Nick made a biting movement with his mouth. The distortion in this response is apparent as he points out that the appendage is crooked and has holes in it. One also hears the idiosyncratic and highly personalized image of a made-up thing called a "Giganter." As the psychologist noted, "His ego remains impotent to meet the demands" and "at times he can only deal with his environment in a fragmented fashion and by distorting reality." A Stanford-Binet was given at this time, and Nick's IQ was 109.

Two and one-half years later, Nick was seen by the present author. The clinical description at that time revealed a "cute, elfin-looking little boy," seated by his mother, nestled under her arm where he sought apparent safety. Although "he walked confidently into the consulting room," this confident air suggested a "pseudo independence." Basically, Nick appeared "uncertain," "afraid," and "hesitant." He became "bored" and "restless," and kept his enlarged hand "deliberately out of sight" hidden behind the edge of the desk. Although friendly, "at no time did I feel we really established a relationship."

During the testing it became clear that failure and inability to answer "was sensed as an inner weakness reactivating great inner anxiety and fear, resulting in disorganization characterized by idiotyncratic remarks intended to be humorous but revealing instead the breakdown in control and thought processes." For example, when asked what he would do if he lost one of his friend's toys, Nick answered, "Ask your turtle to hunt for it." When asked what he would do if he saw a train approach a broken track, he answered, "I'd pull it back by its tail." It was noted that the thought disturbance appeared most clearly when he had to judge and evaluate; that is, when he had to invest himself in a personal way in the answer and "stand by" the response. At these times he sensed the inner feeling of inadequacy and became quite frightened and confused. Consistent with the previous evaluation, he seemed quite frightened and focused his helplessness in what he perceived as a fearful world filled with inner projections and with himself identified as a cripple, as symbolized by the disfigured hand. At this time many of his projective images were seen in a distorted form, representing an effort to rid himself of his own deformity through a reliance on projection. His perception of the first

Rorschach card was no longer a "Giganter" but was now seen as a "four-eyed flying bat." Compared with the first testing, the percept is now closer to reality but still deformed.

If one looks at his Draw-A-Person test at this time, there is a weightlifter clutching barbells above his head—held high with the clasping hands which are drawn in an enlarged, round, and puffy fashion. While the image is static, it is caught in the moment of success—the weights are held high—the hand has begun to function. Unlike two and a-half years ago, the hand is no longer only a primitive and formless claw held uselessly by the side, but it is now a grasping and clutching appendage with strength. The smiling face drawn on the weightlifter clearly conveys a sense of triumph. And yet, the hand is puffy and enlarged, misshapen out of proportion, and involved in a struggle to maintain a burden. It was noted that Nick "seems more focused on himself and the relationship to himself—a focus that reflects an increased ability to cope and adjust. He is no longer impotent to cope, his adjustment is more secure, the disruptions in functioning more intermittent, and the capacity for adaptiveness more certain." His IQ remained about the same as two and one-half years before, with a Full-Scale WISC score of 106. There was, however a noticeable improvement in the Performance score which was now 117—a fact reflecting, perhaps, the increased ability to make use of his hands. His Verbal Scale at this time was 92.

The child who returned for testing in May of 1971, greeted me with a broad smile and a very friendly hello. He was warm responsive, and engaging. He approached the tasks with an easy, self-confident attitude. He was logical and planful, taking pride in his performance. He moved with greater freedom, and the little waif of four and a-half years ago had clearly grown into a sturdy young boy who displayed enthusiasm, motivation, and capability. He was self-assured and confident.

In assessing the test responses, one sees a greater sense of "flexibility and adaptiveness, a sense of being able to invest himself in the tasks." It was further noted: "One senses how much more comfortable he feels with himself, how life is no longer a struggle for survival—but instead, there is room to breathe and move about. There is a feeling that you are going to make it and the pressure is off." Throughout, Nick was thoughtful and reflective, and there was no longer any evidence of confusion or disruption in thought. In fact, what was previously idiosyncratic in a bizarre and distorted sense now bordered on being original in a creative sense. Thus, the ego's ability to cope, adapt, and master seemed much more apparent, and what was regressive disruption now turns into an adaptive regression. "No longer does one sense a boy feeling overwhelmed by life, sensing himself to be helpless and impotent. Now, even though there is still some threat and not all goes uneventfully, the child feels ability and capacity, a growing sense of self that is experienced as capable, reliable, and dependable."

Consistent with this overall impression, Nick's Draw-A-Person test showed genuine artistic ability, and the drawing of the male is now a drawing of a golfer shown in the middle of his golf swing. There is a sense of movement, a sense of freedom of action. Whereas the weightlifter of two years ago had regained the hand but had to struggle with the continuing burden, the golfer of today is freed, the hand is used for pleasure and not to maintain some burdensome struggle. True enough, the hand is still drawn in a somewhat roundish manner, but it is not drawn larger than the left hand and is now in proportion to the rest of the body. It no longer dominates the total person but is more genuinely integrated into the person. It becomes a piece and not the whole. Also, unlike the 1967 picture of a distorted appendage and unlike the hand of two years later that struggled to maintain the burden, this hand seems free to move about. The golfer is not static but is caught in the act of movement.

As noted, one no longer sees evidence of the thought disturbance. When the responses to similar questions are compared, the changes are evident. For example, when asked this time what he would do if he lost one of his friend's toys, he explains, "Find it or pay him back for it." When asked what he would do if he saw a train approaching a broken track, he answers, "Signal it to stop. Don't go into the middle of the track. Wave your hands." The hands have become effective aids and not useless weights. No longer is there confusion under pressure, but judgment and rational, logical reason are present. Nick responds to the first Rorschach card by saying, "a four-eyed dog"—a response given to that same card on which two years ago he saw "a four-eyed bat." But then, as if to emphasize for us the change that has taken place, Nick remarks that instead of trying to recall what he said last time, "I'm trying to thing of something else"—as if to say the past is behind me, let me go on. When questioned later about this remark (about the "four-eyed dog"), Nick indicated "That's what I said before. I'm going to make up some new answers now." From this point on, Nick's answers were generally more appropriate. From time to time deformity was seen in some of the percepts, but it did not dominate the picture as it had two years earlier. Rather, it seemed intermittent as effective judgment held sway over distorted logic.

Consistent with the increased freedom and increased ability is the improvement in the intellectual functioning. In 1967, when he was functioning in the Normal range with an IQ of 109, the psychologist noted: "Although capable of superior intellectual capacities, he is unable to use these in any consistent fashion because his ego remains impotent" as he "can only deal with the environment in a fragmented and distorted fashion." Today most striking aspect of the present evaluation is the noticeable increase in the ego's ability to cope, adapt, and master." Nick's overall WISC IQ is now in the Superior range, with a score of 128. The discrepancy between the Verbal Scale (109) and Performance Scale (145) remains, with the extremely significant improvement appearing most clearly in the Performance area.

It would appear that as the inner image of the self grew from a primitive undifferentiated one into a separate, capable, functioning self it was expressed via the hand as it changed from the primitive clam into a useful functioning appendage. And, as the claw, symbolic representative of the self, became transformed into a hand, it became more and more available for capable, adaptive use—a fact also revealed in the tremendous improvement in the Performance Scale IQ. The deformed hand continues to play a role in his basic sense of identity. Its dominance in his identity has diminished considerably and in proportion to the increased sense of being a capable, separate, competent, and acceptable individual. Increasingly, the deformity of the hand as symbolic of total weakness, of impotence of self, seems to be a thing of the past—a position which Nick himself seems to acknowledge and express. No longer does one sense a boy feeling overwhelmed by life, sensing himself to be helpless and impotent, deformed and crippled. Now, even though there is still some threat and not all goes uneventfully, the child senses ability and capacity, a growing sense of self that is experienced as being capable, reliable, and dependable. One senses how much more comfortable he feels with himself, how life is no longer solely a struggle for survival but contains room to breathe and move about. There is the feeling that he is going to make it and the pressure is off. The claw has indeed become a hand. Psychotic-like organ inferiority has turned into organ functioning.

BIBLIOGRAPHY

1. Busch, Fred. Unpublished Test Report, 1967.
2. Liebowitz, Joel M. Unpublished Psychological Test Report. 1969.
3. Liebowitz, Joel M. Unpublished Psychological Test Report, 1971.

Part V
RESEARCH AND EXPLORATION

Chapter 18

Reactions of Disturbed Children to Natural Crises

BERNICE T. EIDUSON, PH.D.,
LEDA W. ROSOW, M.A., AND
JANET SWITZER, PH.D.*

PILOT STUDY: REACTIONS TO CUBAN CRISIS

What impact does a social emergency situation have on children so anxious that they are patients of a psychiatric clinic? We began investigation of this question during the Cuban crisis when we saw child patients and their parents, waiting for regular appointments at the Clinic, glued to transistor radios they had brought with them (7).

So seldom does the occasion arise for studying the effect and meaning of reality events that actually threaten survival itself, that we have had little opportunity to know whether current events that appear menacing and stressful to adults are seen similarly by children. For this reason it is difficult to know how to prepare children psychologically to face such dangers without making them too anxious to cope intelligently. Our aim in October, 1962, therefore, was to utilize this crisis situation in order to obtain some information about how a group of psychologically dis-

---

* Director of Training, Marianne Frostig School of Educational Therapy.

tressed youngsters viewed an impending disaster and how they attempted to cope with something so overwhelming.

Our study was directed to the following questions:

1. How did this group of children perceive the situation, as evidenced by the kinds of information about the Cuban crisis they brought into their therapeutic hours?

2. How did the children react to their perceptions?

3. Was there any relationship between the accuracy of their information and their subsequent response pattern?

4. Were there any psychological differences betwen those patients who brought some content about the emergency into therapy as compared with those who did not?

The results of this pilot study showed that clinic children were indeed aware of the crisis situation. However, they had absorbed many bits of information which had become unevenly integrated into any consistent picture of what was transpiring in reality. Furthermore, this lack of consistency was a fertile ground for further personally expressed distortion. Fears and anxieties, as well as guilt and depressive reactions, were stimulated. Even feelings of elation appeared when personal needs for massive aggressive action were touched off in this large-scale social action. In some instances transient new symptoms, like school phobias, made their appearance.

It was not possible to establish any statistically significant relationship between diagnosis, chief complaints, or other of the psychologically relevant variables tested, and mode of reaction in coping with anxieties. However, there was clinical confirmation that how much and in what way the child identifies with what goes on—and even recognizes it with some awareness of the danger —seems to be a function of his personality makeup and, more specifically, of the conflicts that are heightened in him. Furthermore, IQ, age, chief reason for referral, or diagnosis did not differentiate the group of children who referred to the Cuban crisis during therapeutic hours from those who did not. Two variables were significant in this regard, however: sex, and use of repression as a major defense mechanism. In regard to the former, there were

2½ times as many boys in the non-reporting group than in the reporting group and less than one-half as many girls.

We felt that our findings were provocative but, growing from a study generated on an impromptu basis, they suffered from a non-rigorous base, a fate shared with other clinical studies done in this area. Recognizing how difficult it is to do a more systematic study if one waits until the disaster strikes, we decided to develop an experimental design which could become operational at a movement's notice.* In line with this aim, we have planned standardized data-collection methods in order to provide quantitative or semi-quantitative data about the clinically relevant aspects of behavior in which we are interested.

In drawing up the design, we took into account certain clues from our pilot work and from the work of others that suggested that it would be desirable to (a) observe many aspects of behavior and whenever possible to compare it with non-disaster behavior; (b) monitor behavior in more than a single situation to study the extent or specificity of the reactions; and (c) observe behavior over a sufficient time to get both disaster and post-disaster reactions.

Furthermore, the vast literature that has been accumulating on disaster behavior, since the "nuclear Damocles sword" turned every natural crisis into a field laboratory for studies of personal behavior, pointed to a number of factors likely to condition disaster behavior. These included (1) spatial proximity to the disaster, personal involvement in it, and other reality factors; (2) characteristics of the social context in which the crisis was experienced, such as primary nature and reactions of the group; (3) certain socio-psychological characteristics of the persons studied, such as sex, age, socio-economic status, diagnosis. Since differences in re-

---

* While drawing up a design in advance was well supported on logical grounds. It posed some psychological problems. For one thing, investigators were teased by staff about hoping for "a good disaster." Secondly, staff interest and enthusiasm in a study which had no beginning data and very little specificity neeed continual regeneration. Immediately following a research conference on the project or during preliminary trial runs on pilot forms, interest was high, but otherwise it flagged. A further complication arose when personnel in the clinic changed; each newcomer had to be introduced to the project rapidly lest he be pressed into service without appropriate training.

gard to some of these factors occur among our patients, it was our intention to utilize these as independent variables and to try to establish their significance for disaster behavior.

We found the generally agreed-upon definition of disaster in the studies of social crises appropriate for our work: "The impinging upon a structured community, or one of its sections, of an external force capable of destroying human life or its resources for survival, on a scale wide enough to excite public alarm, or disrupt normal patterns of behavior, and to impair or overload any of the central services necessary to the conduct of normal affairs or to the prevention or alleviation of suffering and loss. Usually, the term disaster refers to an episode with tragic consequences to a substantial portion of the population—it is a stress on people and on their group and community patterns" (23). The usefulness of this definition for clinical studies such as ours draws support from Miller's comment that the social or group emphases—communal alarm, tragedy and destructive consequences of an unknown and uncertain extent—are readily transposable to individual systems (18). The fight waged by all forms of life, large and small, to maintain their integrity and to continue existence despite threats, dangers and possible destruction, is common to the social group and the individual who is part of this group.

With this definition in mind, this study will become operational, therefore, when official or public recognition of such a disaster is given. It is anticipated that this will be communicated initially, and confirmed, by mass media, or when necessary, by other community channels. Because the geographical distribution and socioeconomic situation of the families coming to the Clinic, the subjects of the study will be a consideration insofar as they are likely to be affected by the disaster. The project investigators will, together, make the decision that appearance of a particular disaster warrants beginning the study.

Our previous work indicated that psychiatrically disturbed children (1) know that a social disaster is occuring, or has occurred;

and (2) they express the reactions to this knowledge in their behavior, verbalizations, fantasies and anxieties. Collation of adult and child responses to disasters by other investigators corroborates that awareness of and disturbances stimulated by crisis situations can be found in every area of function (30, 31).

In our present design, we wanted to be able to identify the areas in which disturbance, if any, was manifest; and to obtain some estimate of the degree of disturbance in these areas. In order to approach this problem we decided to employ two data-collection techniques.

The first is a rating scale, which includes 24 dimensions covering child's overt and intrapsychic behavior as connoted by his play, verbalizations and activity during his therapy hour. The therapist rates the child on each of these parameters by comparing his behavior in the present hour with that of the therapy hour directly preceding. The range of behaviors falls into the four overall categories of (1) general behavior, under which are subsumed specific parameters reflecting motor behavior, level of activity, amount and kind of verbalization, attention, etc.; (2) emotional behavior, including tension, anxieties, mood, aggression, interaction with therapist; (3) fantasies, with attention to both the content and amount and kind of fantasy involvement; and (4) defenses, again including kind utilized, their degree or intensity, and some estimate of whether they suggest adaptive or regressive trends.

Every effort has been made to define the dimensions behaviorally so that agreement on their interpretation is facilitated. To this end, the therapist is further asked to cite the specific evidence in the child's play, verbalizations or behavior during the interview which supports his rating. In addition, he is asked for a narrative description of the total therapy hour. Several therapist ratings of the total hour concern its uniqueness for the patient, the aspects or phases of the transference manifested and the personal material with which the child has been working.

Since our pilot work showed that patients adopted a wide range of behaviors in response to the Cuban crisis, we do not anticipate that a single "disaster pattern" will emerge under more rigorous study. Instead, we shall try to pick up the change evident in the behavior of each individual child, each serving as his own control.

Therapists are asked to compare the child's behavior in the immediate post-crisis hour with that of the last pre-crisis therapy hour.
In regard to each behavioral dimension, the therapist is asked to
note whether the specific behavior noted occurred "more than" or
"less than" or was "no different from" the previous session. The
number of "change" categories provides an estimate of changes
presumed to be a result of the crisis. Direction of change can also
be taken into account.

The assumption that the change seen between the two therapy
sessions is due to the effects of the crisis, will be partially tested in
a pilot non-crisis pretest. In this pretest, conducted under conditions as similar as possible to the crisis plan, therapists will be
asked to compare current interviews with the preceding one. This
will provide an estimate of the amount of change which occurs independent of crisis conditions. This procedure will, hopefully, provide some criterion of variability within the individual child.

The rating scale will be introduced one additional time: the
therapist will be asked to fill it out following termination of the
crisis, the date to be determined by the nature of the crisis. This
latter technique is being employed to complete the pre-, during,
and post-crisis reaction coverage, the need for which Baker has
stressed (3). Because a disaster has a life history whose time
phases have been identified (5, 20, 23, 27), some investigators have
been able to point to analogous stages in an individual's reactions
to a disaster (30), and have even demonstrated that later points
in disaster behavior can only be fully understood by seeing them
as resultants of behaviors adopted at previous stages (29). While
our scales are not refined enough to permit us to contribute much
to this area, they may allow us to identify the extent of the disaster
reaction, and to pick up the previously latent reactors.

The second technique that we are employing is the direct interview with the parent. Planned to take place within 48 hours of the
crisis (either in face-to-face contact or by telephone call), case
workers who see parents will obtain information about the child's
response to the crisis at home. Open-ended questions have been
devised to elicit the circumstances of the child's first information
about the crisis as well as his subsequent behavior and activities.

Our effort to get data about home reactions to the emergency was mainly to extend the data sources, and to elaborate the picture based on therapeutic contacts. However, it drew additional interest from a finding in our pilot work which showed that for some children, responses to the crisis were more regressed at home than at the Clinic. Because we normally think of therapy sessions operating as the stimulus for greater regression, this reversal was provocative, and led us to question factors that affected it.

The interviews with parents had a second purpose: to explore some of the contextual factors that might help us understand the child's initial reaction and information. Two sets of studies by others have pointed to the importance of this area. The first of these are some investigations which point to the importance of physical proximity, or spatial closeness to the disaster areas (19, 21). More accurate or more realistic evaluations of what the potential danger may bring tends to be directly correlated with closeness to point of impact (26). This suggests that reality-testing ability is sharpened by closeness to threatening stimulus. Since in clinical situations this ability is generally thought to suffer under threat, we hope to understand the apparent discrepancy.

Another group of studies calls atention to the psychological and contextual dimensions which attenuate or exacerbate anticipated recations in emergencies. Some of the contextual conditions or states referred to concern the nature of the personal-social environment in which the stress was experienced—such as whether a storm was viewed in a primary group (5), or with the mother/children relationship intact (10); or the nature of role relationships which are established at the time and known to the child, such as an authority person assuming helping status (4); or even kind of group activity during crisis with which the child or his family becomes involved (21, 22). To some limited extent, other pertinent factors as the information available (5), or previous experiences in weathering storms (4) have also been suggested as determinants of disaster behavior. Among the interesting data from these studies is an elaboration of the ways in which crises provide the license for behavior which is normally forbidden, and generate the spontaneous occurrence of group or shared defense reactions (16). We wonder whether child patients utilize or exploit such mechanisms.

In our earlier study, we found that both the amount and the

accuracy of information about the Cuban situation were related to specific reaction patterns (7). For example: when information is accurate it is more likely to be accompanied by direct expressions of bodily or motor manifestations of anxiety, some anticipation of the loss of valued things, and certain intellectual pride at being able to talk with some authority about the situation. Partially accurate information seems to go along with the need for immediate ways of effecting stop-gaps, fantasies or flight, re-stimulation of earlier anxieties, regressions in personal relationships, attempts to deny dangers. If these and related findings are supported and extended by a more rigorous approach, they will have implications for the kind and amount of information a patient should be given when stress is imminent.

THE SILENT PATIENT: THE HANDLING OF AN ERROR SOURCE

One of the problems we became extremely sensitive to in our pilot work was the non-responding children. The "non-reactor" did not spontaneously bring up anything about the Cuban crisis during his therapy sessions, but whether he was *in fact* a non-reactor, or a reactor through silence, or just uninformed about the crisis, we never knew. Nor did we ever know whether factors in the therapy situation itself were more responsible than the crisis for the silence. At best, we could only try to establish some factors which might account for the child's behavior.

To obviate this problem in the more rigorous study, we decided to establish a standardized way of eliciting the child's knowledge about the crisis if he did not spontaneously present it during his therapy hours.* Technically, a series of open-ended questions is introduced by the therapist at a latter point in the hour if it is devoid of anything which can be recognized as relevant to the crisis. The question leads from the general "Has anything unusual

---

* Although interviews had been used effectively in community studies and would provide data that were not spontaneously offered, investigators were wary about using this technique in the clinic setting. Sure that clinicians would be resistive to such planned interventions, we even considered abandoning the interview before exploring its feasibility. To our surprise, staff was comfortable with the procedure. The support given to the project by clinic administration undoubtedly was a strong factor here. Of course, the usual clinical consideration of therapeutic appropriateness will be honored.

happened?" to specific details of the knowledge he has, the place and conditions under which information was obtained, his subsequent actions, reactions of family and friends, and fantasies about the future of the situation the crisis has created. If a child has no knowledge of the crisis and the therapist is thus brought to the point of introducing the subject, the patient's response and subsequent behaviors or fantasies are recorded.

PSYCHOLOGICAL CORRELATES OF DISASTER REACTIONS

Baker has stated that although the nature of the disaster may determine the kind of personal psychological material stimulated in individuals, their individual reactions are a function of their predisaster states (3).

Although descriptions of certain kinds of disasters have built up sufficient data to permit them to be monitored, so that accompanying behavior can be predicted and intelligently assisted, the unique behavioral characteristics stimulated by different kinds of disasters remain to be investigated. For the researcher interested in reactions of individuals, this is an important problem, for detailed studies of single crises suggest that different psychological phenomena are ignited through confrontation with different kinds of stress (15, 25, 31).

Other studies have sensed the importance of the specific nature of the crisis by reporting how its real nature has had to be denied or distorted (1). Bahnson, for example, showed that seriously sick persons projected their threats to life onto external factors, and persons fleeing from the Nazis internalized them, feeling that their safety depended on their own strengths. The meager body of information about different behavior evoked by different crises is overshadowed by the extensive work done on pre-disaster state variables: age (7, 8), developmental phase (8), intelligence level (24), sex (7), socio-economic status (9), defense mechanisms (31), diagnosis (17, 30), presenting psychiatric complaints (7, 31), have all been studied.

Data on the significance of certain psychological variables for an individual's disaster reaction have been provided primarily by small-sample case studies which have had access to depth data.

Therefore, data in this area rest mainly on pathological populations, although generalization of some of the findings to normals has been thought feasible, and to some extent hypotheses generated on clinical-case data have been corroborated by studies on larger-scale normal samples (9, 24).

Our own pilot work was mainly related to the study of certain psychological variables in crisis behavior. We tried to understand them as a function of (1) amount and accuracy of information available; and (2) certain personality characteristics, as IQ, sex, age, referral symptoms, diagnosis, main defense mechanisms. These psychological characteristics were also compared in children who did not react to the crisis so far as we know. Our findings pointed to sex and use of repression as main defense as possibly significant variables. However, the work of other investigators has suggested that we retest the significance of other variables as age, personality pattern and IQ.

In our present design, the total clinic population (children, 2-18 years) automatically becomes subjects of the study by virtue of being patients at the time of the crisis. However, because we do not know what characteristics will comprise the group at the time the study becomes operational, we cannot state what the distribution of breakdown is going to be. At present, we are doing some experimentation with different distribution patterns and refining categorizations within the variables we shall be using. We trust that information obtained from our present group of patients can be ultimately generalized to the actual subjects.

SELECTION AND TRAINING OF DATA COLLECTORS

Every therapist at the Clinic who sees a child and/or a parent in treatment becomes a direct collector of data. Each has been informed about (1) the conditions under which he is likely to act in this capacity; (2) the kinds of data he is expected to collect; and (3) the methods by which data are to be collected, including training on forms to be used. Information about the project has been conveyed at research conferences which have been held regularly.

In addition, each data collector has provided the following back-

ground information about each of the potential subjects for preliminary identification of the population:

(a) Passport data, which identify each patient accordling to
sex, age, school, and provide information which facilitates
ready access to the patient and family;
(b) Psychological data, which concern current symptoms,
character structure, main defense mechanisms and current
diagnosis.

Grinspoon, in noting the problems which studies in this area
create for data collectors and which exacerbate the normally expected variances in their performance, points out that data collectors themselves are often distressed by the disaster (12). This
often results in the mobilization of their personal defense patterns;
we hope to utilize their "resurrected" intellectual defenses for participation in this task. Learning from community studies that persons who engage in their accustomed roles are often found to recover from disaster most quickly, we have designed data-collection
processes in line with customary clinical procedures and functions
wherever possible (4, 6).

While further refinement of data-collection techniques continues,
we are exploring the possibility of giving operational definition to
another variable hypothesized as significant for disaster reactions:
previous experience with "weathering the storm" and with personal
stresses. Because such data are so germane to the therapeutic situation, we feel compelled to find ways to include them.

Our design demands evaluation of intra-individual variation and
comparison among groups which fall within the pathological sphere.
To answer the questions we have posed, no additional population
is necessary. However, we are beginning to think of extending the
planned study to include a group of normal children who could
serve as a control group, and thus provide us with answers to: Are
the reactions of pathologically disturbed children different from
those of normals? If so, in what ways?

In order to maintain the basic plan of the design, we would need
a group of normals who are seen intensively, or at least regularly,
and whose individual behaviors could be systematically monitored
as are those of our original group.

BIBLIOGRAPHY

1. BAHNSON, CLAUS B. Emotional Reactions to Internally and Externally Derived Threats of Annihilation. *The Threat of Impending Disaster.* G. H. Grosser, H. Wechsler and M. Greenblatt, eds. Cambridge: MIT Press, 1964, 21.
2. BAKER, GEORGE W. *Behavioral Science and Civil Defense.* Washington, D.C.: National Research Council, 1962, Publication 997.
3. BAKER, GEORGE W. Comments on the Present Status and Future Direction of Disaster Research. *The Threat of Impending Disaster.* G. H. Grosser, H. Wechsler and M. Greenblatt, eds. Cambridge: MIT Press, 1964, 315.
4. BARTON, ALLEN H. *Social Organization under Stress: A Sociological Review of Disaster Studies.* Washington, D.C.: National Research Council, 1962, Publication 1032.
5. BATES, F. L., FOGELMAN, C. W., PARENTON, V. J., PITTMAN, R. H., and TRACY, G. S. *Social and Psychological Consequences of a Natural Disaster: A Longitudinal Study of Hurricane Audrey.* Washington, D.C.: National Research Council, 1963, Publication 1081.
6. DRAYER, C. S. Psychological Factors and Problems, Emergency and Long Term.*The Annals of Amer. Acad. of Polit. and Social Sciences,* 1957, 309:151.
7. EIDUSON, BERNICE T. A Study of Children's Reactions to the Cuban Crisis. *Mental Hygiene,* 1965, 49:113.
8. ESCALONA, S. *Children and the Threat of Nuclear War.* New York: Child Study Assoc. of America, 1962.
9. ESCALONA, S. Children and the Threat of Nuclear War. *Proc.,* Amer. Ortho. Assoc., March, 1963.
10. FREUD, ANNA, and BURLINHAM, DOROTHY T. *War and Children.* New York: Medical War Books, 1943.
11. FRITZ, C. E., and WILLIAMS, H. B. The Human Being in Disasters: A Research Perspective. *The Annals of Amer. Acad. of Polit. and Social Sciences,* 1957, 309:42.
12. GRINSPOON, LESTER. Fallout Shelter and the Unacceptability of Disquieting Facts. *The Threat of Impending Disaster.* G. H. Grosser, H. Wechsler, and M. Greenblatt, eds. Cambridge: MIT Press, 1964, 117.
13. GROSSER, G. H., WECHSLER, H., and GREENBLATT, M., eds. *The Threat of Impending Disaster.* Cambridge, MIT Press, 1964.
14. KILLIAN, LEWIS M. *An Introduction to Methodological Problems of Field Studies in Disasters.* Washington, D.C.: National Research Council, 1956, Publication 465.
15. KIRSCHNER, DAVID. Reactions to the Death of a President. *Behavioral Science,* 1965, 10:1.
16. LANG, KURT, and LANG, GLADYS ENGEL. Collective Responses to the Threat of Disaster. *The Threat of Impending Disaster.* G. H. Grosser, H. Wechsler and M. Greenblatt, eds. Cambridge: MIT Press, 1964, 58.
17. MENNINGER, ROY. Attitudes toward International Crisis in Relation to Personality Structure. *The Threat of Impending Disaster.* G. H. Grosser, H. Wechsler and M. Greenblatt, eds. Cambridge: MIT Press, 1964, 131.
18. MILLER, JAMES. A Theoretical Review of Individual and Group Psychological Reactions to Stress. *The Threat of Impending Disaster.* G. H.

Grosser, H. Wechsler and M. Greenblatt, eds. Cambridge: MIT Press, 1964, 11.

19. MOORE, H. E. *Tornadoes over Texas.* Austin: University of Texas Press, 1958.

20. MOORE, H. E., BATES, F. L., LAYMAN, M. V., and PARENTON, V. J. *Before the Wind: A Study of the Response to Hurricane Carla.* Washington, D.C.: National Research Council, 1963, Disaster Study No. 19.

21. PERRY, HELEN S., and PERRY, STEWART E. *The School House Disasters.* Washington, D.C.: National Research Council, 1959, Publication 554.

22. PERRY, STEWART W., SILBER, E., and BLOCH, DONALD A. *The Child and His Family in Disaster: A Study of the 1953 Vicksburg Tornado.* Washington, D.C.: National Research Council, 1956, Publication 394.

23. POWELL, JOHN W., FINESINGER, J. E., and GREENHILL, M. H. An Introduction to the Natural History of Disaster. *University of Maryland, Final Contract Report, Disaster Research Project, Psychiatric Institute, Vol. II, 1954.*

24. SCHWEBEL, MILTON. Studies of Children's Reactions to the Atomic Threat. *Amer. J. Ortho.,* 1963, 33:202.

25. SHEATSLEY, P. B., and FELDMAN, J. J. The Assassination of President Kennedy: a Preliminary Report on Public Reactions and Behavior. *Public Opinion Quart.,* 1964, 28:189.

26. WALLACE, A. *Human Behavior in Extreme Situations.* Washington, D.C.: National Research Council, 1956, Publication 390.

27. WALLACE, A. *Tornado in Worcester.* Washington, D.C.: National Research Council, 1956, Publication 392.

28. WALLACE, A. *Tornado in Worcester: An Exploratory Study of Individual and Community Behavior in an Extreme Situation.* Washington, D.C.: National Research Council, 1956, Publication 178.

29. WITHEY, STEPHEN. Sequential Accommodations to Threat. *The Threat of Impending Disaster.* G. H. Grosser, H. Wechsler and M. Greenblatt, eds. Cambridge: MIT Press, 1964, 105.

30. WOLFENSTEIN, MARTHA. *Disaster: A Psychological Essay.* Glencoe, Ill.: Free Press, 1957.

31. WOLFENSTEIN, MARTHA, ed. Children's Reactions to the Death of a President. *Proc.,* Albert Einstein College of Medicine, New York, April 1964.

Chapter 19

Notes on the Strategy of a Child Psychotherapy Project

CHRISTOPH M. HEINICKE, PH.D.

The strategy of research reported below relates to the general question of what factors are likely to be of importance in affecting both the process and outcome of psychoanalytic psychotherapy with children. Of the various models available, three were initially considered. In the first, comparisons are made between a treatment group and a "control" non-treated group. The second involves a comparison of two treatment groups, and the third compares the same group under different treatment conditions. Drawing on the experience of a specific child psychotherapy project, we wish to illustrate that no one model or design is likely to be sufficient, that some designs may be intrinsically difficult to execute, and that a series of sub-projects based on the strategic use of a number of designs is likely to provide the most reliable answers to the complex questions relating to the process and outcome of psychotherapy. Although a considerable number of findings are now available, these are mentioned rather than fully described.

COMPARISON OF TREATMENT AND NON-TREATMENT GROUPS

Our initial approach to psychotherapy research with children involved consideration of the model that had been most frequently used in research reported before 1957: a group of treated children was compared with a non-treated or control group. In assessing the efficacy of child guidance treatment these studies asked what proportion of the treated children can be rated as falling into each of three categories: successful adjustment, partially improved, and no improvement. The question arises as to whether the rate of improvement found (approximately 74%) would not also hold true for children who are accepted for treatment but do not actually receive it. Using as "controls" samples reported on by Witmer and Keller (16) and Lehrman et al (8), and basing his comparisons on the twofold distinction of improvement (whether successful or partial) or no improvement, Levitt (9) noted that the rate of improvement for these controls was almost as high as the pooled percentage based on 17 studies of treated children (72.5 vs. 73.3 percent improvement). He concluded that the evidence "fails to support the view that psychotherapy with 'neurotic' children is effective." Since that time he has brought further evidence to support his view (12).

In a review of essentially the same literature, Heinicke and Goldman (6) reasoned that the comparison of treatment and control groups was best confined to the two studies which included both kinds of samples, and where some effort at comparison had been made. Examination of the data also revealed that one should distinguish between successful adjustment vs. partial improvement, and between the end of treatment and follow-up point.

But the more important result of our review was to point to the intrinsic difficulties of the model of research and particularly of the "control" groups used. Although the question may seem arbitrary, are not a family and child who wait for and then pursue treatment likely to be different from those who do not pursue it? Results of studies (7, 10, 12, 15) of the difference between families who accept treatment and those who do not are conflicting. Levitt (11) finds no differences between these two groups whereas other authors do. He suggests that this conflicting result could be a function of differences in the definition of "defector." But even if one confines oneself to those families who had a full diagnostic work-up and then after a period of waiting refuse treatment, a failure to find a difference at the point of diagnosis between these families and those that accept treatment can be interpreted in various ways. While there may be no difference in severity of symptoms and motivation for treatment, important differences may exist which are neither simple in nature nor easy to detect. Levitt (11) suggests this as a possible explanation.

While thus finding much of interest in the studies using the treatment-control comparison, and realizing that the search for some kind of baseline against which to judge the effects of treatment is a meaningful one, the intrinsic difficulties encountered in using this model of research encouraged us to turn to other designs.

COMPARISON OF TWO TREATMENT GROUPS

The choice of comparing two treatment groups was of course also governed by the interest in a specific variable, namely, the frequency with which a child is seen. Clinical experience had suggested that whether a child is seen once or four times a week is likely to affect the nature of the psychotherapeutic process and outcome. No systematic studies of this factor were, however, available when planning a project begun in 1958. Only Arthur (1) had written about the difference between intensive and less intensive psychotherapy.

Starting with a given theoretical and technical approach to child therapy, that associated with Anna Freud's teachings, one group of 7- to 10-year-old boys was seen once a week and another group was seen four times a week. This variation in frequency cannot be considered a simple independent factor. Despite the use of the same general technical approach, the nature of the psychotherapeutic material produced by the patient it soon different; therefore the utilization and assimilation of this material are different. This in turn leads to variations in the further emergence of material, etc (2). Yet it was felt that the characterization of the cluster of independent process variables associated with differences in frequency and its effect on outcome was the first step in a long-term research strategy. It was anticipated that examination of the differences in the process could suggest which are likely to be the most significant correlates of variation in frequency. For example, it has been hypothesized that the specificity, affect intensity and variety of the transference phenomenon may well be one such significant correlate.

Two psychoanalytic child therapists trained at the Hampstead Child Therapy Clinic treated the children. One therapist saw three pairs of children and the other one. Both had had four years of child psychotherapy experience with children seen on a once- and five-times-a-week basis. All the mothers were seen once a week by a psychiatric social worker or other therapist, and, where appropriate, the fathers also were seen.

The children were all judged to be suitable for psychoanalytic treatment in that permanent and severe symptom formation of a predominantly neurotic character and the retardation of ego and libidinal growth were associated with permanent regressions and fixations (3).

Cases were assigned so as to insure that one group was not over-represented by the more severely disturbed or by certain qualitative constellations (for example, a defensive organization subject to deadlock versus lability). Individual variations are likely to defy matching of groups of cases; as demonstrated elsewhere,* however, the two groups of children did not differ at the beginning of treatment on any of 45 clinical dimensions which differentiated them after treatment.

The two samples of four boys were also characterized by *and did not differ* in regard to the following:

1. They were between the ages of 6 years, 8 months, and 10 years, 5 months.
2. The main reason for referral was a learning disturbance linked to a psychological disturbance.
3. Their difficulties could not be readily linked to the influence of organic impairment or psychotic process.
4. They were either threatened with being held back or had been held back in school.
5. Their rate of academic growth in reading, spelling and arithmetic was below the national average.
6. They scored a Stanford IQ of 91 or better.
7. They came from intact business or professional families.

---

* Unpublished article entitled: "Frequency of Child Psychotherapeutic Session as a Factor Affecting Outcome: Analysis of Clinical Ratings."

8. All treatments were terminated at the request of the parents and with the consent of the therapist.
9. The length of the therapies ranged from between 1½ and 2½ years, the mode being two years for both groups.

Analysis of the data collected has initially focussed on the differential development (outcome) of the two groups of children (5).* Analysis of differences in the therapeutic process has now been initiated.

For the study of differential outcome, data were available for the beginning and end of treatment and one and two years after treatment. The information is derived from sessions with child and parents, from psychological testing, and from interviews with teachers.

At this point in research, it was assumed that the most reliable and valid conclusions about a child are based on all the material at a given point in time. This approach would point to the essential variables and change in variables. It is then possible to develop ways of assessing a certain function and changes in it by using one source of information or test. Unless descriptions of the child are evaluated in the context of his total functioning, conclusions based on them are likely to be misleading. For example, it has been shown (14) that parents disagree on the average 64% of the time in describing the difficulties of their child; that in 60% of these instances the deviant behavior is actually not present; in another 30% one parent failed to report it. Accordingly, the Diagnostic Profile suggested by Anna Freud (3, 4, 13) was used to derive a cross-sectional and integrated statement of the child's developmental status and potential at each of the four assessment points. Studies of the reliability of the Profile construction and of the clinical ratings based on the Profiles have also been undertaken.*

Having formulated all the Profiles, it was possible to compare these for children seen once as opposed to four times a week and to formulate hypotheses reflecting the differences in developmental status and potential at a given assessment point. The specific hy-

---

* See previous note; also, unpublished article: "Frequency of Child Psychotherapeutic Session as a Factor Affecting Outcome: Independent Indices."

* Unpublished article: "Frequency of Child Psychotherapeutic Session as a Factor Affecting Outcome: Analysis of Clinical Ratings."

potheses as well as illustrative details have been reported (5). One general hypothesis reads:

> Other things being equal, children seen on a four- or five-times-a-week basis by comparison with those seen in once-a-week psychoanalytic therapy are likely to give greater evidence of impending and important changes in their total adaptation by the end of treatment. Even more striking, the resolution of the termination of treatment, and the nature of the new integration achieved in the two years after the end of treatment are likely to be associated with a more pronounced growth in adaptation. The clinical findings derived from the Profile, the analysis of the ratings based on the Profile and the analysis of the test results* all support this general hypothesis.

As indicated, data analysis of the process variables is now in progress. A number of differences in the process of children seen four, as opposed to once a week, have been isolated. For example, the libidinal and aggressive transference as well as the transference of defenses typically occur in both treatment situations. Certain features are, however, characteristic of the children seen four times a week. These include: the force of the affects accompanying the transference is greater, especially in the sense of arousing more of a counter-reaction from the therapist; the elaboration of the ideas accompanying the transference is more specific; the variety of themes and defenses transferred is greater; and it is easier to link the transference to current and past object relationships. Moreover, it follows that interpretations of the transference are more effective.

COMPARISON OF ONE GROUP UNDER DIFFERENT TREATMENT CONDITIONS

Given the size and restricted nature of the samples, a next step in the overall research strategy might have been to expand the sample using the same design. Instead it was decided to use the third type of design: comparison of the same group of children under different conditions of the central variable. Although steps

---

* See preceding footnotes.

had been taken to match the two groups of children involved in the group comparison of the study reported above, the complexity of the variables is such that this is not likely to be completely adequate. Comparing the psychotherapeutic process of the child seen once a week with the process of the same child when he is seen four times a week is likely to overcome some of these difficulties.

More important, since the comparison of the two groups seen once vs. four times a week had provided much support for the general hypothesis that frequency of treatment is a significant variable, study of the explicit change in this variable is likely to give more specific clues as to its effects on the psychotherapeutic process. In the sense that a more frequent treatment preceded by a less frequent one is different from one initiated on a more frequent basis, further complications arise. Yet because of the availability of the groups and findings from the previous project, and specifically a group that was seen intensively right from the beginning, such questions can at least be examined. Furthermore, it would be anticipated that after the subproject using the child "as his own control" is finished, the nature of the findings as seen in the total context of all projects will very possibly suggest the use of new designs and methods. What seems clear is that, particularly in this complex area of research, several designs need to be used to provide adequate support for given hypotheses. The use of these designs is, in turn, governed by a strategy of research which exploits the nature of the findings derived from a previous project.

BIBLIOGRAPHY

1. ARTHUR, HELEN. A Comparison of the Techniques Employed in Psychotherapy and Psychoanalysis of Children. *Amer. J. Ortho.*, 1952, 22:484.
2. BIBRING, E. Psychoanalysis and the Dynamic Psychotherapies. *J. Amer. Psychoanalyt. Assoc.*, 1954, 2:745.
3. FREUD, ANNA. Assessment of Childhood Disturbances. *Psychoanalyt. Study of the Child*, 1962, 17:149.
4. FREUD, ANNA. The Concept of Developmental Lines. *Psychoanalyt. Study of the Child*, 1963, 18:245.
5. HEINICKE, C. M. Frequency of Psychotherapeutic Session as a Factor Affecting the Child's Developmental Status. *Psychoanalyt. Study of the Child*, 1965, in press.
6. HEINICKE, C. M., and GOLDMAN, A. Research on Psychotherapy with Chil-

dren: A Review and Suggestions for Further Study. *Amer. J. Ortho.*, 1960, 30:483.

7. LAKE, M., and LEVINGER, G. Continuance Beyond Application Interview in a Child Guidance Clinic. *Social Casework*, 1960, 41:303.

8. LEHRMAN, L. J., SIRLUCK, H., BLACK, B., and GLICK, S., et al. Success and Failure of Treatment of Children in the Child Guidance Clinics of the Jewish Board of Guardians, New York City. *Jewish Bd. of Guardians Research Mono.*, 1949, 1:1.

9. LEVITT, E. E. The Results of Psychotherapy with Children: An Evaluation. *J. Consulting Psychol.*, 1957, 21:189.

10. LEVITT, E. E. A Comparison of "Remainers and Defectors" among Child Clinic Patients. Ibid., 316.

11. LEVITT, E. E. A Comparative Judgmental Study of "Defection" from Treatment at a Child Guidance Clinic. *J. Clinical Psychol.*, 1958, 14:429.

12. LEVITT, E. E. Psychotherapy with Children: A Further Evaluation. *Behavior, Research and Therapy*, 1963, 1:45.

13. NAGERA, H. The Developmental Profile. Notes on Some Practical Considerations Regarding Its Use. *Psychoanalyt. Study of the Child*, 1963, 18:511.

14. NOVICK, JACK, ROSENFELD, EVA, and BLOCH, DONALD A. Situational Variation in the Behavior of Children. Paper presented at the biennial meeting of the Society for Research in Child Development. Minneapolis, Minnesota, 1965.

15. ROSS, A. O., and LACEY, H. M. Characteristics of Terminators and Remainers in Child Guidance Treatment. *J. Consulting Psychol.*, 1961, 25: 420.

16. WITMER, H., and KELLER, J. Outgrowing Childhood Problems: A Study in the Value of Child Guidance Treatment. *Smith College Studies in Social Work*, 1942, 13:74.

Chapter 20

❦

Prolegomenon to a Psychoanalytic Technique in the Treatment of Childhood Schizophrenia*

RUDOLF EKSTEIN, PH.D., AND
SEYMOUR W. FRIEDMAN, M.D.

Psychoanalytic therapy was originally devised to fit the need of adult neurotics and, likewise, the first adaptation of the method to children was made with the infantile neurosis in mind. Since then, in the adult field, the scope of analytic therapy has widened, and, with minor alterations, now serves, besides the neuroses, other categories of disturbances such as psychoses, perversions, addictions, delinquencies, etc. Again, child analysis followed suit extending its field of application in the same directions.

ANNA FREUD

As we consider the task of developing a general technique for the psychoanalytic treatment of psychotic children, we face the apparent paradox of using similar techniques for both psychotic and neurotic children. This poses many questions, inasmuch as this issue is intimately involved with the basic model of psychoanalytic treatment itself, whose limitations and limits, shortcomings, effec-

* This work partially supported by funds from the Annenberg Foundation.

tiveness, and possible improvement are constantly being tested as a valid model and instrument for the treatment of psychotic children.

Freud's introduction of the concepts of the unconscious and the primary process led to a unified view of psychopathology in which normality, neurosis and psychosis were no longer regarded as essentially different and separate. In this unified view, the variety of part-aspects of so complex a disease as schizophrenia could be integrated and synthesized into a total disease condition manifesting itself in a variety of ways. Under the impetus of Freud's synthesis (12, 10) of the differences between neurosis and psychosis within a single conceptual framework of psychopathology, there emerged the essential elements for the outgrowth of a common treatment philosophy and model for dealing with both the psychotic and the neurotic child.

Freud's original topographic (11) and his later structural tripartite models (9) of the personality aptly served the model for classical psychoanalytic treatment of the stable patient whose psychic organization provides the structure for the therapeutic process. Here the significant elements of psychoanalytic treatment, as manifested in the unconscious becoming conscious, the conflict between impulse and defense, between the wish and the reality testing, and between impulsivity and delay functions, could be meaningfully utilized only by a personality of more advanced and stable neurotic psychic organization. The model of treatment consistent with these models of personality organization is the traditional structure in which the free association of the adult or the play activity and verbal productions of the child are met by the interpretive interventions of the therapist. The transference development of the patient is matched by a countertransference and empathy potential of the therapist.

With the neurotic child, the therapist's task is understanding, having like experiences, meeting the patient's controlled and relatively regulated regressions with his own countertransference regressions in the service of professional functioning, matching the patient's inner states with his own inner states, and effectively providing empathy to match the patient's need for psychological "mothering." This is made relatively and reasonably possible by the essential, basic similarity of their psychic functioning. The therapeutic process can proceed with reasonable hope of a successful outcome.

The psychotic child, however, confronts the therapist with a psychic organization of another order. With such a child neither topographic nor structural models of personality organization alone serve for treatment models. Instead, a modification which does not essentially alter the basic elements of these two models is required, one which, we suggest, can be achieved in their synthesis. For our understanding of the nature of the psychic organization of the psychotic child, we are especially indebted to Mahler (14). Her work has clarified the essential difference between autistic and symbiotic psychosis which, together, comprise childhood schizophrenia. By means of her insights we can reconstruct a model of the essential disorder in the development of object relations which characterizes these illnesses and is at the root of the total resultant psychic disturbance.

We can characterize infantile autistic psychosis essentially by its relative failure of affective cathexis of the mother as a human object. This creates a relatively empty inner human-object world over which the autistic child exerts complete and omnipotent control. Symbiotic psychosis can be characterized as a state of object- and self-cathexis but with failure to achieve separation and differentiation of self and object. The ego functions mainly by the delusion of omnipotence derived from the undifferentiated mother-object. We may disregard the primary autistic psychotic child whom we can consider as not existing in pure culture, as Kanner (13) at first held, but rather who always has relative elements of a symbiotic psychotic organization. We can then view the symbiotic psychotic child in either of two ways. In one, he is in a constant, dynamic, inner-turbulent state of movement between the symbiotic state and the stage of separation and individuation, for which symbiosis is the forerunner. In the second, he is regressively pulled toward the autistic position as a retreat from the threatening, devouring and engulfing dangers of the pathogenic symbiosis. For the infant who has had a pathogenic experience within the symbiotic matrix, separation deprives him of his needed delusional omnipotence derived from fusion with the mother. This leads to threatening collapse of the ego and to panic attempts to restore the symbiosis with the mother. In this state of separation and impotence outside the symbiosis, the psychosis serves as the adaptive means to restore ego functioning by restoring the symbiosis with the environment, external objects or therapist. Danger from engulfment by the parasitic mother-object, the negative symbiosis, however, leads to regressive retreat to the autistic position.

We can thus visualize the psychotic state as one in which self object representations are enclosed within the symbiotic sac, separated by a porous osmotic membrane. It is undergoing, without yet having achieved, separation, nor stable cathexis and differentiation of self and object. In this stage only primitive ego functioning exists. It is dominated by primary process and unstable impulse control, in which the thought disorder is characterized by the equations: thought $=$ action; inner reality $=$ outer reality; self $=$ object.

For the psychotic organization we would then postulate a *three-dimensional model combining the topographic and structural models,* and conceive of the structural model as operating in depth. These various levels of consciousness may perhaps best be construed as different layers of psychic organization forming a hierarchy developing out of an undifferentiated archaic phase. In this can be found latent dispositions that will develop into the organizers of a more complex structure within the personality. Such an integrated model allows for a more refined and subtle description of the specific ego deviation suffered by psychotic children. It also permits the concept of fluctuating ego states at various levels of regression and progression. This is characteristic of the functioning of the psychotic psychic organization, which is correlated with the particular form of integration of id, ego and superego functions operating at a given moment and level.

Complementing this three-dimensional model is that of the *symbiotic* sac as the energizing force that fuels the ceaseless fluctuations or the quick, abrupt, deep regressions and the sudden reconstitutive progressions so characteristic of the functioning of such a child's psychic organization. With such models we can offer an explanation of the child's clinical behavior, therapeutic transference manifestations, and of the essence of his life adaptation.

Familiar clinical observation indicates such a child's body-clinging and molding attitudes; his intense preoccupation with and grasping of objects, persons and part of persons; his lightning-like shifts from libidinal to aggressive reactions, when a touch can suddenly deepen into a brutal penetration or tearing, and a kiss can turn into enraged, cannibalistic biting. In his encircling, engulfing, possessing and devouring of parts of the object and of the external environment, we see the id nature of the hungry search for part-objects. This reaching out and grasping of available part-objects reconstitute an autistic-like omnipotent control over a symbiosis which has to be maintained in order to avoid ego collapse and abysmal panic.

Paradoxically, omnipotent control over the symbiosis and the symbiotic partner is desperately needed in order to safeguard the delicate, developing filaments of self and object-differentiation that, overpowered by the dominant, devouring object, are threatened with obliteration. To maintain his precarious balance, to ward off destructive fusion and loss of self, the symbiotic psychotic child's psychic organization has no choice but to impose itself on all available objects. For such a child's only reality is its internal psychic reality, which it cannot fully distinguish from outer reality. Such a child must force its total environment into the mold and image of its own psychic organization, which is all it can master, as if to wipe out all semblance of difference and differentiation that threatens the symbiosis. He literally creates the world, or misperceives the object world, in his own inner image, and is committed to psychotic pantheism.

What seems to be the destruction and nullification of the environment by the deeply disturbed psychotic child is the expression of the savage onslaught of untamed instinctual drives unmediated by effective ego control. This can be understood as the psychotic adaptation of a personality that could not otherwise survive.

This model further enables us to see the forces in dynamic interplay. It highlights the essential similarity of the psychotic psychic organization and the normal neurotic organization, with the significant quantitative differences of ego, id and superego influence, and perhaps with qualitative differences which we cannot identify yet because of unexplored or unclarified areas of etiology (such as the biological, organic areas of heredity, constitution, etc.). Perhaps there is one essential quantitative difference leading to vast qualitative differences between these two basic organizations. This difference lies in the relatively greater effectiveness of the vicissitudes of the impulse-defense conflict in the formation of the neurotic organization, but with greater importance of the influence of a life-and-death struggle in the life of the psychotic personality. This is best depicted in his indecisive, ceaseless struggle for ego control over impulse, for differentiation of self and object, for achievement of ego autonomy through simultaneously differentiation and integration of its various functions. How this occurs depends on the effectiveness of its integrative and synthesizing function and the still unsolved task of neutralization or integration of energies. The psychotic is striving for mediation and integration of the self and external reality to become an effective human being capable of living successfully in the world. He is reaching for the fulfillment of the actuality principle, where trial thought may move towards appropriate action based on genuine option, that is, towards alloplastic behavior.

When we place in apposition to this psychic model the basic model for psychoanalytic treatment, we see the essential and major difference in the treatment of the psychotic child is the role of activity and technique by the therapist. The psychotic child, who is dominated by primary-process thinking, by impulse over delay, and by unstable self-and object-representations of an infinite degree, offers his productions and transferences. The therapist must meet them with his own secondary-process functioning and with a countertransference potential that is significantly challenged (1, 3, 7, 17).

He must competently meet the patient's transference developments with his own countertransference potential while confronted with an extremely difficult problem. He must meet the patient's unpredictable and alien regressions with his own controlled potential for regression; and, in effect, must match the patient's intra-psychic functioning, essentially foreign to him, with his own which is not only foreign but impossibly demanding to the patient. We might even speculate that the therapist is called on to undergo regression to the emotional experience of a symbiotic state that mirrors and reflects the inner symbiotic state of the patient's object relations. Thus enabled to accept the patient's need and demand for symbiosis, he can enter the patient's world but within himself. From there he can cue his response and attitude so that he is available to the patient's need at the same time that he maintains his self-identity; i.e., does not become truly psychotic himself. This enormous demand on the therapist for flexibility and accommodation may be all but impossible to meet; in which case no effective treatment occurs. Assuming that a treatment relationship with such children can be established, however, we cannot rely solely on what we already know about their treatment but must discover more through continued investigation.

The treatment of such children is replete with inherent dilemmas of the kind where the resources and ingredients indispensable to treatment are the very dangers that threaten and terrify the child. We are thus in the constant situation of having to make alliances with monsters of all varieties, nature and degree (4). Some of these unstable alliances are made with deities and mythical heroes. Among the psychotic child's most terrifying monsters are his own thoughts and thinking. At the same time that he cherishes, guards, and even plays with them, he fears them as if they were also alien monsters that can bring destruction to him and his needed objects. The child's thoughts and his thinking are, however, indispensable for the development of the treatment process, even if expressed in action or any non-verbal form of language. When we wish to treat him we also invite him to share and give us his thoughts, or at least invite him to have thoughts which he may or may not share with us, or may communicate in any language he commands. But in so doing we confront him with an immediate task that terrifies him and sets into operation mechanisms that may even destroy the initial treatment situation.

Not only are the child's thoughts potentially monstruous to him, they are often completely alien productions to the therapist, who at first may find them totally incomprehensible and therefore useless. We measure the primary process of the psychotic child's thinking against our own yardstick of secondary-process thinking and thought values and judge his thinking to be a thought disorder. In fact, observation of his thinking and language reveals a very meaningful order (15), although one based on primary-process language and rules of grammar (2) which reflect and represent the functioning of his psychotic psychic organization. Not only do his thinking and language have order, but meaning and purpose which, at least in part, we have come to see as being in the service of the restoration of or struggle against the symbiosis in order to maintain his optimal ego functioning. In effect, the therapist projects his own confusion onto the patient in speaking of the patient's thought disorder when he has not as yet conceived the hidden rules of the patient's thinking.

The patient's thoughts and language, by their private and foreign expression and form, invite the therapist to understand him only in a certain way. That way can be understood as an invitation to a symbiotic relationship. The therapist is to know the patient and his mind so well as to know his strange and foreign thoughts; to understand him on his own level of thinking; to share with him otherwise completely private thoughts and wishes; to maintain his omnipotent control while the symbiotic partner can thus fulfill his needs without even asking—the psychotic version of the non-verbal infant's needs being met by the mother's total empathy and understanding (16). The patient's thoughts, translated into action, are clearly seen as his instrument for consummating a symbiotic union with the external environment, from which he has not yet achieved clear differentiation and over which he must maintain control. His communications to the therapist, in order to be understood and responded to, demand that the therapist, too, think in primary-process language, give up his own secondary-process thinking, and enter into a thought and language symbiosis with the patient, where frequently communication regresses to communion.

The use of the metaphor (6) as an interpretive technique can, among other meanings, be understood in this way: as an entry into the patient's inner world via his language and thinking. The metaphor safeguards the patient's authority and control over the therapist's intrusion by stating the patient's terms. In using the metaphor, the therapist minimizes difference. While introducing himself as a representative of the external world, he does not demand that the patient accept that difference. Use of the metaphor permits the outer world to enter the patient's private world but without demands to cope with a foreign object which he cannot master. Useful and necessary initially and for large stretches of time during treatment, the metaphor outlives its therapeutic purpose as the patient outgrows his need for symbiosis and achieves a more stable and permanent separation and individuation of self from object.

Similarly, in the problem of regression we have another ally that is indispensable for treatment. Under optimal conditions, it serves its positive therapeutic function; out of control, as so readily occurs in the psychotic child, it becomes a monster that can destroy the therapeutic process and dissolve self- and object-cathexis. Here again, the crucial feature is the maintenance of self- and object-cathexis, the optimal state of separation and symbiotic union, but with maintenance of self-cathexis possible for that ego organization. In this situation, the therapist would need to function like the psychological mother, his empathy and understanding directing his distance and closeness to the patient's inner state. He would meet the patient's regressions with his own empathic regressions, like the mother who, for optimal mothering, can gauge the infant's need for dependence, support and need-satisfaction while allowing for distance and stimuli to growth as the infant is ready for these. The therapist's task is to meet empathically the patient's regressive needs, and also his simultaneous or time-appropriate need for growth stimuli. He functions like the grain of sand in the oyster shell which is the irritant that becomes the organizing growth factor.

The therapist's interpretive activity is to adapt within this empathic role. This brings us to a distinction between *interpretation* as the activity pertinent for stabilized self- and object-cathexis, i.e., between two separate people; and *intra-pretation,* the therapist's mode of representing his function within the symbiotic sac, in order to maintain the necessary optimal conditions of self and object separation and union for continued ego functioning. In the relatively weakly differentiated state of internal ego function and structure, thoughts and affects trigger off psychological and motor acts that lead to loss of self and unreachable regressions. In the interpretation of affect to the patient, or of demands for closeness, separation, dependence, or growth that the ego cannot yet master, self-cathexis is lost and uncontrollable panic regressions may occur. And in the interpretation to the patient of his thoughts of fear, self-cathexis is lost. The patient experiences that the therapist, by knowing his thoughts and fears, also has the same fears and cannot protect him. The therapist is no longer a separate observer but a participant in the patient's own self: the patient's self is now lost in the therapist's mind. This leads to loss of object- and self-cathexis and to regressions that may or may not lead to useful therapeutic purpose.

In "Object Constancy and Psychotic Reconstruction" (5), we presented the dilemma of *psychotic object constancy*. We characterized this dilemma in terms of the ego's gross and quixotic distortion of reality testing in which the new or changing object was permitted to exist only in terms of past negative images; i.e., the object existed not as it was in reality but had to be what it was not, therefore being delusional and unreal. To carry the point to an absurd extreme, we can conceive of a similar, almost impossible dilemma confronting the therapist who offers himself as a new object. He, too, must accept the role of a mirror reflection of what the object must be to the self of the psychotic child, i.e., what it is not, and therefore to have to remain unreal. Further, he has simultaneously to remain within and without the symbiotic sac, to move back and forth and yet be at the same place with the patient's regressions and progressions. He has to speak his language, yet not speak but echo. He has simultaneously to be the self of the patient and object, yet remain himself at all times. In short, he has to engage in a host of primary-process maneuvers ad infinitum; a fantastic feat of psychic juggling which, if it were not feasible, could well-nigh make it impossible to treat such a child by means of psychoanalytic psychotherapy.

This may be the reality of analytic work with these children, after all, but this is the question that constantly confronts us. We would like to resolve it not by countertransference impotence or megalomania, but by the scientific curiosity and therapeutic commitment which motivates us in our research, as we develop techniques for treatment and training based on psychoanalytic understanding.

BIBLIOGRAPHY

1. CARUTH, ELAINE, and EKSTEIN, R. Certain Phenomenological Aspects of the Countertransference in the Treatment of Schizophrenic Children. *Reiss-Davis Clin. Bull.*, 1964, 2:80.

2. EKSTEIN, RUDOLF. From Echolalia to Echo: the Psychotic Child's Struggle against, for, and with Language. Summary in *J. Am. Psychoanal. Assoc.*, 1968, 1:117.

3. EKSTEIN, RUDOLF, and CARUTH, E. To Sleep but Not to Dream: on the Use of Electrical Tape Recording in Clinical Research. *Reiss-Davis Clin. Bull.*, 1965, 2:87.

4. EKSTEIN, RUDOLF, and CARUTH, E. The Working Alliance with the Monster. *Bull. of Menninger Clin.*, 1965, 29:189.

5. EKSTEIN, RUDOLF, and FRIEDMAN, S. W. Object Constancy and Psychotic Reconstruction. *Psychoanalyt. Study of the Child*, 1967, 22:357.

6. EKSTEIN, RUDOLF, and WALLERSTEIN, J. Choice of Interpretation in the Treatment of Borderline and Psychotic Children. *Bull. of Menninger Clin.*, 1957, 21:199.

7. EKSTEIN, RUDOLF, WALLERSTEIN, J., and MANDELBAUM, A. Countertransference in the Residential Treatment of Children. *Psychoanalyt. Study of the Child*, 1959, 14:186.

8. FREUD, ANNA. *Normality and Pathology in Childhood. Assessments of Development.* New York: International Universities Press, 1965.

9. FREUD, S. The Ego and the Id (1923). *Standard Edition*, XIX. London: Hogarth Press, 1961.

10. FREUD, S. Formulations Regarding the Two Principles of Mental Functioning (1911). *Standard Edition* XII. London: Hogarth Press, 1961.

11. FREUD, S. The Interpretation of Dreams (1900). *Standard Edition* IV. London: Hogarth Press, 1953.

12. FREUD, S. The Loss of Reality in Neurosis and Psychosis. *Standard Edition* XIX. London: Hogarth Press, 1961.

13. KANNER, LEO. Infantile Autism and the Schizophrenias. *Behavioral Science*, 1965, 4:412.

14. MAHLER, MARGARET. On Child Psychosis and Schizophrenia: Autistic and Symbiotic Infantile Psychoses. *Psychoanalyt. Study of the Child*, 1952, 7:286.

15. MEYER, MORTIMER, and EKSTEIN, R. The Psychotic Pursuit of Reality. Digest in *Am. J. Orthopsychiatry*, 1967, 37:399.

16. SPITZ, RENE. *The First Year of Life.* New York: Int'l. Univ. Press, 1965.

17. WINNICOTT, D. W. Hate in the Countertransference. *Int. J. of Psychoanalysis*, 1949, 30:69.

Chapter 21

Reflections on the Need for a Working Alliance with Environmental Support Systems

RUDOLF EKSTEIN, PH.D.,
SEYMOUR W. FRIEDMAN, M.D.,
ELAINE CARUTH, PH.D.,
AND BEATRICE COOPER, M.S.

We would like to examine some of the therapeutic implications and consequences arising out of the peculiar nature of the interaction between the schizophrenic child and his past and present environment. This is his universe, as one youngster labeled it, and it is a true merging of his inner world and introjects with his outer world where introjects are the substitute for objects. The schizophrenic child and his environment form a kind of undifferentiated unit, analogous to the matrix of the maternal symbiosis in which there is a placental-like interchange between the inner and outer worlds of the child. This interchange is immediately effective in equalizing that which is within and that which is without so that, in effect, differentiation is wiped out and fusion can be re-estab-

The authors wish to express their special thanks to Clara Ballinger whose editorial assistance under demanding circumstances and often beyond the call of duty enabled this paper—and many others—to be published in final form.

lished. A relative lack of differentiation within the psychic organization is paralleled by a lack of differentiation of psychic structure from the environment. Consequently, instead of internal conflict, the predominant conflict is seemingly between the patient and the environment, which has become the externalized projection of his opposing impulses. This is why the inner life of these children frequently seems to mirror and to echo—to reflect but not reflect *upon*—what they have experienced both in the past as well as in their present environment. Their external world seems also to reflect and mirror—to resonate with their inner reality. We may say of these children that they look into reality not to find what is there outside themselves, but rather to find outside themselves what lies within. And all too often the real objects—the current reality figures in their lives—do act out or, more correctly, counteract out, within the countertransference and out of the hate that is engendered in the countertransference (2), in ways that confirm the child's most frightening and dreadful projections. And as the child succeeds in finding or provoking the objects in his outer world to echo the images of his inner world that are the archaic, unstable introjects from his past, he thereby confirms the validity of and strengthens his allegiance to this inner world.

The psychotic child seems to experience reality without distinguishing shadow from substance, inner from outer reality or self from non-self. Our understanding of such a reality requires trying to comprehend the experience of a world emptied of all but one's own thoughts—which, undifferentiated from their concrete imagery, merge with reality, and, mirroring the mind, cannot be distinguished from the mind. Such an inner experience is similar to the man who does not know if he dreams he is a butterfly or if he is a butterfly who dreams he is a man.

A case in point from the clinical reality of the consulting room is Rena (1), a severely regressed schizophrenic girl, whose violently destructive psychotic acting-out can be understood as an attempt to restore and at the same time break away from the negative maternal symbiosis. This symbiosis is like an inner straitjacket in which she is entombed and restrained from her impulsivity, but which, at the same time, enthrones her with a delusional omnipotence that is maintained by the mother-child symbiosis. In a psychiatric re-evaluation* after a number of years of treatment, Rena was described as an extremely sick schizophrenic adolescent. Her illness was manifested by her marked thought disorder reflecting the ego dysfunctioning under severe disintegrative threat, with disorganization, blocking, incoherence, irrelevance, perseveration, condensation, neologisms, word salad, echolalia and autistic logic. At times she manifested hallucinations, false perceptions, and misidentifications. Thought content, expressed in diffuse, fragmented verbalizations, was concerned with many themes, including religious theosophy, color and primitive sexual acting-out behavior. Emotional expression was characterized by blandness and apathy, with shifting and apparent disharmony between affect, response and external stimulus. She manifested numerous peculiar ritualistic mannerisms, stereotypy and catatonic posturing. In action she demonstrated unpredictable behavior, ranging from the use of the toilet, to incontinence and fecal smearing, and from withdrawn passivity to wild activity. When overwhelmed by any kind of disintegrative threat she resorted to violent assaultive behavior, excitement, apathy and confusion.

Psychological evaluations of the child and her mother were also undertaken at that time. The results illustrated the way in which Rena's fragmented inner life mirrored in a bizarre and magnified fashion the inner world of the mother, almost as if to recreate the original matrix within which she had developed and from which she had never grown away. Psychological testing indicated a very regressed schizophrenic girl whose state of disintegration and fragmentation created an overall impression of an animated but not quite animate psychic collage, as it were, with fragments of various aspects of psychic functioning seemingly stuck together haphazardly. No underlying cohesiveness or identity was formed even though one could occasionally get a cue of the remnants of some personality organization. When she spoke—with words, actions or bodily and facial gestures—one felt it was but one of many voices, as if she had a reservoir of isolated, imitative and stereotypic memories (of an echolalic and echopraxic-like nature). Although the observer could often identify what Rena wanted to convey, it could

---

* Conducted by Robert A. Solow, M.D.

not easily be related to whatever was going on externally with her. In similar fashion, she perceived, which is to say, projected onto, those around her as a multitude of fleeting, shifting extrojects and part-objects. These momentarily became the source of gratification of a primitive, instinctual, devouring organization that had never become subordinated to more advanced ego control, and which was incapable of postponement or anticipation, except for very fleeting moments of isolated secondary-process functioning during which were revealed extremely primitive impulse-delay mechanisms.

Psychological testing described Rena's mother as being in a state of extreme distress, torn apart by an intense ambivalence which could not be warded off through the brittle defensive structure available to her. She was particularly helpless in relationship to the maternal figure. Still entangled in her own negative symbiotic fusion, Rena's mother vacillated between seeing herself and/or the other object as omnipotent or impotent, as possessing goddesslike endowments or animal-like defects. She vacillated between her image of Rena as desecrated filth or as consecrated goodness; she felt deeply identified with certain images she had of her daughter, but felt totally alien to others. In short, her perception of the girl was as fragmented, contradictory and unsynthesized as the girl's own inner experience. She could accept in her daughter only the good, the beautiful and the precious—the godlike features that were a projection of her own omnipotent fantasies. She simultaneously rejected the deeply disturbing, damaged, impotent, animal-like aspects, the denied, fragmented bits of self-representation which she projected onto the girl and which the girl had taken in, but in the unpredictable fashion of an eternally revolving kaleidoscope.

Psychological testing highlighted how, separately, neither mother nor daughter was able to achieve any integrated, synthesized personality organization. Clinically, however, we observed that, together, their respective fragmented personalities seemed to achieve a kind of homeostasis which allowed for an apparent capacity to maintain a goal or purpose until their unity was threatened, as, hopefully, would come about after years of treatment. The mother had been able to support an extremely difficult, expensive, demanding, draining treatment program of many years. She could manage this, apparently, as long as she perceived it as restoring the original symbiosis and eliminating those aspects of the psychosis which, in fact, allowed the girl the only separate, albeit psychotic, identity she could achieve. When this separate identity became strengthened through the transference to the analyst and by the utilization of auxiliary therapeutic agents (hospitalization, an occupational therapist, etc.), which provided a nonpathological environment towards which she began to move, both mother and daughter started to act out disruptively. This interference with the treatment program made unavailable those supportive professional services that had begun to substitute for the mother's external nurturing function, just as the transference had begun to substitute for the internal mother representation.

During her six years in treatment, Rena had required constant and intermittent placements, from home to hospital, to a kind of halfway house where she lived with her own nurses; then back home in the care of an aide, then to another hospital, and so forth. The pattern she appeared to follow was one in which she would begin to move away from the negative maternal symbiosis, then become terrified at its loss. Driven to recreate it, she would provoke the environment to counteract out in the image of the bad mother, from whom she was forced to flee and towards whom she was equally impelled to return. The destructive, psychotic acting-out thus maintained the delusional megalomanic position by destroying the opportunity for individuation and separation that the hospital environment potentially could have provided. Her tremendous impulses towards symbiosis would constantly make impotent any persons in her environment unable to withstand the devouring demands that turned them into anaclitic or symbiotic part-objects existing solely for immediate impulse satisfaction. Few people could withstand the powerful psychotic struggle and acting-out that emerged in her battle both to maintain and to break away from the negative maternal symbiosis. Her struggles fluctuated towards and away from entering into a new growth-producing situation, a positive symbiosis with the environmental therapeutic agents which, in collaboration with the therapeutic symbiosis, might lead eventually towards individuation, separation and psychological development.

Her years of treatment were characterized by these powerful and contradictory impulses, which always managed to overwhelm whatever transitory nuclei of ego organization and control that might momentarily emerge out of the evolving positive therapeutic transference. The lack of any synthetic ego function—of any integrated personality organization—led inevitably to the lack of an overall direction in her treatment. All that could be seen was an unsynchronized internal autonomy of part self-representations or self-images, so that she seemed to have no purpose or direction that could be sustained. It was as if her inner processes were so fluid that there was no lasting differentiation between impulse and defense. She was without capacity for cathexis constancy, so to speak, so that any force propelling her in one direction seemed immediately to create its own counterforce of equal magnitude in a different direction. She indicated her desire to leave the hospital, for example, but then led the therapist to a locked gate, communicating thereby her feelings that she could only leave by breaking out violently in psychotic fashion, rather than in the doctor's fashion, which is through the treatment process. She sought to go for a ride with the doctor but led him to a strange car for which there was no key, metaphorically rejecting the "car" for which were available both key and chauffeur in the form of the treatment process and the therapist. Over and over she asked him for what he did not have or else caused the environment to destroy what he did have for her by provoking ejection from that environment. Her own lack of synthetic function seemed always to diminish the integrating power in those who treated her, thereby leading to a disintegrating impact upon the separate elements in her total treatment milieu. Her inability to make use of her environment ultimately turned it into a depriving one. Feeling helpless to take, she made those around her helpless to give, and thus she restored the oneness of nihilistic impotency between her and the environment. This, paradoxically, strengthened the delusional omnipotent inner power and control that guaranteed the psychotic existence and survival.

It is because of such experiences that we wish to explore and define conditions in a *controlled environment* which can provide the kind of autonomous structure that will sustain itself against the impact of such a patient's destructive impulses, without controlling the patient or the illness, and respecting the need for autonomy, albeit a psychotic delusional one. In such an environment, the people continue to function as whole autonomous objects, and can supply the necessary positive nutriment from reality—the external creative obstacle that can enable growth, like the foreign speck in the oyster shell which becomes the "organizer" for the pearl.

Let us describe an hour with the girl at a moment when she appears to have momentarily passed the maternal symbiotic barrier and is ready to enter into the new, positive symbiosis with the therapist. It is an hour of rebirth which she subsequently maintains for several sessions. It leads to a momentary level of integration at such a peak that she is able to say: "I am so sick. How can I help you to help me?" But all this is followed by a violent regression engendered by the panic at leaving the maternal symbiosis. Even the relationship with the therapist is dreaded as a potentially engulfing fusion threat. In the first hour of this sequence, however, she is found in her hospital room by the therapist in a severely regressed condition. Naked, disheveled, her mattress torn up, she is in constant need of a male nurse during her violent periods which alternate occasionally with moments of childish, regressive submissiveness. This alternation forces the nurse, too, to become like a part object that is either experienced as controlling her or else as ministering to her most primitive instinctual needs.

Coming at his regular time, the psychotherapist assumes that her behavior with him is not merely the expression of chaotic impulse but rather is psychotic acting out in the service of communication, but on a primitive appeal-and-signal level. She greets him with her body crouched over at right angles, and is encased in her bedspread while she tears her nightgown to shreds. He interprets her need to hide from him within her secret, autistic world, but reassures her that it is safe to leave it to be with him, or to let him enter it with her. He constantly reaches out for affective contact despite her attacks and withdrawal. Finally, during a momentary level of higher functioning, she bursts out, "I don't want to hurt your feelings." He interprets her desire to protect him, how she gives her whole life to do so, just as she feels her mother gave up her life for her. As he speaks of how she must punish herself out of her fear of hurting him, he interprets the conflict between the wish to have him, and the fear of this wish which turns so quickly into a need to destroy him. He speaks of her undifferentiated love-hate that makes her want to push him out yet grab on to him simultaneously. He restrains her violent assault but maintains the physical contact, until finally the tide goes out and true contact is established. For a brief moment she can give up her fear of losing or destroying him and hence can truly keep in touch with him. This has come about because she had been unable to provoke the assault from him that would have destroyed her but which she constantly invites—feeling powerless and destroyed when she herself is not the all-powerful, megalomanic destroyer.

Thus, with the psychotic tide momentarily at low ebb, cleansed temporarily of the bad object, she gently places her face in his hands as he leaves. Momentarily reborn, with the good object within her revived through the contact with the lifegiving therapist, she requests a bath. It is as if she is cleansing herself of the bad object, the psychic afterbirth, the filth, which is one of the many images assigned to her by the mother. This knowledge gives us some dynamic and generic explanation of the process which we interpret in terms of her fear of destroying or being abandoned and/or destroyed by the lifegiving object. This object, however, is experienced as a corpse which has been destroyed by giving life to her, so that she must give up her own life in return. Like Edgar Allan Poe, she is attached to a deal and deadly host that she feels she has killed; she can only feel the object as a corpse in whose womb she sleeps, and so eventually she must be destroyed herself. As she approaches the object—that is, the lifegiving contact—she assumes both the object and herself to be the negative, bad objects which must destroy each other. The therapist needs to approach her as if she were a dead body that he is to revive by supplying everything the previous dead womb could not. As he becomes an intrusive force, and unwinds the winding sheets, as it were, she becomes like a dessicated mummy and falls apart, a primary-process version of horror mysteries.

Nevertheless, we see evidence that there also exist some elements of an observing ego that reflects about the deadly struggle within her and says that she does not want to hurt him or speak of hating him. We can hope, therefore, even while knowing this level of secondary process cannot yet be maintained, that somehow each peak is an indication of ego function which will eventually develop.

By this time, however, the girl's chaotic behavior has already fragmented the help potential to her in the hospital situation. The administrators have begun to demand that she be withdrawn from the hospital, although they insist that if they could have handled her *entire* treatment they might have been able to maintain her. Thus, within the countertransference, we see how they have been turned into the image of the negative mother whose voice Rena constantly hallucinated as a threatening injunction that she must destroy the therapist rather than leave the mother. We can speculate, perhaps, that the girl has sufficient ego structure for her chaotic behavior to be a kind of psychotic acting-out in which she communicates her thought that she and her doctor are up against an impossible situation. The succeeding hour starts with her maintaining momentarily the regressive position of the newborn baby who can let the doctor take care of her and feed her, as she requests that he give her some water. This necessitates their going out in the ward, where she loses the momentary contact during which she had previously expressed compassion for him and a desire to protect him from herself. On the way to get the water, she becomes violently combative in the hallway, as if, in fear and terror, she must fight the hostile forces around her to get the very sustenance she needs for survival. It is almost as if she must prove to the therapist that the world is an enemy that will turn on them both, that he is helpless to protect her, and that she has only her rage to help her keep alive. Thus, during this hour we see contradictory impulses in which she says, at the same time: "Feed me, don't go away"; and "You can't feed me—powerful forces in me and the world will destroy us both."

We might say, therefore, that this girl preserves delusional, psychotic identity through the psychotic acting-out which, at the same time, destroys her opportunity for true individuation and identity. In addition, her environment, also, is inevitably driven to counteract out with an equivalent force to maintain its delusional control over the girl, even as it is unable to maintain its self-control as an autonomous therapeutic source under the impact of her illness.

Our work with such severely disturbed adolescents and our recognition of the intra-relationship with the environment have helped us recognize the need for understanding the interaction of the multiple therapeutic agencies in the environment which often are involved simultaneously with such patients. We have come to realize the importance of the collateral work with the parents, as well as with the variety of professional therapeutic systems such as private nurses, day hospitals, full-time hospitals, occupational therapists, educational therapists, and so forth. For the very nature of the illness of the schizophrenic makes the contacts with these support systems more of an "intra-action," since if he moves away at all from the maternal symbiosis, it is often only to seek to reestablish it with new objects in the environment. We have seen how the impact upon the environment of the illness of these children is frequently one that totally destroys the integrated yet autonomous functioning of the various agents involved with the patient: the parents, substitute parents, the social worker, occupational therapist, hospital personnel, and so forth. The very lack of synthesized function within the patient is reverberated to and is mirrored by the objects in the environment towards whom the patient develops pathogenic transferences which led Freud to say such patients formed unsuitable transferences for the usual office practice.

Specifically, we are describing the need for a *controlled environment*. That is, for a therapeutic environment that has an autonomy which cannot be destroyed by the patient, and which permits the autonomous functioning of its members as whole objects within a structure unified by the mutual purpose of treating the patient. This concept of a controlled environment may be contrasted with that of controlling environment. The latter, like an externalized superego in the form of authority figures, seeks to control or manipulate the patient rather than to help develop within the patient the self-control of an autonomous, active ego.

This concept of a controlled environment represents a kind of dialectic synthesis of opposing attitudes towards the treatment of the mentally ill, from the earliest harsh attempts to overpower and restrain the mentally ill by means of chains and snake pits; to humane efforts like Pinel's who struck off the chains; to those of Szasz who would close the hospitals and in thereby denying the existence of the illness, would essentially eliminate its treatment. But neither destructive hate nor helpless love is enough; only the insights that develop out of scientific understanding and not merely out of a moralistic or humanistic value system can permit the creation of an adequate treatment program.

Our knowledge of schizophrenia is now such as to make imperative the incorporation of our understanding of the function of environmental support systems into our model of treatment for this disease, which is characterized by a lack of organized, stable, synthesized structure. The fragmented, disorganized, unstable state, in which parts dominate the whole, also describes the impact of this illness upon the environment, which is driven inevitably to mirror the patients' inner fragmentation whenever they begin to externalize their feelings of panic and helplessness.

In order to maintain its delusional omnipotent control, which alone guarantees its psychotic existence, the schizophrenic personality must assume omnipotent control over the object, the therapist, the external environment and any part of the world that becomes its living space. It must impose its own design and organization upon everything from which it draws out the nurturance necessary for its very survival. It thus destroys the capacity of the environment to feed the starving potential for normal living. Instead, the environment is required to feed the pathology with part objects that are in the image of the illness itself, and in this way sustains the helpless, nihilistic, autistic core which creates the world in its own image. Not only the therapist, but the total therapeutic environment must withstand such onslaughts against its integrative capacity to provide a comprehensive, unified program. The child's therapist, the caseworker, the hospital personnel must remain united in their mutuality of goals even as they retain autonomy over their respective functions; that is, they must remain whole objects capable of sharing a purpose while simultaneously retaining individuality of function. Without such an understanding of the need for a total and unified treatment program, the respective healing agents are in the position of the blind men, in the fable of the elephant and the blind men, whose limited and limiting perceptual apparatus leads them to equate the fragmented parts that they perceive with its total identity as a unique creature who encompasses all these various aspects. Thus, even though each "may be partly in the right, in the end they all are in the wrong."

An optimal treatment plan for a schizophrenic child should be derived from a full evaluation of his total intrapsychic and interpersonal structure and functioning. The severity of the illness and its accompanying distortions and deficits of functioning have led to the recognition of the necessity for an integration of the intrapsychic model of treatment into a model involving the totality of the available support systems. It must be organized, however, around the dominant ethic that we deal with a human being whose basic integrity and identity are respected even as his illness is recognized and treated. Restoration of the capacity for inner choice and freedom to function remains our primary goal. Through the understanding of the therapist and the insight of the patient, we can hope—to paraphrase Freud—that where unsuitable transferences existed, treatable ones can be developed. For this we must have available all our total armamentarium of therapeutic facilities in order to offer a rational, unified, united and autonomous treatment program as a substitute for the irrational, disintegrated, symbiotic and ultimately helpless "anti-program" that the patient's illness has heretofore both created and responded to in those around him.

BIBLIOGRAPHY

1. FRIEDMAN, SEYMOUR, W. The Diagnostic Process During the Evaluation of an Adolescent Girl. *Children of Time and Space, of Action and Impulse* by Rudolf Ekstein. New York: Appleton-Century-Crofts, 1966.
2. WINNICOTT, D. W. Hate in the Countertransference. *Int. J. of Psychoanalysis,* 1959, 30:69.

Chapter 22

On the Acquisition of Speech in the Autistic Child

RUDOLF EKSTEIN, PH.D.

Dreifach ist die Leistung der menschlichen Sprache, Kundgabe, Auslösung und Darstellung.

—KARL BUHLER, 1918

In 1934 Karl Bühler published his *Sprachtheorie* (4). This classic offers a conceptual model for mature language, which stimulated much thinking and experimental work among researchers of different empirical and theoretical backgrounds, and its influence and relevance are still felt.

Bühler describes three functions of mature language: expression, appeal and description. He depicts a simplified model of language in this diagram:

Presented on the occasion of the late Karl Bühler's 80th birthday celebration in Santa Barbara, 1960; Chicago Institute for Psychoanalysis, February, 1960; Los Angeles Psychoanalytic Society, March 17, 1960; Topeka Psychoanalytic Society, April, 1960; American Psychoanalytic Association, May, 1960 (Atlantic City, New Jersey); Associacion Psicoanalitica Mexicana, November 23, 1961; Judge Baker Guidance Center, Boston, Massachusetts, May 2, 1962.

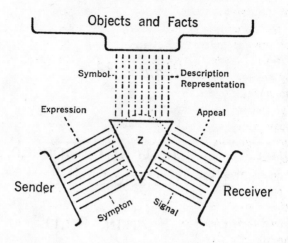

The speaking person, the sender, expresses something about himself, for example, his awareness of inner or outer experience. Were he to do so without any wish to communicate to another person, or perhaps without any capacity for such communication, he would but talk to himself. His self-expression could be considered by observers merely as a symptom of a certain state of mind. If he were intentionally to choose to avoid communication, his behavior could be considered quasi-autistic. He could be diagnosed as autistic in a pathological sense if he were actually unable to avail himself of the communication function of language.

The speaking person does not only express something about himself, a symptom of his inner state of mind, of an inner direction or intention. He may also use language as the means—as Plato put it—"to say something about things," the objects or facts which may be of a physical or psychological nature. He then has acquired the descriptive, the representative, function of language. His words, thus, are not only symptoms for his inner state, but are also symbols for outer or inner reality. These symbols may refer to many different levels of symbolism or to an empirical fact, which has been elaborated by Freud (13) in his discussion of the hierarchy of thought within a range which is defined through the "primary versus secondary process dichotomy." The unavailability, for example, of the functions of time and time-oriented memory would bring to the foreground a language which would not allow the speaker to differentiate consistently between outer and inner worlds or present and past experience. Such language would thus indicate in the "sender" a symptom of permanent or temporary loss of reality testing, an impairment which has been associated with psychotic states.

Finally, the sender, if he can avail himself of the full power of speech, can appeal to the "receiver" of the communication. He gives him a signal in order to influence him in some way. Mature language, then, can be examined in terms of the nature of its functions of description, expression or appeal; it may be understood as symbol, symptom or signal. Any loss or restriction of function in any of these areas may be taken as a sign of emotional or mental illness based on organic and/or functional deficiency and will challenge the investigator of language to raise questions concerning the nature of such loss.

Such questions may be posed in terms of the genesis of the loss, as well as the genesis of available functions. Clinical considerations, at least until very recently, have usually influenced us in searching for the cause of pathology. Studies such as Bühler's strengthen a new and more recent trend in the clinical scientist and encourage us also to ask questions concerning the genesis of available functions. If we wish to repair what has been modified pathologically, or if we wish to restore and encourage growth potentials for functions not as yet available, we will do well to concern ourselves with both available strengths and the genesis of such strengths.

Bühler's model of mature language seems to be in agreement with recent psychoanalytic considerations. In an unpublished lecture, Anna Freud (12) spoke about the normal person as one who is capable of using mature language. She defines mature language in terms of its communication and symbolic function, a definition which is in agreement with Bühler's concept. A child acquires mature language through imitation and identification in a process of socialization, after giving up symbiotic ties and forming object relationships (11, 30). Mature language is, thus, usually an indicator of the person's capacity to form and maintain object relationships; to utilize reality testing; to replace the pleasure principle with the reality principle and impulse by delay; to deal with a widened area of genuine choice.

Bühler's contribution to language theory and to thinking has also been given recognition in recent psychoanalytic literature, such as in Rapaport's "Organization and Pathology of Thought" (23), in Spitz's "No or Yes" (27) as well as in his "Genèse des Premières Relations Objectales" (25); and in Loewenstein's "Some Remarks on the Role of Speech in Psychoanalytic Technique" (19). Reference will be made to these authors as I try to develop my thesis on *how the autistic child acquires part functions of speech*.

The diagnostic category of *early infantile autism* was introduced by Kanner in the early forties. Kanner and Eisenberg restate their position on speech development in the autistic child as follows:

> A second distinctive feature was noted as the failure to use language for the purpose of communication. In three of the eleven cases, speech failed to develop altogether. The remaining eight developed a precocity of articulation which, coupled with unusual facility in rote memory, resulted in the ability to repeat endless numbers of rhymes, catechisms, lists of names, and other semantically useless exercises. The parroting of words intellectually incomprehensible to the child brought into sharp relief the gross failure to use speech to convey meaning or feeling to others. The repetition of stored phrases while failing to recombine words into original and personalized sentences, gave rise to the phenomena of delayed echolalia, pronominal reversal, literalness, and affirmation by repetition (17).

In Travis' *Handbook of Speech Pathology*, Wolpe (30) expresses current, dynamic, clinical thinking on speech difficulties, as does Gertrud Wyatt on stuttering:

> Since the primary function of speech is social communication which in itself implies an interdependence in interpersonal relationships, and which reaches its highest functional value when a oneness in understanding is attained, disturbances in speech, would occur primarily when the interdependent relationship is off balance. Instead of the anticipated understanding resultant from the acquisition of speech there is heightened anxiety and frustration, for the individual finds a widened

rather than a narrowed gap in the area of communication. This is actually what frequently occurs. When the infant is in the babbling stage, the parent is able to coo with him and delight in his dependency. But as the infant moves on to a higher stage in his maturational process, the parent is less and less accepting of his behavior, more and more critical of it, and determined to train the child by imposing demands upon him. The acquisition of speech, equated as it is with maturation, now becomes a symbol of the danger of further maturation, and the child holds tenaciously to infantile speech patterns as symbolic of the period when demands were minimal and when understanding was heightened. Functional disturbances in speech, therefore, would indicate an interference in the normal speech process because of difficulties encountered in the dynamic interaction between the ego and its surrounding forces. Speech, per se, divorced from social interaction would be static and mechanistic and would cease to have any communicative function. Speech is part of the very acculturation of the child and carries with it, therefore, the emotional impacts that any dynamic interaction involves (31).

This general statement does not differentiate among a variety of different pathological forms of speech, nor is it designed for differential diagnosis which might permit us to use the speech difficulty in order to determine the specific syndrome characteristic for the child patient. But it is a beginning in the right direction which has been followed up by more recent work of other contributors to this problem area.

Spitz (27), for example refers to Karl Bühler's formulation on the organization of behavior as a most concise and convincing one. Bühler (4) states that behavior is progressively segregated out of the random disorganized movements of the newborn through the conservation of success—specific movements on the one hand, and the simultaneous elimination of unsuccessful movements on the other. The goal—specific movement—will then be organized into a goal-directed pattern.

Spitz attempts to tackle the problem of speech in investigating preverbal communications (27). He discusses communication in the mother-child duality and defines these communications as: "Every directed or non-directed action of one or more persons, which influences the perception, the feeling, the sensation, the thinking or action of another person in an intentional or unintentional manner" (25). (Similar ideas, to be discussed later, were expressed in "Thoughts Concerning the Nature of the Interpretive Process" (10).) Spitz has investigated pre-verbal communication, that is, phenomena occurring a long time before the use of words or of language proper is acquired (25). He suggests that:

> It will serve to clarify our concepts if we try to enumerate the successive steps in the process of acquiring verbal communication. The first of these steps is the direct discharge of tension in the neonate. This is the step which I have discussed in the article "The Primal Cavity." In the next step of the infant's development a secondary function of this discharge process is acquired; the infant, having developed the functions of perception and memory, links his own discharge, screaming with the tension relief offered by the environment. In the terms of Karl Bühler's language theory, in which he distinguished within the total phenomenon of language three functions, namely expression, appeal and description, the first step just described is expression, while the second step is appeal. Bühler intentionally limited his approach to the descriptive function of language (27).

Spitz suggests that words which designate concrete things and persons are acquired by the child at the end of the first year in the form of "global words," like "ma-ma." Greenson (15) has made the same point in his paper "About the Sound 'MM'," which designates the contentment of the nursing child as well as the echo in the mother's identification with the child's pleasure. The first global word is used by the child to communicate his needs to the libidinal object, that is to the mother, who is also his executive. It signifies, indiscriminately, hunger, boredom, discomfort, etc., and the wish to be relieved of them, just as it signifies biscuit, toy, mother and the desire for these. Other such global words are acquired in the following weeks by the child and a certain measure of specialization of single words is achieved. These first verbal symbols signifying needs manifestly are, to use Karl Bühler's classification, still in the nature of an appeal and not of a description.

Spitz suggests that "a new level of integration is achieved after eighteen months of life. The verbal symbols which are now acquired are used not only for the purpose of appeal, but also for the purpose of description, and specific individual syntax is elaborated." Spitz suggests that this development permits the child to fulfill the function of abstraction. Or, as Kubie (18) has expressed it, "The child has acquired the symbolic function."

When I was investigating the nature of the interpretive process (10), a model of interpretation was suggested which may permit us to study rudimentary aspects of interpretation and communication. Rapaport's primary model of thought (23) was utilized in order to develop a psychoanalytic theory of thought. My suggestion was that the tension-need system of the hungry infant who "communicates" his needs to the mother through crying or restlessness utilizes the appeal function of language. Actually, at first the infant uses only the expressive function, the unintentional signal type of language. It is, however, understood by the mother as an appeal and stimulates her to offer him nourishment and thus to "interpret" the situation. If the baby "communicates" successfully, and is correctly "interpreted" by the mother, a state of affairs exists which presupposes communion between infant and mother —a healthy symbiotic arrangement. In this way a stepping-stone is created which will permit the child to move from the first function of language, the expressive one, to the acquisition of the appeal function. Such language, even though it makes use of words and sentences, is not as yet under dominance of the symbolic function and does not allow for delay. It is really an exchange of unintentional baby signals and intentional maternal acts, and is under the dominance of the pleasure principle. This primitive "language" should really be considered a forerunner of language. It serves to restore homeostasis and is based on the successful achievement of communion which, with incorporation, is directly associated with the togetherness in the root of the word "communication."

A remarkable process, the pre-verbal features of which have been excellently described by Spitz (27) and the logical features of which have been studied by Piaget (21, 22), is observable in the development of language out of impulses, to early imagery, to noun language, to language which consists primarily of the expression of needs (or the expression of restrictions), to fantasy, to secondary-process thinking and reality testing. Isakower (16) has referred to the spoken word in dreams as the expression of the conscience. This idea is expressed in popular usage by "the *voice* of conscience." It can be seen clinically in auditory hallucinations of schizophrenics whose restitutional efforts have regressed to this early development of communication with others and within themselves. The nature of interpretation has been examined within different therapeutic contexts and in reference to patients who have not achieved full capacity for object relationships or symbolic communication. They have given up, in part, the function of descriptive language, which allows for delay and which reflects thinking as trial action. Indication was made of some of the problems which confront us as we communicate with people who are not capable of contact through communication but only through communion in the more primitive sense. Such people fuse the act and the word so that, for them, interpretations become primarily signals which trigger off action rather than stimulate reflection (10).

Reference was made, as in Loewenstein's work (19), to communication devices which are non-verbal and which occur on a different level of consciousness. The sicker or the younger the patient, the more we must rely on means of communication and on interpretation which must consider pre-verbal aspects of language as well as the spoken precursors of mature speech.

The speech problems of the autistic child might lend themselves to a variety of considerations concerning the early functions of language and their acquisition which might prove clinically useful. Bühler's language model can serve as a yardstick against which to measure the task which the autistic child has accomplished; the functions which he has not acquired; the problems that he and the therapist face. They are trying to bring about communion and to form a relationship, initially dominated by utilization of a need-gratifying object and progressively developing to mature communication, which is dominated by the interpretive process. The foundation of this process is the acquisition of mature speech and of mature object relationships. It has frequently been said that the schizophrenic needs contact, communion and communication. No doubt, communication, the use of speech, is the basis for the lasting therapeutic effects, but as Loewenstein stated, "People do not change just because they communicate with each other. What counts in analysis is not communication by itself but *what is being communicated,* on the part of both patient and analyst, what leads to communication, and what psychic processes and changes occur as a result of this communication as such and of its contents" (19). Differentiation has been made between precursors of interpretation and interpretation proper, both of which, however, seem to be equally necessary parts of the total interpretive process (10).

The analytic understanding of the autistic child, a comparatively new interest, as reflected in the literature of the last few years (7) must begin with a consideration of the symptom of autism in reference to available speech development. Kanner believes that one distinctive feature of autism is "the failure to use language for the purpose of communication" (17). The autistic child is described by him as suffering from extreme withdrawal, representing the turning away from intolerable, frustrating and ungiving relationships with parents who could not meet the child's emotional needs, and lead the child to seek comfort in solitude. The child's relationships are described as mechanistic, and its use of others as if they were tools or machines. The autistic child is not capable of genuine human relationships, and his repetitive, mechanical speech is imitative in nature and dominated by echolalia.

Mahler (20) has offered many valuable discussions on the autistic child in dynamic rather than in mere descriptive forms. She sees in autism a special symptom of the disease process, a position which is to defend the child against the symbiotic position, the danger of being devoured by the mother in a pathological relationship. She speaks of autism as the negativism of the symbiotic child. Bleuler (2) discusses symptoms of touching, echopraxia and echolalia and considers them as "phenomena of restitution." This conception suggests that in tactually ascertaining the presence of the object and thus "introjecting" it (identifying with it) through imitation, the patient attempts to regain the world of objects from which he has withdrawn. Echolalia may serve a similar purpose, and the schizophrenic manner of dealing with words could be considered, as Freud has also stated, an attempt at restitution of the lost world of objects.

The adult schizophrenic, in spite of regressive phenomena, retains many functions of adult speech which make it difficult, perhaps, to answer questions concerning the early problems in infantile autism, which are our present concern. Autistic thinking, or as Bleuler has called it, dereistic thinking, is a part of normal development. Spitz speaks about these facts as follows:

> For the child, the feces form a part of his own person. Toilet training is resented as an attempt to deprive him of the liberty of using his self, his body, the sphincters. He will defend these liberties stubbornly. This explanation does not exhaust the various aspects of the anal phase. It purports only to show the role of growing self-awareness in the manifestations of stubbornness during the anal phase.
>
> One of these manifestations is the child's repetitive use of the "No" while doing what the adult wishes him to do. It seems to us that this "No" is a manifesto of independence. It is the same statement, "I have a will of my own and even when it is the same as yours, it is different because it is my own! I am doing this because I want it and I am not doing what *you* want!"
>
> In this example the autistic (dereistic) thinking of the child is very much in evidence. It clearly shows the inappropriate affect, the cleavage between the affect and that which occasions it. In consequence of this cleavage, the message conveyed by the child contradicts the action he performs. This example shows a behavior which is completely normal for the child in his second year. However, this normal action of the child also throws light on the processes of dereistic thinking and inappropriate affect in schizophrenia (27).

The child suffering from infantile autism is characterized by lack of speech, dereistic thinking, and the availability of only archaic forerunners of object relationships which have an autistic or symbiotic taint. Speech development is primarily expressive; dominated by signal and emergency functions of language; has usually mere non-intentional appeal function and only occasionally intentional appeal function. Speech development is also frequently characterized by motoric equivalents of early means of communication, the purpose of which is usually the restoration or the absolute avoidance of communion. Other characteristics of speech development include echolalia and echopraxia, the imitative aspects of which can be considered a forerunner of identificatory processes and an unsuccessful attempt at incorporation.

He who treats such children must be prepared for frustrations of a very strange kind. The therapist soon finds that he is attempting to relate to a child who desperately attempts to use the adult but cannot establish an object relationship; who constantly searches for contact but must destroy it; who hopelessly and unhappily attempts to acquire the means of communication but achieves only a senseless echo. The child reacts to the awareness of being understood with violent, frequently rejecting, motoric acts. Words which exist to express thoughts are received by the child as a signal which triggers off unexpected action. The psychotherapist must deal with children who may not speak for many months, even though they indicate here or there that some of what is communicated to them is understood in primitive ways. The child's utter rejection of him whom he needs most creates a bewildering puzzle for the therapist who can only understand such terror-stricken reactions as something that must have been caused by rejecting, condemning and violent parents. The therapist's anger at the parents can be understood—to paraphrase E. Kris—as *regression in the service of the therapist's ego,* thereby permitting the maintenance of identification with the child. If the therapeutic ego loses control, genuine regressions create "hate in the counter-transference" (29). Frequently, one's own anger in the counter-transference can be tolerated only as it is projected onto the parent or to a colleague in the institutional setting.

The expressions of the autistic child, scarce as they may be, seem to urge us to understand them as an appeal to us. We try to meet the appeal by offering ourselves as the need-gratifying objects. And then—we are rejected. We are experienced as danger to the precarious precursor of identity which the autistic position offers the child.

Much of the foregoing can be seen in an autistic 3½-year-old girl, Nanny, during her psychotherapy on an out-patient basis.*

Nanny, whose twin sister is a comparatively healthy youngster, and whose parents have brought up two older children quite successfully, showed all the characteristics of autistic behavior. Her first weeks in therapy consisted of aimless searching and a wild

---

* I am grateful to Mrs. Leda Rosow for this striking clinical example.

manipulation of the therapist whom she would pull along with her in her chaotic investigation of the clinic's surroundings but whose words she seemingly did not hear. The child's speech behavior was characterized by the dominant use of echolalia. Occasionally, the therapist understood some of the child's echolalia-like communications. When following Nanny through the corridors of the clinic, the therapist could hear her say repeatedly: "Here, Nanny, go." It was as if she were describing her own activities in the third person.

Actually she was repeating the therapist's description of her activities. In an attempt to maintain some kind of communication with Nanny, the therapist had decided to describe in simple words what was happening, what Nanny was doing. The echolalia was of such a kind that it suggested the interpretation that it was the child's attempt to repeat what the therapist had said; that is, to describe her own actions, and thus to incorporate descriptive statements as well as occasional commands. The seemingly meaningless echolalia of the first few weeks changed. It turned into a practice in which it seemed clear that the child imitated, without apparent awareness, the voice of the therapist or, as it were, the voice of a commanding conscience to which Nanny now listened. The child's aimless act, through the "description" of the therapist, had now become a task, and the description of the therapist had become a command within the matrix of the autistic-symbiotic struggle.

A few weeks after the development had been noted and was continuing, the mother reported that as they were driving home, Nanny verbalized repeated short sentences. These were actually verbatim statements of the therapist's communications to her, which she was mechanically repeating. It became clear that the therapist had gained some foothold in the child's primitive inner life. Echolalia, rather than an empty and mechanistic repetition of words, a parrot-like imitation, seemed to be in this case, an attempt to introject the therapist, to incorporate her voice, and to become her. Rather than hearing the "voice of conscience," Nanny repeated the voice of the therapist and thus tried to use the therapist's communication as a quasi-organizer of her own inner life. One could look at this as an attempt to restore the introject which was lost and which could be maintained only if a quasi-auditory hallucination was maintained. Echolalia then could be considered as the motoric and verbal substitute for the auditory hallucination. It is as if Nanny now could weave her fantasies of having the therapist with her around the spoken word. The spoken word is comparable to the toy, the external object around which a fantasy or delusion may be woven. Echolalia then could be considered a forerunner of more advanced psychotic play, the nature of which has been discussed in a recent paper (8).

It is interesting that the clinicians have used the term "echolalia" in order to stress the mechanistic, blindly imitative, hardly human characteristics of autistic speech. On the surface, popular usage holds the same view. A German proverb says: *"Wie man in den Wald hinein ruft, so kommt es heraus."* The phenomenon of sound being thrown back by the woods as one calls into the woods, is actually used as the simile which suggests that "communication may be any directed or non-directed action of one or more people, who thus influence perception, feeling, sensation, thinking or action in one or more other people in an intentional or unintentional manner" (27). Even the autistic child, incapable as she is of communication on a higher level, *responds,* and the response itself depends on the nature of what is expressed by the therapist. The autistic child, then, has neither completely lost nor, as yet, completely achieved the capacity for understanding, for mature communication. She works with primitive speech elements and many archaic forerunners of the organum of language, which indicate strongly that she can be reached, albeit in a primitive way only. The functions of expression and appeal, even though they are not fully developed, dominate the communication scene. The appeal value of the therapist's voice has not yet become a permanent introject. It must be constantly restored through echolalia, a form of self-appeal, a forerunner of internal language and thought of silent inner speech.

Nanny gave the impression that she was trying in vain to incorporate the love object. The endless repetition of the therapist's simple orders, suggestions or descriptions were not fully "swallowed," but were only endlessly repeated.

One of the child's motoric activities, a precursor of play, was her interminable occupation with the water fountain. This seemed to refer to Nanny's attempt to restore the mother object. Whenever the mother was out of sight, the child would endlessly play with water and continually drink large amounts of it, as if to restore a situation of nurture. The use of echolalia, also serving the restoration of the object, or at least serving the primitive maintenance of some form of primitive object relationship, characterized this particular phase of treatment. The echolalia activity of the autistic child could be considered the child's attempt to make herself independent of the love object by introjecting, or repeating its appeal function.

Echolalia, a primitive form of imitation, a failure in the achievement of permanent introjections and identifications, is an attempt to acquire the capacity for object relationships and the capacity of speech by the installment plan, as it were. I am reminded of the Viennese dialect expression which refers to installment payments as "*abstottern,*" to stutter it off.

Brenner discusses the importance of identification for the child's acquisition of language and he suggests that:

> Simple observation will show us that the child's acquisition of motor speech depends in considerable measure on the psychological tendencies to imitate an object in the environment or, in other words, to identify with it. It is perfectly true that a child cannot learn to speak until his central nervous system has matured sufficiently and that the acquisition of language as a whole is far from being simply a process of imitation. Nevertheless it is true that children ordinarily speak in imitation, at least at first. That is to say they repeat sounds that adults say for them, and learn to say them in imitation of an adult, very often as part of a game. Moreover, it is most instructive to observe that every child talks with the same "accent" as do the adults and other children of his environment. Intonation, pitch, pronunciation, and idioms are all copied exactly if the child's hearing is normal. So exactly, indeed, that it makes one wonder whether what we ordinarily call "tone-deafness," that is, the inability to detect relative differences in pitch, can really be congenital. However that may be, we can have no doubt that identification plays a very great role in the acquisition of this particular ego-function that we have called motor speech" (5).

We may speak of the autistic child's lack of communication only if we think in terms of mature language. If the communication function of language is primarily thought of in terms of description, of symbolic expression, then indeed we will find the young autistic child severely handicapped and we may think of our patient as being unable to "communicate." If, however, we consider other functions of speech, such as expression, appeal, contacting, signaling, imitation and restoration of part objects, we will be inclined to give up the designation of "autistic" as a diagnosis and to see in it rather a special phase of psychotic illness. Even an older child patient, who regresses to an autistic position, does not completely withdraw, but rather withdraws from or gives up symbolic communication.

The attempt of the patient to restore communion whenever necessary may constitute a regression or a fixation at a level of development characterized by the shifting positions between positive nurture within a symbiotic communion and the autism of sleep after satisfaction has been achieved. The dream could be considered as the normal hallucination of the healthy, containing among other functions a normal form of echolalia. Echolalia or echopraxia in the waking stage, however, represents a pathological form, and could be looked upon as a quasi-dream. This way of looking at echolalia and echopraxia is a useful device as long as it does not mislead us to overstep the boundaries of this analogy. The therapist who succeeds in becoming a part of the system of echolalia and of delayed echolalia, as was true in the case of Nanny, has created a transference-like condition, analogous to the one of the patient who dreams of the analyst. Nanny's therapist thus stepped into the child's dream and became a part of a new, common, comparatively undifferentiated matrix. Out of this, a new form of echolalia might grow, which could lead to symbolic speech, an acquisition characteristic of the descriptive function of language.

Bak (1) suggests that the internal image "appears in almost clean culture in automatic obedience, in the echolalias and echopraxias" and "is a part of [the schizophrenic's] symptomatology and comes under the heading of ego restitution." He wonders as to how the "furthering of the same mechanisms" is to "lead to appropriate behavior and clinical improvement." He expresses "doubts that the mechanisms of object-finding and identification would account for it." And he wonders as to what else there is to account for the higher integration of the ego. It seems to me that Wexler's (28) experience with adult patients and my own with very young child and adolescent patients (6) do not suggest that the internalization of the therapist's image is *the* cause for change but rather allows for the creation of the transference track upon which the psychotherapeutic process may proceed. We are simply speaking of a modified technique to allow for the establishment and maintenance of the therapeutic situation rather than trying to account for all agents of change.

Nanny's small language vocabulary is further restricted by a group of implied rules for usage. These rules must be discovered by us as we study the natural habitat of this child's language, thereby enabling ourselves to reconstruct this very habitat; that is, the state of her psychic functioning, the degree, quantitatively as well as qualitatively, of the "disturbance in the reciprocal identification between mother and child" (31). We can thus reconstruct the available capacity for the maintenance or formation of object relationships in whatever precursor form they may appear. We may also be able to reconstruct existing conflict and crises in the psychosexual and psychoaggressive development as they occur within the matrix of impoverished ego maturation and development.

Echolalia is a phenomenon under constant change as the inner dynamics of the child and the vicissitudes of the therapeutic relationship change. At the end of one session and at a time when the child was screamingly unruly and chaotic, the therapist spoke to Nanny about the necessity to stop. The violent and archaic movements of the child gave the impression that she did not hear or understand her therapist. After the therapist's repeated comments concerning ending and leaving, Nanny suddenly and unexpectedly stopped screaming and kicking and said quietly, "Nanny, say bye-bye!" These words were not directed to the therapist. They were said in seeming self-absorption—as if Nanny had carried on a dialogue with herself—and they clearly represented the mother's repeated demands. In regard to the mother, they constituted an expression of delayed echolalia; in regard to the therapist, an indirect response, which indicated that the patient had understood her. It is as if Nanny suddenly recalled her mother's order, which, rather than executing, she now repeated in parrotlike echolalia-bound fashion.

Echolalia here served not only the function of restitution, the restoration of the mother's voice, but was also in the service of the recognizing ego. We deal here with an example of "regression in the service of the ego," albeit a psychotic ego (a formulation suggested by Ernest Kris). As Nanny regresses to echolalia, the delayed imitation of her mother's voice, we note that this *selected regression,* as it were, now permits her to understand and to deal with a new situation by making it into an old and familiar one. Every mental act of recognition, of insight, is an act of reducing the new to the old and the familiar. Otherwise, such a neutral act must be experienced chaotically with mechanical and blind reliance on the auxiliary ego of the mother. But the mother's organizing capacity cannot become part of the child's mentality except as it desperately tries to identify with the mother through the primitive echolalia response.

At a later point of the treatment process, Nanny pulled the therapist back and forth through different parts of the clinic, implying an aimless searching for objects which she has in mind but seems able neither to name, nor to know in a conscious sense. The therapist said to the child as they arrived at the door which led to the street: "It is raining." Nanny followed with, "It's wet." There is the possibility that the child did not respond to the therapist but made an independent statement which by chance corresponded to the therapist's comment. Barring this, her short sentence provides a beautiful and simple example of how she moved from the use of stereotyped and delayed echolalia limited to the service of restitution and imitation of objects. The echolalia of her response was in the service of the recognizing ego and demonstrated the capacity of rephrasing somebody else's statement. While seemingly a repetition and, as such, still related to echolalia, it was clearly, an indication that words were being grasped as symbols rather than as mere signs or signals, that a beginning had been made in the acquisition of the representative, the descriptive function of language.

At the end of one session, approximately six months later, the child's mother came to the therapist to say: "I have something encouraging to tell you. Until now Nanny never showed any signs that she had learned anything from you. But now I know that she has learned something, because she says two things that you always say. She says, '*No, no, no, you mustn't do that,*' and that's what she always hears you say, because I never say anything like that. She also says to herself—again your way of putting it—as she does something, '*That's the way!*' "

We might look at the mother's observation as a confirmation of our earlier interpretation of delayed echolalia, and, even more, we may see in it an example of a clearer and more highly developed use of the therapist. We may think of Nanny's walking through her world in the way that we think of an airplane landing, guided by radar rather than by the pilot's direct observations. Nanny's "radar" are the therapist's commands and assurances. As she echoes the therapist, her own voice, "No, no, you mustn't do that," guides one aspect of her activity. She thus establishes the forerunner of a super-ego. Approved activities of Nanny are accompanied by the delayed echolalia response. "That's the way," and serve as forerunner of ego-ideal functions. She travels on these two beams supplied by the therapist and thus lands safely. Blind flying may not always be the safest way but it is the only way when one is surrounded by dense and impenetrable fog. The therapist's injunctions and approvals, when genuinely internalized, turn echolalia responses into stable ego functions, thus replacing blind flying with genuine reality testing.

This schematized and over-simplified use of clinical data does not do justice to the fantastic difficulties one encounters when working with such children. Nevertheless, even schematic, over-simplified thinking may permit conjectures which might lead to technical suggestions for the treatment of such patients. Their chaotic behavior, their non-conventional responses, and their lack of capacity to communicate on levels on which we are able to respond put us in the situation of a person lost in the primeval forest and searching desperately for the way out. Such a person might be overwhelmed by millions of impressions, but might not find a sign from which to glean a cue as to the direction which will lead him into known, explored and cultivated territory. Not even a ray of sunlight comes through in sufficient strength since the thick ceiling of the foliage screens the forest floor. The therapist of such children will find frequently that there seems to be no familiar sign on which to attach a tactical maneuver or from which to derive a strategic plan built on a possible rationale. The therapist might find that Bühler's formulation (3) on the organization of behavior, according to which behavior is progressively segregated out of random disorganized movements and directed toward goal-specific movements and goal-directed patterns, does not seem to hold for both therapist and patient. It is as if the therapist repeats the experience of the mother who desperately but vainly attempts to arrive at a relationship with her child which is based on reciprocal identification.

But as the therapist follows the most *dominant speech event,* the echolalia phenomenon, he finds himself in a situation comparable to that of the explorer who suddenly discovers an open spot in the forest, accessible to sunlight and allowing him to synchronize the time on his watch and the shadow patterns and thus to find his bearings. Echolalia thus becomes meaningful and opens for him an access to primitive communion-communication. It is as if he, rather than the child, has to give up random-disorganized movements, and has to strenghen success-specific movements in the achievement of contact with the patient. Rather than expecting that the child can identify with him, he imitates the child, follows its actions and puts them into words and imitative acts. The child's echolalia is met by the therapist's advanced echolalia, a translation of the child's acts into the therapist's symbols. He thus reaches the child in terms of living himself into the world of the child. The child's autism grows into a symbiosis which is based not on commands or on expectations, but on understanding by the therapist. By saying what the child does, he echoes the patient and becomes the partner in the child's search for contact, and offers strength which will allow the patient to replace the unsuccessful imitation with his capacities. Thus, the child may acquire capacity for identification and symbolic language through the therapist's willingness to become, temporarily, like the child. The demand on the child to identify with the more mature person results in echolalia, a symptom through which the child tries to imitate and indicates that it cannot complete the act of imitation. This is a symptom which is replaced with the less threatening gift of the therapist; that is, his effort to become the patient's extension. Instead of persistently demanding that the child identify with the world of the adult, the therapist persistently intrudes into the inner world of the child. He does this by means of imitation of acts and with descriptive words, through quasi-echopraxia and echolalia as it were. Since the therapist expresses no more than the child's appeal, the child learns to understand itself against the matrix of a child-dominated symbiosis. It may thus be able to give up the autistic position it assumed as a defense against negative symbiosis. Since this poses an impossible task and forces the child into failure, trying to meet the task and failure are combined in echolalia.

These few remarks neither explain sufficiently the success of such therapeutic maneuvers nor do they throw much light on the etiology of this illness. But they do seem to allow us to enter an unknown area which, once there, we may open to more consistent and formal research. These recesses of the mind, pre-verbal in origin, must be understood if we wish to understand more fully the dynamics of language development and its meaning in terms of first relationships. It is not arbitrariness that popular conception speaks of *"Muttersprache,"* mother tongue," when it refers to one's native language. Greenson (14) has pointed this out when he contended "that the early mechanisms of auditory incorporation and identification necessary for learning to speak and learning a new language are decisively influenced by the outcome of the conflicts between mother, breast, and child." Schwing's therapeutic "motherliness" (24), a suggestion for the opening phase of psychotherapy with adult schizophrenics, also has its place, in modified form, in our therapeutic work with such children. It gives them a new mother-tongue through which expression turns into successful appeal and, thus, allows for description, completing hereby the development of language, characteristic for *homo sapiens*. This triple accomplishment of mature language was stated by Karl Bühler in 1918: *"Thrice is the function of human language, expression, appeal and representation."*

BIBLIOGRAPHY

1. BAK, ROBERT C. Discussion of Dr. Wexler's Paper. *Psychotherapy with Schizophrenics.* Eugene B. Brody and Frederick C. Redlich, editors. New York: International Universities Press, Inc., 1952, pp. 201-207.

2. BLEULER, EGON. *Dementia Praecox oder Gruppe der Schizophrenien.* Leipzig: Deuticke, 1911.

3. BUHLER, KARL. *Die Geistige Entwicklung des Kindes.* Jena: Gustav Fischer, 1924.

4. BUHLER, KARL. *Sprachtheorie.* Jena: Verlag von Gustav Fischer, 1934.

5. BRENNER, CHARLES. *An Elementary Textbook of Psychoanalysis.* New York: International Universities Press, Inc., 1955.

6. EKSTEIN, RUDOLF. Vicissitudes of the "Internal Image" in the Recovery of a Borderline Schizophrenic Adolescent. *Bulletin of the Menninger Clinic,* 1955, 29:86-92.

7. EKSTEIN, RUDOLF, BRYANT, KEITH, and FRIEDMAN, SEYMOUR W. Childhood Schizophrenia and Allied Conditions. *Schizophrenia—A Review of the Syndrome.* Leopold Bellak, editor. New York: Logos Press, 1958.

8. EKSTEIN, RUDOLF, and FRIEDMAN, SEYMOUR W. On the Meaning of Play in Childhood Psychosis. *Dynamic Psychopathology in Childhood.* Lucie Jessner and Eleanor Pavenstedt, editors. New York: Grune & Stratton, 1959.

9. EKSTEIN, RUDOLF, WALLERSTEIN, JUDITH, and MANDELBAUM, ARTHUR. Counter-Transference in the Residential Treatment of Children—Treatment Failure in Childhood Symbiotic Psychosis. *Psychoanalytic Study of the Child,* 1959, 14:186-218.

10. EKSTEIN, RUDOLF. Thoughts Concerning the Nature of the Interpretive Process. *Readings in Psychoanalytic Psychology.* Morton Levitt, editor. New York: Grune & Stratton, Inc., 1959.

11. FENICHEL, OTTO. *On the Psychoanalytic Theory of Neurosis.* New York: W. W. Norton & Co., 1945.

12. FREUD, ANNA. The Concept of Normality. Unpublished. Medical Faculty Lecture, University of California at Los Angeles, April 2, 1959.

13. FREUD, SIGMUND. Formulations Regarding the Two Principles of Mental Functioning (1911). *Collected Papers,* Vol. IV. London: Hogarth Press, 1949.

14. GREENSON, RALPH R. The Mother Tongue and the Mother. *International Journal of Psychoanalysis,* 1950, 31:1-6.

15. GREENSON, RALPH R. About the Sound "MM . . ." *Psychoanalytic Quarterly,* 1954, 33:234-239.

16. ISAKOWER, OTTO. Spoken Words in Dreams. *Psychoanalytic Quarterly,* 1954, 23:1-6.

17. KANNER, LEO, and EISENBERG, LEON. *Early Infantile Autism, 1943-1955.* Psychiatric Research Reports of the American Psychiatric Association, April, 1957.

18. KUBIE, LAWRENCE S. The Distortion of the Symbolic Process in Neurosis and Psychosis. *Journal of the American Psychoanalytic Association,* 1953, 1:59-86.

19. LOEWENSTEIN, RUDOLPH M. Some Remarks on the Role of Speech in Psychoanalytic Technique. *International Journal of Psychoanalysis,* 1956, 37:460-467.

20. MAHLER, MARGARET. On Child Psychosis and Schizophrenic, Autistic and Symbiotic Infantile Psychoses. *Psychoanalytic Study of the Child*, 1952, 7:286-305.

21. PIAGET, JEAN. *Play, Dreams and Imitation in Childhood.* New York: W. W. Norton, Inc., 1951.

22. PIAGET, JEAN. *The Origins of Intelligence in Children.* New York: International Universities Press, Inc. 1952.

23. RAPAPORT, DAVID. *Organization and Pathology of Thought.* New York: Columbia University Press, 1951.

24. SCHWING, GERTRUD. *A Way to the Soul of the Mentally Ill.* New York: International Universities Press, Inc., 1954.

25. SPITZ, RENE A. Genèse des Premières Relations Objectales. *Revue Française de Psychanalyse*, 1954, 18:479-575.

26. SPITZ, RENE A. The Primal Cavity. *Psychoanalytic Study of the Child*, 1955, 10:215-40.

27. SPITZ, RENE A. *No and Yes—On the Genesis of Human Communication.* New York: International Universities Press, Inc., 1957.

28. WEXLER, MILTON. The Structural Problem in Schizophrenia. *Psychotherapy with Schizophrenics.* Eugene B. Brody and Frederick C. Redlich, editors. New York: International Universities Press, Inc., 1952, pp. 179-201.

29. WINNICOTT, D. W. Hate in the Counter-Transference. *International Journal of Psychoanalysis*, 1949, 30:69-74.

30. WOLPE, ZELDA S. Play Therapy, Psychodrama and Parent Counseling. *Handbook of Speech Pathology.* Lee Edward Travis, editor. New York: Appleton-Century-Crofts, Inc. 1957, pp. 991-1024.

31. WYATT, GERTRUD. Mother-Child Relationship in Stuttering in Children. Unpublished dissertation, 1958.

Chapter 23

From Impulse Expression to Object Relations through Conflict Resolution between Impulse and Object

PETER D. LANDRES, M.D.

The effect on the psychotic child of the struggle between his impulse expression and the parents' efforts at control through a punitive reaction is commonly known to therapists. There are bizarre, disruptive, aggressive, hyperactive, and self-destructive behavioral manifestations. Sometimes there is autistic withdrawal; sometimes there is silly behavior. The child's ego seems overwhelmed, and autonomous ego functions needed for the learning of necessary skills are interfered with. Parents often seem too helpless and paralyzed to be anything but punitive or rejecting in their response to the child's behavior. The parental response and the child's reaction become internalized so that the therapist may be seen as an animated manifestation of forbidden impulses or as a forbidding shadow of the punitive parents.

The patient in therapy appears dominated by the need for drive and impulse expression (2, 7, 8, 11). With latent schizophrenic or borderline psychotic children, this often leads to a therapeutic dilemma, often conceptualized as a control struggle. Helping the patient to gain control is a goal of most therapeutic approaches, whether they be analytic, eclectic, or behavior modifying. These efforts are usually short-lived and result in temporary improvements which last only as long as the therapeutic relationship is maintained in combination with some form of external controls. The external controls very often become dominant and substitute for absent internal controls; regression is common, and therapists become discouraged.

Therapeutic models of treatment vacillate between the polarities of emphasis on control to emphasis on impulse expression (4). The former leads to an improvement in the child's behavior while the latter leads to an improvement in the patient-therapist relationship. However, control is not the basic issue, nor is drive expression or drive repression. The therapist's dilemma actually is the child's. No matter what the child does he cannot maintain an internal object image or an external object relationship, nor can he maintain controls (5, 8, 10, 11). Drive expression is vital for these children. They can only maintain the internal object image upon which their own self-image is founded by continual drive expression because they have not developed enough ego structure out of drive-object interactions to do otherwise (6, 9, 10). The restriction of impulse expression leads to the containment of drives which results in the loss of the ability to maintain object relationships. Clinically, this appears as psychotic behavior. When the drives are expressed, the parents respond punitively to the hostility and aggression in their child's emotional demands. Infantile oral and sexual elements in the child's behavior also help prevent the parents from responding adequately. In the struggle to contain the unacceptable elements, the children lose their parents' image out of their anger towards their parents. Since self- object images are still in an early developmental state and require both external object relations and drive expression for their maintenance, the children are in a state of object loss panic (1). This panic leads them either to abandon object contact and return to autistic withdrawal or to maintain object contact through psychotic behavioral symptom formation.

The ego-disrupting attempts to contain object-seeking drives are particularly evident in the school setting where the children are required to control their impulses. At school these children must simultaneously control their "unwanted" thoughts and actions, while they remember and perform what is expected of them. However, because these children need to have continual tangible evidence of their parental object ties, they cannot repress their impulses. Therefore, they react to the pressure to repress "unwanted" thoughts and actions as they would to impulse control. This response leads either to autistic withdrawal or psychotic behavioral symptoms.

The treatment of a six-year-old latent schizophrenic child first made me aware of this phenomenon. His behavior was continually impulsive, provocative, or destructive. All attempts to enter into a relationship with him failed, as did any attempts to control his behavior (3). When I first took him into treatment, I noticed that he tensed up and flinched after episodes of provocative or destructive behavior. I focused my attention on this, and he was later able to tell me that he was afraid that I would strike him. After he told me of his fear of me, he again exhibited all manner of psychotic behavior which led him to break off contact with me. He then seemed to enter into a state of panic. During the course of treatment he frequently broke off contact with me through psychotic behavior, and at these times he would often express his panic through laughter and giggling. It was this laughter and giggling which led me to believe that he was struggling to establish some form of object tie. This belief was confirmed for me when my interpretation of his fear that I would retaliate led him to quiet down for short periods of time.

To illustrate further my thesis that the internalization of the parental punitive reaction disturbs the object-maintaining impulse expression in latent schizophrenic and borderline psychotic children, I wish to use the case of six-year-old Fred Woods. He was referred to the Reiss-Davis Child Study Center because of his bizarre and hyperactive behavior, short attention span, regressive fetallike posturing, preoccupation with sensual stimulation, and daydreaming. The patient's school was especially concerned with his unprovoked, disruptive, hyperactive, silly, and aggressive behavior. The mother was apprehensive about his behavior at home where he ate crayons and pulled his hair. He suffered from nightmares and from terrifying hallucinations of monsters and attacks by bugs. He reacted to these with frantic, aggressive self-injury and appealed to mother for help. The diagnostic team made the diagnosis of schizophrenia in childhood, latent type. This finding was based on the patient's overall functioning at the borderline psychotic level of adjustment with moments of psychosis. The disorder manifested in severe ego impairment which resulted in thought disorder, loss of reality testing, impaired symbiotic object relationships, and a primitive shifting sense of identity. The personality organization was prone to regression. I saw Fred for the initial interviews but was his second therapist; his first saw him for eight months prior to leaving the clinic. I saw him for the first time some six weeks after the departure of his first therapist. The first therapist felt that Fred "had been able to make use of psychotherapy, principally by partially identifying with some aspects of the therapist, including the quality and capacity of verbalization, the capacity for delay, and the capacity to plan and to consider the implications of action."

In presenting the following case material my intent is to focus on language, drawings, and cutouts in which scatological and sexual expressions enter, both to the patient's pleasure and distress. The aim is to demonstrate not only impulse expression and the internalized punitive parental reaction, but also the consequent impairment of autonomous ego functioning.

Children like Fred struggle between their wish to do schoolwork and their ability to do so. Their attention span is limited, and they often manifest some of the above-mentioned psychotic behavior. Their work is usually incorrect and messy. When they draw they have difficulty making images. These difficulties result from their attempts to maintain a tie to the mother in their schoolwork. With their ego organization based on maintaining the internal object representation through drive-based impulse expression, any attempt to draw images or to write symbols is accompanied by such drive-based impulse expression.

The first hour to be discussed is the ninth therapy hour. It demonstrates how the expression of drives has an exhibitionistic connection to the mother. The fusion of aggressive and libidinal impulses seems to be a primitive defense mechanism which allows the maintenance of the maternal tie. There is also evidence of identity confusion which is connected with the wish to fuse with the mother.

Fred took some scotch tape and paper to make a book to take home to his mother. He asked me whether it should be a "gorilla or an animal book," so I indicated that though he was asking me what to do, it was his mother he really wanted to please. He decided it would be an "animal" book. He had me hold it straight and then he taped it together. He started drawing a giraffe but drew a picture of what he called "poops" coming out of its tail region. He was surprised and dismayed at what he had drawn, so I commented that something had appeared that he hadn't wanted to appear. Then he drew six legs instead of four so I remarked how difficult it was to control things. He said: "I know. I saw a giraffe. How many [legs] should it have?" He thought a giraffe had four legs but he also thought that he had noticed six. He was perplexed. He erased the picture and started over again. This time he made four legs but then he almost erased them all. Out of his fear that the book would fall apart, he wanted to retape it. As he worked, he became concerned that he would ruin the tape. He showed me how careful he was not to "mess up."

As he started to draw on another piece of paper he began to tell me about his friend, Fred N., who was an Indian, and who had his "same first name and middle name," George, but who had a different last name. He went on to tell me that there were other differences between them. He told me that he had two other friends with the same name which was confusing for him, though he said that he knew the difference. Then he talked about "drawing" his name. He had flatus as he spoke about "cutting a fart" and called it a "bad" word. He told me he did it while he was putting "3" and "3" on paper so I asked him if he had done so in a moment of excitement. He wanted his sister to know about it and added that he would make such an explosion that everyone would know about it. I commented on how much he wanted to "make a fart" and have his mother admire it. Then he started to write his name on the piece of paper. He wrote "FRED WO" and began to say what he called "bad words": "fart, poops, tits," etc. I commented how all these words "appeared and interfered" with his ability to finish what he was doing. He tried to write his name again but didn't get further than writing "FRED" before he started scribbling with a pencil and said more of his "words." I told him "all of these thoughts about 'tits' and things like that are so exciting that they make you stop what you are doing." He answered that he had to draw and proceeded to draw breasts which he called "titties" and then put in eyes and a mouth. He went on to draw both male and female sexual organs, becoming excited as he did so. I commented on all the "exciting" things that he had drawn and how hard it was to draw without the "exciting" things. He responded by wanting to know if I had a son and if so was his name John.

The material demonstrates that what appears to be only a control struggle around impulse expression is also a struggle to maintain object ties. When the therapist is able to make interpretations which do not inhibit impulse expression while empathizing with the patient's struggle, a transference of the wish to fuse with the mother appears.

Material from the 37th therapy hour demonstrates how Fred had internalized his fear of a punitive, rejecting mother. He was caught in a struggle between the wish to express his impulses, in order to maintain his tie with the mother, and the wish to control these same impulses, in order to avoid her displeasure and physical punishment.

When he came to the room, he hid something from me which he said was "private." Then he showed me that it was a picture of a man defecating. He took a piece of paper and wanted both of us to cut the paper with scissors. He cut out two shapes, wondering what they were. He decided they were racing cars and that I could have one of them. He thought that the shapes I cut out were snakes. I commented that my shapes must seem dangerous, whereupon he said that I was making bunnies. At this time I decided that because of his concern with making or drawing feces, I would cut out poop shapes. He became worried about the shapes because he perceived them as "bad words." I commented that his fear was that "poop words" would hurt him. He began associating with "poops" to "poo" to "fart" to "pee" to "pussy" and said that he was going to say all the other words that he could think of that were "slap words," that is, words for which he would be slapped by his mother. I helped him try to find words which were not "slap words," but no matter how we tried, he would associate back to "slap words." As he continued to make shapes and draw with me, he continued to make pictures and shapes of feces. Finally he decided he would make something out of the feces. He attached some Kleenex to three of the feces shapes that he had connected together. Then he asked me to make some hearts which he added to his feces shapes and said that he would attach his creation to the wall of the office. He made a second construction to take home, but instead of putting the first construction up on the wall, he hid it so that nobody else could get it.

The attempts of children like Fred to use normal representational processes fail because of the struggle between the containment and the expression of their impulses. This struggle weakens their ability to maintain the internal object tie to the mother. Their representations become mother-connected, and, therefore, symbolic. We are able to treat these children because they reenact the impulse-expression, fusion-identity struggle with each attempt at creation.

In the 39th therapy hour we see the result of this expressed graphically in an attempt both to draw and write object-image representation. Fred shows how he tries to defend against impulse expression by using part for whole, and fragmenting the "bad" words. Towards the end of the hour he drew a picture of a little boy and then a picture of a little girl. He wrote out the word "fucker" and said: "The little girl is ugly. She is small." Then he drew the figure of a large woman and said: "She is nice and pretty. She's big. She doesn't like to hear the word 'fucker'." He wrote the letters "E R" and asked what they were. I pointed out his fear that he had written the word "fuck" and not just the "E R" as he had wanted. He told me that he would cut the word "fucker" into a jigsaw so he could fool everybody, because then only he would know its meaning.

In the 40th hour there is an attempt to maintain both the impulse expression and the connection to the mother through a written verbal representation (written words) of drive-connected impulse expression. In Fred's case the ability to do this indicates a strengthening of the ego.

Towards the end of the hour he drew a gun, a large cloud, a little

cloud, and a very tall house with two stories. He wrote the word
"doee" on the bottom of the picture and asked me if I knew what
it was. I said it was "doo." He asked me if I could write the word
"shit" for him and then showed me that he could write the words
"fuck" and "fucker." He cut the words "fuck" and "shit" out of
the paper and told me with a smile of excitement that he was going
to show them to his mother. I commented that it must be exciting
to be able to show the words to mother instead of having to say
them. Then he showed me the cutout which said "shit" and said
that he knew how to spell it, but once having written it became
unsure of its meaning. I pointed out that he was still afraid of
the "poops" coming out in his pictures which was why he wanted
to know if he had been able to "draw" them.

The 42nd therapy hour demonstrates the emergence of autonomous symbolic representation out of uncontrolled impulse expression. In the middle of the hour, he asked me to write the word
"mother" on a piece of paper which was the shape of feces and on
which he had written the word "shit." Then he played in a scattered way first writing "doo," making "don" out of it, then "donn,"
followed by "doonna," then "donna," and finally a new word,
"sorry."

When children like Fred can express their impulses without the
object loss panic caused by the punitive parental reaction, autonomous ego function begins to be free for schoolwork. The capacity
for symbolic object representation appears because both the impulse and object are represented in the symbolic object. This allows
the beginning of the superego function of censorship without the
resultant loss of the primitive object tie. One observes the emergence of some judgmental and critical ego functioning which permits the child to appraise his own work perceptually. The capacity
to reestablish and maintain the object tie to the mother in her
physical absence may also appear through the use of symbolic
representation.

In the 60th therapy hour Fred told me that he wanted to draw
something "sexy." He drew the back of a woman with what he
called "her you-know-what." He kept making mistakes in the
drawing and asked me to do it for him. I told him I couldn't because I didn't know how, but if he would help me by telling me

what he wanted to draw, I would be glad to do so. He had me draw the profile of a woman with two legs, buttocks which he called "butt" on the back, breasts which he called "boobs" in front, and a face. When it was finished he drew the eyes, mouth, and nose in the top of the head. He also added a nipple to the breast. Then he told me that he wanted to make the picture into a person and tried to erase the breasts in order to do so. He was upset when he couldn't erase the breast totally. He reminded himself that earlier he had intended to copy what I had drawn. He started to redraw the figure but changed his mind, deciding that he would not be able to show it to his mother because she would be angry when she saw that he had drawn in a breast. I commented, "It is difficult to make a drawing when you know Mother is going to be angry at what you want to look at." He repeated that he only wanted to look, he only wanted to see. Then he drew a tepee with doors. He told me what he was going to draw prior to drawing the picture and was able to do so without any mistake. When he had drawn the tepee, he reminded himself that he needed a way inside and added the doors.

He had to remove the "sexy" expression of the drive derivative impulse (his wish to see his mother's exciting body parts) from his drawing of mother in order to make it acceptable as a "person." As a result he created a symbol of mother, a tepee with doors. This demonstrates the beginning of Fred's ability for symbolic object representation. This symbol has as its latent content the image of Fred's mother and the expression of his voyeuristic wishes towards her. The following hour, the 61st therapy hour, demonstrated the emergence of a new ability to project and re-create an object out of memory. In that hour Fred played the "dot" game in which he drew a series of dots on a piece of paper seemingly at random, and then connected them with lines in order to make a face emerge.

In the case cited, the expressions of scatological words of anal and phallic origin and the drawing of anal and phallic body parts and bodily functions occurred at the times when the patient was struggling with the transference situation. Throughout the therapeutic work the impulsive expressions of both libidinal and aggressive drives were represented in drawings, cutouts, and words. The seemingly psychotic behavior may represent a regressed relationship in which the child attempts to restore an early state of attachment through the expression of impulses which he hopes will elicit a positive response from mother. The therapist interpreted the punitive expectations and maintained a supportive and helpful attitude which resulted in the child's establishment of a relatively positive transference which, in turn, freed some autonomous ego function from conflict.

BIBLIOGRAPHY

1. BURGNER, MARION, and EDGECUMBE, R. Some Problems in the Conceptualization of Early Object Relationships, Part II: The Concept of Object Constancy, *Psychoanalyt. Study of the Child*, 1972, XXVII:315.
2. EKSTEIN, R., and CARUTH, E. Psychotic Acting Out: Royal Road or Primrose Path, *Children of Time and Space, of Action and Impulse*. New York: Appleton-Century-Crofts, 1966.
3. EKSTEIN, R., and FRIEDMAN, S. W. A Technical Problem in the Beginning Phase of Psychotherapy with a Borderline Psychotic Boy. *Children of Time and Space, of Action and Impulse*. New York: Appleton-Century-Crofts, 1966.
4. EKSTEIN, R., and FRIEDMAN, S. W. On Some Current Models in the Psychoanalytic Treatment of Childhood Psychosis. *The Challenge: Despair and Hope in the Conquest of Inner Space*. New York: Brunner/Mazel, 1971.
5. EKSTEIN, R., and WALLERSTEIN, J. Observations on the Psychology of Borderline and Psychotic Children. *Psychoanalyt. Study of the Child*, 1956, IX:30.
6. FREUD, A. The Mutual Influences in the Development of Ego and Id. *Psychoanalyt. Study of the Child*, 1952, VII:42.
7. GELEERD, E. R. A Contribution to the Problem of Psychoses in Childhood. *Psychoanalyt. Study of the Child*, 1946, II:271.
8. GELEERD, E. R. Borderline States in Childhood and Adolescence, *Psychoanalyt. Study of the Child*, 1958, XIII:279.
9. HARTMANN, H. The Mutual Influences in the Development of Ego and Id. *Psychoanalyt. Study of the Child*, 1952, VII:9.
10. MAHLER, M. S. On Human Symbiosis and the Vicissitudes of Individuation. Vol. I, *Infantile Psychosis*. New York: Int. Univ. Press, 1968.
11. WEIL, A. P. Disturbances of Ego Development. *Psychoanalyt. Study of the Child*, 1953, VIII:271.

Chapter 24

❧

Clinical Considerations Concerning the Expansion of Language Space: From the Autistic to the Interpersonal*

RUDOLF EKSTEIN, PH.D., AND
J. THOR NELSON, PH.D.

Disturbances in language development and speech often accompany psychopathology in children. Such disturbances can range from the relatively mild and transitory to the profound and seemingly unalterable. Often there exists a parallel between the degree of psycholological disturbance and the extent of impairment in speech and language functions. In conditions of severe psychological disturbance, such as childhood autism, speech and language development itself are invariably affected. The ways in which such functions are affected are many, but principally it is the autistic child's manner of communication with others which is most influenced. Kanner (7), in his initial description of early infantile autism, states that the failure to use language for the purpose of communication is one of the hallmarks of the disorder. This has remained as one of the classic indications of autism, although not the only one (11).

However, the extent to which there exists a failure to use lan-

* Paper presented in slightly different form at the American Psychological Association Annual Convention, New Orleans, 1974.

guage for the purpose of communication differs among children whose speech functions are grossly affected. They may be relatively mute, or their speech primarily echolalic in nature. For others, if some speech is present, it may be atonal and arrhythmic, lacking inflection, and failing to convey emotion. However, children with such gross impairments in speech and language development do not constitute the entire population of children who possess an autistic disturbance. While such impairment is highly recognizable and fits into the stereotyped way of thinking about such children, in actuality the childhood autism disturbance in the communication function can be more subtle.

Many autistic children possess expressive speech. The language development of such children can be basically intact. They can express their needs and wishes through the use of language and in certain situations can communicate with little or no observable degree of disturbance. However, even though language is available for such children, and oftentimes at a rather advanced level, it nevertheless is affected by the autistic condition in a manner as striking as for those whose communication is primarily echolalic.

Basically, the autistic child's language is a solitary one—it does not include others, except in a most rudimentary way. It is a private language, developed for the self and not for interpersonal relations. It is a language in which the primary audience is the self, not another. It is unending soliloquy, a monologue which never evolves into a true dialogue. The autistic child's inability to progress from a monologue to a dialogue, which includes recognition of the individuality of the other person, is one of his most striking characteristics. While he may give the impression of communicating, the communication is the sort which denies the individuality of the other. The function of the person can be understood and acknowledged by the autistic child, and in this way he copes rather effectively with many situations in life. This coping is comparable to the way, in the course of our everyday lives, we respond to certain others in terms of their functioning. For example, when we buy something from someone across a store counter, an interaction occurs, but one which is developed from the buyer and seller functions. The personal characteristics of the seller may or may not enter into the picture for us, as buyers. It is a routine and fairly impersonal interaction. For the autistic child, however, all of his interactions are structured along such lines—routine, impersonal, and deanimating.

Thus, in many respects, the autistic child can communicate with people via language. When analyzed, however, it is seen that the nature of the communications emphasizes expression or appeal, and not the more descriptive or representational functions, called by Bühler (1) the essence of symbolic communication. While language exists for the autistic child, it is an incomplete communication system which does not allow the individuality of the other to emerge. The feelings, thoughts, opinions, and attitudes of the other are rigorously excluded. Therefore, while the autistic child may be quite capable of functioning fairly effectively in his communications in many spheres of everyday life, he is always at a loss in the truly interpersonal sphere, which acknowledges a separateness and individuality of the other. In this sphere, the essence and very nature of the autistic disorder is manifestly present.

Elsewhere (*Reiss Davis Clinic Bulletin,* No. 2), Ekstein and Caruth discuss the function of language in the development of object relationships. Following Mahler's model (10), they suggest that as the infant in normal development proceeds through an age-appropriate autistic and then symbiotic phase that is eventually resolved through individuation, so, too, does normal language development proceed along such a course. They describe this process as an expansion of the language space, the *Sprachraum.* The language space of the child expands as his object relationships develop.

The psychotherapy of children with autistic disturbances is exceedingly difficult. Many of the difficulties are due to the fact that such children seemingly deny the very existence of the therapist as a human being. Even if the therapist is acknowledged as an external object, his opportunity to establish an emotional relationship necessary for the therapeutic work is extremely limited. This impenetrability of the autistic child is understood by researchers and clinicians in varying ways, ranging from a solely neurological explanatory viewpoint to a solely psychological one. Our viewpoint is based upon the ideas of Mahler (9, 10). She identifies in the early mental life of the infant normal phases through which he passes on the path to the development of object relationships. If these phases are mastered successfully, the infant gains the capacity to differentiate from nonself and eventually he will perceive the people around him as objects separate from himself. As his psychological development continues, he separates from the maternal figure through certain processes of separation and individuation. This ultimately leads to the capacity to achieve object and self-representations, stable identifications, and to a psychic organization capable of functioning according to the reality of the principle (2, 3).

Within this framework, the dilemma for the autistic child is that a meaningful reciprocity with an external object involves the risk of a loss of a precariously developed sense of self. This loss of a sense of self occurs through a fusion of the self with the object. When such a fusion occurs, the boundaries between self and object are lost. This is akin to a feeling of annihilation in the child, in that the separateness of the self and object is no longer present. From this point of view, autism becomes a means by which the child retains an element of self in a threatening and potentially most dangerous world. Since the autistic child would rather deny the human existence of the object than face the threat of fusion, psychotherapy with such children is most formidable. And yet, it is through the psychotherapy of such children that basic mental processes associated with this disorder can be identified and understood so that the solitary and psychotic nature of the disorder can be overcome.

In line with this aim, the following clinical material gives particular emphasis to the expansion of the language space—*Sprachraum*—of an autistic five-year-old girl during the course of her psychoanalytically oriented psychotherapy. As her language space expands, so does her ability to allow the therapist to become an object differentiated from herself and thus, eventually, therapeutically helpful to her.

At the time of her referral here, Celeste was five years and six months of age. She is a somewhat small girl with a shy, pale, and fragile appearance. As noted by the psychiatrist in the initial evaluation, "Her way of looking at people or the environment is indecisive and full of aversion. She glances briefly, and then looks into space." This characteristic, along with her physical appearance, gives her an ephemeral, evanescent quality. Referral to the clinic followed an odyssey for help on the part of her parents as they tried to cope with Celeste's peculiar and bizarre behavior.

At the time of her evaluation, Celeste was described by the parents as a most withdrawn child. She preferred play of a solitary nature to activities with peers. She would carry on conversations with an imaginary character which only she could see, named Ya-Ya. She would sit and rock endlessly, unless interrupted. In the special nursery school in which she was enrolled, her ability to participate in classroom activities was limited. She would sit and stare into space, rubbing her long hair or a piece of yarn across her face in a dreamy manner. Oftentimes she would lie on the floor and play with her hands, seemingly oblivious to the playing children next to her. Her speech was extremely infantile in manner and her coordination poor. Because she was pigeontoed, she possessed a peculiar gait, which was only emphasized by her characteristic hand-flapping behavior as she went from one place to another. While her appearance caused mothers to be reluctant to allow their children to play with her, she got along with them fairly well when she did interact with them.

Her parents, both college graduates, had noticed their daughter's peculiar behavior for some years and had made a variety of attempts to understand and deal with it. A sister, some two and a-half years younger than Celeste, was developing along normal lines and this only highlighted for the parents Celeste's peculiar behavior.

The evaluation process revealed a youngster with a basic diagnosis of schizophrenia in childhood, characterized by a typical and bizarre behavior, gross immaturity and unevenness in development, infantile speech, delusions, and hallucinations. She did, however, possess certain strengths in her personality organization which led the diagnostic team to believe that she might benefit from treatment. Treatment began when Celeste was five years and nine months. It consisted of psychoanalytically oriented psychotherapy sessions three times a week. Also, her parents were each seen on an individual basis once a week by a social worker.

Three phases in Celeste's treatment will be described, with a particular emphasis upon her behavior of the period and its relationship to the expansion of her language space and to the therapeutic process itself.

Her behavior in her early therapy sessions was most solitary. She sat in her chair and played with her hands or a piece of Kleenex tissue she would bring with her. Occasionally she would play with her ponytail holder, which had on it two small balls of a bright color. In the course of her play she chattered almost constantly. While it was difficult in the beginning to understand all of what she said, certain words and phrases would be quite clear. Her speech had a singsong lilt to it with a rhythmic, repetitive quality. Nevertheless, it was unmistakable that her behavior was that of a person engaged in an internal dialogue. While that dialogue was clearly a monologue, it had about it an interactive quality. Questions would be asked and then answered by her. Comments would be made and responded to by her. Over a number of sessions it became clear that her hands were animated objects for her, and it was they who were involved in the dialogue, spoken in their behalf by Celeste. While her hands represented a variety of figures, they primarily were referred to as "doggies." Each dog would chatter to himself or depict certain activities before the therapist as Celeste sat in her chair and played, seemingly oblivious to where she was or whom she was with.

A Kleenex tissue served as a primary vehicle for her play. She would bring one or two pieces with her to the session and then use the tissue in various ways. For example, she would tear the tissue into small pieces and the shredded bits would represent "cheeses," which the dogs would eat with gusto. Sometimes one dog would eat all the cheeses, leaving none for the others. As one dog would complain, it would be laughed at by the other. Celeste herself would laugh with apparent glee at its misfortune. Sometimes a larger piece of tissue would be identified as a little boy, and he would get no cheeses because all would be eaten by the dogs. Such themes of eating and being without were brought into the sessions in her play, although the themes were relatively simple and unelaborated.

As is typical in the early treatment process of such severely disturbed children, there were constricted and circumscribed fields of activity in several significant spheres. Her relationship to the therapist was minimal. She acknowledged him more by her lack of attention to, than through any involvement with, him. She asked no questions of him, nor did she make any comments about coming to the clinic. Both her actual and psychological play spaces were extremely circumscribed (4, 5). In these early sessions she literally would spend the entire time playing in her chair. She evinced no interest in the toy cabinet or its contents. Once, when she did not bring a tissue, she was offered one from the therapist's desk. She refused, and had one dog comment, "That's yucky." Her psychological play space was also constricted. No elaborated or refined play occurred, but only repetitive actions, depicting a certain scene, played over and over again. Most of the activities she depicted had a brief duration as though there was a short circuit which prevented anything too involved or developed to be presented. The characters of the dogs, represented by her hands, sometimes seemed like actors in search of a plot (8). Many of the activities were repeated again and again in a mechanical and stereotyped way.

Finally, her language space itself was quite limited. While the figures represented by her hands would engage in a dialogue, it was one in which all the words were supplied by Celeste. In short, while it had the appearance of a dialogue, it was in actuality a monologue. Her language space was clearly autistic in nature, in that it was entirely solitary. It was a language space characterized by a preoccupation with the self as audience. In a way, her speech at this time might be compared to those private thoughts of a person as he talks to himself in the planning of some action. The internal speech is designed for the self, and if it were to be said to another person, it would be expressed in a far different manner. For Celeste, however, her language space at this time did not allow for the ability to use speech in a way to allow inclusion of another person.

During these early sessions the therapist's role was less than a participant's, but a bit more than merely an observer's. He attempted to follow whatever activities were being depicted and to an extent to verbalize his understanding of them. Sometimes he would take on the reactions of one of the characters in her current playlet or sympathize with the plight of one of her characters. In this way he would be responsive to her. Always, however, he was a follower. He could only develop or build upon that which she initiated. If, for example, he would have a character ask a question of the other, or be different in any way from the role ascribed by her, he was completely ignored. Thus, the therapist was allowed to play the part of an echo. He was not yet at the point of being given the opportunity to be an interpretative echo, in which he could make conscious and available to Celeste that which is conveyed to him by her play (3). He was still far from becoming a mirror to the activities enacted by Celeste, for the mirror has more autonomy than the echo, since it has the capacity of reflecting someone other than the self.

The above clinical material characterizes the picture of this autistic child which emerged during her early sessions. As can be seen, her behavior was extremely constricted in several significant spheres of activity. Also, it was behavior which had a fragmented, discontinuous quality to it. Nevertheless, it presented the beginning of a process, and the apparent fragmentation represented the forerunner of structure.

The second phase in Celeste's therapy represented a period of some forty sessions after the beginning period. Slowly but surely, over the course of these sessions, there occurred an expansion of her activities. Changes could be noticed—changes significant for the developing role allowed the therapist, both in the sessions and in her intrapsychic life. Her actual play space increased and deepened. She was able to move first from the chair to the floor around it, and then to the space between herself and the therapist's chair, and finally even to where he was seated. As she did this, her psychological play as well increased to some degree. Also, instead of ignoring the presence of the therapist, she began to make use of him in her play. Naturally, his role was circumscribed and only, so to speak, on command.

For example, one playlet consisted of the following: Celeste, through the vehicle of the dogs, ordered the therapist to close his eyes. He echoed the fact that he was to close his eyes, and then did so. She then placed on the top of his shoes some tiny pieces of shredded tissue and told him to open his eyes, which he echoed and did. Then, he was allowed to become more than an echo, for he exclaimed over the tissue on his shoetop. Quickly he was told to close his eyes, and she brushed away the pieces of paper. Upon being told to open his eyes he did so, and then exclaimed that the tissue was gone. This was a source of great delight for Celeste and became the signal for her to repeat the activity. One is reminded of the play of the child described by Freud, as he dropped over the side of a bed a spool of thread, which he then repetitively and gleefully wound up again and again (6).

Also, there occurred a small but significant expansion of her language space, in that now the therapist was allowed to have words, or lines, although the part assigned to him was admittedly a small one. His role allowed for little individuality or creative interpretation. It was as though she was an authoritarian stage director who directs the actors with a heavy hand, leaving them no opportunity to be any way other than the way he outlines for them. Thus, the assignment of the role to the therapist occurred essentially within an autistic framework, since it allowed him no individuality or self-expression. He was but an extension of her, as are the soldiers who respond to the marching orders of the drill sergeant. While the sergeant yells his commands, thereby acknowledging the presence of the soldiers, their opportunity for self-expression is minimal. In a similar manner, Celeste directs the therapist.

Then, during the course of her play, a matter of significance occurred. There was established by the therapist a figure with whom communication could occur with one of the figures controlled by Celeste. The therapist's figure was identified as a "little boy" and was represented by the therapist's forefinger and middle finger of his right hand. By the emergence of this figure, there were created increasing opportunities for communication, since he could talk with the "pretty lady," a figure fashioned out of tissue and controlled by Celeste. The therapist now had a vehicle by which he could move from the roles heretofore limited to him by Celeste's need to control him. By his ability to manipulate the figure of the little boy, he had a measure of autonomy that was denied to him before. Of course, the sphere of independence was quite circumscribed and very closely monitored by Celeste. The little boy was allowed to become involved in the playlets developed by Celeste but he still had to follow her directions. In the beginning, in fact, Celeste carefully dictated almost every word that the boy was to say. Later, she would instruct him to respond to a particular situation with a specific emotion, which gave the therapist a greater degree of freedom.

At this point in her therapy a repetitive story was enacted by Celeste. After her entrance into the office she would sit on her chair and either through a tissue figure or by a crook of her finger, invite the "little boy" to visit her. The therapist would then move from his chair onto the floor, and with his fingers walk over to where Celeste was sitting. He would be in a merry mood, whistling happily, and delighted over the invitation offered to him by the "pretty lady." However, as he climbed to the top of the stairs of her house, represented by the seat of the chair in which she sat, he would be met by a large and ferocious dog which would literally kick him out. As the boy fell to the floor below, he would cry out in terror and surprise, much to the delight of Celeste. Then, upon her urging, the boy would again ascend the stairs, only again to be attacked and knocked around. Eventually, however, over the course of several sessions, the boy was allowed to enter the house. However, it was necessary to feed the dog great amounts of bones, cakes, and candy. A great deal of time was spent in the feeding, which was necessary to appease the dog's voracious appetite. This play, simple as it was, was repeated over and over, and always at the beginning of a session.

In this play Celeste seemed to be setting up certain conditions of approach—conditions which might later enable the therapist to become more of a real person in the psychotherapeutic process. Significantly, for a considerable period of time, there was little activity between the little boy and the pretty lady once he had placated the dog with food and gained entrance into the house. It was as though Celeste could envision only the approach, and not the activity once the approach had been accomplished. Nevertheless, one is able to see the expansion that has occurred in her play, and how it has become more elaborated and developed. While the therapist was essentially to speak only those lines given him, he was allowed greater opportunities for the expression of emotion on the part of the figure represented by his fingers. Always, however, this figure was controlled by Celeste through her instructions to the therapist. In actuality, the "little boy," i.e., the psychotherapist, had no life of his own, except that which she gave him.

At a later point in Celeste's treatment, some seventy sessions from the period just discussed, considerable expansions have occurred in several areas. She is now able to play with some of the toys in the toy cabinet, although not all of them. She now walks freely around the office. Her play is more elaborated and developed and it is not presented in so fragmented a manner. Often it consists of various playlets acted out by figures created by her. While there is still an emphasis upon the preparation for the play, rather than on the play itself, it is a more developed activity.

Her language space has expanded, in terms of there being greater opportunities for communication between patient and therapist, or at least their representatives. To say that her communications have passed from the autistic to the truly interpersonal is not true at this point. Her ability to relate directly to the therapist is still absent. In fact, in her own way, she still controls him as much as ever. There has emerged in the course of the therapy the knowledge that Dr. Nelson, as well as Celeste herself, are "monsters." There has never occurred any direct communication between the monsters, much less between the real people who are Celeste and Dr. Nelson. Always, the communication is between go-betweens or intermediaries, that is, between various figures which have been established in the course of our play. The "little boy and the "pretty lady" are such figures, and there are others. Her wish to prevent a more personal relationship with the therapist continues. Her ability to afford the opportunity for a relationship in which each of them can participate in an interpersonal manner is still prevented by the autistic disorder. This is so, even when the most pedestrian matters are discussed. Once, for example, Dr. Nelson commented upon her hair, and how it was done up in a different style that day. Celeste almost visibly pondered this comment, and then said that the monster's mother had done it in this way. She then added a comment about how the monster represented by Dr. Nelson was "yucky," presumably for making such a comment.

By making everything about her in the third person she effectively maintains that distance so required by the autistic disorder. While it appears that a relationship occurs between patient and therapist, it is one which is still under her firm control. It does not allow for the therapist to be different, or at least too different, from

the way she wants him to be. As a person, he seemingly is not recognized or acknowledged by Celeste. Nevertheless, there obviously
is now a recognition of him as an object outside of herself. This
object is not truly separate or independent, because of her great
control of him. She is still delusional in that she believes that she
is in control of the object. But while still maintaining control, she
has nevertheless allowed the therapist significantly greater areas
of involvement with her. While she clings to the delusion of control
by placing him in various roles, she acknowledges his capacity for
independence simply by her controlling manner.

In other words, if there truly was no recognition of him as an
object with a will of his own, there would be no need to be so controlling of him. Slowly but surely his ability for independent action
is more openly voiced by her. For example, she will say to him that
he walked too quickly behind her on the way to the office. For this,
he will be given a ticket. Or, she will involve him in various guessing games, such as one in which he is to guess which color crayon
is the prettier. Naturally, the little boy is instructed to guess the
wrong color by her. But even through this action there emerges a
recognition that he could, if not properly instructed, guess the correct color. The extent to which the therapist can become a reflective or interpretative voice is still limited, but the opportunities for
such a role have increased significantly from the time of her entrance into therapy. While the clinical treatment continues, analytic therapy has yet to move beyond a technique which must be
considered but a steppingstone in the expansion of her language
space and in her opportunity to develop viable and meaningful
object relationships. In a sense, that which has occurred to this
point is but a precursor of what is yet to unfold.

There exists in San Diego, California a replica of the Globe
Theater, in which a repertory group stages plays by Shakespeare
during the summer months. As the audience gathers before a performance, wandering among the small shops or simply relaxing on
the village green members of the acting troupe in their colorful
Renaissance costumes mix among the crowd, entertaining them.
The actors' task at this point is to prepare the audience for the
play—to help them make a transition from the twentieth century
to the sixteenth century, better to appreciate the play yet to come.

During this preplay, the actors appear in no particular order nor according to a plot. Then, as the preplay ends, the audience enters the theater. They look at the program, where the characters are named, and listed in order of appearance. Now, as the actors appear, the play takes form, and the drama and conflict develop.

With Celeste, it is still the time of the preplay. There is not yet content, not yet true conflict, not yet a true involvement with the psychotherapist, and not yet a true engagement with people. There is merely a kind of stage setting and mood setting, as with the actors on the green. For the psychotic child, however, this is not a choice, not an option, but a must. At this point, Celeste must use the therapist as a sort of stage prop. He will be useful for the play to come, but at this time cannot be allowed to be himself. He can only be an externalization of one of the internal figures of the drama to be enacted by Celeste. Just as the early object relationships of this psychotic child were empty and of an autistic character, so will the therapist be seen in autistic terms in the transference configuration, and thus be nothing more than a prop. However, as he permits himself to be used in this way, and realizes the opportunities for action available to him, he will appear more and more in her activities, and will make the transition from a prop to a real person.

BIBLIOGRAPHY

1. Buhler, K. *Sprachtheorie*. Jena: Fischer, 1934.
2. Ekstein, R. *Children of Time and Space, of Action and Impulse*. New York: Appleton-Century-Crofts, 1966.
3. Ekstein, R. *The Challenge: Despair and Hope in the Conquest of Inner Space*. New York: Brunner/Mazel, 1971.
4. Ekstein, R., and Caruth, E. From the Infinite to the Infinitesimal—the Play Space of the Schizophrenic Child. *Reiss-Davis Clin. Bull.*, 1973, 2:89.
5. Erikson, Eric H. Studies in the Interpretation of Play: Clinical Observations of Play Disruption in Young Children. *Genetic Psych. Monographs*, 1940, XXII:557.
6. Freud, S. Beyond the Pleasure Principle (1920). *Standard Edition*, Vol. 18. London: Hogarth Press, 1950.
7. Kanner, L. Autistic Disturbances of Affective Contact. *Nervous Child*, 1943, 2:217.
8. Liebowitz, J. Story-Telling in Search of a Plot. *Reiss-Davis Clin. Bull.*, 1972, 2:112.

9. MAHLER, M. On Childhood Psychosis and Schizophrenia: Autistic and Symbiotic Psychoses. *Psychoanal. Study of the Child*, 1952, 7:286.
10. MAHLER, M. *On Human Symbiosis and the Vicissitudes of Individuation.* New York: Int. Univ. Press, 1968.
11. ORNITZ, E. M. Childhood Autism: A Review of the Clinical and Experimental Literature. *Calif. Medicine*, 1973, 118:21.

Part VI

EDUCATION AND SCHOOL

Chapter 25

✳

Psychoanalysis and Education: An Historical Account*

RUDOLF EKSTEIN, PH.D., AND
ROCCO L. MOTTO, M.D.

. . . the relationship of psychoanalysis to education is complex. In a first approach the inclination may be to characterize it as one between a basic science and a field of application. Psychoanalytic propositions aim at indicating why human beings behave as they do under given conditions. The educator may turn to these propositions in his attempts to influence human behavior. The propositions then become part of his scientific equipment which naturally include propositions from other basic sciences. *In any relationship between a more general set of propositions and a field of application outside the area of experience from which these propositions were derived, a number of factors must be taken into account. The more general propositions, in this instance those of psychoanalysis, must be formulated in a way that permits their operation in the field, here that of education.* The process of application is likely to act as a test of the validity of the propositions or of the usefulness of their for-

* Read at the Panel on Psychic Development and the Prevention of Mental Illness, Midwinter Meeting of the American Psychoanalytic Association, December 9, 1961, New York City.

> mulation. Hence we are dealing not merely with a process of diffusion of knowledge from a "higher" to a "lower" level, from the more "general" to the "applied" field, but with a *process of communication between experts trained in different skills in which cross-fertilization of approaches is likely to occur.*
>
> ERNST KRIS (1948)

Through most of the history of psychoanalysis we find bridges which lead from the area of psychoanalysis to the area of education. There has always been a strong relationship between these two endeavors, although the nature of this relationship has been a changing one. The changes occurred both in terms of the readiness of a specific social scene to make use of psychoanalysis in different areas of application, and the readiness of psychoanalysis itself to become available to special fields of application. The degree and the nature of this mutual readiness depend on social as well as on certain scientific issues. It will be the purpose of this communication to trace the historic development of the relation of these two fields in order to learn about the social and scientific climate which gave rise to different experimentation. This paper may thus throw some light on questions that confront us today as we wish to explore the ways in which experts in both fields may be able to collaborate.

Our concern is not merely with the contribution of psychoanalysis to the prevention of pathology, but rather to the facilitation of positive growth. We do not wish to think of education as a preventive force, but rather as a force which releases growth potentials and fosters development and maturation in a positive way. Perhaps our review will allow us to see whether we merely express a semantic difference in a more optimistic mood, or whether we might add another important dimension to psychoanalysis beyond the therapeutic and preventive application.

The first reception of psychoanalysis in medicine, as well as in the social sciences and the field of education, was a hostile one. Consequently, we find a paucity of direct attempts to deal analytically with the child before the First World War, and even fewer attempts to apply analysis to problems of education or parent guidance. Beyond Freud's "Little Hans" (1909) and the outstanding exception of Hug-Hellmuth's work, we find but few traces of such interest in the literature which reach into the pre-war period. During the post-war era there was a resumption of psychoanalytic work, and we find suddenly an avalanche of contributions—a situation not unlike the immense growth of psychoanalysis in America after the Second World War. One has the impression that the end of the military holocaust released positive forces permitting the questioning of old educational institutions and methods. The questioning fostered experimentation in the field of education, and thus offered an opportunity for psychoanalysis to extend its contributions.

As we quote from the literature we do not mean to be exhaustive. Instead, we hope to give representative samples in order to follow the psychoanalytic climate as it affects educational experimentation. In Switzerland, an island of peace, Oskar Pfister addressed the pedagogues as early as 1916 in a summer course of the Swiss Pedagogic Society. He spoke to them on the issue "What Does Psychoanalysis offer to the Educator?" In this address he described psychoanalysis as a form of education and suggested that Freud was a great pedagogue. He referred to psychoanalysis, as did Freud and many others, as *Nacherziehung*.

After the war a number of educational experiments, usually in connection with war orphans or with children who faced a variety of difficulties, were made and described by their respective originators. Bernfeld (1921) reports on *Kinderheim Baumgarten;* this report speaks of a "serious experiment with new education." Schmidt (1924) also offers a report about a children's home in Moscow, and thus describes "psychoanalytic education in Soviet Russia." Aichhorn's famous *Wayward Youth* (1925) refers to his experience in a children's home with delinquent children; his experimentation goes back to his pre-analytical period but was understood and interpreted by him after he had received psychoanalytic training. These publications, between 1921 and 1925, refer to work of short duration. In spite of the writers' enthusiasm, which ran parallel to the new spirit in central Europe when revolutions replaced empires with republics, their experiments broke down because of external pressure and the lack of trained personnel. The liberation from

dominating leaders led to a new society which Paul Federn, who
was then very interested in the application of psychoanalysis to the
child, analyzed in a publication of 1919. He described the new
social scene as a fatherless society. In this contribution on the psychology of the revolution, he suggested that the father-son motive
had suffered the most severe defeat. However, he thought that this
motive was so basically and deeply anchored in family education
and in inherited feeling deep inside of humanity that it would
most likely prevent the success of a completely "fatherless society"
(22).

This spirit of the post-year era influenced the thinking of analysts of those years for quite a long time and led to many enthusiastic publications, such as Wittels' *The Liberation of the
Child* (1927), which ends:

> This will take a long time. In carrying out the new plan diffi-
> culties and unforeseen problems appear. But the fundamental
> thought is simple: Leave your children alone. Do not educate
> them, because you cannot educate them. It might be better if
> the teachers were to write a thousand times in their copy book,
> "I should leave the children alone!" instead of having the chil-
> dren write, "During school sessions one is forbidden to speak!"
> One speaks of the century of the child. But this will begin only
> when the adults will understand that the children have to
> learn less from them than they have to learn from the
> children (64).

It is easy to see that at the time the basic contribution of psychoanalysis to education was a protest against the old forms of
society, as typified by the Victorian age of suppression. Progressive
education was seen as a liberation of the instincts, as a struggle
against trauma, as favoring laissez-faire, with a minimum of intervention on the part of educators and parents. Much of the literature of those days, such as a contribution by Pfister (1929), was
concerned with "the faults of parents":

> The Pädaanalyse (pedagogical analysis) fights, therefore, the
> education of categorical ordering and forbidding, which re-
> quires blind cadaver-like obedience without giving the child
> understandable reasons and without letting the child under-
> stand that the parents act not because of despotic needs,

but because they are guided by consideration for the child's welfare (50).

Those were the days in which there was a struggle against limits, and a constant fear of traumatization. As sophisticated a writer as Bernfeld, to whose credit is the first *Psychology of the Infant* (1925), sums up infancy as the phase of life which reaches "from the trauma of birth to the trauma of weaning."

It is not only naive enthusiasm as exemplified through Wittels' contribution, but sometimes also the somber recognition of limits of and for the educator which find reflection in the literature. Siegfried Bernfeld's *Sysiphus or the Boundaries of Education* (1925) describes as the two boundaries the unconscious forces in the child on the one hand, and the social forces on the other. These limit the educator and may frequently give him the feeling of a Sysiphus who faces endless and hopeless tasks. Bernfeld defined education as "the reaction of Society to the facts of maturation and development." He thus forces us to take a look at societal forces as well as the inner forces of the child in order to move from a naive application of psychoanalysis to a more sophisticated one which includes those societal forces. Those familiar with this book will remember his invention of Citizen Machiavell (i), who was to be elected Minister of Education. Machiavell (i), knowing the insights of modern sociology as well as psychoanalysis, invents an educational system to serve a reactionary society by slowly molding the child into the willing tool of these future anti-Semitic, nationalistic and war-minded rulers.

In the meantime, psychoanalytic training organizations developed. Centers of influence, as far as the application of psychoanalysis to education was concerned, sprung up in many places. The first organized expression of a concentrated effort in relating these two fields was the *Zeitschrift für Psychoanalytische Pädagogik*, which first appeared in October, 1926, with articles by Meng of Stuttgart and Schneider of Riga. In later years we find, among other contributors, Aichhorn, Federn, Anna Freud, Friedjung, Hoffer, Storfer, Wittels of Vienna; Lou Andreas-Salomé of Gottingen; Marie Bonaparte of Paris; Chadwicke, Eder, Barbara Low of London; Ferenczi of Budapest; Furer of Zurich; Landauer of

Frankfurt; Bernfeld and Müller-Braunschweig of Berlin; Piaget of Neuchâtel; Vera Schmidt and Wulff of Moscow; Tamm of Stockholm; and Zullinger of Bern. This *Zeitschrift* lasted until the invasion of Austria in 1938; its last editor was Willie Hoffer with the collaboration of Aichhorn, Federn, Anna Freud, Meng and Zulliger. There were at least six issues each year, and during some years the publishers brought out fifteen issues. The spirit of this journal is well described in Schneider's lead article in the first issue:

> Psychoanalysis as a therapeutic procedure, which undertakes to make conscious the unconscious and to restore subsequently the missed order, was always properly considered a pedagogical procedure. One spoke of *Nacherziehung*, of post-education. It was therefore in the nature of the matter that pedagogues began to utilize psychoanalytic procedures with educational intentions.
>
> After all this we may say: *Psychoanalysis serves the pedagogue* once *as* "the science of the inconscious psyche" and enlarges for him the necessary psychological knowledge, and then gives him *a new means of education,* a procedure which is capable through interventions into the unconscious to bring about psychic order. Its applicability reaches, therefore, mainly into the area of pedagogical methodology. If and how far this methology can also help determine the questions of goals is not easy to decide: This task reaches far beyond the area of psychology and, therefore, also beyond the area of psychoanalysis (59).

This first programmatic paper, "The Area of Application of Psychoanalysis for Pedagogics," carried the early enthusiasm which was bringing psychoanalytic insigts to the field of education, but it also bore the seeds of theoretical and practical dilemmas. It opened a new field and confronted us with the new questions arising out of these first experiments.

Schneider and many of the early authors, who published in the *Zeitschrift für Psychoanalytische Pädagogik,* tried to differentiate between psychoanalysis and pedagogy. They saw in the one a therapeutic procedure and in the other a technique for education. At the same time, and this was the trend of the time, both procedures were somehow fused. Both were thought to be educational, and no clear boundary lines between them were established. Analysis was seen as post-education, and much of pedagogy was seen as a form of therapy. But because there were many serious attempts at clarification of this issue, this first phase, in which education and therapy were undifferentiated, is better described as phase-dominance than phase-exclusiveness.

The mainstream of interest concerning the application of psychoanalysis in the life of the child was expressed in the late twenties by teachers. Many of them, originally kindergarten or elementary-school teachers, became the first child analysts. Psychoanalytic pedagogy and child analysis, sociologically speaking, derived from the same social matrix, the teaching profession. At that time, much of what was taught to the teachers centered around the early maturation of the child.

We think, for example, of Anna Freud's famous "Introduction to Psychoanalysis for Teachers" (1931), her four lectures originally published in 1930 and given to the teachers at the Children's Centers in Vienna. These lectures deal with infantile amnesia and the oedipus complex; the infantile instinct life; the latency period; and the relation between psychoanalysis and pedagogy. She discusses the "definite danger arising from education" and the nature of the restrictions imposed upon the child. She speaks of the psychoanalyst as one "who is engaged in therapeutic work of resolving such inhibitions and disturbances in the development" and who, thus, learns "to know education from its worst side." But she also warns against the exaggeration of this impression. She struggles with and argues against the one-sidedness of such views, trying to take a second look at the positive aspects of education. She describes the work of Aichhorn in his *Wayward Youth*, and tries to outline an educational task which keeps a balance between the danger of the "injurious effect of too great repression" and the equal danger of "the lack of all restraint." She suggests that "the task of a pedagogy based on analytic data is to find a via media between these extremes—that is to say, to allow to each stage in the child's life the right proportion of instinct gratification and instinct restriction." This is a far cry from the previously quoted view point of Wittels in his *Liberation of the Child* in which he seems to indicate that the adults, the teachers, should abdicate their role. Anna

Freud suggests that there is not yet analytical pedagogy, but that there are individual educators who are interested in this work.

She sees the main application of analysis to education—we believe that this is also true in the American scene today—as experimental and as a hopeful indication for the future. But she also maintains "that even today psychoanalysis does three things for pedagogics." She refers to the criticism of existing educational methods; the increase of the teacher's knowledge of human beings, including an understanding of the relations between the child and the educator; and, finally, his knowledge of the use of analysis as a therapeutic method for those children who have suffered injuries "which are inflicted . . . during the process of education."

It can be seen now that the temper of the times from the twenties to the thirties changed the psychoanalytically oriented educator. He was no longer stressing almost exclusively the liberation of the instincts and the crusade against the faults of parents and educators. Instead, he was beginning to stress the creation of an optimum situation in which his orientation was to help the child grow toward maturity on a middle road which avoided the pathological trauma of too much strictness as well as unlimited indulgence. This new trend is reflected also in Anna Freud's discussion of the concept of the rejecting mother (1955).

The first application of psychoanalysis to the field of education, as we note in the new efforts following the First World War, was an expression of protest, a demand for the new. The second step was one in which specific techniques were evaluated through actual application.

Burlingham described this new phase of psychoanalytic pedagogy in 1937 when commenting on "the problem of the psychoanalytic teacher":

> In recent years the number of those called by us "psychoanalytic pedagogues" has steadily increased. All these pedagogues have gone through their own analysis; they have been introduced to psychoanalytic theory through theoretical courses; and they have participated in seminars where they could report difficult cases from their children's groups and where they could try together with an analyst to employ the fundamental principles of analysis to their practical work. The pedagogues

work in this way on the slow development of psychoanalytic pedagogy (11).

In her paper in the training course for psychoanalytic pedagogues (*Lehrgang für Psychoanalytische Pädagogen*), Burlingham describes her accumulated experience in training educators. The first difficulty which she reported stemmed from the original, initial phase of application of psychoanalysis to education—the counterpressure against outmoded repressive educational techniques. The second difficulty was one which had to do with the misconception of the function of the pedagogue; he identified with his own therapist and saw himself as a child analyst rather than as an educator. Interpretation was the only reliable tool for him, and the role of education was seen as a therapeutic one. The third misconception which Miss Burlingham discussed could be called the "parent-blaming doctrine." According to this doctrine every educational problem would be resolved, not through the educational techniques of the teacher, but through analysis of the parent and manipulation of the environment.

The discussions in the next few years attempted to examine these three issues and to offer suggestions for the necessary differentiation.

We mention papers such as Steff Bornstein's on "Misunderstandings in the Application of Psychoanalysis to Pedagogy" (1937), and Editha Sterba's on "School and Educational Guidance" (1936). These attempt to tackle the problem concerning the means by which the educator may draw knowledge from the field of psychoanalysis but not apply himself as a child analyst. Sterba's paper summarized the situation with:

> It must not be stressed that in comparison to child analysis these interpretations (in education) are altogether incomplete and too much related to the situation. But the dynamic changes, which developed in consequence of these interpretations, demonstrate that in terms of that which was to be achieved, they were effective and sufficient in spite of their incompleteness. For the goals of the teacher which were decisive for the cases discussed, these interpretations did suffice. We must guard ourselves, of course, against believing that children so educated could be called "analyzed." We have

simply gained some insights into the actual symptomatic picture, nevertheless, sufficient to make possible for the child to continue in school and to function in his home environment.

The fruitfulness of such collective work between the analyzed educator and the child analyst cannot be doubted after what has been discussed (61).

According to this differentiation, child analysts would make complete use of interpretation. The analytically oriented pedagogue would resort to interpretive means only in relation to the situational crisis, and then only as much as was necessary to help the child with the current educational task. Such differentiation, however, does not clearly explain the qualitative difference between the two fields. It refers more to problems of education as we encounter them in the kindergarten, nursery-school situation, the home or, perhaps, in the primary grades. It does not, therefore, help us to relate much of our psychoanalytic insights to problems of education in which there is a didactic task; in which the educator is primarily a teacher. It also continues to stress primarily the incidents in the life of the child in which there are symptomatic disturbances, the beginnings of pathological crises, rather than ordinary education.

During this period, then, psychoanalysis offered the educator inspiration, identification and an opportunity for the critique of available techniques. It facilitated the task of creating a new technique without yet having accomplished the job. This new demand for scientific techniques of education was well expressed by Erikson when, in 1930, he said:

> It is surely no coincidence that the desire for a science of education should appear on the scene at the moment when, in the form of psychoanalysis, the truth of the healing power of self-knowledge is again establishing itself in the world. And to this truth much has been added since the times of Socrates, namely, a method. If education earnestly seeks to rebuild on a new conscious basis of knowledge and intelligence, then it must demand radical progress to the point where clear vision results in human adjustment. Modern enlightenment can best achieve this through psychoanalysis (19).

Many of the concepts of psychoanalysis were applied in individual remedial work with children as well as in the classroom situation. The papers of Zulliger (1926, 1930), Redl (1932, 1933, 1934) and Buxbaum (1931, 1936) apply analytic understanding to the classroom situation.

Anna Freud (1962) (28) has called to the attention of the authors a similar development in England which found expression in the literature through many contributions of J. C. Hill, an inspector of schools in London. It was he who arranged Anna Freud's first public addresses to teachers in London in October, 1938. While much of his work is theoretically influenced by the first phase we are discussing, we find that the actual practical applications are very much in accord with our current interests.

The Viennese group started to experiment with kindergarten systems, with elementary schools, as well as with infant observation. The occupation of Austria, part of the upheavals in Europe which finally led to the Second World War, destroyed much of this training work and opened our eyes more fully to the relationship of social systems to the problem of education and the applicability of psychoanalysis as a social force. Bernfeld's warnings in *Sysiphus* were now being understood as, later, the frightful prediction of Orwell's *1984* would be, but Bernfeld was not the only one to relate psychoanalysis, education and the social system.

Alice Balint's book, *The Early Years of Life—a Psychoanalytic Study,* originally published in Hungary in 1931, republished in England in 1953 and here in 1954, makes this point most eloquently. Her ending sums up this phase of the relationship between psychoanalysis and education:

> In conclusion, a few words as to the relation between education and civilization. The study of various people shows that there can hardly be any method of education which is not practicable. From the greatest imaginable freedom to the most cruel tyranny, everything has been practiced and the children have borne it. It is only the particular civilizations themselves that cannot tolerate a deviant system of education. There is no absolute pedagogy, no absolute mental hygiene. Changes in a civilization must be underpinned by corresponding educational measures, if they are to last. It follows conversely that reforms in education necessarily bring about a change in the civilization, even when that was not the conscious intention. For every improvement affects the whole of a given situation. Hence pedagogics is the most revolution-

ary of all sciences. Perhaps the inconspicuous "improvements" in methods of education are the prime mover in cultural evolution, for every educational system has its defects and tends towards change (3).

These notions of Bernfeld and Balint which forced us to look at the "reality" of the child as part of a dynamic, ever-changing social reality have led to many studies. Perhaps the best-known exponent of the attempt to understand educational systems culturally as well as analytically has been Erikson. In *Childhood and Society* (1950), he examined educational systems of primitive tribes and reflected on the concept of identity in American, German and Russian society.

As far as publications are concerned, there was a comparative void between 1938 and 1945, the end of the Second World War. However, some of the early group undertook to understand the psychological elements of democratic and totalitarian education. One such was Ekstein (1939), who compared educational devices used in totalitarian systems with those applicable to a democratic society.

The comparative silence in these seven years is no indication that either the analysts or the analytically oriented educators had given up their work. The European analytical organizations had been destroyed, and the attempt to build up equivalents in England and in the United States had been hampered, of course, by the war. Two volumes, published toward the end of the conflagration, are lasting testimonies to this effort. Both volumes, by Anna Freud and Dorothy Burlingham, describe the educational and research work in three war-time nurseries in England.

No sooner did the war end than we find, this time in the United States, a new publication, the heir, as it seems to us, of the *Zeitschrift für Psychoanalytische Pädagogik*. We refer to *The Psychoanalytic Study of the Child*. Perhaps even the change in name is important: the stress of the earlier journal was on application while the stress of this new annual is on study, on research. The early enthusiasm from the days of the "Psychoanalytic Movement *(Psychoanalytische Bewegung)*" was transformed into organized scientific work. Hoffer, one of the prime participants in the *Lehrgang* in Vienna, wrote on "Psychoanalytic Education" in the first issue of the new annual (1945). His was essentially a descriptive study of those early days, and he, too, mentions that, beginning with the days of Hug-Hellmuth, the attempt was made to disentangle analytic and educational processes. He speaks of Melanie Klein's negative attitude toward education, and he writes of the "crying need for longitudinal research in personality development" in order to help the educator acquire more insight into the child.

This first issue contained a variety of papers by analysts who originally belonged to the central European group and who, now, participated in the development of psychoanalysis as well as its application to education in a new country. We think of Fenichel's paper, "Means of Education," and Editha Sterba's contribution, "Interpretation and Education," as well as Erikson's papers on two Indian tribes and Edith Buxbaum's on "Transference and Group Formation" (all 1945). A paper by Ruben (1945), "A Contribution to the Education of Parents," seems to have been the beginning of a lasting interest as reflected in some of her 1960 work.

This second phase seems to differ vastly from the first. We must remember the fact that the social scene for psychoanalysis is a different one. Analysts in Europe worked primarily in private practice; had few clinical facilities nor any social-agency structure; and did not work in close contact with general psychiatry. In the States, psychoanalysts work hand-in-hand with psychiatrists, clinical psychologists and social workers. We find, therefore, that the relationship to the teaching profession and to school systems is a rather different one. Many of the original child analysts came from the teaching profession in Europe, while the American training system made no provisions for such opportunities.

The colleges for teacher's training had comparatively little use for psychoanalysis. This may well have much to do with the fact that progressive educational theory and philosophy were influenced in the States by John Dewey, whose work was compared with that of Freud in a recent volume by Levitt (1930), *Freud and Dewey*. Oberndorf (1953), in his history of psychoanalysis in America, actually believes that we owe Dewey a great deal for his work which made the country ready for analysis:

> The third reason for the widespread acceptance of psychoanalysis is due to another philosopher whose theories affected

education fundamentally and radically. In all psychotherapy the re-educative factor plays an important, perhaps an indispensable, part. Just at the time when the new psychotherapy, psychoanalysis, was slowly but surely affecting American psychiatry, a powerful figure advancing a new theory in the educational field was making his bid for recognition in New York City. In 1904 John Dewey became Professor of Philosophy at Columbia University, and for the next 25 years his ideas about education dominated the instruction of students at Columbia's Teacher's College. Dewey, greatly influenced by James' pragmatic philosophy, regarded James as a pioneer in his perception that experiences "an intimate union of emotion and knowledge." So Dewey in the theory of education insisted that learning is an experience of individual experimentation to be opened by those who participate in it. The basis for learning in a child should allow a maximum freedom of initiative rather than the absorption of facts from books or teachers.

The widely scattered alumni of Teachers' College have introduced this form of teaching through experimentation and practice, in the schools throughout the land. The psychoanalytic accentuation of the importance of early occurrences in the life of the individual, especially the traumatic ones, were not far removed from the experimental values through which childhood growth could be molded. The educators in schools, public and private, elementary and collegiate, were ready to welcome and to understand the psychoanalytic psychiatrist as an aid and co-worker in preparing students for adaptation in the democratic society. They found that interpretive psychiatry assisted in solving the problems of both normal and deviant cases (45).

We do not quite share Oberndorf's optimism. Rather, we believe that the clinical application of psychoanalysis, the stress on its therapeutic application, has created a social problem which is different from the one in central Europe, and actually should be described as a second phase. In the first phase it was almost possible to think of analysis as post-education, as a kind of progressive pedagogy. But in the second phase, psychoanalysis has become so much a part of the medical psychiatric scene, that only the therapeutic application is stressed. It is almost forgotten during the training of the physician that there are many applications of psychoanalysis beyond the therapeutic one. We find, therefore, that the analyst, the psychiatrist, clinical psychologist and the social worker look at education, as well as at all other activities, in terms of therapy or prevention. Many of the teachers who become interested in analysis ask for help with their deviant problems. If they do identify with psychoanalytic science, it is as "educational therapists."

Only the first volume of *The Psychoanalytic Study of the Child* contains a group of papers under the sub-heading "Problems of Education." In the second volume (1946), this sub-heading changes to "Problems of Education and Sociology," and contains the contributions of Erikson and Peller, but later volumes have given up this sub-division. We read, rather, about therapeutic nursery schools, frequently attached to child guidance clinics, and most of the experiments with analytically oriented education are now basically seen as therapeutic ventures. Psychoanalytically oriented educators are now frequently attached to clinical institutions, such as child guidance clinics, therapeutic nurseries, residential treatment centers and children's hospitals. The contact with the ordinary school system is a comparatively peripheral one which serves, at best, as a bridge for the severely disturbed child for whom treatment is needed. The primary interest is the deviant child who needs treatment and the cry is for prevention. Thus a situation has arisen which seems to leave little room for the educator except as a frustrated, second-class therapist or as a seeker of training opportunities ultimately leading to the clinical field. A good example for the development of this point of view can be found in a comment by Alpert (1941) in her paper on "Education and Therapy":

> Educational group therapy may be considered a period of intensification of an intelligent educational program, as it should be conducted from day to day. An intelligent educational program is one in which the subject matter and the approach to it are sufficiently challenging to the children to afford them ample opportunity for sublimation; one in which the teacher is as interested in the personality of the pupils as she is in the subject she is teaching; one in which group discussions are conducted informally and purposively. Such an educational program is as feasible in public schools as in private schools.
>
> While planning for mental health should be a requirement

of all responsible education, the progressive type of schools has a special responsibility in approximating this goal, because in it the personality of the child is encouraged to reveal itself more completely and is, therefore, more accessible to mental hygiene through education. Though most schools, gravely acknowledge this responsibility, opportunities for mental hygiene inherent in education have scarcely been tapped. The mental hygiene program usually operates more indirectly through teacher-child relationship, disciplines, home-school relationship. This paper will discuss a more direct and specialized use *of the educational setting for the purpose of mental health* (2) (Italics ours).

A similar stress on the mental helath aspect was expressed in 1953 by Blos in a paper on "Aspects of Mental Health in Teaching and Learning," as well as in Berman's "Mental Hygiene for Educators" (1953) and Weinreb's "Report of an Experience in the Application of Dynamic Psychiatry in Education" (1953).

This attitude of helping some teachers to move toward psychoanalysis but ultimately leading to their identification with its therapeutic aspect, was also expressed by Pearson in his volume, *Psychoanalysis and the Education of the Child,* published in 1954. His recommendations remind one of the *Lehrgang für Psychoanalytische Pädagogen.* While one cannot help but identify with his essential purpose, the creation of a more permanent bridge between psychoanalysis and education, one also realizes that the original problem of differentiation is not yet resolved. He says:

> It would seem to me that all psychoanalytic institutes which give instruction in psychoanalysis of children and adolescents could increase their services to the community by carefully selecting certain students to be students in the institute. These teachers might be chosen partly from among instructors in schools of education and partly from those in the school system itself. They should be given exactly the same instruction as are the psychiatric students in the course of psychoanalysis of children. They should have the same preliminary personal analysis and the same theoretical instruction, and should attend the same clinical and technical seminars. They should conduct a supervised psychoanalysis of at least one adult and three or four children. In this way they would learn by theory and practice the principles of psychoanalysis. When a teacher

had completed such a course, he can return to the school as a reputable consulting psychoanalyst. If after completing his course he should desire to devote himself entirely to psychoanalysis, as many pediatricians who have had psychoanalytic training have done, then the institute should demand that he limit his practice to the psychoanalysis of children in cases referred by a physician-psychoanalyst and under his supervision. If the personal psychoanalysis has been really successful —and no such student should be permitted to complete his training otherwise—the teacher's increased ability to adjust to reality will enable him to accept these necessary restrictions with good grace and in good faith. There are relatively more teachers than physicians who show an intuitive ability to understand and work with children, and so the practice of psychoanalysis of children would actually be benefited by this procedure. It would be hoped, however, that teachers with such intensive training would prefer to employ their knowledge of psychoanalysis in the field of education rather than in the practice of psychoanalytic therapy. As I said before, the procedure I have suggested would not lower but raise the standards of the American Psychoanalytic Association (47).

This point of view favors utilizing the resources of people, who are interested in children and who show intuitive talents to supply a gifted group of child therapists. In recent years such child psychotherapeutic training programs have been started. The best-known example is the Hampstead program for child psychotherapists, conducted so successfully and creatively by Anna Freud and her collaborators. In addition, there are some beginnings in the States, such as the program in Cleveland. Nevertheless, this does not solve the problem which we now are posing, the problem of strengthening education as a positive and creative force.

Tracing the history of psychoanalysis and education reveals, then, two essentially different phases. The first phase occurred in Europe. Its main characteristics were: enthusiasm; protest; and the slow beginning of the application of psychoanalysis to the training of child analysts and pedagogues. This last-named characteristic was the basis of questioning the differences between education and child analysis. The first phase, then, was one in which psychoanalysis was considered an educational procedure.

The second phase, after the Second World War, was characterized by experimentation in the Anglo-Saxon countries, particularly the United States. The psychoanalytic study of the child, no longer in need of the early protest movement, has become more fully a serious professional and scientific issue. Technical questions have been raised, but much of what has been developing in America and in England has been either in the field of therapeutic endeavors or in the field of prevention. Frequently the teacher sees himself, or is invited by us to see himself, as an educational therapist. The accent has changed from analysis as post-education to education as prevention of emotional illness, but some of the basic issues of differentiation still concern us.

Is it possible now to think of a third phase in the making, a phase in which there are two distinct fields, both benefiting from psychoanalysis as a scientific body of knowledge? Such future development was anticipated by Kris, when, as early as 1948, he wrote "On Psychoanalysis and Education." He envisioned "a process of communication between experts trained in different skills in which cross-fertilization of approaches is likely to occur" (41).

The influence of psychoanalysis on the school teacher and on modern education started, of course, with the deviant child. With the introduction of the school psychologist and with the focus on finding techniques which would be of service to the group of deviant children, psychoanalysis was a constant force on the educational scene. This concern for the deviant child has in recent years been quite well summarized in two volumes. The first of these, edited by Nelson B. Henry, called *Mental Health in Modern Education* (1955), is a volume in which there are many friendly comments on the contribution of psychoanalysis. One of its contributors, Olson, Dean of the School of Education at the University of Michigan, had already expressed himself on the psychoanalytic contribution to education. He wrote, "Originally designed for work with children who are ill, dynamic conceptions have proliferated so as to dominate or influence many modern approaches to the understanding and education of children in general" (46). His book (1949) makes much use of basic psychoanalytic knowledge, but its focus is on the achievement of mental health.

Another contribution, *Professional School Psychology*, was edited by Monroe G. and Gloria B. Gottsegen (1960). This volume is primarily concerned with the role of the school psychologist, and has a strong bias, of course, in the direction of psychotherapy and diagnostic testing. Its articles deal with different illnesses of children in addition to the adjustment problems of the major deviant groups of children. Among the contributions of analysts is one by the present authors. It deals with the borderline child in the school situation and suggests that:

> Teachers and psychotherapists will help each other best if each will accept the difference of the other's function as a prerequisite to successful collaboration. The maturity of a free society is reflected in the degree to which the notion of the "average" person, the insistence on adjustment to the mass personality, is replaced by the acceptance of individual differences. There is no better place to test the maturity of our concepts of freedom than in our educational system (18).

This is very much in accord with the spirit expressed by Kris.

A recent volume by Krugman (1958), *Orthopsychiatry and the School,* expresses the same spirit and sees the psychoanalyst as a consultant in the school system, with the diagnostic ability to prescribe therapy when called for. He is not seen as a potential collaborator for educational problems with the average, the so-called normal child.

But there is a function beyond the issue of mental health that the school must fulfill. Peller's discussion (1956) brings us nearer to a clarification of this task. She says that:

> good education is not characterized by its degree of permissiveness or strictness. . . . The pendulum may swing all the way back from over-indulgence to strict discipline and still miss the essential. A school may be very permissive, take a very lenient attitude toward some of the child's instinctual needs, and consider academic work a necessary evil, something that children naturally dislike. In consequence, it will postpone academic learning, reduce the study load, and for the ineducable rest impose passive acceptance upon the child (49).

She speaks about the need to cathect activities and interest and she describe the process of sublimation. She discusses the libidinal charge on activities, be they collective activities or solitary pursuit.

She thus includes, beyond the problem of the interpersonal relationships, the learning task of the school and leads us to techniques to help the children meet this task. Education is not only seen in terms of mental health and the prevention of ill health, but in the didactic terms of growth, enrichment and meeting tasks of life. The educational problem moves, then, out of the area of mental health toward the problem of learning, the acquisition of knowledge and skills. It seems to us that the new dimension which is thus created must lead to a new task in the rapprochement between psychoanalysis and education.

In an unpublished communication, Gerhart and Maria Piers (1955) speak about "Learning Theories and the Psychoanalytic Process." They discuss different kinds of learning and submit that analytic insights and constructs, combined with what we can learn from the learning theories, offer us three basic models of learning: "Learning by repetition; by insight; and learning through identification" (52). Actually, all three forms of learning can be observed in the therapeutic process, and will find their equivalent in the kind of learning that goes on in education.

The question as to how one is to combine existing capacities for learning at different age levels with existing techniques of teaching seems to be the issue for him who wishes to develop insights into processes of learning and teaching.

The psychoanalyst may then well be the resource person for the educator. The analyst can help the teacher use psychoanalytic insights and constructs in order to apply them to a process which is not therapeutic in nature but has as its purpose, training and education, the acquisition of knowledge, skills and social attitudes. The task of the educator is not to resolve unconscious conflicts, nor to cure the symptom of the deviant child, but rather to utilize analytic insights toward the teaching process.

So far, most of our experiences in collaboration with teachers and therapists have concerned children who were in both processes at the same time. Buxbaum, in Seattle, is engaged in such a collaborative study with co-workers in the teaching profession. Many schools for children whose problems do not permit them to use the public-school system work with analysts and clinicians on a similar level. We are concerned with the question of whether a third phase could be developed. In this phase, the collaboration between teacher and psychoanalyst could lead to the development of positive teaching techniques, rather than merely the avoidance of mental health risks or the fostering of good mental health.

It was in 1909 that Freud published the first analysis of a child. The study of Little Hans is the beginning of a powerful scientific and social influence on modern education. Freud's discussion of this case leads to:

> Hitherto education has only set itself the task of controling or, it would often be more proper to say, of suppressing the instincts. The results have been by no means gratifying, and where the process has succeeded it has only been to the advantage of a small number of favored individuals, who have not been required to suppress their instincts. Nor has anyone enquired by what means and at what cost the suppression of the inconvenient instinct has been achieved. Supposing now that we substitute another task for this one, and aim instead at making the individual capable of becoming a civilized and useful member of society with the least possible sacrifice of his own activity; in that case the information gained by psychoanalysis, upon the origin of pathogenic complexes and upon the nucleus of every nervous affection, can claim with justice that it deserves to be regarded by educators as an invaluable guide in their conduct toward children. What practical conclusions may follow from this, and how far experience may justify the application of those conclusions within our present social system, are matters which I leave to the examination and decision of others (29).

The third phase that we talk about is the envisioned collaboration between teachers and analysts, deriving applied principles from the same generic body of psychoanalytic knowledge. Whether it may actually lead to the development of new techniques; to new forms of collaboration; to a concept which includes, not only therapy and prevention, but also techniques which will more fully "enable the individual to take part in culture and to achieve this with the smallest loss of original energy" remains an open question. Since the Second World War, we have seen that in many places in Europe much of the original achievements described in the first part of this paper has disappeared. We must realize, consequently, that this third phase will depend, in part, on the strength and the interest of analysts who will encourage such development and participate in it.

One of the present authors has indicated in "Reflections on Parallels in the Therapeutic and the Social Process," how the applicability of discoveries and, sometimes, the very discoveries themselves, seem to be related to the *Zeitgeist,* to the ups and downs of history. We have seen educational techniques more readily influenced by psychoanalysis and by psychological considerations whenever society is, relatively, relaxed. In such periods there may be social experimentation, including attempts to discover better means of education. In times of acute stress, we pay less attention to the individual; we speak of crash programs, in which education of the individual child is subordinated to goals which are frequently far beyond the interest of the individual child Thus, this may not be a good time to attempt to predict the third phase.

Moreover, it is well to remember that whenever one describes historical trends for an open or an implied purpose, one must learn to cope with the danger of interpreting the past in the shadow of one's wishes for the future rather than in the light of actual reality. But even remembering this, one must acknowledge that seemingly impossible, Utopia-like tasks are sometimes made feasible through the inspiration of leaders.

We wish, then, to end this contribution on such a note. During the first Reiss-Davis Institute for Teachers in 1960, one of the authors told the teachers that the first public lectures Anna Freud gave in London in 1938, after the exodus from Austria, were directed to teachers. A teacher in the audience came up to the speaker later and said that this address had revived sentimental memories and strengthened still further her interest in psychoanalytic education. She had been present at that meeting in London, too, and she added, with pride: "But I have known Anna Freud much, much longer than that. She was my teacher in Vienna when I went to first grade."

REFERENCES

1. AICHHORN, AUGUST. *Wayward Youth.* Leipzig, Vienna, Zurich: International Psychoanalytic Publishers, 1925.

2. ALPERT, AUGUSTA. Education as Therapy. *Psychoanalytic Quarterly*, 1941, 10:468-474.

3. BALINT, ALICE. *The Early Years of Life—A Psychoanalytic Study.* New York: Basic Books, Inc., 1954.

4. BERMAN, L. Mental Hygiene for Educators: Report on an Experiment Using a Combined Seminar and Group Psychotherapy Approach. *Psychoanalytic Review*, 1953, 40:319-332.

5. BERNFELD, SIEGFRIED. *Kinderheim Baumgarten* (The Baumgarten Children's Home—A Report on a Serious Experiment in Modern Education). Berlin: Judische Verlag, 1921.

6. BERNFELD, SIEGFRIED. *The Psychology of the Infant.* Vienna: Springer, 1925.

7. BERNFELD, SIEGFRIED. *Sysiphos oder die Grenzen der Erziehung* (Sysiphus or the Boundaries of Education). Leipzig, Vienna: Internationaler Psychoanalytischer Verlag, 1925.

8. BLOS, PETER. Aspects of Mental Health in Teaching and Learning. *Mental Hygiene*, 1953, 37:555-569.

9. BORNSTEIN, STEFF. Misunderstandings in the Application of Psychoanalysis to Pedagogy. *Zeitschrift für Psychoanalytische Pädagogik*, 1937, 11:81-90.

10. BRUNER, JEROME S. *The Process of Education.* Cambridge, Mass.: Harvard University Press, 1961.

11. BURLINGHAM, DOROTHY. Problem of the Psychoanalytic Educator. *Zeitschrift für Psychoanalytische Pädagogik*, 1937, 11:91-97.

12. BUXBAUM, EDITH. Question Periods in a Class. *Zeitschrift für Psychoanalytische Pädagogik*, 1931, 5:263-265.

13. BUXBAUM, EDITH. Problems of Group Psychology in the Schoolroom. *Zeitschrift für Psychoanalytische Pädagogik*, 1936, 10:215-240.

14. BUXBAUM, EDITH. *Your Child Makes Sense.* New York: International Universities Press, 1949.

15. EKSTEIN, RUDOLF. A Refugee Teacher Looks on Democratic and Fascist Education. *Education*, October, 1939:101-109.

16. EKSTEIN, RUDOLF. Reflections on Parallels in the Therapeutic and the Social Process. *Values in Psychotherapy.* Charlotte Buhler, editor. New York: Free Press of Glencoe, 1962, pp. 181-194.

17. EKSTEIN, RUDOLF. The Boundary Line between Education and Psychotherapy. *Annual Report.* Los Angeles: Reiss-Davis Clinic for Child Guidance, 1960-61, pp. 14-15.

18. EKSTEIN, RUDOLF, and MOTTO, Rocco L. The Borderline Child in the School Situation. *Professional School Psychology.* Monroe G. and Gloria B. Gottsegen, editors. New York: Grune and Stratton, Inc., 1960, pp. 249-262.

19. ERIKSON, ERIK H. Psychoanalysis and the Future of Education. *Psychoanalytic Quarterly*, 1935, 4:50-68.

20. ERIKSON, ERIK H. Ego Development and Historical Change. *Psychoanalyt. Study of the Child*, 1946, 2:359-396.

21. ERIKSON, ERIK H. *Childhood and Society.* New York: Norton and Co., 1950.

22. FEDERN, PAUL. On the Psychology of Revolution; the Fatherless Society. *Der Aufsteig, Neue Zeit-und Streitschriften*, 1919, 12-13. Vienna: Anzengruber, 29 pp.

23. FENICHEL, OTTO. Means of Education. *Psychoanalytic Study of the Child,* 1945, 1:281-292.

24. FREUD, ANNA. *Introduction to Psychoanalysis for Teachers.* London: Allen and Unwin, 1931.

25. FREUD, ANNA, and BURLINGHAM, DOROTHY. *War and Children.* New York: Medical War Books, 1943.

26. FREUD ANNA, and BURLINGHAM, DOROTHY. *Infants without Families.* London: Allen and Unwin, 1943.

27. FREUD, ANNA. *An Inquiry into the concept of the Rejecting Mother.* New York: Child Welfare League of America, February 1955.

28. FREUD, ANNA. Personal communication ,1962.

29. FREUD, SIGMUND. The Analysis of a Phobia in a Five-Year-Old Boy. *Collected Works.* Standard Edition, 10:3-149. London: Hogarth Press, 1955.

30. GOTTSEGEN, MONROE G., and GLORIA B., editors. *Professional School Psychology.* New York: Grune and Stratton, 1960.

31. HENRY, NELSON B. *Mental Health in Modern Education.* Chicago: University of Chicago Press, 1955.

32. HILL, J. C. *Dreams and Education.* London: Methuen & Co., 1926.

33. HILL, J. C. *The Teacher in Training.* London: Allen and Unwin, 1935.

34. HILL, J. C. A New Technique of Teaching. Presidential Address, National Association of Inspectors of Schools and Educational Organizers. Annual Conference, London, 6th, 7th and 8th October, 1938.

35. HILL, J. C. Freud's Influence on Education. Presidential Address, Annual Conference of National Association of Inspectors of Schools and Educational Organizers. Annual Conference, London, 8th October, 1949.

36. HOFFER, WILLIE. Psychoanalytic Education. *Psychoanalytic Study of the Child,* 1945, 1:293-307.

37. HUG-HELLMUTH, HERMINE VON. Analysis of a Dream of a 5½-Year-Old Boy (Analyse eines Traumes eines fünfeinhalbjährigen)." *Zentralblatt für Psychoanalyse und Psychotherapie,* 1912, 2:122-127.

38. HUG-HELLMUTH, HERMINE VON. *A Study of the Mental Life of the Child.* James J. Putnam and Mabel Stevens, translators. Washington: Nervous and Mental Diseases Publishing Co., 1919.

39. HUG-HELLMUTH, HERMINE VON. On the Technique of Child-Analysis. *International Journal of Psychoanalysis* (Rosalie Gabler and Barbara Low, translators), 1921, 2:287-305.

40. HUG-HELLMUTH, HERMINE VON. *A Young Girl's Diary.* Eden and Cedar Paul, translators. London: Allen and Unwin; New York: Thomas Seltzer,, 1921.

41. KRIS, ERNST. On Psychoanalysis and Education. *American Journal of Orthopsychiatry,* 1948, 18:622-635.

42. KRUGMAN, M. *Orthopsychiatry and the School.* New York: American Orthopsychiatric Association, 1958.

43. LEVITT, MORTON. *Freud and Dewey.* New York: Philosophical Library, Inc., 1960.

44. MAYER, MARTIN. *The Schools.* New York: Harper & Brothers, 1961.

45. OBERNDORFF, C. P. *A History of Psychoanalysis in America.* New York: Grune and Stratton, 1953.

46. OLSON, WILLARD C. *Child Development.* Boston: Heath & Co., 1949.

47. PEARSON, GERALD. *Psychoanalysis and the Education of the Child.* New York: Norton & Co., 1954.
48. PELLER, LILI E. Incentives to Development and Means of Early Education. *Psychoanalytic Study of the Child,* 1946, 2:397-415.
49. PELLER, LILI E. The School's Role in Promoting Sublimation. *Psychoanalytic Study of the Child,* 1956, 11:437-449.
50. PFISTER, OSKAR. The Faults of Parents. *Zeitschrift für Psychoanalytische Pädagogik,* 1929, 3:172-184; 205-211; 251-291.
51. PFISTER, OSKAR. *What Does Psychoanalysis Offer to the Educator.* Leipzig: Julius Klinkhardt, 1917.
52. PIERS, GERHART and MARIA. Learning Theories and the Psychoanalytic Process. Unpublished.
53. REDL, FRITZ. The Educational Duties of a Homeroom Teacher. *Die Wiener Schule,* 1932: 12.
54. REDL, FRITZ. We Teachers and Examination Anxiety. *Zeitschrift für Psychoanalytische Pädagogik,* 1933, 7:378-400.
55. REDL, FRITZ. The Concept of "Learning Disturbance." *Zeitschrift für Psychoanalytische Pädagogik,* 1934, 8:155-177; 319-349.
56. RUBEN, MARGARETE. A Contribution to the Education of Parents. *Psychoanalytic Study of the Child,* 1945, 1:247-262.
57. RUBEN, MARGARETE. *Parent Guidance in the Nursery School.* New York: International Universities Press, Inc., 1960.
58. SCHMIDT, WERA. *Psychoanalytic Education in Soviet Russia—Report on the Experimental Children's Home in Moscow.* Vienna: Internationaler Psychoanalytischer Verlag, 1924.
59. SCHNEIDER, ERNST. The Area of Application of Psychoanalysis for Pedagogy. *Zeitschrift für Psychoanalytische Pädagogik.* October, 1926, 1:2-6.
60. SMOLEN, ELWYN M. and JENSEN, CAROLYN E. Educational Director in a Child Guidance Clinic: Report of a Pilot Project. Presented at Annual Meeting of the American Orthopsychiatric Association, Chicago, February 26, 1960.
61. STERBA, EDITHA. School and Educational Guidance (Schule und Erziehungsberatung). *Zeitschrift für Psychoanalytische Pädagogik,* 1936, 10:141-201.
62. STERBA, EDITHA. Interpretation and Education. *Psychoanalytic Study of the Child,* 1945, 1:309-318.
63. WEINREB, JOSEPH. Report of an Experience in the Application of Dynamic Psychiatry in Education. *Mental Hygiene,* April, 1953, 2:283-293.
64. WITTELS, FRITZ. *Die Befreiung des Kindes* (The Liberation of the Child). Stuttgart, Berlin, Zurich: Hippokrates-Verlag, 1927.
65. ZULLIGEER, HANS. *Psychoanalytic Pedagogics. A Report on Mass Education and Individual Education.* Zurich: Orell Füssli, 1926.
66. ZULLIGER, HANS. *Loosened Chains. Psychoanalysis in School Education.* Dresden: Alvin Hinkle, 1926.
67. ZULLIGER, HANS. Psychoanalysis and Leadership in School. *Imago,* 1930, 16:39-50.
68. ZULLIGER, HANS. Failures in School. *Zeitschrift für Psychoanalytische Pädagogik,* 1930, 4:431-441.

Chapter 26

A Psychoanalytic Approach to Individualized Day Care: The Development of the Culver City Children's Center

CHRISTOPH M. HEINICKE, PH.D.

"But we can and must do more. Psychoanalysis must not merely be considered a therapeutic application, although this application is the center of our activity. Because of many years experience in this area, we are stressing work with teachers, with public and private school systems, and with parents. We are speaking about the application of psychoanalysis to preschool and school education as it is designed for the average, the normal child. There is enormous need for this application in all areas, including the economically, culturally or otherwise deprived ones. Such work must be directed towards parents in all school systems on every grade level" (23). When this was said, Reiss-Davis' work in building a bridge from psychoanalysis to education and vice versa had already been underway for several years. The most immediate root of the Culver City Children's Center Project was, therefore, the consultation work reported on in "Issues in Collaboration" (*Reiss-Davis Bulletin Clinic*, 1972, No. 1).

As we consulted with the total faculty of two of the elementary schools, we became painfully aware that there were many children who were simply not prepared to enter kindergarten and failed to progress academically from this point on. One felt that they were very likely reachable. Nevertheless, the ordinary resources and even the special classes of the school system were often unable to help these individual children and keep them from disrupting the learning process. Despite the intense devotion of the teaching staff and some initial progress, there would suddenly be horrendous fights on the playground or acts of seemingly innocent vandalism. Since I participated in the attempt to cope with these difficulties, I felt their consequences intensely. This then was one of the most cogent reasons that I accepted the invitation from both the Culver City School District and Community Coordinating Council to develop a day care center. It was soon clear that without this community-based interest the present effort would not have been realized.

As one would expect, however, there were many other reasons for further collaboration between the Culver City School District and the Reiss-Davis' Division of Research. More than a decade had been spent in research on the process and outcome of psychoanalysis with elementary school children suffering from a learning disturbance. This work had indeed further convinced us that intensive, long-term treatment of these children was often the only lasting way of insuring their progressive development (11). A review of other methods of helping these children did not suggest any dramatic or more efficient alternatives to such treatment (7). For example, literature on tutoring of children revealed that these learning-disturbance children did improve while the tutoring was in effect but went back to their former rate of improvement once the relationship to the tutor was terminated. But even though psychoanalysis seemed the appropriate treatment for many children who were one or two years behind in their academic work, its tremendous cost both in terms of time and professional training could not be ignored. Without wishing to suggest that treatment resources should be replaced, we did feel that they could be usefully complemented. Our efforts were directed at attempting to detect potential learning difficulties at an earlier age and to employ resources that would promote the development of these children.

Still another experience encouraged us to work on the longitudi-

nal study of young children. We experimented with a great variety
of methods of checking the reliability of the reports of therapists.
While we concluded that certain aspects of the material can be
reliably reported by the therapist, we were also persuaded by our
experience that tape recording and observation through a one-way
mirror interfered with the clinical task of child psychoanalysis. In
search for other means of enhancing and/or confirming the data
derived from the therapist's report, we reasoned that observational
data which can more readily be checked for reliability would be a
real asset. That is, we thought that the data on the treatment of
the child would be greatly strengthened by having available earlier
intensive longitudinal observations of that child's behavior in the
preschool and family setting. Psychoanalyzing children who are
part of a longitudinal study had some time ago been recommended
and applied by Ernst Kris and his colleagues (21). We felt that
this approach should be applied more extensively. As of writing,
two such children who were observed by one team of observers in
preschool are being treated by a separate clinical team in the
primary school period (10). From this vantage point, intensive
longitudinal observation and the observations gathered during the
child analysis are two complementary but independent ways of
studying the total development of a child.

Another root in the development of the Children's Center is to
be found in the longitudinal studies of the effects of mother-child
separation (15). Central to this effort was the attempt to delineate
specifically the impact of object relations and disruptions of object
relations on ego development. It was noted that two-years-olds
who were separated from their families and placed in a residential
nursery showed various signs of the disruption of ego functioning.
Severe forms of hostility were expressed; they became intensely
greedy, lost all previously established sphincter control, and after
about two weeks of separation were using next to no words. Most
fascinating were the developments following the reunion with the
parents. After a period of extreme testing and provocation, the
affectionate tie to the parents was restored and all of the ego functions subsequently returned to their previous level. It is not certain
that the separation had not left some permanent damage, but what

can be stressed here is the responsiveness of ego functioning of the two-year-old being separated from his parents.

Combining this interest in mother-child separation with that of attempting to assess the forerunners of learning disturbances led us to that phase of life when most children separate from their parents to enter nursery school. We anticipated that assessments at this developmental point might well permit us to differentiate between those children who would continue to develop successfully to the point of kindergarten and those who were already showing difficulty in shifting from the psychological base of the family to a new one with the adults and peers in the nursery school. Collaboration with the Center for Early Education, Los Angeles, made a preschool setting available for our first pilot study.

Before initiating this work, we reviewed the literature to determine what was known of observable variables in preschool that would predict later learning difficulties in reading (7). As a function of this review and of our actual research experience, the concept of the child's orientation seemed one of the most workable and promising of such variables. The choice of a conceptualization closely linked to ego functioning revealed our interest in developing this part of our knowledge. Since we were constantly working within the framework of the Anna Freud Developmental Profile (5), we thought of task orientation as an additional "line of development." These lines combine both drive and ego considerations.

The tasks we initially used to observe the child are the goal-directed motor activity of wood-gluing, and the listening-comprehension task of hearing a story. In these situations the various behavior related to the child's task orientation could be observed. Consistent with the total emphasis on the child's engagement in new relationships and activities, we focused initially on the child's engagement in the particular task being observed. *Engagement* in the listening-comprehension task was judged by the child's ability to attend and volunteer actively as opposed to withdrawing. In this situation as well as in the goal-directed motor activity, we paid particular attention to the child's ability to persist in the activity. We saw this persistence as one index of the child's ability to tolerate frustration.

Closely related, but focusing more on the child's ability to tolerate anxiety, is his *compliance with the definition of the task situation*. Can the child follow the teacher's instructions and respond to her efforts at control? Does he disrupt by interfering with others, either by making personal demands or by hitting other children or running from the group?

The child's *productivity* was also assessed. How frequently was he able to answer the teacher's question and how appropriate were his answers? In the wood-gluing work, did he produce what was called for, and if so, how extensive was his production? What *pride* and what *pleasure* did the child show in appropriate answers to certain requests or the production of certain articles? We also assessed the child's capacity for *creativity and imagination*. Were his answers unique and fresh without being bizarre? Did he combine material in a new way without losing integration? We also noted whether the child was sucking his thumb, holding a blanket, or masturbating and so forth, as evidence of the child's tendencies towards regression.

Kagan and Moss (16) reported that the child's involvement in task mastery at age three to six predicted the same achievement behavior from six to ten years, as well as his intellectual achievement from 10 to 14 years. I.Q., as assessed at age six, was also associated to the above two measures. Several studies have demonstrated the relationship between the components of task orientation, as assessed in kindergarten, and reading performance from grades one through five. De Hirsch et al. (2) included only two personality variables, ego strength and work attitude, in their kindergarten test battery, but each was predictive of later reading performance. Attwell, Orpet, and Meyers (1) reported the following kindergarten test behavior variables as relating to fifth-grade reading: the ability to concentrate on the test tasks; the effort displayed; the interest shown in the task; the self-confidence in approaching the task, and the manual dexterity shown. In brief, there was already much evidence to indicate a broad association between components of task orientation as assessed in preschool and the child's reading performance in the elementary school. Needed, however, was delineation of the more specific details of this broad association. Before summarizing the results of our pilot study, it is necessary to indicate the nature of our methodology described more fully elsewhere (14).

The longitudinal information on the child is provided by intensive observations made in the preschool setting by at least three different observers. These are scheduled to provide representative and constant as well as daily samples of behavior, particularly during the first five months of the child's entrance into preschool. After this, until the end of the second year of school, a minimum of one observation period per week is planned for. The observer is in the room approximately half an hour, is guided by a general set of headings derived from the Anna Freud Developmental Profile (5) and is giving a complete descriptive account of what he has observed immediately after leaving the child. Following this, he may add certain interpretive comments to the description. The observer also speaks to the teacher and often has the opportunity to observe the parent-child interaction.

At predetermined points in the two-year span, special assessments are added to provide additional cross-sectional observations. These include systematic categorized observations of the child's task orientation, his performance on intelligence tests, standard teacher reports, a play interview with each child, and films on the child's behavior in various task situations. A variety of methods of data analysis has been developed to handle this information. The longitudinal data are abstracted into a series of periods of development, the so-called period analysis, and the cross-sectional data are dealt with in terms of the developmental profile and ratings derived from it.

The major longitudinal information on the parent-child relationship is provided by the interviews and observations of the parents and child in the home. These data are supplemented by many observations made on the parents in the preschool, especially during the first two weeks when the parents are asked to remain in the vicinity of the child.

So far, the results of the first pilot study of ten children have been published in two ways. We initially focused on the description of the step-by-step process whereby two three-year-old girls adapted to preschool and, in particular, to certain tasks which were part of the curriculum. For example, we could eventually conclude from these detailed studies that Jean, one of the girls, had in the past experienced and re-experienced during entrance into nursery school, that people make an initial engagement but then depart. All her commitments, including those to the task, reflected the expectation that abandonment would follow. Characteristically, she would flee the situation first. It was particularly through the reassurance that she would not be abandoned and could be loved as a girl that Teacher Esther in important ways eventually enhanced her development (13).

A second mode of presentation deals with certain rating and test scores available on all ten children for the two-year span. In this effort we focused on the association of the child's task orientation with other variables. Systematic ratings and scored observations of the child's task orientation at three years, five months were indeed correlated with similar ratings and scores at four and five years. Of the various components of task orientation, the nature of the engagement in the task was most consistent; that is, it intercorrelated to the greatest extent. This, one would expect from previous research findings.

Of greater interest is the fact that in this middle-class sample, the children who were engaged in the tasks of the preschool showed the greatest engagement or concentration while being given the WPPSI at age five. Moreover, the children who showed the least general engagement or concentration performed less well on the Performance than on the Verbal items of that task. Initially, this was quite puzzling. Examination revealed that the children, who were low on the performance items, showed a particularly striking deficit on the subtests entitled "Picture Completion" and "Mazes." Both of these subtests can be interpreted as arousing unresolved conflicts in the area of separating psychologically from the mother. Thus, on the Maze subtest the child is asked to trace the path whereby the baby chick returns to his mother. There was further substantiation for the hypothesis that the testing situation, and especially these two performance scale subtests, aroused unresolved conflicts around separation and individuation. Children who had difficulty with the subtests also had difficulty separating from the nursery schoolroom and remaining alone with the examiner. The intensive longitudinal data describing their entrance into preschool also revealed an inability to resolve the issue of moving from their home and the family to a new base and to the adults and then the peers in the nursery school.

The systematic ratings of the child's ability to move psychologically from home to school during the first five months of school are correlated with the ratings of task orientation made at that time and later in the two-year span.

It must be noted that we are aware that many factors may be influencing the cluster of variables involved in the successful adaptation to preschool. A variety of research, including our own, does stress, however, the importance of the quality of the previous and ongoing parent-child relationship as one such factor. First of all, therefore, we generated a number of ratings of such parent-child dimensions as warmth, limit-setting, etc. We then developed a profile of such ratings for each of the families. One profile of parent-to-child relationships can be described as follows: The mother showed an adequate level of warmth; her psychological availability was very clearly defined; she encouraged new relationships; she definitely set limits; in addition, she exerted pressure for independent achievement, particularly in the academic area. It is clear that this type of profile will have to be greatly elaborated to do justice to our observations as we expand the number of families studied. Even in this pilot effort we could, nevertheless, establish statistically significant correlations between this profile, as assessed at six weeks after entrance into preschool, to ratings of task orientation assessed throughout the two-year span and test scores as derived from the child's WPPSI test performance at age five. That is, children whose parent-child relationships were described by the above profile rated high on task orientation, and performed evenly on both verbal and performance IQ subtests.

A second pilot study is now focusing on the preschool *day care* program of the Center for Early Education. The staff of the Center had alerted me to the fact that the development of many of the children there was not proceeding in a desirable manner. This emerged most clearly in terms of the greater difficulty that the preschool staff had in handling these children when compared with the children attending the half-day program. Accordingly, we followed these three-year-olds entering the day care program in the fall of 1969. As it happened, only two children and their families started at that time so they constitute the total sample. In addition to the previous types of observations, including contacts with the working mothers, the development of the children was followed by filming them in certain task situations five, ten, and twenty months after their entry into the program (9). This film shows these two children with others involved in the task of wood-gluing, the manipulation of playdoh, and listening in a group to a story entitled, "Are You My Mother?" The film is a visual addition to a monograph now in preparation (12).

Some of the tentative conclusions that emerged from our observations of the child and mother as they entered day care are: 1) The manner in which the mother and child enter the day care program reflects an essential component of their relationship. 2) The nature of that relationship, and especially whether the child has an inner expectation that he will be cared for, is very significant in determining whether he will make use of the new relationships offered in the program. 3) The continued availability of a caretaker, such as a grandmother, to whom the child has a relationship, will greatly facilitate the transition from care in the home to care in the center. 4) The impact of the loss of parent is likely to be less if the child has a chance to adjust to the half-day care program before being moved to the full day care stay (8).

In addition to the above, our initial and subsequent observations stress the importance of providing adequate and fairly nonstructured relationship opportunities in the early months of entrance into day care. To illustrate from the forthcoming monograph: "From the first day of school Amy again entered with assertive questions of 'Where is this— where is that?' she did bring back the doll that she had been given on a previous short visit and pointed out that the doll's eyes were gone. She was anxious about this aggression of hers but could be reassured. One was immediately impressed by the lack of physical contact between mother and child, but they did maintain a verbal communication, with Amy holding her mother through such statements as, 'Mommy, I'm painting. Mommy, look at this.'

"Amy made her first commitment to the painting which she entered with great concentration, but was also soon wildly dripping the paint on the newspaper. 'It's dripping, Mommy, it's dripping,' she cried out in a loud voice that all could hear. The head teacher had to begin to respond with some form of limits. More important, Amy now attempted to make a series of personal contacts. She first of all wanted the mother to come over and sit with her, but mother turned her over to the head teacher. The latter did start to sit down but as new children came in this was inevitably interrupted. Then a very warm student teacher, Susan, began to help her with the picture, label it, and in this way she produced three pictures that were eventually taken home and in which Amy showed considerable pride. But another child now called Susan away, and Amy then attempted a relationship with Jonathan. Jonathan seemed again to promote her relaxing, but he then suddenly missed his mother and asked her to come over and sit by him. She did this. Again anxious, Amy called to her mother, saying, 'I'm not finished painting yet.' It was said in a way as if to invite the mother and to hold her in this activity. The mother remained seated in her chair. When her mother failed to come over, Amy attacked Jonathan slightly, taking some of his paints away. He was passive and therefore it did not lead to any kind of a scene. From this Amy then turned to a student teacher, Ellen, and for a considerable period of time involved herself at playdoh." We feel that the continued availability of one person would have greatly assisted Amy in making a more adequate adaptation.

We were equally impressed by the need for developing a particular kind of supportive relationship, not only for the day care child, but for the working mothers involved. We anticipated that with families not of middle-class background such casework would have to veer heavily towards the supportive. But even with the middle-class families, one often was compelled to help the mother organize certain aspects of daily life. It was particularly necessary to provide the judgment of another adult against which the working mother, in this case also divorced, could reach some sense of confidence.

These conclusions, reached from our own pilot research, were supported by a review of other efforts as preschool intervention.

The challenge of enhancing the competence of the preschool child and particularly the task orientation of children from poverty, single-parent homes can clearly be met in a variety of ways. Edwards and Stern (4) report evidence favoring programs which include the systematic presentation of a curriculum with well-defined objectives. However, they stress that the information on the advantage of structured curriculum approaches is by no means uniform and a great deal more investigation is needed (3). In comparing four types of programs, ranging from the highly structured to the traditional or less structured, Karnes et al. (18) found that the degree of structure did not explain the results. The so called "traditional" program involving intensive interaction with the teacher was nearly as effective as the highly structured one. Even more striking, in many studies, gains made during the structured programming are lost in the period after the program (19). More recently, Weikart (24) reported the results of a seven-year study contrasting a very structured behavior-modification approach to language training developed by Bereiter and Engelman with his own cognitively oriented curriculum and a more "traditional," less-structured child-centered approach. As administered by Weikart and his staff, all programs were successful in leading to permanent gains in IQ and reading achievement of poverty children entering the program at three years of age. If anything, the most structured approach was less effective. In interpreting the success of all programs, Weikart has stressed the importance of staff support, supervision, and planning. Most important, extensive service was provided to the families to help them realize their own goals.

Other recent research has also re-emphasized the tremendous importance of working not only with the child—as is usually the case in the more structured programs—but also of attending to the family situation to which the child returns daily. One of the first studies that reported a post-program decrement, but a smaller one, was the Early Training Project (20). Unlike other programs, this one stressed a comprehensive, intensive approach, including home visits and direct work with parents. Since then the successful work of Karnes (17), Levenstein (22), Gordon (6), and others has focused on helping the mother to become more competent in dealing with and instructing her child. Of great interest here is that one of the important correlates of these programs is the increased competence and lack of depression in the mothers themselves.

With all these considerations in mind we have now developed the initial outlines of a service to be initiated in the Culver City Children's Center. The carefully planned but individualized curriculum will allow the child the maximum opportunity to engage at the level of his interest. In addition, we will provide the relationship opportunity of a mature volunteer who will be asked to come to the preschool approximately three times a week for a four- to six-hour span. Besides the volunteer, both the head teacher and the student teachers will be organizing the major schoolroom situations.

To provide adequate support and understanding for the mother, experienced social workers will maintain continuous contact with the families involved. The needs of each family will be initially formulated and a general approach worked out for best meeting these needs. We envisage that much of the activity will be supportive in nature and almost of an advocacy character, but we stress that it will always be based on our fullest understanding of the family inter-relationships.

A third essential component to our service effort will be the constant integration of that service under the leadership of the Program Co-ordinator (the author) as he maintains contact with each of the individuals and with the team as a whole in weekly staff meetings. That is, within an individualized open framework classroom situation, psychoanalytic experience will be used to plan for and continuously assess the development of each child and family.

The methodology previously used in the pilot studies will be applied as part of a systematic design that has been worked out for the new project. In a variety of ways we shall assess whether the service provided does indeed have a significant impact on these children of working, under-privileged mothers. If effective, the Culver City Children's Center could well serve as a demonstration model. In any case, our understanding of the impact of the quality of object relationships on ego functioning ought to be greatly enhanced.

BIBLIOGRAPHY

1. ATTWELL, A. A., ORPET, R. E., and MEYERS, E. C. Kindergarten Behavior Ratings as a Predictor of Academic Achievement. *J. of School Psych.* 1967, 6:43.

2. DE HIRSCH, K., LANSKY, J., and LANGFORD, W. *Predicting Reading Failure: A Preliminary Study of Reading, Writing and Spelling Disabilities in Preschool Children*. New York: Harper & Row, 1966.

3. DICKIE, J. P. Effectiveness of Structured and Unstructured (Traditional) Methods of Language Training. *Language Remediation for the Disadvantaged Preschool Child*, M. A. Brottman, ed. Monographs of the Society for Research in Child Development, 1968, 33, No. 124.

4. EDWARDS, J., and STERN, C. A Comparison of Three Intervention Programs with Disadvantaged Preschool Children. *J. of Spec. Ed.*, 1970, 4:205.

5. FREUD, A. *Normality and Pathology in Childhood*. New York: Int. Univ. Press, 1965.

6. GORDON, I. Stimulation via Parent Education. *Children*, 1969, 16:47.

7. HEINICKE, C. M. Learning Disturbance in Children. *Manual of Child Psychopathology*, B. Wolman, ed. In press.

8. HEINICKE, C. M. Parental Deprivation in Early Childhood: A Predisposition to Later Depression? *Separation and Depression: Clinical and Research Aspects*, E. C. Senay, chm. Symposium of the Amer. Assoc. for the Advancement of Sci., 1971. In press.

9. HEINICKE, C. M. Film: *Day Care and the Child's Task Orientation*, 1971.

10. HEINICKE, C. M. In Search of Supporting Evidence for Reconstructions Formulated during a Child Psychoanalysis. *Reiss-Davis Clin. Bull.*, 1970, 7:92.

11. HEINICKE, C. M. Frequency of Psychotherapeutic Session as a Factor Affecting Outcome: Analysis of Clinical Ratings and Test Results. *J. of Abnor. Psych.*, 1969, 74:553.

12. HEINICKE, C. M., WEITZNER, L., LAMPL, E., LIEBOWITZ, J., WAX, D., and PORTNOY, N. Relationship Opportunities in Day Care and the Child's Task Orientation: Three-year-old Amy and Julie. Unpublished.

13. HEINICKE, C. M., BUSCH, F., CLICK, P., and KRAMER, E. Parent-Child Relations, Adaptation to Nursery School and the Child's Task Orientation: A Contrast in the Development of Two Girls. *Individual Differences in Children*. J. C. Westman, ed. In press.

14. HEINICKE, C. M., BUSCH, F., CLICK, P., and KRAMER, E. A Methodology for the Intensive Observation of the Preschool Child. *Individual Differences in Children*. J. C. Westman, ed. In press.

15. HEINICKE, C. M., and WESTHEIMER, I. *Brief Separations*. New York: Int. Univ. Press, 1965.

16. KAGAN, J., and MOSS, H. A. *Birth to Maturity*. New York: John Wiley & Sons, 1962.

17. KARNES, M. B. *A New Role for Teachers: Involving the Entire Family in the Education of Preschool Disadvantaged Children*. Urbana: Univ. of Illinois Press, 1969.

18. KARNES, M. B., TESKA, J. A., and HODGINS, A. S. The Effects of Classroom Intervention in the Intellectual and Language Development of 4-Year-Old Disadvantaged Children. *Amer. J. of Orthopsychiat.*, 1970, 40:58.

19. KARNES, M. B., TESKA, J. A., and HODGINS, A. S. *A Longitudinal Study of Disadvantaged Children Who Participated in Three Different Preschool Programs*. ERIC Document Reproduction Service, 1968, ED-26-338.

20. KLAUS, R., and GRAY, S. The Early Training Project for Disadvantaged

Children: A Report after Five Years. *Monographs of the Society for Research in Child Development,* 1968, 33, No. 4.

21. KRIS, E. The Recovery of Childhood Memories in Psychoanalysis. *Psychoanalytic Study of the Child,* 1956, 11:54.

22. LEVENSTEIN, P. Cognitive Growth in Preschoolers through Verbal Interaction with Mothers. *Amer. J. of Orthopsychiat.,* 1970, 40:426.

23. MOTTO, R. L., CAMPBELL, M., EKSTEIN, R., FRIEDMAN, S., HEINICKE, C., and MEYER, M. A Reaffirmation at a Time of Crisis: Concerning the Philosophy and the Scope of Work at the Reiss-Davis Child Study Center. *Reiss-Davis Clin. Bull.,* 1970, 7:2.

24. WEIKART, D. *Early Childhood Special Education for Intellectually Subnormal and/or Culturally Different Children.* Washington, D.C.: National Leadership Institute in Early Childhood Development, 1971.

Chapter 27

The Influence of Psychoanalysis on Education and School

RUDOLF EKSTEIN, PH.D.

But there is one topic which I cannot pass over so easily—not, however, because I understand particularly much about it or have contributed very much to it. Quote the contrary: I have scarcely concerned myself with it at all. I must mention it because it is so exceedingly important, so rich in hope for the future, perhaps the most important of all the activities of analysis. What I am thinking of is the application of psychoanalysis to education, to the upbringing of the next generation. I am glad that I am at least able to say that my daughter, Anna Freud, has made this study her life-work and has in that way compensated for my neglect.

—SIGMUND FREUD

"Whose heart is full, his mouth runneth over." I believe you can all appreciate how grateful I am for the honor of being asked to deliver the Freud Lecture for 1970, an invitation which brings me back to my native city in an official capacity after more than three decades. To Anna Freud I owe the theme of this lecture: the influence of psychoanalysis on education and school. This area of

Freud Lecture, read June 15, 1970, before the Sigmund Freud Society of Vienna. Translated by the author from the original German.

340

ideas and endeavor originally led me to psychoanalysis in the 1930's and has remained an important interest influencing my professional activities, particularly during the last ten years, and leading to a series of publications.

When, in 1938, I was forced to go to a foreign land, I took with me a few books. Those who had either approved the burning of books or who had silently accepted their burning would probably have considered them the valueless remainders of a world lost. But for me these books were deep, inner support that helped me turn the foreign country into a new home. One of them, a small but unforgettable volume by Thomas Mann, described *The Coming Victory of Democracy* (18). During the first half of that fateful year, 1938, when Austria was occupied, he spoke in America about his intention of settling there:

> Four years ago I visited America for the first time, and since then I have come here each year. I was delighted with the atmosphere that I found here, because it was almost free of the poisons that fill the air of Europe—because here, in contrast to the cultural fatigue and inclination to barbarism prevalent in the Old World, there exists a joyful respect for culture, a youthful sensitivity to its values and its products. I feel that the hopes of all those who cherish democratic sentiments in the sense in which I have defined them, must be concentrated on this country. Here it will be possible—here it *must* be possible—to carry out those reforms of which I have spoken; to carry them out by peaceful labour, without crime and bloodshed. It is my own intention to make my home in your country, and I am convinced that if Europe continues for a while to pursue the same course as in the last two decades, many good Europeans will meet again on American soil. I believe, in fact, that for the duration of the present European dark age, the centre of Western culture will shift to America. America has received much from Europe, and that debt will be amply repaid if, by saving our traditional values from the present gloom, she can preserve them for a brighter future that will once again find Europe and America united in the great tasks of humanity.

A few years earlier, on the occasion of Freud's eightieth birthday, Mann gave a talk on "Freud and the Future." The book (17) containing this lecture also accompanied me into emigration.

Thomas Mann describes "the fundamental temper of that more
blithely objective and peaceful world, which the science of the unconscious may be called to usher in." He states prophetically:

> Its mingling of the pioneer with the physicianly spirit justifies
> such a hope. Freud once called his theory of dreams "a bit of
> scientific new-found land won from superstition and mysti-
> cism." The word "won" expresses the colonizing spirit and
> significance of his work. "Where Id was, shall be Ego," he epi-
> grammatically says. And he calls analysis a cultural labour
> comparable to the draining of the Zuider Zee. Almost in the
> end the traits of the venerable man merge into the lineaments
> of they grey-haired Faust, whose spirit urges him
>
> > "to shut the imperious sea from the shore away,
> > Set narrower bounds to the broad water's waste."
> > "Then open I to many millions space
> > Where they may live, not safe-secure, but free
> > And active. And such a busy swarming I would see
> > Standing amid free folk on a free soil."
>
> The free folk are the people of a nature freed from fear and
> hate, and ripe for peace.

Through the words of Thomas Mann I am attempting to make
clear that I believe psychoanalysis can influence education only in
a civilization based essentially on a free order of society. Moreover,
within the social and cultural values of such an order, individual-
ism must have an esteemed place. That is, the goals and rights of
the individual—not just the goals of the state or the political-power
apparatus—must be valued and respected. These values were being
almost completely negated in Europe at that time, and many of us
felt that they could only be maintained somewhere far away from
our native land.

I shall describe the history of pedagogic interest in psychoanalysis in order to make clear that those of us who came to the United
States were not satisfied simply to hold on to old traditions. We
intended to build upon and enlarge the knowledge and skills we
had brought from Europe.

What, then, was the historic and scientific situation before 1938?
In an abbreviated way, I would like to touch upon what I have
dealt with more thoroughly and conscientiously in an earlier work

(5). And I will again refer to a few books and scientific journals that accompanied me, first to England and, later, to the United States.

For instance, there were the eleven volumes of the *Zeitschrift für psychoanalytische Pädagogik,* published between 1926 and 1937. One of the first editors was Heinrich Meng; and during the last years, Willi Hoffer, my first teacher in the *Lehrgang für psycho-analytische Pädagogen,* was the editor. The editorial board during the last years was composed of August Aichhorn, Paul Federn, Anna Freud, Heinrich Meng, Hans Zulliger—psychoanalysts whose contributions have created the basis for generations of research workers in the area of education and psychoanalysis.

At the risk of simplifying matters too much, I would like to characterize this period as the phase of development of a new school of pedagogy, namely psychoanalytic pedagogy. In studying the different contributions of those eleven years between 1926 and 1937, one finds that there was not as yet a serious attempt to separate the therapeutic function from the educational one. Freud himself often referred to psychoanalysis as a second education, and many of the pedagogues spoke about *Heilpädagogik,* therapeutic education. The educators who found their way to psychoanalysis frequently moved from the field of education to therapeutic application, and became child analysts. A more exhaustive examination of the facts might demonstrate, I believe, that this inner development—the change in goal directions from education to therapeutic ones—involved not only scientific issues, as yet scientifically unsolvable, but had to do with the political and social climate. The social order in Central Europe had changed, but the hopes of the young republics were soon lost in the ensuing political and economic chaos. The island that could be maintained the longest was the therapeutic application of psychoanalysis.

I wish to speak now about a contribution that made an enormous impression on many searching young intellectuals: Siegfried Bernfeld's *Sisyphus or the Boundaries of Education,* published in 1925. This book, together with Bernfeld's other works, helped set goals for a generation of psychoanalysts and psychoanalytically oriented pedagogues. Bernfeld sees the educator as a Sisyphus, the hero of Greek antiquity who tried again and again to bring about the impossible, only ever to be thwarted by the gods who defeated his efforts and forced him endlessly to start anew. Bernfeld tells us that the educator must fight against two limits of education that are almost impossible to overcome: the unfavorable order, or perhaps even disorder, of society; and the obstacle of the unconscious in the child's mind. Many years later, Friedrich Hacker (14) discussed this dilemma once more. In a consideration of the problems of modern criminal psychology, he put the question to us: Is it man that fails or is it society? Bernfeld's views were influenced by Freud's instinct theory and by Marxist ideology. The idealism of the teacher can lead to a scientific profession, Bernfeld suggested, only if the educator both understands the specific civilization he lives in and recognizes as well the boundaries of the unconscious. Bernfeld's pessimism caused us to overlook, at that time, the fact that boundaries are not simply obstacles, but can also serve to produce the capacity to live and to grow within limits, as well as beyond them. Boundaries are not merely limiting forces; they must also be considered as inner organizers that make goals realizable. Again and again, Bernfeld expresses the hope that the application of fundamental psychoanalytic principles will be possible some day in an ideal society. He states: "In such an ideal society it will be perhaps an indifferent issue as to how children grew up, that they will become, in any case, just and fair human beings by means of identification. There is no way out from inner ambivalence and doubt. The scientist is not ashamed of it; he exaggerates these doubts and ambivalences in order to hopefully overcome them in the future" (2).

I do not know whether hoping for the realization of an ideal society, or idealizing the profession of the educator, makes education any easier. Perhaps most of us need ideals in order to work towards a better reality or to be able, at least, to bear with reality, but we must not permit Utopian expectations and hopes to keep us from careful scientific work.

The first experiments in psychoanalytic pedagogy were primarily concerned with the faults of the societal order (2), the faults of parents (20), the suppression of childhood sexuality, the lack of sexual enlightenment, the oppressive machinery of the school, and similar questions. The first psychoanalytic attempts were a critique of the existing educational philosophy, and they were constantly directed towards the construction of a system of progressive education. Many such experiments were undertaken during those post-war years in Europe, but all of them suffered, more or less, from what we can see now was the childhood disease of psychoanalytic pedagogy. This was that their emphasis was primarily on the liberation of the child (23), the faults of parents, and the necessity for a new system of education. These attempts were an understandable protest against the old, as well as an attempt to bring about something new, but they were not sufficiently self-critical.

Wilhelm Hoffer himself, one of the leading figures of that time, spoke critically about these first years in the first volume of *The Psychoanalytic Study of the Child*—the American successor to the *Zeitschrift für psychoanalytische Pädagogik*. He said that there was a "crying need for the results of longitudinal research on personality development. No amount of successful child analysis and no miracles that well-trained educators and parents may report, can replace a prolonged experiment with children and adolescents from birth to maturity. Only after the experience of such research shall we be able to assess whether or not it is possible to prevent or modify early traumas, and to what extent the ego's faculty to integrate id tendencies can be developed and utilized" (16).

The first heroic phase in the relationship between education and psychoanalysis—more a critique of society than a self-critical phase —ended with the onset of the Second World War. In turning to the second phase, I base the discussion primarily on my experiences in the United States. The new annual, *Psychoanalytic Study of the Child* dealt only in its first volume with education and psychoanalysis. Interest in problems of education was not very strong in American psychoanalytic literature between 1945 and 1965, mostly because psychoanalysis in America has been medically oriented. Lay analysts have played a smaller part than in Europe, and the training of psychoanalysts since 1938 has included mainly psychiatrists. The interests of psychoanalysis were therapeutic or directed to the prevention of emotional and mental illness. The volumes cited were filled with papers on theory and clinical practice; only in recent years have some of us been committed once more to the restoration of a bridge between psychoanalysis and education. Psychoanalysis, of course, influenced many social institutions, as, for example, social work, hospital work, and the mental-health movement, but the emphasis of the twenty years prior to 1960 was largely therapeutic and preventative.

Educators did show some interest in psychoanalysis, but mainly in using psychoanalytic insights for those children who brought pathogenic conflicts into the school situation. We were occupied with children suffering from learning difficulties and with those who needed psychotherapeutic help. Teachers seemed to insist that psychoanalytic insights be used only as clinical insights. The psychologists, the clinicians—analytically oriented or from other schools of thought—were hardly in the center of education, and were, on the whole, occupied with those situations which schools and educators could not handle. During the first European phase, psychoanalysis and pedagogy formed a new but isolated unity of psychoanalytic pedagogy, but not in the second phase taking place in America. There, psychoanalysis and education were considered as separate functions, and psychoanalysis did not contribute to general education but was occupied primarily with the sick child. Thesis is followed by antithesis.

This rough outline, which simplifies everything and which exaggerates, as every simplification does, leads us now to the third phase which has occupied many colleagues and myself during the last ten or fifteen years.

I see this third phase as a synthesis, in which education and psychoanalysis represent separate fields of application. It we look beyond the application of psychoanalysis as a therapy, we can see in it a basic science dealing with the development of psychic organization and the function of personality. We are then able to ask in which way psychoanalytic insights and theories may contribute to education. Psychoanalysis is one of the many basic sciences that must be accessible to the educator in order to allow him earnestly and competently to carry out his work in society. We do not want to fuse education and psychoanalysis but we do want to create a bridge between them. During the first phase, we observed learning-disturbed children, and, sometimes, also teaching-disturbed teachers, and we often asked in which way these learning and teaching disturbances could be helped. We suggested then that child analysis and the didactic analysis of the pedagogue was the answer. I am still convinced that many of the problems that we face with children go beyond the possibilities of education. They are problems that do not allow for realistic solutions by teacher or parent. Other measures, in terms of social work or in terms of therapy or, sometimes, in terms of political action, have to be undertaken. I believe now as strongly as I did then that it would be most desirable if as many professional educators as possible would undergo a personal analysis so that they would have full contact with themselves and with the child and adolescent. There are few educators—and August Aichhorn who gave us the classic, *Wayward Youth* (1), was one of them—who have the gift of real empathy. Aichhorn had the capacity to feel deeply into the heart of the child and the adolescent, and was able to develop this gift without his own analysis. But even he spoke about the necessity and value of the analysis of the pedagogues, after he had gone through such training. It permitted him to turn his intuitive talent into a rational and teachable technique.

But I suggest that the value of psychoanalysis, as far as its application to education and school is considered, goes far beyond its therapeutic aspects. My view is that we should not only be occupied with neurotic, psychotic, or delinquent children and youth. We should also consider the average child, the gifted child, the normal parents, and that all educators have a right to utilize fully the insights of psychoanalysis. The beginning of psychoanalysis, of course, is its clinical history. But the genius of Freud soon recognized that insights derived from sick people are but magnified versions of insights which can be applied to all people. This is also true for the application of psychoanalysis to the problems of education and school.

The progress of our science as far as education is considered has to do with just this new development. That is that we have much to contribute to normal school situations, to better educational work with children, towards influencing educational institutions, and to the training of teachers in early education, in elementary school, in high school, and in the university. I should like to report on some tentative experiments that have occupied us during the last ten or more years. I do this to emphasize that the aim of this lecture is not only to treasure the past, to honor our old teachers and Freud, but to state that Freud's psychoanalysis remains a living science which always grows and continually gives us new tools. Out of Freud's thoughts and suggestions we derive applications which, as Thomas Mann suggests, will create an educational system in which "the free folk are the people of a future freed from fear and hate, and ripe for peace."

In the last few years during which it was possible for me to evolve courses for pedagogues—a kind of Americanized continuation of the *Lehrgang für psychoanalytische Pädagogen*—I have tried to teach psychoanalysis in a way that permits its insights to help us understand the child as a learner. I have attempted to interpret the concepts of learning capacity and learning readiness of the child, as well as the teaching capacity and teaching readiness of the teacher.

I might add, in order to be fair to the topic of this essay, that I have also been occupied with notions concerning the educational capacity and readiness of educators and parents. The German language has no simple translation for the concept of capacity and readiness for "parenting." Once I suggested, half jestingly and half seriously; that the mother's breast was the first curriculum for the infant. She is thus the first teacher who, through the way that she feeds him, becomes the first representative of social reality, and confronts him with the task of recognizing and accepting the world, as well as of acquiring an adequate style with which to solve this task. In the early days of psychoanalysis we often described the world of the infant as a frustrating one. Our first insights were insights about obstacles, as we spoke of the need to substitute the reality principle for the pleasure principle. Slowly, we began to speak not only about the principle of frustration but also about the principle of gratification. We began to recognize that a certain equilibrium between frustration and gratification makes it possible for the infant to solve and to master the first tasks which reality sets before him.

This first drama between mother and child makes it possible for the child to develop the capacity to live in the specific culture of which he is a part, as Freud described in *Beyond the Pleasure Principle* (11). Out of this conflict, out of these obstacles that can be overcome, grow the psychic capacities—through the discovery of object, of mother, and of self—to leave the world of the pleasure principle and enter the world of the reality principle. This first conflict and its positive resolution lead to the capacity for solving tasks. Erikson (8) tells us that it is at this time that basic trust is developed—confidence in the mother, confidence in other people, and self-confidence. Freud spoke of this early trust as that which creates a fundamental optimism that will make it possible to face future tasks. Karl Bühler suggested that these first positive attempts at solution produce *Funktionslust*—pleasure in functioning— a very important side product of the solution of those conflicts which contribute to the development of learning capacity and learning readiness. Charlotte Bühler has always stressed the positive meaning of reality, and Piaget also speaks of reality as the necessary nutriment, the nourishment, without which learning and growing are impossible.

During its beginning phases, psychoanalysis stressed frustration, since it was then occupied with therapeutic problems; only later was it recognized that reality, such as the love of mother, can and must be a giving one. It is therefore no coincidence that we use many analogies, many similes, which relate education and schooling with the first feeding experiences of the infant. We speak of the Nürnberger funnel, certainly an outdated notion of teaching; we refer to intellectual and emotional food, the digesting of knowledge, the regurgitating of lessons, and so on. One takes knowledge into oneself, and sometimes one cannot digest it and spits it out. The early trust in the mother and self-confidence—or mistrust and lack of self-confidence—are not stable achievements; they shift back and forth in life as new experiences and relationships develop. This is also characteristic of the way in which the child deals with teachers. With each pupil, of course, the teacher inherits the sins and virtues of its parents and has to deal with the problem of using the existing capacity of the child in the school situation. We suggest that a serious theory of learning and teaching must come to grips with human relations, with object relations. The metaphor of the Nürnberger funnel assumes that the empty vessel of the mind of the child can somehow be filled in an impersonal way with the milk of knowledge. It suggests that the psychic apparatus can be considered a purely mechanical structure which needs only to be filled up like the tank of an automobile in order to function. Psychoanalysis has contributed much to the study of human relations, and can offer the teacher much. It can help enable him to create for the child a positive, giving school reality in which the child learns to master positive obstacles—a mastery which also changes, widens, and deepens the learning capacity and learning readiness of the child.

The teachers of kindergarten and elementary-school children were the first ones who could apply the insights of psychoanalysis. This is because it is almost impossible for them to overlook the extent to which learning during the early years depends on human relations, and how much the child's need to acquire love, and his fear of being hated and punished, affect his learning readiness and learning capacity.

The wish to be successful in the learning situation, to get good marks on report cards, or to acquire other signs of love and reward, is never completely lost in life. There is certainly a connection between the first good mark in school which the six-year-old acquires, and the joy of the aging person at being assigned a task that honors him, or on being given an honorary title. Learning for love—the need to adjust in order to be ready for something new, in order to be acknowledged—is only one of the many aspects which later define maturity, learning capacity, and learning readiness. I am speaking therefore, as is evident, about a dynamic concept, a capacity in man which constantly develops and takes on new components.

It should be clear by now that I intend to develop thoughts which apply certain developmental studies of psychoanalysis to issues of education and school. I am referring to the contributions of Anna Freud and her many students, especially those studies in which she determines that one can understand the normal development of the child better if one utilizes the concept of *developmental lines* (10). I also refer to Erik Erikson's thoughts about the epigenetic ground plan, which is characteristic for all people under normal and favorable conditions of life (8).

I have utilized these studies in order to stimulate educators and teachers to develop a *learning profile,* as a means of applying Anna Freud's studies to questions of education and teaching.

The first phase in the development of the infant, the oral phase, stretches over an area of development that offers insights concerning the meaning of object relations; this area of analytic research has been treated creatively by René Spitz in his beautiful volume, *The First Year of Life* (22). Psychoanalysis has also examined other aspects, other fragments concerning learning, which contribute to an integrated theory of learning. I am turning now to the anal phase. Seen from the point of view of education, this phase allows us to construct in the child the psychic capacity for self-regulation, as well as—even though this seems to be contradictory—the capacity to accept outer control and authority. This inner struggle from the phase of final weaning to the phase of toilet training, allows the child to develop the capacity for inner self-regulation within the boundaries of the family and society. I refer to the problem of discipline—outer and inner—which is never completely mastered and which, when unresolved, can destroy both learning and teaching capacity. Many of the teaching methods and learning theories that have occupied educators are primarily concerned with the problem of discipline. Many theories have overstressed it; currently we are again being engulfed by the idea that one can educate only by steering the behavior of children by positive and negative reinforcements, rewards and punishments. This model of conditioning is a very old one, if we recall the dogs of Pavlov or the pigeons of Skinner. I have suggested earlier that even the learning of the infant is influenced by the "steering" of the mother—the gratification of nursing and frustration at weaning. We have no reason to reject the importance of these insights, or the experiments involving issues of education and school that are directed towards the modification of behavior. It is indeed correct that during the phase of toilet training—the child's battle to achieve autonomy and to accept boundaries—the problem of inner discipline and direction is constantly studied by the external world and influenced through reward and punishment, through the bestowal or withdrawal of love and gratification, or through actions of anger and hate. All these methods will continue to be a part of future learning and teaching. But we also have to recognize that a modern theory of learning has the task of integrating the human aspects, the relationships between men, as well as the merely mechanical, the external steering that can be done, for example, by teaching machines.

We see then that psychoanalysis suggests the creation of a new theory of learning which grows beyond the one-sided schools. At approximately the time school life starts, we observe a third phase in human development: in Freud's words, the phallic phase, motivated by curiosity and initiative. Erikson tells us that the successful solution of the oedipal complex does more than create the conscience, the superego, and the ego ideals, or at least their forerunners. It must also be seen as the decisive factor for producing in the child either initiative or, in the case of inner defeat, apathy. The child's curiosity, his wish to understand the world, to understand his origins, to discover the sexual and social secrets of his parents, must always encounter some obstacle in every and any kind of social order. We find some societies in which there is no real place for curiosity and where the primitive system of social organization permits only imitation. In such a society, there is no progress, no real adaptation in a creative sense; it remains static. Its education merely emphasizes what already exists, defending a dead tradition and unable to identify with a dynamic one that permits the improvement of society and of man. We can imagine social orders —and we have many signs of that in our world today—in which there are no inhibitions, no obstacles, no boundaries for this curiosity and initiative. In such a social order—really, a social disorder —there would be no education. As early as 1919, Federn predicted that this kind of society would be a fatherless society (9), as Mitscherlich has also indicated more recently (19); its children and adolescents would be impulsive, destructive, and unable to develop true, tamed initiative.

During the time of the development of initiative, we must help the child acquire the capacity to sublimate the first expressions of curiosity in a way that really contributes to learning. Piaget has contributed much, as have the Gestalt psychologists, to the observation of the development of logic in the child. It is during this time that the capacity for insight, for interpreting the world, grows, and this capacity and readiness for insight influences the process of learning and makes it possible to solve tasks on a higher plane.

We have determined then that psychoanalysis tells us people learn because of and through human relations; they learn through outer stimuli, through repeating and mastery, through the acceptance of external tasks; and finally they learn by means of having their curiosity satisfied through insight. We may, therefore, say that a psychoanalytic theory of learning will have to examine and understand object relations, the external stimuli which force repetition, as well as the problems of learning via insight. The first phase of learning, of course, has much to do with affect; and learning theories without understanding of affects and feelings—the problems of loving and hating, of separating from and of longing for the love object—isolate us from understanding the total person.

In the earlier phases of psychoanalytic understanding we were particularly concerned with the effect of early conditions on development. Later on, we understood more and more the value of studying external stimuli, and we saw the boundaries of education not simply as rejection and frustration but also as possibilities for steering the child to utilization of the school and social worlds in a positive way.

In the psychoanalytic treatment of patients we always understood, that we must go far beyond our early insights. We were aware, as Gerhart and Maria Piers (21) once pointed out, of the importance of human relations, of object relations, in the concept of transference. The concept of transference, also extremely important in its application in education, has to do with object relations. The concept of working through, the continuous repetition, has to do with those aspects of learning that can be influenced by outer stimuli. But the main concept of psychoanalytic treatment —that of interpretation—deals with those aspects of learning that are based on insight, on understanding, on the capacity to solve tasks, on creative intuition. Bernfeld stressed even in those early days how much the concept of interpretation is related to insights and to concepts of Gestalt psychology.

As the child grows up, his learning capacity and readiness develop to higher forms. The early forms are never completely given up, however; they remain, although sometimes they are repressed or crippled. The only change is that new forms arise and dominate later phases. Hartmann and Kris stressed the concept of phase dominance in order to permit us to understand that we are dealing with a dynamic development of psychic life. The human relationships, the repetition of tasks through external stimuli, the learning through insights, the thirst for knowledge, are but different stages and steps of learning capacity and learning readiness. At times, we can observe certain regressions which throw the student back to earlier levels and which sometimes fixate him at old points of development.

May I suggest that the ideological war between different theories of learning represents a kind of repetition for the development of the child. This leads me to the thought that the teaching capacity and readiness of the educator, of the teacher, also go through a similar development. I have occupied myself with examining the psychic evolvement of the *teacher becoming* and have suggested what steps he must go through before he acquires a mature professional identity (7). He undergoes approximately the same fate, if on a higher level, as every human being who must go through a series of identity crises before he can say about himself, what he is, what he wants to be, and what he wants to move towards.

In an ideal world of education which we sometimes dream up in utopian fashion, we would like to see the learning profile of the child brought into accord with the teaching profile of the teacher. That is, a child who can not learn only through disciplined repetition but is ready to work towards insights should be matched with a teacher who can teach in a fashion that permits the child's capacities for new insights to grow.

This thought leads me to a new problem. I suggested first that through psychoanalysis we can understand the child as a learner, as being capable of education. I spoke about the need to study learning profiles in order to grasp the child as a learner. We do not think of the child as an empty blackboard, a sort of *tabula rasa* upon which we etch knowledge and skills. We think of him as an active, steadily developing psychic instance whose learning capacity constantly changes and presents an immense task for all of us who want to deal with the problem of teaching on a scientific and serious basis. We then have to turn away from questions simply about

the child, and start to think about the training of teachers, about
the development of the educators as well as of the parents.

This last decade has made it possible for me to be actively engaged in these tasks. I speak not only of influencing young students
who want to became teachers but also of the postgraduate educa-
tions of active teachers. I am referring also to experiments which
we have conducted in the school system to help teachers with
educational and teaching problems. What can I share with you in
the time given me to convey some idea of the wide area of this
work?

Passive learning must slowly be changed into active learning. If
the teacher wants to teach successfully, to educate positively, he
will soon grasp that only he who never stops learning can be a good
teacher. Teaching I consider an active form of learning. The poet
Wordsworth, who speaks of the child as the father of the man, has
stimulated me to suggest that the student be considered the father
of the teacher.

In direct work with teachers—lectures, seminars, individual conferences, observation of teaching activity, the literature, and, occasionally, analysis—I succeeded in going at least a small way
beyond the old books. As I came to these teachers and began to
share with them psychoanalytic contributions to pedagogy, we
discovered together a few new questions. Sometimes we invited important educators and psychoanalysts who answered some of these
questions and then posed new ones. We have turned passive yearning—passive studying of our area of work—into creative, active
learning. These experiences are published in many papers and have
led me to publish a book that describes ten years of work at Reiss-
Davis Child Study Center. This book (6) was enriched by the
work of colleagues who helped me with this new experiment.

Since Vienna might be considered the cradle of the application
of psychoanalysis to education, you will allow me a bit of local
patriotism in telling you that a number of Viennese contributed
to this volume: Bruno Bettelheim, Edith Buxbaum, Lili Peller,
Maria Piers, and Fritz Redl. The title of this volume describes a
process: *From Learning for Love to Love of Learning*. Learning for
personal motives—nourished mainly by longing and fear and motivated by the pressure of society and home—is slowly internalized.

If it is really successful it changes so that out of it grows a love of learning, and love for a profession or for a science. How many men—students or teachers—can say they have really gone through these phases of development? But Goethe must have meant just that when he said that inheritance of the fathers must be acquired and internalized, before one may really call it one's own.

Heinz Hartmann, the great psychoanalyst and son of Ludo Hartmann, founder of Viennese adult education, discovered the concept of adaptation within the new ego psychology, and made clear why the development from learning because of outer force to love of learning can take place. Neutral and conflict-free areas of the psychic apparatus make just that possible. He made it clear that psychoanalysis was not only a psychology of conflict, not only a theory of the unconscious, not only an instinct theory, but also the theory of successful identifications, of creative adaptations. It leads from the resolution of inner conflicts to the solution of creative tasks. Through these contributions of ego psychology all of psychoanalysis has become richer. We now bring to the educator not only a new human attitude but also the possibility of improving teaching and new educating techniques.

The science of education, of course, has to battle with an immense problem which it has in common with all non-technical sciences that deal with social issues. Heinz Hartmann clearly recognized this when he wrote:

> The second field in which analysis has been widely, though much less systematically, used for practical purposes is pedagogy. But here the situation, as to the problem of values, is different to begin with. In pedagogy there is no single goal accepted as unquestionably as is health in medicine. Social, moral, and other values are constantly to be considered. In the use of pedagogical techniques moral values cannot simply be put into parentheses, as they are in psychoanalytic technique. One has to face the differences in this respect between religious and nonreligious, between individualistic and conformist educational goals, between the aims of being a "good citizen" in a democratic or totalitarian society, and so on; yet there are, of course, also common elements in the ideas and practices of child rearing (15).

Perhaps one might even say that the contribution of psychoanalysis may somehow overcome all of these obstacles, and that the differences throughout the world pose only varied technical and theoretical tasks for us, about which the insights of psychoanalysis and the general sciences of education have much to say. May I mention two examples of serious educational research, each occupied with completely different educational tasks but both undertaken by Viennese? I wish to mention first a small study which does, and ought to, have immense social meaning in America: *Wages of Neglect* (4). By Robert Coles and Maria Piers, this book is about young black children in Mississippi who live under the oppressive influence of unbelievable poverty. Maria Piers and her American colleague, Robert Coles, tried to teach the mothers of these children the rudiments of educating, the meaning of feeling, of touching, of speech, of learning, of play, and the significance of identification. They compared these neglected children with those in a study which comes from Anna Freud's Hampstead Clinic and deals with the treatment and education of six small children who were saved from a Nazi concentration camp. The work of Maria Piers, the dean of the Erikson Institute for Early Childhood Education in Chicago, demonstrates what one can do with the most important, fundamental concepts of psychoanalysis in order to make them education-effective.

I wish to mention another study which Bruno Bettelheim describes in *Children of the Dream* (3). In this book he compares the education in the kibbutz, the Socialist agricultural communes in Israel, with American education. His work is concerned not only with the young child but also with youth; not only with elementary school but also with high school and touches on college education. We have observed how the whole world seems to be confronted with unsolvable problems in the form of student disorders, the problem of narcotics, the lack of identification of youth with society and the adult world. At times, we ask what education may contribute to the solution of these questions. The alienation of youth is not only a normal phase which must take place during puberty and adolescence. In its present exaggerated form, it becomes the symptom of a widening gap, a deeper alienation, which isolates the adult world and poses new questions for us.

As Hartman (15) touched upon, the psychoanalyst who is occupied solely with his patients can somehow go beyond the social system and can contribute to the restoration of inner psychic functions. He limits himself to treat and not to educate. He resolves conflicts, but he leaves it up to the patient to find his own life goals.

The educator, on the other hand, is not in the same situation. He may attempt to stay between the generations, and to identify both with the child and with the world of the adult so that he represents a bridge which the child can use to cross over into the adult world. He also may, and should, try to improve the world of adults, and he will then be confronted with political and social values. Regardless of how neutral he remains, he is still an educator; the word *educator* implies, after all, that the educator must lead the child out of its early stages towards higher goals.

Perhaps this suggests that the educator, too, must lead himself out of stages that are outdated, and that he has the moral obligation not only to enlighten the child but also the world of the adult, and to lead it.

And this leads me back to that hero of antiquity whom Bernfeld sees as the first educator—Sisyphus, who endlessly tried and endlessly failed. In thinking about the identity of the teacher, his professional identity, I thought of another hero of antiquity—of Prometheus. It was he who brought fire to the children of this earth, who taught them mastery of fire by means of which it was possible to build a civilization. He brought this knowledge to the children of earth, however, without the consent of the gods. He could not bring about an agreement with the ruling establishment, and in rebelling against them he was punished by the gods. But Zeus did not forever remain a god of vengeance, and Pallas Athene came to rule in Athens. And in a social system dominated not by the military spirit of Sparta but guided by the democratic spirit of Pallas Athene, Prometheus no longer was a wrongdoer but an example to society; in his honor, there was an annual day of festivity, a torch race, to symbolize learning and progress.

Many years ago when I listened to youth leaders in Vienna, they told us, over and over again, that we must oppose the idea of force with the force of an idea. I think of Freud's influence, his influence on the world—without armies and without guns, without creating fear and serving only insight. Will the force of his ideas some day be stronger than the idea of force?

I am here from America—a country that gave me the chance to turn into reality what I learned in my first home. This great country, that has made it possible for so many people of the Old World to find a new home, that fought to maintain the best of Europe's values, just as Thomas Mann predicted; this giant, that can send people to the moon, exists now in deep social crisis. Let us not forget, if we want to educate this world correctly, if we are to contribute to progress, that this crisis—America's crisis—is also the crisis of all other countries, and that all of us, each in his own area, will have the task of transforming this crisis into an *Aufbaukrise*, a crisis of construction. I spoke about the boundaries of education and I might very well talk about the boundaries of politics. Are these the boundaries of a Sisyphus? Or are they the boundaries of a Prometheus, who was honored and idealized in Athens? What has Freud, whom we honor today, to say about this question? In 1930 he wrote:

> Thus I have not the courage to rise up before my fellowmen as a prophet, and I bow to their reproach that I can offer them no consolation: for at bottom that is what they are all demanding—the wildest revolutionaries no less passionately than the most virtuous believers.

The fateful question for the human species seems to me to be whether and to what extent their cultural development will succeed in mastering the disturbance of their communal life by the human instinct of aggression and self-destruction. It may be that in this respect precisely the present time deserves a special interest. Men have gained control over the forces of nature to such an extent that with their help they would have no difficulty in exterminating one another to the last man. They know this, and hence comes a large part of their current unrest, their unhappiness and their mood of anxiety. And now it is to be expected that the other of the two "Heavenly Powers," eternal Eros, will make an effort to assert himself in the struggle with his equally immortal adversary. But who can foresee with what success and with what result? (12).

Freud has remained our teacher, not consoling but insight-giving.

Permit me to paraphrase Goethe in order to characterize the significance, the importance of Sigmund Freud, for all of us—for Vienna and the world:

"What thou hast inherited from Sigmund Freud, acquire it to make it thine and thee."

BIBLIOGRAPHY

1. AICHHORN, AUGUST (1925). *Wayward Youth. Psychoanalysis and Correctional Education; 10 Introductory Lectures.* New York: Whiting Press, 1935.
2. BERNFELD, SIEGFRIED. *Sisyphos oder die Grenzen der Erziehung.* (Sisyphus or the Boundaries of Education.) Vienna, Leipzig: Internationaler Psychoanalytischer Verlag, 1925.
3. BETTELHEIM, BRUNO. *The Children of the Dream. Communal Child Rearing and American Education.* New York: Macmillan, 1969.
4. COLES, ROBERT, and PIERS, MARIA. *Wages of Neglect—New Solutions for the Children of the Poor.* Chicago: Quadrangle, 1969.
5. EKSTEIN, RUDOLF, and MOTTO, Rocco. Psychoanalysis and Education—An Historical Account. *Reiss-Davis Clin. Bull.,* 1964, 1:7.
6. EKSTEIN, RUDOLF, and MOTTO, Rocco. *From Learning for Love to Love of Learning.* New York: Brunner/Mazel, 1969.
7. EKSTEIN, RUDOLF. Psychoanalytic Reflections on the Emergence of the Teacher's Professional Identity. *Reiss-Davis Clin. Bull.,* 1970, 1:5.
8. ERIKSON, ERIK H. *Childhood and Society.* New York: W. W. Norton, 1950.
9. FEDERN, PAUL. *Zur Psychologie der Revolution: Die vaterlose Gesellschaft.* (On the Psychology of Revolution: The Fatherless Society.) Leipzig, Wien: Anzengruber Verlag, 1919.
10. FREUD, ANNA. *Normality and Pathology in Childhood—Assessments of Development.* New York: Int. Univ. Press, 1965.
11. FREUD, SIGMUND. Beyond the Pleasure Principle (1923). *Standard Edition.* XIX. London: Hogarth Press, 1961.
12. FREUD, SIGMUND. Civilization and Its Discontents (1930). *Standard Edition,* XXI. London: Hogarth Press, 1961.
13. FREUD, SIGMUND. New Introductory Lectures on Psycho-Analysis (1932). *Standard Edition,* XXII. London: Hogarth Press, 1964.
14. HACKER, FRIEDRICH. *Versagt der Mensch oder die Gesellschaft? Probleme der modernen Kriminalpsychologie.* (Who Fails: Men or Society?) Wien: Europa Verlag, 1964.
15. HARTMANN, HEINZ. *Psychoanalysis and Moral Values.* New York: Int. Univ. Press, 1960.
16. HOFFER, WILLI. Psychoanalytic Education. *Psychoanalyt. Study of the Child,* 1:293.
17. MANN, THOMAS. *Freud, Goethe, Wagner.* New York: Alfred A. Knopf, 1937.
18. MANN, THOMAS. *The Coming Victory of Democracy.* London: Secker & Warburg, 1938.
19. MITSCHERLICH, ALEXANDER. *Society without the Father.* New York: Harcourt, Brace & World, 1969.

20. PFISTER, OSKAR. Elternfehler (The Faults of Parents). *Zeitschrift für Psychoanalytische Pädagogik,* 1929, 3:172.
21. PIERS, GERHART, and MARIA. Modes of Learning and the Analytic Process. *Selected Lectures, Sixth International Congress in Psychotherapy. London,* 1964. Basel, N.Y.: S. Karger, 1965.
22. SPITZ, RENE A. *The First Year of Life.* New York: Int. Univ. Press, 1965.
23. WITTELS, FRITZ (1927). *Set the Children Free!* New York: W. W. Norton, 1933.

INDEX